INTERNATIONAL
Vital Records
Handbook

INTERNATIONAL
Vital Records
Handbook

Thomas Jay Kemp

3rd Edition

GENEALOGICAL · PUBLISHING Co. Inc.

First Edition (published as *Vital Records Handbook*), 1988
Second Edition, 1990
Third Edition copyright © 1994
by Thomas Jay Kemp
All Rights Reserved
Published by Genealogical Publishing Co., Inc.
Baltimore, 1994
Second printing 1995
Library of Congress Catalogue Card Number 94-77221
International Standard Book Number 0-8063-1424-9
Made in the United States of America

Dedicated to my wife Vi
and children Andrew and Sarah

CONTENTS

INTRODUCTION

At one time or another all of us need copies of birth, marriage, or death certificates for driver's licenses, passports, jobs, Social Security, family history research, or for simple proof of identity. But the fact is that the application forms needed to obtain copies of vital records, to say nothing of fees and special requirements, vary from state to state and from country to country, often necessitating a tedious and time-wasting exchange of correspondence before the appropriate forms can be obtained and the correct procedures followed. The *International Vital Records Handbook* is designed to put an end to all that, as it offers instructions and a complete, up-to-date collection of vital records application forms from nations throughout the world, thus simplifying and speeding up the process by which vital records are obtained, regardless of the number or type of application forms required.

Divided into two parts, this new 3rd edition of the *International Vital Records Handbook* contains the latest forms and information for each of the fifty states and also furnishes details about records that were created prior to statewide vital records registration; then, in alphabetical sequence, it covers all the other countries of the world, giving, where available, their current forms and instructions; and since most non-English-speaking nations have neither a centralized vital records registration system nor application forms of any kind, this work provides as a substitute a list of national and provincial record repositories or key addresses of other institutions that might be of assistance.

Application forms issued by the various civil registration offices and the current procedures for obtaining a birth, marriage, or death certificate are given, where available, for each state, province, territory, or country. Simply photocopy the form you need, follow the instructions, and send the fee and the completed form to the appropriate record office.

In obtaining copies of vital records it should be kept in mind that copies of the original certificate might be on file in several different jurisdictions, depending on the country. For example, if a vital record is not available from a state office of vital records, you should check with the appropriate county or city office to see if they have a copy. Similar records are also kept by the various religious denominations, and some copies and originals are held by archives and libraries the world over.

As a matter of policy, the Family History Library of The Church of Jesus Christ of Latter-day Saints in Salt Lake City has microfilmed millions of vital records from church and civil registers all over the world. This ongoing and extraordinary program has made the Family History Library the world's largest repository of vital records. A catalog of its microfilm holdings can be viewed at any of the 1,800 Family History Centers here and abroad. For further information on the library system write to: The Family History Library, 35 North West Temple Street, Salt Lake City, Utah 84150.

1. United States

UNITED STATES

Send your requests to:

Passport Services
Correspondence Branch, Room 386
U.S. Department of State
1425 K Street, NW
Washington, DC 20522-1705

(202) 647-0518

Cost for a certified Birth Certificate	$10.00
Cost for a certified Marriage Certificate	$10.00
Cost for a certified Death Certificate	$10.00

Vital records are kept by state and local registrars in the United States. If the birth, marriage, divorce, or death occurred inside the United States, you need to consult the listing in this book for the state where the event occurred.

If the event occurred in another country and the person was a United States citizen or his dependent, contact Passport Services.

If the event occurred in another country and the person was a member of the Army, Navy, Marines, or Air Force, contact the Secretary of Defense, Washington, DC 20301. If the person was a member of the Coast Guard, contact the Commandant, P.S., U.S. Coast Guard, Washington, DC 20226.

If the event occurred on the high seas while the vessel or aircraft was outbound from the United States or at a foreign port, contact Passport Services of the U.S. Department of State. If the vessel or aircraft was inbound and first docked in the U.S. after the event occurred, write to the registrar in the state where it arrived.

Vital records information is also maintained by the Social Security Administration. It is possible to obtain a copy of an original application for Social Security services. Please see the instruction form given.

The Family History Library of The Church of Jesus Christ of Latter-day Saints in Salt Lake City, Utah has copies of the Social Security Administration Death Files. For details on their holdings please consult your nearest Family History Center.

PASSPORT SERVICES/SEARCH REQUEST FORM

DATE _____   PURPOSE OF REQUEST _____

NAME AT (CIRCLE ONE)
BIRTH/DEATH/MARRIAGE _____

NAME AFTER ADOPTION (IF APPLICABLE) _____

DATE OF (CIRCLE ONE)   COUNTRY OF (CIRCLE ONE)
BIRTH/DEATH/MARRIAGE _____   BIRTH/DEATH/MARRIAGE _____

FATHER'S NAME _____
COUNTRY & DATE OF BIRTH _____

MOTHER'S NAME _____
COUNTRY & DATE OF BIRTH _____

IF YOU ARE IN POSSESSION OF A REPORT OF BIRTH/DEATH OR CERTIFICATION
OF BIRTH/MARRIAGE PLEASE ENCLOSE A COPY TO AID IN OUR FILE SEARCH.

PASSPORT - FIRST ENTRY TO U.S.

NAME OF BEARER _____
DATE OF ISSUE _____   PASSPORT NBR. _____
DATE OF AMMENDMENT (IF PASSPORT NOT ISSUED TO SUBJECT) _____

CURRENT PASSPORT INFORMATION

NAME OF BEARER _____
DATE OF ISSUE _____   PASSPORT NBR. _____

SIGNATURE _____
          (SUBJECT OR GUARDIAN)
ADDRESS _____
TELEPHONE NBR. _____
          (BETWEEN 9 AM AND 5 PM)

PLEASE STATE WHICH DOCUMENT AND HOW MANY.   COST $10.00 EACH.

REPORT OF BIRTH (FS 240)   _____   (ONLY ONE COPY AVAILABLE)
CERTIFICATION OF BIRTH (DS 1350) _____   (MULTIPLE COPIES AVAILABLE)
REPORT OF DEATH (OF 180)   _____   (MULTIPLE COPIES AVAILABLE)
CERTIFICATE OF WITNESS TO
MARRIAGE   _____   (MULTIPLE COPIES AVAILABLE)

RETURN THIS FORM WITHIN 30 DAYS TO:

Passport Services RM 386
1425 K Street, N.W.
Washington, D.C. 20522-1705

02/92

Social Security Number Record
Third Party Request for Extract or Photocopy

Mail to: Office of Central Records Operations
Baltimore, Maryland 21201

Refer to: **SPPE-1**

<u>INSTRUCTIONS</u> – <u>Print or type all data</u>. <u>Sign in ink</u>. <u>Allow 4 to 6 weeks</u> for <u>a reply</u>.

AS A REPRESENTATIVE OF THE PERSON WHOSE FULL IDENTIFYING INFORMATION IS SHOWN BELOW, I HEREBY REQUEST AN EXTRACT OR PHOTOCOPY OF THAT PERSON'S APPLICATION(S) FOR A SOCIAL SECURITY NUMBER.

SOCIAL SECURITY NUMBER (if known)	FULL NAME NOW USED	
NAME SHOWN ON LAST SOCIAL SECURITY CARD (if different from full name now used)		
FULL NAME AT BIRTH		
DATE OF BIRTH (month, day, year)		
PLACE OF BIRTH (city, county, and state or foreign country)	SEX ☐ MALE ☐ FEMALE	
FULL MAIDEN NAME OF MOTHER (whether living or dead)		
FULL NAME OF FATHER (whether living or dead)		

☐ The person I represent has completed and signed the authorization shown below which is required to release this confidential information to me since I am not a court-appointed legal representative.

☐ I am attaching a certified copy of my current court-appointment as this person's legal representative to obtain the release of this confidential information to me. Please return this copy with my reply.

PENALTY STATEMENT (read before signing)
Deliberately furnishing or causing to be furnished false information on this form is punishable by fine, or imprisonment, or both under federal law.

SIGNATURE OF REPRESENTATIVE	DATE
STREET ADDRESS	CITY, STATE, AND ZIP CODE

AUTHORIZATION TO RELEASE CONFIDENTIAL INFORMATION TO A THIRD PARTY – I am the person to whom this request pertains; and I hereby authorize the Social Security Administration to release an extract or photocopy of my Social Security number application(s) to my representative whose signature and address appear above.

SIGNATURE (do not print unless this is your usual signature)	DATE
STREET ADDRESS	CITY, STATE, AND ZIP CODE

NOTE: A printed signature or a signature by mark (X) must be witnessed below by two adults.

(1) SIGNATURE	(2) SIGNATURE
STREET ADDRESS	STREET ADDRESS
CITY, STATE, AND ZIP CODE	CITY, STATE, AND ZIP CODE

Department of Health and Human Services
Social Security Administration

Form **SSA-L997** (2-83)

ALABAMA

Send your requests to:

Alabama Department of Public Health
Center for Health Statistics
Office of Vital Records
P.O. Box 5625
Montgomery, Alabama 36103-5625

(205) 242-5033

For Marriage Records before August 1936 write to:

Probate Judge
County Courthouse
(County Seat), Alabama

For Divorce Records before 1950 write to:

Clerk
Court of Equity
(County Seat), Alabama

Cost for a certified Birth Certificate	$12.00
Cost for a certified Marriage Certificate or Divorce Decree	$12.00
Cost for a certified Death Certificate	$12.00
Cost for a duplicate copy, when ordered at the same time	$4.00

Birth and death records are on file at the Office of Vital Records from January 1908. Births are filed under the father's name by the date and place where the event occurred. Marriage records are on file from August 1, 1936 and divorce records from January 1, 1950.

If your request is urgent you may call and charge your certificate to your Visa, Discover, or MasterCard. There is a $36.50 total charge for this service, which includes the cost of the certificate and postage.

The Alabama Department of Archives and History (624 Washington Avenue, P.O. Box 300100, Montgomery, AL 36130-0100; Tel. 205-242-4435) has copies of birth, marriage, divorce, and death records.

The Family History Library of The Church of Jesus Christ of Latter-day Saints in Salt Lake City, Utah has microfilmed many of the original and published vital records and church registers of Alabama. For details on their holdings please consult your nearest Family History Center.

ALABAMA

APPLICATION FOR CERTIFICATION OF A VITAL EVENT WHICH OCCURRED IN ALABAMA

The service fee is $12.00 for a birth, death, marriage or divorce record search, which covers the cost of one certified copy. The fee is $15.00 to amend a record, $20.00 to prepare a new certificate of birth after adoption or legitimation or to file a delayed certificate, which also covers the cost of one certified copy of the record. For additional copies of the same record ordered at the same time, the fee is $4.00 for each additional copy. If you wish to have a document expedited, you must include $10.00 extra, and mail the request to us by an overnight express mail service. Make check or money order payable to State Board of Health. DO NOT SEND CASH. Fees nonrefundable.

CHECK THE BLOCK UNDER THE TYPE OF EVENT WHICH YOU ARE APPLYING FOR AND COMPLETE THAT SECTION ONLY. DO NOT REQUEST TWO DIFFERENT TYPES OF EVENTS ON THE SAME FORM.

		DO NOT WRITE IN THESE SPACES
BIRTH ☐ Number of copies requested ___	FULL NAME AT BIRTH _____ DATE OF BIRTH _____ RACE _____ SEX _____ COUNTY OF BIRTH _____ HOSPITAL _____ FATHER'S FULL NAME _____ MOTHER'S FULL MAIDEN NAME _____	FEE FILE NUMBER
DEATH ☐ Total Number of copies requested ___	DECEASED FULL NAME _____ DATE OF DEATH _____ RACE _____ SEX _____ AGE _____ COUNTY OF DEATH _____ FULL NAME OF HUSBAND OR WIFE _____ Starting with 1991 deaths, certificates may be issued without a cause of death. Indicate the number of copies you want issued. WITH CAUSE OF DEATH ___ WITHOUT CAUSE OF DEATH ___	ADDITIONAL INFORMATION REQUESTED EVIDENCE REQUESTED AMENDMENT FORM MAILED INFORMATION LETTER MAILED
MARRIAGE/ DIVORCE ☐ Number of copies requested ___	HUSBAND'S FULL NAME _____ WIFE'S FULL MAIDEN NAME _____ DATE OF MARRIAGE/DIVORCE _____ COUNTY OF MARRIAGE/DIVORCE _____ IF MARRIAGE, COUNTY WHERE LICENSE WAS ISSUED _____	ADVISED RECORD NOT ON FILE NUMBER OF CERTIFIED COPIES ISSUED

APPLICANT **WARNING** Falsely Applying for Record is against the law	**WARNING:** Falsely applying for a record is subject to a penalty upon conviction of up to three months in the county jail or a fine of up to $500. Code of Ala. 1975, §13A-10-109. SIGNATURE OF APPLICANT _____ DATE _____ (By signing, I certify that I have a proper interest in obtaining this record) STREET _____ DAYTIME PHONE NUMBER ( )_____ CITY _____ State ____ Zip ____ AMOUNT ENCLOSED _____ RELATIONSHIP (To Person whose record is being requested) _____
CHANGES ☐	ARE YOU REQUESTING ANY **CHANGES** ON THE RECORD YOU ARE APPLYING FOR? IF YES, CHECK THIS BLOCK AND STATE THE CHANGES YOU WANT MADE.
Where to mail this form:	Alabama Department of Public Health Center for Health Statistics P.O. Box 5625 Montgomery, Alabama 36103-5625

DO NOT TEAR

FEE PAID

(This is a mailing insert. PRINT name and address of person to whom the certified copy is to be mailed)

DO NOT WRITE IN THIS SPACE

Certificate of _____

MAIL TO:

Name _____

Street _____

City _____ State ____ Zip ____

THIS WILL BE YOUR RECEIPT AFTER WE PROCESS IT AND RETURN IT TO YOU.

ADPH-F-HS-14/Rev. 7-92

ALASKA

Send your requests to:

Bureau of Vital Statistics
P.O. Box 110675
Juneau, Alaska 99811-0675

(907) 465-3392

Cost for a certified Birth Certificate	$10.00
Cost for a plastic Birth Card	$10.00
Cost for a Heritage Birth Certificate	$35.00
Cost for a certified Marriage or Divorce Certificate	$10.00
Cost for a certified Death Certificate	$10.00

The Bureau of Vital Statistics has birth, marriage, and death records from January 1, 1913 and divorce records from January 1, 1950.

If your request is urgent you may call and charge your certificates to your Visa or MasterCard. There is a $10.00 fee for this service. Express Mail service is also available at an additional charge of $9.95.

The Alaska Historical Library has an extensive collection of records. Contact them at the Alaska Department of Education, Division of Libraries and Archives (State Office Building, 8th Floor, P.O. Box G, Juneau, Alaska 99811-0571; Tel. 907-465-2925).

The Family History Library of The Church of Jesus Christ of Latter-day Saints in Salt Lake City, Utah has microfilmed many of the original and published vital records and church registers of Alaska. For details on their holdings please consult your nearest Family History Center.

BUREAU OF VITAL STATISTICS
P.O. Box 110675
Juneau, Alaska 99811-0675
(907) 465-3392

VITAL RECORDS ORDER FORM

PLEASE SPECIFY TYPE OF RECORD NEEDED AND QUANTITY OF EACH

Type	Qty.
Birth Certificate	
Plastic Birth Card	

Type	Qty.
Marriage Certificate	
Divorce Certificate	

Type	Qty.
Death Certificate	
Heritage Birth Certificate $35.00	

1. NAME ON RECORD:	(First)	(Middle)	(Last)	Sex:

2. NAME OF SPOUSE: (For Death, Marriage, Divorce Records Only)

3. DATE OF BIRTH	DATE OF DEATH	DATE OF MARRIAGE	DATE OF DIVORCE

4. PLACE OF BIRTH	PLACE OF DEATH	PLACE OF MARRIAGE	PLACE OF DIVORCE **ALASKA**

5. FATHER'S NAME:

6. MOTHER'S FIRST & MAIDEN NAMES:

7. NAME OF AGENCY OR PERSON ORDERING RECORD:

8. YOUR RELATIONSHIP TO THE PERSON NAMED ON LINE 1:	DAYTIME PHONE NUMBER:

PLEASE NOTE: The <u>fee</u> for each item requested is **$10.00**. If the requested record cannot be found, the **$10.00** search fee must be retained, and a statement of search will be issued.

PLEASE ENCLOSE THE CORRECT FEE WITH THIS APPLICATION

Make check or money order payable to: **BUREAU OF VITAL STATISTICS**

The Alaska Vital Records Office has the following records:

Births in Alaska since 1913   Deaths in Alaska since 1913
Marriages in Alaska since 1913   Divorces in Alaska since 1950

In accordance with Alaska Statute 18.50, in addition to having one's own record, a birth record can be furnished to the parents, guardian or respective representative. If you do not fall into one of the above categories, we will need written permission from one of the eligible persons. The written consent must accompany return of this form. We can send the copy directly to the registrant if the address is available.

Your mailing address must be entered below:

NAME		
STREET		
CITY	STATE	ZIP CODE

MAIL TO: VITAL STATISTICS, P.O. BOX 110675, JUNEAU, ALASKA 99811-0675

Form 06-8000
VS-7 (Rev. 7/93)

ARIZONA

Send your requests to:

> Office of Vital Records
> Arizona Department of Health Services
> 2727 West Glendale Avenue
> P.O. Box 3887
> Phoenix, Arizona 85030-3887

(602) 255-3260

Send your requests for Marriage or Divorce Certificates to:

> Clerk
> Superior Court
> (County Seat), Arizona

Cost for a certified Birth Certificate	$9.00
Cost for a computerized Birth Certificate	$6.00
Cost for a certified Death Certificate	$6.00

The Arizona Office of Vital Records has birth records from 1884 and death records from 1887. Your request must be accompanied by a copy of a photo ID card witnessed by a notary public. For marriage and divorce records contact the Clerk of the Superior Court in the county where the event occurred.

If your request is urgent you may FAX (602) 249-3040 and charge your certificates to your Visa, Discover, or MasterCard. There is a $5.00 fee for this service.

The Arizona Department of Library, Archives and Public Records, Archives Division (1700 West Washington, Phoenix, AZ 85007; Tel. 602-542-4159) has early Arizona marriage records from the counties.

The Family History Library of Salt Lake City, Utah has microfilmed many of the original and published vital records and church registers of Arizona. For details on their holdings please consult your nearest Family History Center.

ARIZONA DEPARTMENT OF HEALTH SERVICES
VITAL RECORDS SECTION

REQUEST FOR COPY OF BIRTH CERTIFICATE

DATE					
	ENCLOSED $ _____ AMOUNT	IN _____	FOR _____	CERTIFIED PHOTO COPY $9 (FEE INCLUDES $1.00 SURCHARGE)	(1950 TO PRESENT ONLY) CERTIFIED COMPUTERIZED COPY $6

I. BIRTH CERTIFICATE OF:

FOR OFFICE USE ONLY

FULL NAME AT BIRTH		DATE OF BIRTH	SEX
PLACE OF BIRTH (City, County, State, Hospital)	MOTHER'S MAIDEN NAME (First, Middle, Last)		MOTHER'S BIRTHPLACE
HOSPITAL OR FACILITY	FATHER'S FULL NAME		FATHER'S BIRTHPLACE

DATE ISSUED

STATE FILE NUMBER

II. PERSON MAKING REQUEST — PRINT PLAINLY - RETURN ADDRESS

WARNING: False application for a birth certificate is a punishable offense.

For the protection of the individual, certificates of vital events are NOT open to public inspection. Signature of applicant MUST BE NOTARIZED OR this form must be accompanied by a copy of a valid Government Issue picture I.D. which contains the applicant's signature.

Your Signature ☞ _____

YOUR NAME _____

YOUR ADDRESS (Number and Street) _____

(TOWN, STATE, ZIP CODE) _____

RELATIONSHIP TO PERSON NAMED IN CERTIFICATE (e.g. parent, attorney, etc.)	FOR WHAT PURPOSE DO YOU NEED THIS COPY?	TELEPHONE NO. (Optional)

Send completed application and correct fee to:
OFFICE OF VITAL RECORDS
Arizona Department of Health Services
P.O. Box 3030
Phoenix, Arizona 85030

SUBSCRIBED AND SWORN TO OR AFFIRMED BEFORE ME THIS _____ DAY OF _____

NOTARY'S SIGNATURE

MY COMMISSION EXPIRES

ADHS/ADM/Vital Records VS-15A (Rev. 9-92)

ARIZONA DEPARTMENT OF HEALTH SERVICES
OFFICE OF VITAL RECORDS

APPLICATION FOR COPY OF DEATH CERTIFICATE

DATE				COPIES OF THE FOLLOWING DEATH CERTIFICATE	**FOR OFFICE USE ONLY**
	ENCLOSED $ _____ AMOUNT	IN _____	FOR _____		

1. NAME OF DECEASED - First, Middle, Last	IF ANOTHER LAST NAME (except by marriage) WAS EVER USED ENTER HERE

STATE FILE NUMBER

2. DATE OF DEATH - Month, Day, Year	SEX	SOCIAL SECURITY NUMBER (necessary for positive identification)

DATE ISSUED

3. PLACE OF DEATH - Hospital or Residence	Town or City	County — ARIZONA

THE FEE IS $6 FOR EACH CERTIFIED COPY

4. IF MARRIED, IS WIFE/HUSBAND OF DECEASED NOW LIVING? ☐ YES ☐ NO	IF YES, LIST NAME - First, Middle, Last

5. HOW WILL COPIES BE USED?	ARE COPIES TO BE USED FOR U.S. GOV'T CLAIMS? ☐ YES ☐ NO	IF YES, LIST EACH TYPE OF CLAIM

WARNING: False application for a death certificate is a punishable offense.

For the protection of the individual, certificates of vital events are NOT open to public inspection. Signature of application MUST BE NOTARIZED OR this form must be accompanied by a copy of a valid Government issued picture I.D. which contains the applicant's signature.

6. SIGNATURE OF APPLICANT (The regulations require a signed application)	RELATIONSHIP TO THE DECEASED?

7. TYPE OR PRINT NAME AND CORRECT MAIL ADDRESS BELOW

NAME _____

STREET ADDRESS OR P.O. BOX NUMBER _____

CITY AND STATE _____ ZIP CODE _____

SEND COMPLETED APPLICATION AND CORRECT FEE TO:
OFFICE OF VITAL RECORDS
Arizona Dept. of Health Services
P.O. Box 3887
Phoenix, Arizona 85030-3887

SUBSCRIBED AND SWORN TO OR AFFIRMED BEFORE ME THIS _____ DAY OF _____

NOTARY'S SIGNATURE

MY COMMISSION EXPIRES

ADHS/ADM/Vital Records VS-158 (Rev. 11/89)

ARKANSAS

Send your requests to:

Arkansas Department of Health
Division of Vital Records
4815 West Markham Street, Slot 44
Little Rock, Arkansas 72205-3867

(501) 661-2336, (800) 637-9314 (inside Arkansas), FAX (501) 663-2832

For earlier records contact:

County Clerk
County Courthouse
(County Seat), Arkansas

Cost for a certified Birth Certificate	$5.00
Cost for a plastic Birth Card	$5.00
Cost for a certified Marriage or Divorce Certificate	$5.00
Cost for a certified Death Certificate	$4.00
Cost for a duplicate copy, when ordered at the same time	$1.00

Birth and death records are on file from February 1, 1914. Marriage records have been kept from January 1, 1917 and divorce records from January 1, 1923. Incomplete birth and death records for Little Rock and Fort Smith are available from 1881.

The Arkansas History Commission (Multi-Agency Complex, Capitol Mall, 2nd Floor, Little Rock, AR 72201; Tel. 501-682-6900) has marriage records from selected counties from 1814.

If your request is urgent you may call (501) 661-2726 and charge your request to your Visa, Discover, or MasterCard. There is an additional fee of $5.00 for this service.

The Family History Library of The Church of Jesus Christ of Latter-day Saints in Salt Lake City, Utah has microfilmed many of the original and published vital records and church registers of Arkansas. For details on their holdings please consult your nearest Family History Center.

DATE _____

ARKANSAS DEPARTMENT OF HEALTH
DIVISION OF VITAL RECORDS
4815 WEST MARKHAM STREET
LITTLE ROCK, ARKANSAS 72205-3867

BIRTH CERTIFICATE APPLICATION

Only Arkansas births are recorded in this office. There are no original birth records for events which occurred before February 1, 1914. The fee is $5.00 per certificate copy or birth registration card. This fee must accompany the application. Send check or money order payable to the Arkansas Department of Health. DO NOT SEND CASH. Of the total fee you send, $5.00 will be kept in this office to cover search charges if no record of the birth is found.

INFORMATION ABOUT PERSON WHOSE BIRTH CERTIFICATE IS REQUESTED (Type or Print)			
1. FULL NAME AT BIRTH	FIRST NAME	MIDDLE NAME	LAST NAME
2. DATE OF BIRTH	MONTH DAY YEAR	SEX & RACE	AGE LAST BIRTHDAY
3. PLACE OF BIRTH	CITY OR TOWN COUNTY	STATE	ORDER OF THIS BIRTH (1st, 2nd, 3rd, etc.)
	NAME OF HOSPITAL OR STREET ADDRESS	ATTENDANT AT BIRTH	
4. FULL NAME OF FATHER	FIRST NAME	MIDDLE NAME	LAST NAME
5. FULL MAIDEN NAME OF MOTHER (NAME BEFORE MARRIAGE)	FIRST NAME	MIDDLE NAME	MAIDEN NAME

If this child has been adopted, please give original name if known. _____

Has a copy of this certificate been received before? _____

If this is a delayed certificate, when was it filed? _____

What is your relationship to the person whose certificate is being requested? _____

What is your reason for requesting this certificate? _____

Is the person whose record is being requested still living? _____

Signature and telephone number of person requesting this certificate: _____

DO NOT WRITE IN THIS SPACE

Searcher	
Index	
Delayed	Prior
Volume No.	
Page No.	Yr.

BIRTH REGISTRATION CARD
(ACTUAL SIZE 3 3/8" X 2 1/8")

Arkansas Department of Health
Division of Vital Records
BIRTH REGISTRATION CARD

CERTIFICATE
NUMBER
NAME:
BIRTHDATE:
TOWN
COUNTY
THIS CERTIFIES THAT THE ABOVE IS A TRUE ABSTRACT OF THIS PERSON'S BIRTH RECORD WHICH IS FILED WITH THE STATE REGISTRAR.
HENRY C. ROBINSON, JR.
STATE REGISTRAR

CERTIFICATION OF BIRTH
(ACTUAL SIZE 7 1/2" X 6 1/2")

STATE OF ARKANSAS
ARKANSAS DEPARTMENT OF HEALTH
DIVISION OF VITAL RECORDS
CERTIFICATION OF BIRTH
DATE FILED: DATE ISSUED:
CERTIFICATE NUMBER:
NAME: SAMPLE
BIRTHDATE: SEX:
TOWN: COUNTY:
MOTHER'S MAIDEN NAME: AGE:
MOTHER'S BIRTH PLACE:
FATHER'S NAME: AGE:
FATHER'S BIRTH PLACE:
SEAL
Henry C. Robinson Jr
State Registrar
168661
THIS DOCUMENT IS VOID WITHOUT A COLORED BACKGROUND THE BACK OF THIS DOCUMENT CONTAINS AN ARTIFICIAL WATERMARK.

FOR CHARGE CARD CALLS ONLY-
Call (501) 661-2726 to charge copies to a VISA or MASTERCARD.

VISA   MasterCard

CHARGE CARD FEE IS $5.00, IN ADDITION TO FEE FOR EACH CERTIFIED COPY REQUESTED.

ALL TYPES OF COPIES ARE LEGAL PROOF OF BIRTH

	HOW MANY
COPY OF ORIGINAL RECORD ($5.00 EACH)	
CERTIFICATION OF BIRTH** ($5.00 EACH)	
BIRTH CARD ($5.00 EACH)	
AMOUNT OF MONEY ENCLOSED $	

** If Certification of Birth cannot be issued, copy of original record will be substituted.

Please **PRINT** below the name and address of the person who is to receive the copy(s) or card(s).

_____

_____

_____   ZIP _____

Any person who willfully and knowingly makes any false statement in an application for a certified copy of a vital record filed in this state is subject to a fine of not more than ten thousand dollars ($10,000) or imprisoned not more than five (5) years, or both. (Arkansas Statutes 82-527.)

VR-7   9-28-90

ARKANSAS DEPARTMENT OF HEALTH
DIVISION OF VITAL RECORDS
4815 WEST MARKHAM STREET
LITTLE ROCK, ARKANSAS 72205-3867

MARRIAGE OR DIVORCE RECORD APPLICATION

Only Arkansas events of marriage or divorce are filed in this office. Marriage records start with 1917 and divorce records with 1923. The fee is $5.00 per certified copy of a marriage or divorce coupon. This fee must accompany the application. Send check or money order payable to the Arkansas Department of Health. DO NOT SEND CASH. Of the total fee you send, $5.00 will be kept in this office to cover search charges for each record not found in our files.

FILL IN FOR A MARRIAGE RECORD

NAME OF GROOM _____

MAIDEN NAME OF BRIDE _____

DATE OF MARRIAGE _____

Month   Day   Year

COUNTY IN WHICH LICENSE WAS ISSUED _____

FILL IN FOR A DIVORCE RECORD

NAME OF HUSBAND_____

NAME OF WIFE _____

DATE OF DIVORCE OR DISMISSAL _____

Month   Day   Year

COUNTY IN WHICH DIVORCE WAS GRANTED/DISMISSED _____

_____

PLEASE ANSWER ALL QUESTIONS

What is your relationship to the parties named on the requested record?
_____

What is your reason for requesting a copy of this record?_____
_____

Signature and telephone number of person requesting this record:
_____

DO NOT WRITE IN THIS SPACE	
Searcher _____	
Index _____	
Volume No. _____	
Page No. _____	Yr. _____

DO NOT DETACH

THIS IS A MAILING INSERT. **PRINT** NAME AND ADDRESS OF PERSON TO WHOM THE CERTIFIED COPY IS TO BE MAILED.

THIS IS NOT AN INVOICE.

NO. OF COPIES REQUESTED
(Fee is $5.00 per copy)
Marriage _____
Divorce _____
Amount of Money Enclosed _____

NAME _____

ADDRESS _____

CITY _____ STATE _____ ZIP _____

VR-9

Any person who willfully and knowingly makes any false statement in an application for a certified copy of a vital record filed in this state is subject to a fine of not more than ten thousand dollars ($10,000) or imprisoned not more than five (5) years, or both. (Ark. Statutes 82.527)

—3689

DATE _____

DEATH CERTIFICATE APPLICATION

Only Arkansas deaths are recorded in this office. There are no original death records for events which occurred before February 1, 1914. The fee is $4.00 for the first copy and $1.00 for each additional copy of the same record ordered at the same time. The fee must accompany the application. Send check or money order payable to the Arkansas Department of Health. DO NOT SEND CASH. Of the total fee you send, $4.00 will be kept in this office to cover search charges if no record of the death is found.

INFORMATION ABOUT PERSON WHOSE DEATH CERTIFICATE IS REQUESTED (Type or Print)

FULL NAME OF DECEASED _____
First   Middle   Last

DATE OF DEATH _____ AGE OF DECEASED _____ SEX _____ RACE _____

PLACE WHERE DEATH OCCURRED _____
City   County   State

If Unknown,
Give Last Place of Residence _____
City   County   State

NAME OF FUNERAL HOME _____

ADDRESS _____

NAME AND ADDRESS OF ATTENDING PHYSICIAN _____

If deceased was an infant, was it stillborn? _____

What is your relationship to the person whose certificate is being requested? _____

_____

What is your reason for requesting a copy of this record? _____

Signature and telephone number of person requesting this certificate:

_____

DO NOT WRITE IN THIS SPACE	
Searcher	
Index	
Delayed	Prior
Volume No.	
Page No.	Yr.

DO NOT DETACH

THIS IS A MAILING INSERT. PRINT NAME AND ADDRESS OF
PERSON WHO IS TO RECEIVE THE COPY OR COPIES.
THIS IS NOT AN INVOICE

FOR CHARGE CARD CALLS ONLY-
Call (501) 661-2726 to charge copies to a VISA or
MASTERCARD.

CHARGE CARD FEE IS $5.00, IN ADDITION TO FEE FOR
EACH CERTIFIED COPY REQUESTED.

COPIES REQUESTED	
	HOW MANY
ONE COPY $4.00	
ADDITIONAL COPIES $1.00 EACH	
AMOUNT OF MONEY ENCLOSED $	

_____

_____

VR-8   **1-91**   -3688

CALIFORNIA

Send your requests to:

Office of the State Registrar of Vital Statistics
Department of Health Services
304 S Street
P.O. Box 730241
Sacramento, California 94244-0241

(916) 445-2684

For earlier records contact:

County Clerk
County Courthouse
(County Seat), California

Cost for a certified Birth Certificate	$13.00
Cost for a certified Marriage or Divorce Certificate	$13.00
Cost for a certified Death Certificate	$9.00

The Office of the State Registrar has birth, marriage, and death records from July 1, 1905 to the present. They also offer certificates of record for divorces from 1962 to June 1984. For earlier records contact the County Clerk in the county where the event occurred.

If your request is urgent you may FAX (800) 858-5553 and charge your certificates to your Visa or MasterCard. There is an additional $5.00 charge for this service.

The California State Archives (201 North Sunrise Avenue, Roseville, CA 95661; Tel. 916-773-3000) has marriage records from the counties from the late 1800s to the early 1900s.

The Family History Library of The Church of Jesus Christ of Latter-day Saints in Salt Lake City, Utah has microfilmed many of the original and published vital records of California. They have microfiche copies of the statewide marriage indexes from 1960 to 1981 and statewide death indexes from 1903 to 1988. For details on their holdings please consult your nearest Family History Center.

APPLICATION FOR CERTIFIED COPY OF BIRTH RECORD

INFORMATION

Birth records have been maintained in the Office of the State Registrar of Vital Statistics since July 1, 1905. The only records of earlier events are delayed birth certificates and court order delayed birth certificates registered as provided by law.

INSTRUCTIONS

1. Use a separate application blank for each different record of birth for which you are requesting a certified copy. Send $13.00 for each certified copy requested. If no record of the birth is found, the $13.00 fee will be retained for searching as required by statute and a Certification of No Record will be sent.

2. Give all the information you have available for the identification of the record of the registrant in the spaces under registrant information. If the information you furnish is incomplete or inaccurate, it may be impossible to locate the record. If this person has been adopted, please make the request in the adopted name.

3. Complete the applicant information section.

4. Indicate the number of certified copies you wish and include with this application sufficient money in the form of a personal check, postal or bank money order (international money order only for out-of-country requests), made payable to the State Registrar of Vital Statistics; the fee is $13.00 for each certified copy. Mail this application with the fee to Office of Vital Records and Statistics, 304 S Street, P.O. Box 730241, Sacramento, CA 94244-0241.

CERTIFICATE INFORMATION—PLEASE PRINT OR TYPE.

Name on Certificate—First Name	Middle Name	Last Name or Birth Name if Married
City or Town of Birth		Place of Birth—County
Date of Birth—Month, Day, Year (If unknown, enter approximate date of birth.)		Sex
Name of Father—First Name	Middle Name	Last Name
Name of Mother—First Name	Middle Name	Last Name (Maiden Name)

APPLICANT INFORMATION—PLEASE PRINT OR TYPE.

Purpose for Which Certified Copy Is to Be Used	Today's Date	Phone Number—Area Code First
Name of Person Completing Application (Please print.)	Signature of Person Requesting Record(s)—Your Signature ➤	
Address—Street	City	State—ZIP Code
Name of Person Receiving Copies if Different from Above	Number of Certified Copies Requested	Amount of Money Enclosed
Mailing Address for Copies if Different from Above	City	State—ZIP Code

---

DO NOT WRITE IN SPACE BELOW—FOR REGISTRAR.

BIRTH

APPLICATION FOR CERTIFIED COPY OF MARRIAGE RECORD

INFORMATION

Marriage records have been maintained in the Office of the State Registrar of Vital Statistics since July 1, 1905 through _____*1986*_.

INSTRUCTIONS

1. Use a separate application form for each different record of marriage for which you are requesting a certified copy. Send $13.00 for each certified copy requested. If no record of the marriage is found, the $13.00 will be retained for searching as required by statute and a certificate of search will be sent.

2. Give all the information you have available for the identification of the record of marriage in the spaces under bride and groom information. If the information you furnish is incomplete or inaccurate, it may be impossible to locate the record.

3. Complete the applicant information section.

4. Indicate the number of certified copies you wish and include with this application sufficient money in the form of a postal or bank money order (International Money Order only for out-of-county requests), made payable to the Office of Vital Records and Statistics, 304 S Street, P.O. Box 730241, Sacramento, CA 94244-0241. The fee is $13.00 for each certified copy.

BRIDE AND GROOM INFORMATION—PLEASE PRINT

Name of Groom—First Name	Middle Name		Last Name	
Date of Birth	Place of Birth		Name of Father of Groom	
Maiden Name of Bride—First Name	Middle Name		Last Name	
Date of Birth	Place of Birth		Name of Father of Bride	
Date of Marriage—Month, Day, Year	If Date Unknown, Enter Year(s) to be Searched		County of Issue of License	County of Marriage

APPLICANT INFORMATION—PLEASE PRINT

Enter Purpose or Which Certified Copy is to be Used	Today's Date	Your Telephone Number—Area Code First
Please Print—Name of Person Completing Application	Signature of Person Requesting Record(s)—Your Signature ➤	
Address—Street	City	State—ZIP Code
Mailing Address for Copies if Different Than Above	Number of Certified Copies Requested	Amount of Money Enclosed
Mailing Address—Street	City	State—ZIP Code

DO NOT WRITE IN SPACE BELOW—FOR REGISTRAR

VS 113 (2/94)

APPLICATION FOR CERTIFIED COPY OF DEATH RECORD

INFORMATION

Death records have been maintained in the Office of the State Registrar of Vital Statistics since July 1, 1905.

INSTRUCTIONS

1. Use a separate application blank for each different record of death for which you are requesting a certified copy. Send $9 for each certified copy requested. If no record of the death is found, the $9 fee will be retained for searching as required by statute and a certificate of search will be sent.

2. Give all the information you have available for the identification of the record of the decedent in the spaces under Decedent Information. If the information you furnish is incomplete or inaccurate, it may be impossible to locate the record.

3. Complete the Applicant Information section.

4. Indicate the number of certified copies you wish and include with this application sufficient money in the form of a postal or bank money order (International Money Order only for out-of-country requests), made payable to the Office of Vital Records and Statistics, 304 S Street, P.O. Box 730241, Sacramento, CA 94244-0241.

DECEDENT INFORMATION—PLEASE PRINT OR TYPE

Name of Decedent—First (Given)	Middle	Last (Family)	Sex
Place of Death—City or Town	Place of Death—County	Place of Birth	Date of Birth—Month, Day, Year
Date of Death—Month, Day, Year—or Period of Years to be Searched		Social Security Number	
Mother's Maiden Name	Name of Spouse (Husband or Wife of Decedent)		

APPLICANT INFORMATION—PLEASE PRINT OR TYPE

Enter Purpose for Which Certified Copy is to be Used	Today's Date	Your Phone Number ( )
Name of Person Completing Application	Signature of Person Requesting Record(s)—Your Signature ➤	
Address—Street	City	State / ZIP Code
Name of Person Receiving Copies if Different Than Above	Number of Certified Copies Requested	Amount of Money Enclosed
Mailing Address for Copies if Different from Above—Street	City	State / ZIP Code

DO NOT WRITE IN SPACES BELOW—FOR REGISTRAR USE ONLY.

VS 112 (2/94)

COLORADO

Send your requests to:

Vital Records Section
Colorado Department of Health
4300 Cherry Creek Drive South
Denver, Colorado 80222-1530

(303) 692-2200, (303) 756-4464, FAX (800) 423-1108

Send your requests for Marriage Certificates and early vital records to:

County Clerk
County Courthouse
(County Seat), Colorado

Send your requests for Divorce Certificates to:

Clerk
District Court
(County), Colorado

Cost for a certified Birth Certificate	$12.00
Cost for verification of a Marriage or Divorce Record	$12.00
Cost for a certified Death Certificate	$12.00
Cost for a duplicate copy, when ordered at the same time	$6.00

The Vital Records Section has birth records from 1910 and death records from 1900. In addition, they have an index to marriage and divorce records from 1900 through 1939 and from 1975 to the present. The index gives the names of the persons married or divorced, the date, and the county where the event occurred.

If your request is urgent you may call or FAX the Vital Records Section and charge your certificates to your Visa, Discover, or MasterCard. There is a $4.50 fee for this service.

The Colorado Historical Society (1300 Broadway, Denver, CO 80203; Tel. 303-866-2305) has an extensive collection of records.

The Family History Library of The Church of Jesus Christ of Latter-day Saints in Salt Lake City, Utah has microfilmed many of the original and published vital records and church registers of Colorado, including the state marriage index from 1900 to 1992. For details on their holdings please consult your nearest Family History Center.

Application for Certified Copy of Birth Certificate

(Colorado has birth records for the entire state since 1910)

INFORMATION ABOUT PERSON WHOSE BIRTH CERTIFICATE IS REQUESTED -- type or print

Full Name* at Birth	First	Middle	Last	
Date of Birth	Month	Day	Year	
Place of Birth	City	County	State	Colorado
Full Name of Father	First	Middle	Last	
Maiden Name of Mother	First	Middle	Maiden	

Reason for Request	Is this person deceased? ☐ Yes ☐ No

Signature of Person Making Request	Relationship to Registrant	Date

Address	City	State	Zip	Daytime Phone ( )

*If adopted, use adopted name.

Fees: $12 for first copy (or search of files when no record is found)
$6 for each additional copy of the same record ordered at the same time
$4.50 per order convenience charge for use of VISA or MasterCard

Include appropriate additional fees if you wish your certificate returned certified mail, Express Mail, or Federal Express.
Make check or money order payable to Vital Records Section. Please do not send cash.

Types of Service: Apply in person--same day (lobby hours are from 8:30 am to 4:30 pm)
Mail in your application with check or money order--mailed within 2 weeks
Fax us a copy of your order with VISA or MasterCard number--mailed next day***

For Credit Card Use:**   VISA No. _____ Exp. Date _____
MasterCard No. _____ Exp. Date _____

**Convenience charge to be added

- -

Please complete this area also

DO NOT DETACH

| Number of copies ordered_____ |
| Amount of order $ _____ |

PRINT name and address of person to whom
the certified copy is to be issued over the counter,
or mailed:

_____
Name

_____
Address

_____
City/State/Zip

ADRS 2 (Rev. 10/92)

APPLICATION FOR A VERIFICATION OF A MARRIAGE RECORD
(Please complete the form as far as your information will allow.)
(Please Print or Type.)

Vital Records Section
Colorado Department of Health
4300 Cherry Creek Drive South
HSVRD-VR-A1
Denver, Colorado 80222-1530

FEES: $12.00 per copy or per search of files if no record is found.
$5.00 per additional index searched.
We have the following indices:
~~1900~~-1939; 1975-present
1900-

Name of Bride _____

Name of Groom _____

Date of Marriage _____

Place of Marriage _____

This office will not have a record of the marriage if the county did not forward the information for the State Index.

_____   _____
Your signature   Street

(   )_____   _____
Your day time telephone number   City   State   ZIP

If possible, please include a self-addressed, long envelope with your order. Make your check or money order payable to Vital Records.

10/92

Application for Certified Copy of Death Certificate
(Colorado has death records for the entire state since 1900)

INFORMATION ABOUT PERSON WHOSE DEATH CERTIFICATE IS REQUESTED -- *type or print*

Full Name at Death	First		Middle		Last	
Date of Death	Month			Day		Year
Place of Death	City		County		State	Colorado

Reason for Request		Age at Time of Death	State of Birth
Signature of Person Making Request		Relationship to Deceased	Date

Address	City	State	Zip	Daytime Phone ( )

Fees: $12 for first copy (or search of files when no record is found)
$6 for each additional copy of the same record ordered at the same time
$4.50 per order convenience charge for use of VISA or MasterCard

Include appropriate additional fees if you wish your certificate returned certified mail, Express Mail, or Federal Express.
Make check or money order payable to Vital Records Section. Please do not send cash.

Types of Service: Apply in person--same day (lobby hours are from 8:30 am to 4:30 pm)
Mail in your application with check or money order--mailed within 2 weeks
Fax us a copy of your order with VISA or MasterCard number--mailed next day**

**For Credit Card Use:*   VISA No. _____ Exp. Date _____
MasterCard No. _____ Exp. Date _____

*Convenience charge to be added

- -

Please complete this area also

DO NOT DETACH

Number of copies ordered_____
Amount of order $ _____

PRINT name and address of person to whom
the certified copy is to be issued over the counter,
or mailed:

_____
Name

_____
Address

_____
City/State/Zip

Certified copies of certificates are also available in the county where death occurred.

CONNECTICUT

For records from July 1, 1897 to the present write to:

Connecticut Department of Public Health and Addiction Services
Vital Records Section
150 Washington Street
Hartford, Connecticut 06106-4476

(203) 566-1124

Certificates are also available from:

Town Clerk
Town Hall
(Town), Connecticut

For Divorce Records write to:

Clerk
Superior Court
(Town), Connecticut

Cost for a certified Birth Certificate	$15.00
Cost for a wallet-size Birth Certificate	$15.00
Cost for a certified Marriage Certificate	$5.00
Cost for a certified Death Certificate	$5.00

The Vital Records Section has copies of vital records from July 1, 1897. Original records are on file with each town clerk, who can also issue certificates. The town clerks generally have the records from the year their town was formed.

The Connecticut State Library (231 Capitol Avenue, Hartford, CT 06115; Tel. 203-566-3056) has the Barbour Index to Connecticut Vital Records, which indexes records from the 1600s to the mid-1800s. It also has the Hale Index to Cemetery Inscriptions; the Hale Index to Marriage and Death Notices (which appeared in early Connecticut newspapers); and microfilm copies of pre-1900 vital records from the town clerks. The Connecticut Historical Society (1 Elizabeth Street, Hartford, CT 06105; Tel. 203-236-5621) also has an extensive collection.

The Family History Library of The Church of Jesus Christ of Latter-day Saints in Salt Lake City, Utah has microfilmed many of the original and published vital records of Connecticut. For details on their holdings please consult your nearest Family History Center.

REQUEST FOR COPY OF BIRTH CERTIFICATE

VS.39B REV 8/84

Mail request with fee or bring to:

STATE OF CONNECTICUT, DEPT. OF HEALTH SERVICES

Vital Records Section

150 Washington St., Hartford, Conn. 06106

PLEASE PRINT.   *DO NOT MAIL CASH*

I. BIRTH CERTIFICATE OF:

FULL NAME AT BIRTH

DATE OF BIRTH | SEX

PLACE OF BIRTH (Town, Hospital)

II. PARENTS OF PERSON NAMED IN BIRTH CERTIFICATE:

FATHER'S FULL NAME | FATHER'S BIRTHPLACE (State)

MOTHER'S MAIDEN NAME | MOTHER'S BIRTHPLACE (State)

RESIDENCE OF PARENTS AT TIME OF THIS BIRTH

TYPE OF COPY (See explanations below)	LEGAL FEE	NO. OF COPIES	AMOUNT ATTACHED
Full certified copy	$15.00		$
Certification of birth	$15.00		$

Full certified copy: Sufficient for all legal purposes. If requester is a minor (under 18 years of age), parent or guardian must sign this request

Certification of birth: Wallet-size certificate, sufficient for Social Security, school, driver's license, and working papers

III. PERSON MAKING THIS REQUEST

Your Name

Your Address | (No. and Street)

(Town, State) | (Zip Code)

▲ Your Signature

*For the protection of the individual, certificates of vital events are **not** open to public inspection.*

A full certified copy can be obtained by registrant 18 or over, parent, or legal representative.

A birth certification can be obtained by registrant 16 or over, parent, spouse or legal representative.

RELATIONSHIP TO PERSON NAMED IN CERTIFICATE (e.g. parents, attorney) | REASON FOR MAKING REQUEST

REQUEST FOR COPY OF MARRIAGE CERTIFICATE
VS-39M 3-88

Mail request with fee or bring to:

STATE OF CONNECTICUT, DEPT. OF HEALTH SERVICES

Vital Records Section

150 Washington Street, Hartford, Conn. 06106

PLEASE PRINT

GROOM	FULL NAME *(First)*	*(Middle)*	*(Last)*
BRIDE	FULL NAME BEFORE MARRIAGE *(First)*	*(Middle)*	*(Last)*

DATE OF MARRIAGE *(Mo./Day/Year/)*	PLACE OF MARRIAGE *(Town)*

PERSON MAKING THIS REQUEST	YOUR NAME		Legal fee is $3.00 per copy.
	YOUR ADDRESS *(No. and Street)*		NO. OF COPIES WANTED / AMOUNT ATTACHED $
	(Town, State)	*(Zip Code)*	YOUR SIGNATURE ►

REQUEST FOR COPY OF DEATH CERTIFICATE
VS-39M Rev. 6-83

Mail request with fee or bring to:

STATE OF CONNECTICUT, DEPT. OF HEALTH SERVICES

Vital Records Section

150 Washington Street, Hartford, Conn. 06106

PLEASE PRINT.

DEATH CERTIFICATE OF:	FULL NAME *(First)*	*(Last)*	SEX	DATE OF DEATH (OR DATE LAST KNOWN TO BE ALIVE) *(Mo., Day, Yr.)*
	PLACE OF DEATH *(Town)*	DATE OF BIRTH *(Month, Day, Year)*		PLACE OF BIRTH *(Town, State or Foreign Country)*
	FATHER'S NAME	MOTHER'S NAME		IF MARRIED, SPOUSE'S NAME

PERSON MAKING THIS REQUEST	YOUR NAME		Legal fee is $3.00 per copy.
	YOUR ADDRESS *(No. and Street)*		NO. OF COPIES WANTED / AMOUNT ATTACHED $
	(Town, State)	*(Zip Code)*	YOUR SIGNATURE ►

DELAWARE

Send your requests to:

Office of Vital Statistics
Division of Public Health
P.O. Box 637
Dover, Delaware 19903-0637

(302) 739-4721

Send your requests for Divorce Records to:

Clerk   or   Clerk
Family Court   Prothonotary Office
(Town), Delaware   (Town), Delaware

Cost for a certified Birth Certificate	$5.00
Cost for a certified Marriage Certificate	$5.00
Cost for a certified Death Certificate	$5.00
Cost for a duplicate copy, when ordered at the same time	$3.00

The Delaware Office of Vital Statistics has birth records from 1921 and death and marriage records from 1953. Earlier records are held by The Bureau of Archives, Hall of Records (P.O. Box 1401, Dover, DE 19901; Tel. 302-739-5318). They charge $5.00 per copy for these records.

If your request is urgent you may call and charge your certificates to your Visa, Discover, or MasterCard. There is a $5.00 fee for this service, plus the express mail charges.

The Family History Library of The Church of Jesus Christ of Latter-day Saints in Salt Lake City, Utah has microfilmed many of the original and published vital records of Delaware. They have microfilm copies of the statewide birth records and their indexes from 1861 to 1913, marriage records and their indexes from 1680 to 1850, and death records and their indexes from 1855 to 1910. For details on their holdings please consult your nearest Family History Center.

_____
Today's Date

_____
Number of Copies

APPLICATION FOR BIRTH CERTIFICATE
COMPLETE ALL ITEMS REQUESTED BELOW AS ACCURATELY AS POSSIBLE

_____
Full Name at Birth of Person Whose Record is Requested - If Name Has Ever Been Changed Please Give Details on Back

_____   _____
Date of Birth (Month, Day, Year)   *Place of Birth (Hospital)*

_____
Full Maiden Name of Mother

_____
Full Name of Father

_____
If Known, Name of Doctor or Midwife

_____
For What Purpose is Certificate Needed

PLEASE COMPLETE
YOUR NAME AND
MAILING ADDRESS

NAME _____

STREET ADDRESS _____

TOWN _____ STATE _____

ZIP CODE _____

FEE: $5.00 for first copy. $3.00 for each additional copy of same record requested at same time.

A certified copy of the original birth record has entered thereon the name, birthdate, birthplace, names of parents and personal particulars. This copy is used for all purposes.

If the record is not found $5.00 will be retained as the search fee.

Insufficient fee being returned $ _____

If a check with the incorrect fee is being returned do not alter. make another check.

Today's Date

Number of Copies

APPLICATION FOR MARRIAGE CERTIFICATE
COMPLETE ALL ITEMS REQUESTED BELOW AS ACCURATELY AS POSSIBLE

FULL NAME OF GROOM _____

FULL MAIDEN NAME OF BRIDE _____

PLACE OF MARRIAGE _____

DATE OF MARRIAGE _____

NAME OF OFFICIATING MINISTER _____

* * * * *

MAIL COPY TO . . . .   NAME _____

STREET ADDRESS _____

TOWN _____

STATE _____ ZIP CODE _____

Fee for a certified copy is $5.00 for the first copy.

$3.00 for each additional copy of same record requested at same time.

Include fee with appplication - Make payable to the Office of Vital Statistics.

If the record is not found $5.00 will be retained as the search fee.

Insufficient fee being returned.

OFFICE OF VITAL STATISTICS
P.O. Box 637
Dover, Delaware 19903

_____
Today's Date

_____
Number of Copies

APPLICATION FOR A CERTIFIED COPY OF A DEATH CERTIFICATE
(Complete items requested below accurately as possible)

_____   _____
Name of decedent   _Race_

_____   _____
Date of decease   _Place of decease_

_____   _____
Full name of decedent's father   _Full maiden name of mother_

_____
For what purpose is certificate needed

SEND COPY TO . . . .   _____
                        Name

                        _____
                        Street/Development/Rural Delivery/Box Number

                        _____
                        City/Town   _State_   _Zip Code_

Fee - $5.00 for first copy. $3.00 for each additional copies of same record requested at same time.

Payable to. . . . OFFICE OF VITAL STATISTICS

If the record is not found the fee will be retained for the search.

Insufficient fee being returned _____

If a check with the incorrect fee is being returned do not alter. Make another check.

DOCUMENT NO. 35-05-002/86/02/17 PH - 252

DISTRICT OF COLUMBIA

Send your requests for Birth and Death Certificates to:

Vital Records Branch
Government of the District of Columbia
Department of Human Services
613 G Street, N.W., 9th Floor
Washington, DC 20001

(202) 727-9281

Send your requests for Marriage Certificates to:

Marriage Bureau
Superior Court of the District of Columbia
500 Indiana Avenue, N.W., Room 4485
Washington, DC 20001-2131

(202) 879-4848

Send your requests for Divorce Certificates to:

Domestic Relations
Superior Court of the District of Columbia
500 Indiana Avenue, N.W., Room 4230
Washington, DC 20001-2131

(202) 879-4848

Cost for a certified Birth Certificate	$18.00
Cost for a computerized short form Birth Certificate	$12.00
Cost for a certified Marriage Certificate	$10.00
Cost for a certified Divorce Certificate	$5.00
Cost for a certified Death Certificate	$12.00

The Vital Records Branch has birth and death records from August 1, 1874. Marriage records are available from 1811 to the present and must be ordered from the Superior Court.

If your request is urgent you may call and charge your certificates to your Visa, Discover, or MasterCard. There is a $6.00 charge for this service.

The Washingtoniana Division of the Martin Luther King Memorial Library (901 G Street, N.W., Washington, D.C. 20001; Tel. 202-727-1213) has an extensive collection.

The Family History Library of The Church of Jesus Christ of Latter-day Saints in Salt Lake City, Utah has microfilmed original and published vital records of the District of Columbia. For details on their holdings please consult your nearest Family History Center.

GOVERNMENT OF THE DISTRICT OF COLUMBIA
DEPARTMENT OF HUMAN SERVICES

RETURN OF CORRESPONDENCE

The attached request is being returned for the following reason(s):

[ ] Fee for Birth Records: $12.00 per copy Computer (short form); $18.00 per Archival (long form) payable in advance. **Death records $12.00**

[ ] Check of Money Order MUST be made payable to the D.C. **TREASURER**

[ ] The information given is insufficient for a through search. Please complete the form below and return to this office:

> 613 G St., N.W.
> 9th Floor
> Washington, D.C. 20001

[ ] The District of Columbia registers only birth/deaths that occur in the District of Columbia.

[ ] **NO RECORDS REGISTERED PRIOR TO 1874.**

[ ] <u>**APPLICATION FOR CERTIFIED COPY OF BIRTH CERTIFICATE**</u>(S)
   [Please Print]
   Choice of Certificate: [ ] COMPUTER (short form) $12.00
                           [ ] ARCHIVAL (long form) $18.00

Name at Birth:_____
         (First)   (Middle)   (Last)

D.O.B.   Place of Birth (DC) Hospital or Street Address Sex

Father's Name   Mother's Maiden Name
Purpose:_____ Relationship:_____
Signature:_____
Mailing Address:_____

DHS-13 [Rev 1/89]

[ ] <u>**APPLICATION FOR CERTIFIED COPY OF DEATH CERTIFICATES**</u>(S)
   [Please Print]
Full Name of Deceased:_____
Race (optional)_____
D.O.D.:_____ Place of Death in D.C.:_____
If Date of Death not known, then date last alive:_____
Age at Time   Name of   Name of
of Death:_____ Spouse:_____ Father:_____
Last known address of deceased:_____
Name of Funeral Director:_____
Mailing Address:_____

DHS-14 (Rev 1/89)

WARNING: Vital Records are not public records. Vital Records may **be issued only to the registrant, members of his/her family, or persons acting on behalf of the registrant of his/her estate.**

Send your requests to:

> State of Florida
> Department of Health and Rehabilitative Services
> Vital Statistics
> P.O. Box 210
> Jacksonville, Florida 32231-0042

(904) 359-6900

For Marriage and Divorce Certificates before June 6, 1927 write to:

> County Clerk
> County Courthouse
> (County Seat), Florida

Cost for a certified Birth Certificate	$9.00
Cost for a commemorative Birth Certificate	$30.00
Cost for a certified Marriage Certificate	$5.00
Cost for a certified Divorce Certificate	$5.00
Cost for a certified Death Certificate	$5.00
Cost for a duplicate copy, when ordered at the same time	$4.00

The first state law requiring registration was passed in 1899. However, the Office of Vital Statistics has birth and death records from 1917, with some birth records dating back to 1865 and some death records to 1877. They have marriage and divorce records from June 6, 1927 to date.

If your request is urgent you may mark it "rush" for an additional charge of $10.00. You may also call (904) 359-6911 and charge your certificates to your Visa or MasterCard for a $10.00 rush fee plus a $4.50 service charge.

The Special Collections Department of the University of South Florida Library (4202 East Fowler Avenue, Tampa, FL 33620; Tel. 813-974-2731) has the original marriage records and indexes for Hillsborough County from 1840 to 1980.

The Family History Library of The Church of Jesus Christ of Latter-day Saints in Salt Lake City, Utah has microfilmed many of the vital records of Florida, including the state marriage index from 1927 to 1969 and the state death index from 1877 to 1969. For details on their holdings please consult your nearest Family History Center.

FULL NAME AT BIRTH (Registrant)	First	Middle	Last	
If name was changed since birth, indicate new name here ⟶	First	Middle	Last	
BIRTH NUMBER (if known)			Social Security Number (if known)	Age
DATE OF BIRTH (required for search)	Month	Day	Year	Sex
PLACE OF BIRTH	Hospital	City	County	FLORIDA
FATHER'S NAME	First	Middle	Last	
MOTHER'S MAIDEN NAME (name before marriage)	First	Middle	Last (Maiden)	

FEES ARE NONREFUNDABLE and subject to change without notice.

A BIRTH RECORD SEARCH REQUIRES ADVANCE PAYMENT OF A <u>NONREFUNDABLE</u> SEARCH FEE OF $9.00*

This fee entitles the applicant to one computer certificate for births from 1968 through present, or a photocopy for births from 1967 back to 1865, or a wallet-size card on all the above years, or a certified no-record statement if no record is found .... Record ☐   Wallet Card ☐

Additional computer certifications, photocopies, or cards are $4 each when ordered at the same time as the initial search .... Number of Records ☐   No. of Cards ☐

If a photocopy is requested for computer years (1968 to present) instead of the computer certification a fee of $14 is required; each additional photocopy at that time is $4 .... Number of Records ☐

RUSH ORDERS: An additional $10 per application is required if you wish rush service. Your envelope must be marked "RUSH" .... YES ☐   NO ☐

COMMEMORATIVE CERTIFICATE NOW AVAILABLE: signed by the Governor of Florida; large size suitable for framing; $25 if ordered at the same time as certificate record, $34 if ordered separately, allow 4-6 weeks for delivery .... YES ☐   NO ☐

TOTAL ENCLOSED: Check or money order payable to U.S. dollars to Vital Statistics .... PLEASE DO NOT MAIL CASH   TOTAL ENCLOSED _____

Florida Law imposes an additional service charge of $15 for dishonored checks.

Applicant's Signature	Applicant's relationship to registrant
Home Phone Number / Work Phone Number	Name and Address for mailing, if different from residence
Residence Address / Apt. No.	
City, / State / Zip Code	

HRS Form 726, Oct 90 (Obsoletes previous editions which may not be used)
(Stock Number: 5740-000-0726-8)

*$2 of this fee is for Crimes Against Children; $1.50 is for Child Welfare Training

HRS

State of Florida, Department of Health and Rehabilitative Services
APPLICATION FOR MARRIAGE RECORD FOR LICENSES ISSUED IN FLORIDA

	First	Middle	Last	Race
NAME OF GROOM				
NAME OF BRIDE	First	Middle	Last	Race
DATE OF MARRIAGE (approximate month & day)	Month	Day	Specify exact year or series of years to be searched	
PLACE LICENSE ISSUED	City or Town		County	FLORIDA

AVAILABILITY: Marriage records from June 6, 1927 are available at this office. Beginning with 1972, the marriage application is an integral part of the record issued here. Other marriage documents are obtainable only from the county court which issued them.

FIRST YEAR SEARCH FEE: (includes one certified record or a "no record found" statement) **$5.00**

ADDITIONAL YEARS: $2 per year. The maximum search fee is $55 regardless of the total number of years to be searched

ADDITIONAL RECORDS: when ordered at the same time. $4 each. . . . .

RUSH ORDERS (optional): $10 per order. Envelope must be marked "RUSH" . . . .

FOR JACKSONVILLE PICKUP SERVICE OR FOR MASTERCARD OR VISA CHARGES, TELEPHONE (904) 359-6911
FEES ARE NON REFUNDABLE AND SUBJECT TO CHANGE WITHOUT NOTICE

COMMEMORATIVE CERTIFICATE NOW AVAILABLE: signed by the Governor of Florida; large size suitable for framing; $25 . . .
if ordered at the same time as a certified record, $30 if ordered separately, allow 4-6 weeks for delivery.

TOTAL ENCLOSED: Check or money order payable in U.S. dollars to Vital Statistics. . . . .
Florida Law imposes an additional service charge of $15 for dishonored checks.

PLEASE DO NOT MAIL CASH

Applicant's Signature		Name and Address for mailing, if different from residence
Applicant's Name (must be typed or printed)		
Residence Address	Apt. No	
City, State, Zip	Telephone No.	

MAIL THIS APPLICATION TO VITAL STATISTICS, P.O. BOX 210, JACKSONVILLE, FL 32231-0042

HRS Form 261, Oct 90 (Obsoletes previous editions which may not be used)
(Stock Number: 5740-000-0261-4)

PLEASE TYPE OR PRINT CLEARLY

HRS

State of Florida, Department of Health and Rehabilitative Services

APPLICATION FOR DISSOLUTION OF MARRIAGE RECORD (DIVORCE OR ANNULMENT) GRANTED IN FLORIDA

PLEASE TYPE OR PRINT CLEARLY

NAME OF HUSBAND	First	Middle	Last
NAME OF WIFE	First	Middle	Last
DATE OF DISSOLUTION (approximate month & day)	Month	Day	Specify exact year or series of years to be searched
PLACE LICENSE ISSUED	City or Town	County	FLORIDA

AVAILABILITY: Dissolution records from June 6, 1927 are available at this office. All other dissolution documents, including copies of final decrees, are obtainable only from the Clerk of Circuit Court of the County where granted.

FIRST YEAR SEARCH FEE: (includes one certified record or a "no record found" statement)...... $5.00

ADDITIONAL YEARS: $2 per year. The maximum search fee is $55 regardless of the total number of years to be searched ......

ADDITIONAL RECORDS: when ordered at the same time. $4 each ......

RUSH ORDERS: $10 per order (optional). Envelope must be marked "RUSH" ......

FOR JACKSONVILLE PICKUP SERVICE OR FOR MASTERCARD OR VISA CHARGES, TELEPHONE (904) 359-6911

FEES ARE NON REFUNDABLE AND SUBJECT TO CHANGE WITHOUT NOTICE

TOTAL ENCLOSED: Check or money order payable in U.S. dollars to Vital Statistics ...... PLEASE DO NOT MAIL CASH

Florida Law imposes an additional service charge of $15 for dishonored checks.

Applicant's Signature	Name and Address for mailing, if different from residence
Applicant's Name (must be typed or printed)	
Residence Address	Apt. No	
City, State, Zip	Telephone No.	

MAIL THIS APPLICATION TO VITAL STATISTICS, P.O. BOX 210, JACKSONVILLE, FL 32231-0042

HRS Form 260, Oct 90 (Obsoletes previous editions which may not be used)
(Stock Number: 5740-000-0260-6)

State of Florida, Department of Health and Rehabilitative Services

APPLICATION FOR DEATH RECORD FOR DEATH WHICH OCCURRED IN FLORIDA

NAME OF DECEASED (Registrant)	First	Middle	Last	Race
SOCIAL SECURITY NO. (if known)				Sex
DATE OF DEATH (approximate month & day)	Month	Day	Specify exact year or series of years to be searched	
PLACE OF DEATH		City or Town	County	FLORIDA
NAME OF FUNERAL DIRECTOR				

BEFORE ORDERING, PLEASE READ THE BACK OF THIS FORM.

FEES ARE NONREFUNDABLE and subject to change without notice.

FIRST YEAR SEARCH FEE: (includes one certified record or a "no record found" statement) $5.00

ADDITIONAL YEARS: $2 per year. The maximum search fee is $55 regardless of the total number of years to be searched

ADDITIONAL RECORDS: when ordered at the same time. $4 each . . . .

RUSH ORDERS: $10 per order (optional). Envelope must be marked "RUSH" . . . .

FOR JACKSONVILLE PICKUP SERVICE OR FOR MASTERCARD OR VISA CHARGES, TELEPHONE (904) 359-6911

TOTAL ENCLOSED: Check or money order payable in U.S. dollars to Vital Statistics . . . .

PLEASE DO NOT MAIL CASH

Florida Law imposes an additional service charge of $15 for dishonored checks.

Applicant's Name (must be typed or printed)		Applicant's Signature	
Home Phone Number	Work Phone Number	CAUSE OF DEATH REQUESTED (see back of form for eligibility)	YES ☐ NO ☐
Residence Address		Apt. No.	Relationship to deceased (must be completed when cause of death is requested)
City	State	Zip Code	

MAIL THIS APPLICATION TO VITAL STATISTICS, P.O. BOX 210, JACKSONVILLE, FL 32231-0042

HRS Form 727, Jan 91 (Replaces Oct 90 edition which may be used)
(Stock Number: 5740-000-0727-6)

PLEASE TYPE OR PRINT CLEARLY

GEORGIA

Send your requests to:

Georgia Department of Human Resources
Vital Records Service
47 Trinity Avenue, S.W., Room 217-H
Atlanta, Georgia 30334-1201

(404) 656-4750

Earlier records are available from:

Clerk
County Probate Court
(County Seat), Georgia

Divorce Records are available from:

Clerk
Superior Court
(County Seat), Georgia

Cost for a certified Birth Certificate	$10.00
Cost for a certified Birth Card	$10.00
Cost for a certified Marriage Certificate	$10.00
Cost for a certified Death Certificate	$10.00
Cost for a duplicate copy, when ordered at the same time	$5.00

The Georgia Department of Human Resources has birth and death records from January 1, 1919 and marriage and divorce records from June 1952.

If your request is urgent you may call and charge your certificates to your Visa, Discover, or MasterCard. There is a $5.00 fee for this service, plus $15.50 if you want your certificate to be shipped by overnight Federal Express.

The Georgia Department of Archives and History (300 Capitol Avenue, S.E., Atlanta, GA 30334; Tel. 404-656-2350) has marriage and divorce records for various years depending on the county.

The Family History Library of The Church of Jesus Christ of Latter-day Saints in Salt Lake City, Utah has microfilmed original vital records of Georgia. For details on their holdings please consult your nearest Family History Center.

BIRTH CERTIFICATE REQUESTS

Please indicate below the type and number of copies requested and forward this form with either a money order or certified check for the correct amount, made payable to the Georgia Department of Human Resources.

[　]Full size copy $10.00　[　]Wallet size copy $10.00　[　]Total Number　[　]Amount
　　Additional Copies　　　　　Each additional　　　　　　of Copies　　　　Received
　　$5.00 each at this time　　$10.00 at this time　　　　Requested　　　$_____
　　　　　　　　　　　　　　　BIRTH RECORDS ONLY

FILL IN INFORMATION BELOW CONCERNING PERSON WHOSE BIRTH CERTIFICATE IS REQUESTED

Name at birth: _____
　　　　　　　(first　　　　　　(middle)　　　　　　　　(last)

Date of birth: _____ Age:_____ Race:_____ Sex:_____

Place of birth: _____
　　　　　　　(hospital)　　(city)　　　(county)　　　(state)

Full name of father: _____

Full name of mother before marriage: _____

DEATH CERTIFICATE REQUESTS

FILL IN INFORMATION BELOW CONCERNING DECEDENT

Name: _____

Date of death: _____ Age:_____ Race:_____ Sex:_____

Place of death: _____
　　　　　　　(hospital)　　(city)　　　(county)　　　(state)

If married, name of husband or wife:_____
Occupation of deceased:_____
Funeral director's name:_____
Name of doctor:_____
Place of burial:_____
　　　　　　　(city)　　　　　　　(county)　　　(state)

MAILING ADDRESS

List below name and address of person to whom certificate is to be mailed and indicate their relationship to the person whose name is on the certificate:

Name:_____ Relationship:_____

Address:_____
　　　　(No. & Street or RFD and Box No.)　　　(Apt. No.)

_____
　　　(city)　　　　　　(state)　　　　　(zip code)

MARRIAGE CERTIFICATE REQUESTS

Please indicate below the type and number of copies requested and forward this form with either a money order or certified check for the correct amount, made payable to the Georgia Department of Human Resources.

[   ] Full size copy $10.00;
       Additional copies are
       $5.00 each at this time

[   ] Total Number of
       Copies Requested

NOTE: Records prior to June 9, 1952 must be requested at the Office of the Probate Judge in the county where the license was issued. If you are requesting a marriage certificate prior to this date, complete this application and mail it to the County's Probate Court's Office in which the marriage was granted. Contact their office concerning their fee requirements, as their prices may differ from our prices.

COMPLETE ALL INFORMATION FOR THE MARRIAGE RECORD BEING REQUESTED:

Groom's Name_____
              (First)   (Middle)   (Last)

Bride's Name_____
              (First)   (Middle)   (Maiden)

Date of Marriage_____
              (Month)   (Day)   (Year)

Place of Marriage_____
              (City)   (County)   (State)

Signature of Requestor_____

Relationship (if other than Bride or Groom)_____

MAILING ADDRESS

List below the name and address of person to whom certificate is to be mailed; then, indicate relationship to the person whose name is on the certificate.

Name:_____Relationship:_____

Address:_____
            (No. & Street)   (Apartment Number)

        _____
            (City)   (State)   (Zip Code)

Send your requests to:

State Department of Health
Research and Statistics Office
Vital Records Section
1250 Punchbowl Street, Room 103
P.O. Box 3378
Honolulu, Hawaii 96801-3378

(808) 961-7327

Cost for a certified Birth Certificate	$2.00
Cost for a certified Marriage Certificate	$2.00
Cost for a certified Divorce Certificate	$2.00
Cost for a certified Death Certificate	$2.00

The Hawaii Vital Records Section has birth, marriage, divorce, and death records from 1853.

The State Archives (Iolani Palace Grounds, Honolulu, HI 96813; Tel. 808-548-2355) and the State Library (478 South King Street, Honolulu, HI 96813; Tel. 808-548-4165) both maintain indexes to all birth and marriage notices (1850-1950) and obituary notices (1836-1950) from Hawaiian newspapers.

The Family History Library of The Church of Jesus Christ of Latter-day Saints in Salt Lake City, Utah has microfilmed many of the original and published vital records of Hawaii. They have made microfilm copies of the statewide birth registers from 1901 to 1916 and death registers from 1909 to 1916. For details on their holdings please consult your nearest Family History Center.

STATE OF HAWAII, DEPARTMENT OF HEALTH
RESEARCH AND STATISTICS OFFICE

REQUEST FOR CERTIFIED COPY OF **BIRTH** RECORD
(ATTACH $2.00 FOR EACH COPY. DO NOT SEND CASH BY MAIL)

	FIRST	MIDDLE	LAST
NAME ON CERTIFICATE			

	MONTH	DAY	YEAR		CITY OR TOWN	ISLAND
DATE OF BIRTH:				PLACE OF BIRTH:		

	FIRST	MIDDLE	LAST
FATHER'S NAME:			

	FIRST	MIDDLE	MAIDEN NAME
MOTHER'S NAME:			

NUMBER OF COPIES _____	AMOUNT ATTACHED $ _____

ALL ITEMS MUST BE COMPLETED IN FULL TO PERMIT THIS OFFICE TO COMPLY WITH THIS REQUEST. FOR THE PROTECTION OF THE INDIVIDUAL, CERTIFICATES OF VITAL EVENTS ARE NOT OPEN TO PUBLIC INSPECTION.

RELATIONSHIP OF REQUESTOR TO PERSON NAMED ON CERTIFICATE

REASON FOR REQUESTING A CERTIFIED COPY

SIGNATURE OF REQUESTOR:	TELEPHONE NUMBERS
	RES.:
PRINT OR TYPE NAME OF REQUESTOR:	BUS.:

MAIL TO: {

NAME

NO. AND STREET OR P. O. BOX

CITY	STATE	ZIP

FOR OFFICE USE ONLY

Index Searched		Volumes Searched		Date Copy Prepared
From	To	From	To	
Year	Volume	Certificate		Receipt Number

RS 135 (Rev. 1/84)

STATE OF HAWAII, DEPARTMENT OF HEALTH
RESEARCH AND STATISTICS OFFICE

REQUEST FOR COPY OF **MARRIAGE** OR **DIVORCE** RECORD
(ATTACH $2.00 FOR CERTIFIED COPY)

AMOUNT ATTACHED $ _____	MARRIAGE NO. OF COPIES _____	DIVORCE NO. OF COPIES _____

GROOM'S NAME:	FIRST	MIDDLE	LAST

BRIDE'S NAME:	FIRST	MIDDLE	LAST

DATE OF	MARRIAGE: OR DIVORCE:	MONTH	DAY	YEAR

PLACE OF	MARRIAGE: OR DIVORCE	CITY OR TOWN	ISLAND

ALL ITEMS MUST BE COMPLETED IN FULL TO PERMIT THIS OFFICE TO COMPLY WITH THIS REQUEST. FOR THE PROTECTION OF THE INDIVIDUAL, CERTIFICATES OF VITAL EVENTS ARE NOT OPEN TO PUBLIC INSPECTION.

RELATIONSHIP OF REQUESTOR TO PERSONS NAMED ON CERTIFICATE

REASON FOR REQUESTING A CERTIFIED COPY

SIGNATURE OF REQUESTOR:	TELEPHONE NUMBERS RES.:
PRINT OR TYPE NAME OF REQUESTOR:	BUS.:

MAIL TO:
NAME

NO. AND STREET OR P. O. BOX

CITY   STATE   ZIP

FOR OFFICE USE ONLY		
Index Searched	Volumes Searched	Date Copy Prepared
From To	From To	
Year Volume	Certificate	Receipt Number

RS 137 (Rev. 1/84)

STATE OF HAWAII, DEPARTMENT OF HEALTH
OFFICE OF HEALTH STATUS MONITORING

REQUEST FOR CERTIFIED COPY OF **DEATH** RECORD

ATTACH $2.00 FOR EACH CERTIFIED COPY	AMOUNT ATTACHED $ _____ _____	NUMBER OF COPIES REQUESTED: _____

	FIRST	MIDDLE	LAST
NAME OF DECEASED:			

	MONTH	DAY	YEAR
DATE OF DEATH:			

	CITY OR TOWN	ISLAND
PLACE OF DEATH:		

RELATIONSHIP OF REQUESTOR TO PERSON NAMED ON CERTIFICATE	REASON FOR REQUESTING A CERTIFIED COPY

SIGNATURE OF REQUESTOR:	TELEPHONE NUMBERS
	RES.:
PRINT NAME OF REQUESTOR:	
	BUS.:

ADDRESS OF REQUESTOR:	NO. AND STREET OR P. O. BOX

CITY	STATE	ZIP

ALL ITEMS MUST BE COMPLETED IN FULL TO PERMIT THIS OFFICE TO COMPLY WITH THIS REQUEST. FOR THE PROTECTION OF THE INDIVIDUAL, CERTIFICATES OF VITAL EVENTS ARE NOT OPEN TO PUBLIC INSPECTION.

MAIL TO:

PLEASE COMPLETE ONLY IF MAILING TO PERSON OTHER THAN REQUESTOR.

NAME
NO. AND STREET OR P. O. BOX

CITY	STATE	ZIP

FOR OFFICE USE ONLY		
Index Searched	Volumes Searched	Date Copy Prepared
From To	From To	
Year	Volume	Certificate	Receipt Number

OHSM 136 (REV. 10/89)

COMPLETE ALL ITEMS

Send your requests to:

> State of Idaho
> Department of Health and Welfare
> Vital Statistics Unit
> 450 West State Street
> Boise, Idaho 83720-5450

(208) 334-5980

Earlier Marriage and Divorce Records are available from:

> County Recorder
> County Courthouse
> (County Seat), Idaho

Cost for a certified Birth Certificate	$8.00
Cost for an heirloom Birth Certificate	$30.00
Cost for a wallet-size Birth Card	$8.00
Cost for a certified Marriage or Divorce Certificate	$8.00
Cost for a certified Death Certificate	$8.00

The Idaho State Office of Vital Statistics has birth and death records from July 1, 1911 and marriage and divorce records from May 1, 1947.

If your request is urgent you may call and make arrangements to FAX your request and charge your certificates to your Visa, Discover, or MasterCard. There is a $5.00 fee for this service, plus express delivery charges.

The Family History Library of The Church of Jesus Christ of Latter-day Saints in Salt Lake City, Utah has microfilmed many of the original and published vital records of Idaho. For details on their holdings please consult your nearest Family History Center.

BIRTH CERTIFICATE APPLICATION

(For Persons Born in Idaho)

MAIL TO: **VITAL STATISTICS**
450 W. State Street
Boise, ID 83720-5450

Name on Certificate _____
(First)   (Middle)   (Last)

Place of Birth _____ File Number _____
(City)   (County)   (If Known)

If Home Birth Give Exact Address _____

Date of Birth _____ Sex _____
(Month)   (Day)   (Year)

Father's Name _____

Mother's Maiden Name _____

Purpose _____   Check if Applicable: ☐ RUSH
                                                                             ☐ Twin Birth

Signature of Applicant _____

Address _____
(Street)   (City)   (State)   (Zip)

Relationship _____

Number of Copies Requested: ____ Certified Copy ____ Birth Card ____ Heirloom Certificate

Fees: Certified Copy – $8.00
        (A certified copy is normally required for passport, social security, school entrance, driver's license, etc.)
        Heirloom Certificate – $30.00
        ($15.00 of the fee is automatically deposited to the CHILDRENS DEFENSE TRUST ACCOUNT to help combat Child Abuse)
        Birth Card – $8.00
        Search Fee – $8.00
        (A search fee is charged for each search of the files, even though a record may not be found. When a record is found, the search fee covers the cost of one certified copy of the record.)
        Filing Fee – $10.00
        (A filing fee is required by statute for new certification creation and amendments regarding paternity, adoptions, court order name changes, and delayed registrations.)

Name _____

Street _____

City _____ State _____ Zip _____

HWH-0160

APPLICATION FOR A MARRIAGE CERTIFICATE

Address correspondence and make money order payable to:

VITAL STATISTICS UNIT

Department of Health and Welfare
Division of Health
Statehouse
Boise, Idaho   83720

FULL NAME OF GROOM _____

FULL NAME OF BRIDE _____

DATE OF MARRIAGE _____

CITY AND COUNTY OF MARRIAGE _____

SIGNATURE OF APPLICANT _____

ADDRESS _____

RELATIONSHIP TO ABOVE PERSONS _____

Number of certified copies requested: _____
The fee for each certified copy and/or search is $8.00.

NOTE: *Marriages have been filed with the State office since May, 1947. Prior to that time, they are filed with the County Recorder of each County in the State.*

APPLICATION FOR A DIVORCE CERTIFICATE

Address Correspondence and make check or money order payable to:

VITAL STATISTICS UNIT
Department of Health and Welfare
Statehouse
Boise, ID   83720

To avoid errors and unnecessary delays, write or print clearly in ink.

FULL NAME OF PLAINTIFF _____

FULL NAME OF DEFENDANT _____

DATE OF DIVORCE _____

CITY AND COUNTY OF DIVORCE _____

PERSON MAKING REQUEST _____

ADDRESS _____

RELATIONSHIP TO ABOVE PERSONS _____

The fee for each certified copy and/or search is **$8.00.**

THIS IS **NOT** A DIVORCE CERTIFICATE

NOTE: *Divorces have been filed with the State office since May 1947. Prior to that time they are filed with the County Recorder of each County in the State.*

HW-0161

APPLICATION FOR AN IDAHO DEATH CERTIFICATE

Note: Death records have been filed in Idaho since July 1911.

ADDRESS CORRESPONDENCE AND MAKE MONEY ORDER PAYABLE TO: **VITAL STATISTICS**
450 W. State Street
Boise, ID 83720

1. Full name of deceased at death _____

2. Place of death _____
   (City/Town)   (County)

3. Date of death _____
   (Month/Day/Year)   (If unknown, need approximate year or range to search)

4. Signature of applicant _____

   Address _____

   Relationship to person named in item #1 _____

5. If legal representative — name and relationship of client to deceased _____

PLEASE COMPLETE THE FOLLOWING (if known):   Purpose _____

Birth Date _____ Birth Place _____ Spouse _____
           (Month/Day/Year)   (City/State)

Mother's Maiden Name _____ Father's Name _____

Number of certified copies requested: _____ The fee for each certified copy and/or search is **$8.00.**

Send your requests to:

Illinois Department of Public Health
Division of Vital Records
605 West Jefferson Street
Springfield, Illinois 62702-5097

(217) 782-6553

Send your requests for Marriage Certificates to:

County Clerk
County Courthouse
(County Seat), Illinois

Send your requests for certified Divorce Decrees to:

Clerk of the Circuit Court
(County Seat), Illinois

Cost for a certified Birth Certificate	$15.00
Cost for a short form Birth Certificate or Birth Card	$10.00
Cost for a commemorative Birth Certificate	$40.00
Cost for a verified Marriage or Divorce Record	$5.00
Cost for a certified Death Certificate	$15.00
Cost for a short form or uncertified Death Certificate	$10.00
Cost for a duplicate copy, when ordered at the same time	$2.00

The Illinois Department of Public Health has birth and death records from January 1, 1916 and marriage and divorce records from January 1, 1962. They will verify a marriage record but will not issue a certificate. For a marriage certificate write to the County Clerk. For copies of vital records before 1916 write to the County Clerk of the county where the event occurred.

If your request is urgent you may call and charge only your birth certificates to your Visa or MasterCard. There is an additional $17.00 fee for this, which includes shipping.

The Illinois State Archives (State Archives Building, Springfield, IL 62756; Tel. 217-782-4682) has an index to deaths from 1916-1942, and is preparing an index to marriages from the earliest records to 1900. Fifty-five counties are partially indexed. There is a $.50 charge per page of the index or documents copied.

The Family History Library of The Church of Jesus Christ of Latter-day Saints in Salt Lake City, Utah has microfilmed many of the original vital records of Illinois, including the index to deaths from 1916 to 1938 and death records from 1916 to 1942. For details on their holdings please consult your nearest Family History Center.

APPLICATION FOR SEARCH OF BIRTH RECORD FILES

The fee for a search of the files is $10.00. If the record is found one CERTIFICATION or BIRTH CARD is issued at no additional charge. Additional certifications or birth cards of the same record ordered at the same time are $2.00 each. The fee for a FULL CERTIFIED COPY is $15.00 Additional certified copies of the same record ordered at the same time are $2.00 each. Please indicate below the type and number of copies requested and return this form with the proper fee. DO NOT SEND CASH. Make check or money order payable to: Illinois Department of Public Health.

CERTIFIED COPY $15.00 Each	CERTIFICATION $10.00 Each	BIRTH CARD (wallet size) $10.00 Each
Amount Enclosed:$_____	Amount Enclosed:$_____	Amount Enclosed:$_____
for_____copies	for_____copies	for_____copies

FULL NAME: First   Middle   Last

PLACE OF BIRTH: Street, RFD., Hosp.   City or Town   County

DATE OF BIRTH: Month   Day   Year   SEX: BIRTH NUMBER IF KNOWN:

FATHER:

MOTHER: Maiden Name   Married Name

Application Made By:

NAME:
(written signature)

STREET ADDRESS:

CITY: STATE: ZIP

YOUR RELATIONSHIP TO PERSON:

Mail Copy to (if other than applicant):

NAME:

STREET ADDRESS:

CITY   STATE: ZIP

INTENDED USE OF DOCUMENT:

NOTE: Birth certificates are confidential records, and copies can be issued only to persons entitled to receive them. The application must indicate the requestor's relationship to the person and the intended use of the document.

VR. 180 (5/87R)-DIVISION OF VITAL RECORDS-605 WEST JEFFERSON STREET-ILLINOIS DEPARTMENT OF PUBLIC HEALTH, SPRINGFIELD, ILLINOIS 62702

APPLICATION FOR SEARCH OF DEATH RECORD FILES

The fee for a search of the files is $10.00. If the record is found, one *CERTIFICATION is issued at no additional charge. Additional certifications of the same record ordered at the same time are $2.00 each. The fee for a **FULL CERTIFIED COPY is $15.00. Additional certified copies of the same record ordered at the same time are $2.00 each.

The fee for a 5 years search for genealogical research is $10.00. If found, one UNCERTIFIED copy of the record will be issued at no additional charge. Each additional year searched is $1.00. NOTE: STATE DEATH RECORDS BEGAN JANUARY 1, 1916.

* A CERTIFICATION shows only the name of deceased, sex, place of death, date of death, date filed, and certificate number.

** A FULL CERTIFIED COPY is an exact photographic copy of the original death certificate.

CERTIFIED COPY $15.00 Each	CERTIFICATION $10.00 Each	GENEALOGICAL RESEARCH
Amount Enclosed:$_____	Amount Enclosed:$_____	Amount Enclosed:$_____
for _____ copies	for _____ copies	for _____ year search

(DO NOT SEND CASH) Make check or money order payable to: Illinois Department of Public Health.

FULL NAME OF DECEASED:	First	Middle	Last

PLACE OF DEATH:	Hospital	City or Town	County

DATE OF DEATH:	Month	Day	Year	SEX:	RACE:	OCCUPATION:

DATE LAST KNOWN TO BE ALIVE:	Month	Day	Year	LAST KNOWN ADDRESS:	MARITAL STATUS:

DATE OF BIRTH:	Month	Day	Year	BIRTHPLACE: (City and State)	NAME OF HUSBAND OR WIFE:

FULL NAME OF FATHER OF DECEASED:	FULL MAIDEN NAME OF MOTHER OF DECEASED:

APPLICATION MADE BY:	MAIL COPY TO: (if other than applicant)
NAME:	NAME:
FIRM NAME: (if any)	FIRM NAME: (if any)
STREET ADDRESS:	STREET ADDRESS:
CITY: STATE: ZIP:	CITY: STATE: ZIP:

VR 280 (5/87R) DIV. OF VITAL RECORDS, ILLINOIS DEPT. OF PUBLIC HEALTH, SPRINGFIELD, IL. 62702

INDIANA

Send your requests for birth and death certificates to:

Indiana State Department of Health
Vital Records
1330 West Michigan Street
P.O. Box 1964
Indianapolis, Indiana 46206-1964

(317) 633-0276

For Marriage Certificates and Divorce Records write:

Clerk of the Court
County Courthouse
(County Seat), Indiana

Cost for a certified Birth Certificate	$6.00
Cost for a certified Death Certificate	$4.00
Cost for a duplicate copy, when ordered at the same time	$1.00

The Indiana State Department of Health has birth certificates from October 1907 and death records from January 1900. While marriage certificates are only kept in each county, the state does have an index to marriages from January 1958 to the present.

The Family History Library of The Church of Jesus Christ of Latter-day Saints in Salt Lake City, Utah has microfilmed many Indiana vital records. For details on their holdings please consult your nearest Family History Center.

INDIANA STATE DEPARTMENT OF HEALTH
VITAL RECORDS

MR# _____ Date Rec'd. _____

☐ Your fee of $ _____ was received and is being held pending return of information requested below.

☐ Please remit additional fee of $ _____

Application for Search and Certified Copy of Birth Record
Please Complete All Items Below

Original birth records filed with this office begin October 1907. If birth occurred before this date, contact the health officer in the county where the birth occurred.

Full Name at Birth _____

Could this birth be recorded under any other name? Yes _____ No _____
  If yes, please give name _____

Has this person ever been adopted? Yes _____ No _____
  If yes, please give name AFTER adoption _____

Place of Birth: City _____ County _____

Hospital _____

Date of Birth: _____ Age Last Birthday _____

Full Name of Father: _____
(If adopted, give name of adoptive father)

Full Maiden Name of Mother: _____
(If adopted, give name of adoptive mother)

Purpose for which record is to be used: _____

Your relationship to person whose birth record is requested: _____

FEES: $6.00 required before search can be made. Search fee is not refundable. (Includes one (1) certified copy if found.)
$1.00 each additional copy of same record issued at the same time.

Telephone Number of Applicant:
Home (___) _____
AC
Work (___) _____
AC
Extension _____

Total Certificates _____ Total Fee $ _____

Signature of Applicant _____

Mailing Address _____

City and State _____ Zip _____

*Identification is required (i.e., photocopy of driver's license, work identification card, etc.) unless payment is made by the applicant's personal check.

PRINT name and address of person to whom the certified copy is to be mailed, if different than stated above.

Name: _____

Street or Route: _____

City or Town: _____ State: _____ Zip: _____

SEND TO:

Indiana State Department of Health
1330 West Michigan Street
P.O. Box 1964
Indianapolis, IN 46206-1964

State Form 35485   SDH06-040R
Rev. 6/92   FORM 7/VR1

INDIANA STATE DEPARTMENT OF HEALTH
VITAL RECORDS SECTION

1330 West Michigan Street
P.O. Box 1964
Indianapolis, IN 46206-1964

MR# _____   Date Rec'd _____

☐   Your fee of $_____ was received and is being held pending return of information requested below.

☐   Please remit additional fee of $_____

DEATH RECORDS IN THE STATE VITAL RECORDS OFFICE BEGIN WITH 1900

Death Registration in Indiana began in 1882. Prior to 1900, records of death are filed ONLY with the Local Health Department in the county where the death actually occurred.

There are **no indexes** to the state death certificates from 1900 through 1918. The specific CITY or COUNTY of death must be provided for searches in this period and the search is limited to **one county** for each Search Fee ($4.00) paid.

Application for Search and Certified Copy of Death Record
Please Complete All Items Below

Name of Deceased _____   Was this a stillbirth? _____

Date of Death _____

Place of Death (City) _____ (County) _____ INDIANA

SEARCH FEE - $4.00: If the exact date of death is not known, please indicate the **five (5) year period** to be searched. An additional $4.00 is required for **each additional five (5) year period searched, or COUNTY SEARCHED from 1900-1918.** Search fees are nonrefundable.

Date of birth of deceased (if known) _____

Father's Name _____   Mother's Maiden Name _____

Your relationship to the person named on this record? _____

Purpose for which the record is to be used? _____

Signature of Applicant _____

Printed Name of Applicant _____

Street Address _____

City _____   State _____   Zip Code _____

Telephone Number _____

Total Certificates: _____   Total Fee: $_____

State Form 36174
SDH06-023
Rev. 9/92   VRFORM11.VR1

Send your requests to:

Iowa Department of Public Health
Vital Records Bureau
Lucas State Office Building, 4th Floor
321 East 12th Street
Des Moines, Iowa 50319-0075

(515) 281-4944, FAX (515) 281-4958

For records before July 1, 1880 write to:

Clerk
District Court
(County Seat), Iowa

Cost for a certified Birth Certificate	$10.00
Cost for a certified Marriage Certificate	$10.00
Cost for a certified Death Certificate	$10.00

The Iowa Department of Public Health has birth, marriage, and death records from July 1, 1880. They do not issue divorce certificates.

If your request is urgent you may call (515) 281-5871 and charge your certificates to your Visa, Discover, or MasterCard. There is a $5.00 fee plus an additional express mail charge for this service.

The State Historical Society of Iowa (600 East Locust Street; Des Moines, IA 50319; Tel. 515-281-3007) has Iowa birth and death records from 1880 and marriage records from 1880 to 1916, with some county records dating back to 1835. The dates vary by county.

The Family History Library of The Church of Jesus Christ of Latter-day Saints in Salt Lake City, Utah has microfilmed many of the original and published vital records and church registers of Iowa. For details on their holdings please consult your nearest Family History Center.

APPLICATION

For a Certified Copy of a Vital Record
Instructions on Other Side of this Page

_____ 1. Type of record: Birth _____ Death _____ Marriage _____

_____ 2. Name on record: _____
(Note: If marriage record application, include names of bride and groom.)

_____ 3. Date of event: _____

_____ 4. City and/or county of event: _____ _____
(City) (County)

_____ 5. Father's full name: _____
(Please complete ONLY if this is a birth or death application.)

_____ 6. Mother's full <u>maiden</u> name: _____
(Please complete ONLY if this is a birth or death application.)

_____ 7. Has the name on the record ever been changed by a legal procedure?

_____ Yes _____ No

If yes, what type of legal procedure: _____ Adoption _____ Paternity Action

_____ Legal Name Change

Please provide previous name: _____

_____ 8. Purpose for this copy: _____

_____ 9. Number of copies requested ($10.00 per copy): _____

_____ 10. Applicant's signature: _____

_____ 11. Applicant's relationship: _____
(Copies of the certificate are issued only to the person named on the certificate; members of the immediate family; legal guardians or legal representatives. If you are the legal guardian or legal representative, please furnish a copy of the document authorizing guardianship or representation.)

Applicant's daytime telephone number: _____

_____ 12. Name and address of person to receive the certified copy:

☐ PICK UP

_____

☐ MAIL

_____

_____

CPK-72964 588-0225 (Rev. 7/93)

Send your requests to:

Kansas State Department of Health and Environment
Office of Vital Statistics
Landon State Office Building
900 S.W. Jackson
First Floor, Room 151
Topeka, Kansas 66612-2221

(913) 296-1400

For earlier records write to:

Clerk of the District Court
District Court
(County Seat), Kansas

Cost for a certified Birth Certificate	$10.00
Cost for a wallet-size Birth Certificate	$10.00
Cost for a certified Marriage or Divorce Certificate	$10.00
Cost for a certified Death Certificate	$10.00
Cost for a duplicate copy, when ordered at the same time	$5.00

The Office of Vital Statistics has birth and death records from July 1, 1911, delayed birth certificates from 1875, marriage records from May 1, 1913, and divorce records from July 1, 1951.

If your request is urgent you may call and charge your certificates to your Visa, Discover, or MasterCard. There is a $5.00 fee for this service.

The Family History Library of The Church of Jesus Christ of Latter-day Saints in Salt Lake City, Utah has microfilmed many of the original and published vital records and church registers of Kansas. For details on their holdings please consult your nearest Family History Center.

KANSAS DEPARTMENT OF HEALTH AND ENVIRONMENT
OFFICE OF VITAL STATISTICS

APPLICATION FOR CERTIFIED COPY OF BIRTH CERTIFICATE

BIRTH CERTIFICATES ARE ON FILE FROM JULY 1, 1911 TO PRESENT

THIS REQUEST MAY BE REJECTED UNLESS ALL ITEMS ARE COMPLETED AND CORRECT FEES SUBMITTED

I hereby declare that as the applicant for a certified copy of the certificate described below, I have direct interest in the matter recorded and that the information therein contained is necessary for the determination of personal or property rights, pursuant to K.S.A. 65-2422 (c). FOR THE PROTECTION OF THE INDIVIDUAL, CERTIFICATES ARE NOT OPEN TO PUBLIC INSPECTION.

Signature of person
making request _____   Today's
                                              Date _____

Relationship to person
named on record _____   Daytime
                                               Phone No. (___) _____

Reason for Request _____
(Please be specific)

One identification is required of anyone requesting and/or picking up a vital record.

Applicant's Identification No. _____

BIRTH INFORMATION (All items must be completed) **(PLEASE PRINT OR TYPE)**

Name on record _____
               (First)   (Middle)   (Last)   Present age of this person _____
Date of birth _____   Date of death, if applicable _____
               (Month)   (Day)   (Year)

Place of birth _____ _____
               (City)   (County)   (State)   Name of hospital (if known)

Name of mother _____   Birthplace _____
               (First)   (Middle)   (MAIDEN) SS# _____
                                                                    (if known)
Name of father _____   Birthplace _____
               (First)   (Middle)   (Last)   SS# _____
                                                                    (if known)
Birth order of this child (1st, 2nd, etc.) _____ Race _____ Sex _____

Adopted? Yes ____ No ____   Is request for record prior to adoption? Yes ____ No ____

Original name, if known _____

Print name & address of person to receive record(s)

_____   Number of Copies Requested
            (Name)
_____   _____ Certified Copy
         (Street Address)   _____ Wallet Size Card

_____
(City)   (State)   (Zip)   TOTAL FEE: _____

PLEASE ENCLOSE A SELF-ADDRESSED STAMPED ENVELOPE   Fees expire 12 months from date pd.

Form VS-235   Rev. 7-1991

KANSAS DEPARTMENT OF HEALTH AND ENVIRONMENT
OFFICE OF VITAL STATISTICS

APPLICATION FOR CERTIFIED COPY OF MARRIAGE CERTIFICATE

MARRIAGE RECORDS ARE ON FILE FROM MAY 1, 1913 TO PRESENT

THIS REQUEST MAY BE REJECTED UNLESS ALL ITEMS ARE COMPLETED AND CORRECT FEES SUBMITTED

I hereby declare that as the applicant for a certified copy of the certificate described below, I have direct interest in the matter recorded and the information therein contained is necessary for the determination of personal or property rights, pursuant to K.S.A. 65-2422(c). FOR THE PROTECTION OF THE INDIVIDUAL, CERTIFICATES ARE NOT OPEN TO PUBLIC INSPECTION.

Signature of person
making request _____

Today's
date _____

Relationship to person
named on record _____

Daytime
phone no. (___) _____

Reason for request _____
(Please be specific)

One identification is required of anyone requesting and/or picking up a vital record.

Applicant's Identification No. _____

MARRIAGE INFORMATION (All items must be completed) **(PLEASE PRINT OR TYPE)**

Groom (full name) _____

Date of
Birth _____

Bride (maiden and previous
married surname) _____

Date of
Birth _____

Date of marriage _____
                                   (Month)   (Day)   (Year)

County in which marriage license was issued _____

City or town in which marriage took place _____

Print name & address of person to receive record(s)

_____
(Name)

Number of certified
copies requested _____

_____
(Street Address)

_____
(City)   (State)   (Zip)

TOTAL FEE: _____

PLEASE ENCLOSE A SELF-ADDRESSED STAMPED ENVELOPE

Fees expire 12 months from date pd.

Form VS-237 Rev. 1991

KANSAS DEPARTMENT OF HEALTH AND ENVIRONMENT
OFFICE OF VITAL STATISTICS

APPLICATION FOR CERTIFIED COPY OF DIVORCE CERTIFICATE

DIVORCE RECORDS ARE ON FILE FROM JULY 1, 1951 TO PRESENT

THIS REQUEST MAY BE REJECTED UNLESS ALL ITEMS ARE COMPLETED AND CORRECT FEES SUBMITTED

I hereby declare that as the applicant for a certified copy of the certificate described below, I have direct interest in the matter recorded and that the information therein contained is necessary for the determination of personal or property rights, pursuant to K.S.A. 65-2422(c). FOR THE PROTECTION OF THE INDIVIDUAL, CERTIFICATES ARE NOT OPEN TO PUBLIC INSPECTION.

Signature of person
making request _____

Today's
date _____

Relationship to person
named on record _____

Daytime
phone no. (___) _____

Reason for request _____
(Please be specific)

One identification is required of anyone requesting and/or picking up a vital record.

Applicant's Identification No. _____

<u>DIVORCE INFORMATION</u> (All items must be completed) **(PLEASE PRINT OR TYPE)**

Husband (full name) _____

Wife (maiden and married name) _____

Date divorce was granted _____
　　　　　　　　　　　(Month)　　　　(Day)　　　　(Year)

County in which divorce was granted _____

Date of this marriage _____

Print name & address of person to receive record(s)

_____
　　　　　　(Name)

Number of certified
copies requested_____

_____
　　　(Street Address)

_____
(City)　　　(State)　　　(Zip)

TOTAL FEE: _____

PLEASE ENCLOSE A SELF-ADDRESSED STAMPED ENVELOPE

Fees expire 12 months from date pd.

Form VS-238　Rev. 1991

KANSAS DEPARTMENT OF HEALTH AND ENVIRONMENT
OFFICE OF VITAL STATISTICS

APPLICATION FOR CERTIFIED COPY OF DEATH CERTIFICATE
DEATH CERTIFICATES ARE ON FILE FROM JULY 1, 1911

THIS REQUEST MAY BE REJECTED UNLESS ALL ITEMS ARE COMPLETED AND CORRECT FEES SUBMITTED

I hereby declare that as the applicant for a certified copy of the certificate described below, I have direct interest in the matter recorded and the information therein contained is necessary for the determination of personal or property rights, pursuant to K.S.A. 65-2422(c).   FOR THE PROTECTION OF THE INDIVIDUAL, CERTIFICATES ARE NOT OPEN TO PUBLIC INSPECTION.

Signature of person
making request _____

Today's
date _____

Relationship to person
named on record _____

Daytime
phone no. (__) _____

Reason for request _____
(Please be specific)

One identification is required of anyone requesting and/or picking up a vital record.

Applicant's Identification No. _____

DEATH INFORMATION (All items must be completed) **(PLEASE PRINT OR TYPE)**

Full name of deceased _____

Date of death _____ Place of death _____
    (Month)   (Day)   (Year)   (City)   (County)   (State)

Check if stillbirth _____ Race _____ Sex _____

Residence at death _____ Marital status at death _____

Name of spouse (if applicable) _____

Father's name/mother's maiden name _____

Age at time of death (or birthdate) _____ Place of birth _____

Funeral home _____

City/County where buried _____

Print name & address of person to receive record(s)

_____
                (Name)

Number of certified
copies requested _____

_____
            (Street Address)

_____
    (City)   (State)   (Zip)

TOTAL FEE: _____

PLEASE ENCLOSE A SELF-ADDRESSED STAMPED ENVELOPE

Fees expire 12 months from date pd.

Form VS-236 Rev. 1991

KENTUCKY

Send your requests to:

Department for Health Services
Office of Vital Statistics
275 East Main Street
Frankfort, Kentucky 40621-0001

(502) 564-4212

For vital records from 1852 to 1862 and 1872 to 1910 contact:

Public Records Division
Kentucky Department for Libraries and Archives
300 Coffee Tree Road
P.O. Box 537
Frankfort, Kentucky 40602-0537

(502) 875-7000

Cost for a certified Birth Certificate	$7.00
Cost for a wallet-size Birth Certificate	$7.00
Cost for a certified Marriage or Divorce Certificate	$6.00
Cost for a certified Death Certificate	$6.00

The Office of Vital Statistics has birth and death records from January 1, 1911 and marriage and divorce records from June 1, 1958. Earlier marriage and divorce records are available from the County Clerk or Clerk of the Circuit Court, respectively, of the county where the event occurred.

If your request is urgent you may call and charge your certificates to your Visa, Discover, or MasterCard. There is a $5.00 fee for this service. Overnight Federal Express Service is available for an additional charge.

The Public Records Division of the Kentucky Department for Libraries and Archives has microfilm copies of the vital records from 1852 to 1910 and the indexes to vital records from January 1, 1911 through 1954. For further information see *A Guide to Kentucky Birth, Marriage and Death Records 1852-1910,* published by the Public Records Division in 1988.

The Family History Library of The Church of Jesus Christ of Latter-day Saints in Salt Lake City, Utah has microfilmed many of the original and published records of Kentucky. They have microfilms of the birth records from 1874 to 1878, 1907 to 1910, and 1939 to 1954; marriage records from 1875 to 1878 and 1906 to 1914; and death records from 1874 to 1878, 1905 to 1910, and 1939 to 1954. There are indexes to birth and death records from 1911 to 1954, marriage records from 1972 to 1990, and death records from 1911 to 1986. For details on their holdings please consult your nearest Family History Center.

VS-37
(Rev. 5/92)

COMMONWEALTH OF KENTUCKY
DEPARTMENT FOR HEALTH SERVICES
STATE REGISTRAR OF VITAL STATISTICS

APPLICATION FOR BIRTH CERTIFICATE

Please Print Or Type All Information Required On This Form

Full Name at Birth _____ Sex _____

Date of Birth _____ Ky. County of Birth _____

Mother's Full Maiden Name _____

Father's Name _____

Name of Attending Physician or Midwife _____ Hospital _____

Has Original Certificate Been Changed? If So, To _____

Have You Ever Received a Copy Before? ☐ Yes ☐ No ☐ Unknown

If Yes, When? _____
                    Year

_____ Phone: _____
(Signature of Applicant)   (Area Code)   (Number)

Office Use Only
Vol. _____
Cert. _____
Year _____
Date _____
Initials _____

Relationship To Person Named On Certificate _____

A **$7.00** search fee must accompany this application. The fee cannot be returned. If the certificate is on file you will receive one copy. Additional copies are $7.00 each. Make check or money order payable to "Kentucky State Treasurer". When complete, mail the entire form to Vital Statistics, 275 East Main, Frankfort, Kentucky 40621.

Check Type Of
Copy Desired

☐ Full Size Copy - **$7.00** Each Copy - Quantity Desired _____

☐ Billfold Size Birth Card - **$7.00** Each Copy - Quantity Desired _____

(Kentucky School Systems will not accept billfold size birth certificates)

Print Name and Mailing Address of Person to Receive the Certificate.

This Portion is a Mailing Insert and Will Be Used to Mail the Copy You Have Requested.

_____
Name

_____
Street Number & Name

_____
City — State — Zip Code

IF YOU HAVE NOT RECEIVED THE CERTIFICATE(S) YOU REQUESTED WITHIN 30 DAYS FROM THE POSTMARKED DATE OF MAILING, PLEASE CONTACT THE OFFICE OF VITAL STATISTICS AT: 502-564-4212

APPLICANT'S PHONE: _____
                         (Area Code)   (Number)

VS-230
(Rev. 5/92)

COMMONWEALTH OF KENTUCKY
DEPARTMENT FOR HEALTH SERVICES
State Registrar of Vital Statistics

APPLICATION FOR MARRIAGE/DIVORCE CERTIFICATE

Please Print or Type All Information Requested on This Form.

Please Circle Type of Record Requested.

Full Name of Husband _____

Maiden Name of Wife _____

County In Which   (Marriage License)   (Divorce Decree)   Granted _____
                              (Circle One)

Date of   (Marriage)   (Divorce)   _____
                     (Circle One)   (Mo.)   (Day)   (Year)

Name of Applicant _____

Address _____

The Information I Am Requesting Concerns
(Marriage)   (Divorce)
(Circle One)

Office Use Only
Vol. _____
Cert. _____
Year _____
Date _____
Initials _____

Please Indicate Quantity Desired _____

A $6.00 fee must accompany this application. The fee cannot be returned. If the certificate is on file you will receive one copy. Additional copies are $6.00 each. Make check or money order payable to "Kentucky State Treasurer". When complete, mail the entire form to Vital Statistics, 275 East Main Street, Frankfort, Kentucky 40621.

Print Name and Mailing Address of Person to Receive the Certificate.
This Portion is a Mailing Insert and Will be Used to Mail the Copy you
Have Requested.

_____
Name

_____
Street Number & Name

_____
City-State-Zip Code

VS-31
(Rev. 5/92)

COMMONWEALTH OF KENTUCKY
DEPARTMENT FOR HEALTH SERVICES

State Registrar of Vital Statistics

APPLICATION FOR DEATH CERTIFICATE

Please Print or Type All Information Required on This Form.

Full Name of Deceased _____

Date of Death _____   KY County in Which
              (Mo.)   (Day)   (Year)   Death Occurred _____

Did Death Occur In a Hospital?   ☐ Yes ☐ No   Age at Death _____

If "Yes" Give Name of Hospital _____

Name of Attending Physician _____

Name of Funeral Director _____

Address _____
       (Street)   (City)   (State)

Name of Applicant _____

Address _____
       (Street)   (City)   (State)

_____   Phone _____
    Signature of Applicant   (A/C) (Number)

Official Use Only

Vol. _____

Cert. _____

Year _____

Date _____

Initials _____

A $6.00 fee must accompany this application. The fee cannot be returned. If certificate is on file you will receive a copy. Additional copies are $6.00 each. Make check or money order payable to "Kentucky State Treasurer". When complete, mail the entire form to: **Vital Statistics, 275 East Main Street, Frankfort, Kentucky 40621.**

Please Indicate Quantity Desired _____

Print Name and Mailing Address of Person to Receive the Certificate.
This Portion is a Mailing Insert and will be used to Mail the Copy you Have Requested.

_____
Name

_____
Street Number & Name

_____
City - State - Zip Code

LOUISIANA

Send your requests to:

Louisiana Department of Health and Hospitals .
Office of Public Health
Vital Records Registry
325 Loyola Avenue
P.O. Box 60630
New Orleans, Louisiana 70160-0630

(504) 568-5150, (504) 568-5152, FAX (504) 568-5391

For Birth Records over 100 years old and Death and Orleans Parish Marriage Records over 50 years old write to:

Louisiana State Archives
P.O. Box 94125
Baton Rouge, Louisiana 70804-9125

(504) 922-1206

For Marriage Records outside of Orleans Parish write:

Parish Clerk
(Parish Seat), Louisiana

Cost for a certified Birth Certificate	$10.00
Cost for a wallet-size Birth Certificate	$7.00
Cost for a certified Marriage Certificate	$5.00
Cost for a certified Death Certificate	$5.00

---

all births over 100 yrs old & other vital records over 50 yrs old to Archives

The Louisiana Vital Records Registry has birth records for the last 100 years and marriage and death records for the last 50 years. Earlier records are held by the Louisiana State Archives. The Vital Records Registry does not provide divorce records.

If your request is urgent you may call and charge your certificates to your Visa or MasterCard. There is a $15.50 additional charge for this service.

The Family History Library of The Church of Jesus Christ of Latter-day Saints in Salt Lake City, Utah has microfilmed many of the original and published vital records and church registers of Louisiana. For details on their holdings please consult your nearest Family History Center.

Louisiana State Archives
Archives and Records Section
P.O. Box 94125
Baton Rouge LA 70804-9125

DEPARTMENT OF HEALTH AND HOSPITALS
OFFICE OF PUBLIC HEALTH
VITAL RECORDS REGISTRY

APPLICATION FOR CERTIFIED COPY OF BIRTH/DEATH CERTIFICATE

PHS 520A   (Rev. 7/92)

FOR SERVICE BY MAIL: SUBMIT CHECK OR MONEY ORDER PAYABLE TO VITAL RECORDS. MAIL TO: VITAL RECORDS REGISTRY, P.O. BOX 60630, NEW ORLEANS, LA 70160. **PLEASE DO NOT SEND CASH.** IF NO RECORD IS FOUND, YOU WILL BE NOTIFIED AND FEES WILL BE RETAINED FOR THE SEARCH.

☐ BIRTHCARD   BIRTHCARD: $ 7.00
☐ BIRTH CERTIFICATE   BIRTH CERTIFICATE: $10.00
☐ DEATH CERTIFICATE   DEATH CERTIFICATE: $ 5.00

*See Note Below:
NAME AT BIRTH/DEATH (FIRST, MIDDLE, LAST)

DATE OF BIRTH/DEATH   SEX

CITY OF BIRTH/DEATH   PARISH OF BIRTH/DEATH

FATHER'S NAME (FOR BIRTH RECORD ONLY)

MOTHER'S MAIDEN NAME - BEFORE MARRIAGE (FOR BIRTH RECORD ONLY)

HOW ARE YOU RELATED TO THE PERSON WHOSE RECORD YOU ARE REQUESTING?_____

PRINT YOUR ADDRESS:
Name_____

Street or
Route No._____   Number of
                                                 Copies Requested: _____
City
and State_____
                              ZIP CODE   Total Fees Due $_____
Home   Office
Phone No._____ Phone No._____

I AM AWARE THAT ANY PERSON WHO WILLFULLY AND KNOWINGLY MAKES ANY FALSE STATEMENT IN AN APPLICATION FOR A CERTIFIED COPY OF A VITAL RECORD IS SUBJECT UPON CONVICTION TO A FINE OF NOT MORE THAN $10,000 OR IMPRISONMENT OF NOT MORE THAN FIVE YEARS, OR BOTH.

Signature of Applicant _____

*PLEASE NOTE: Birth records **over 100 years** old and Death records **over 50 years** old are obtained by writing the Louisiana State Archives, P.O. Box 94125, Baton Rouge, LA 70804-9125. Please make check PAYABLE TO: Secretary of State.

CERTIFICATE TO BE MAILED TO:

Name_____
Street or
Route No. _____
City
and State_____
                              ZIP CODE

SEARCH METHOD	EMPLOYEE	DATE
TRANSMITTAL:	_____	____
COMPUTER:	_____	____
MICROFILM:	_____	____
BOOK INDICES:	_____	____
CHARITY CARDS:	_____	____
DELAY CARDS:	_____	____
HAND SEARCHED:	_____	____
OTHER (INDICATE)		
_____	_____	____
_____	_____	____
CERTIFICATE #	_____	

DEPARTMENT OF HEALTH AND HUMAN RESOURCES
OFFICE OF PREVENTIVE AND PUBLIC HEALTH SERVICES
VITAL RECORDS REGISTRY

APPLICATION FOR CERTIFIED COPY OF MARRIAGE CERTIFICATE

PHS 520C

(Rev. 9/87)

FOR SERVICE BY MAIL: SUBMIT CHECK OR MONEY ORDER PAYABLE TO VITAL RECORDS. MAIL TO: VITAL RECORDS REGISTRY, P.O. BOX 60630, NEW ORLEANS, LA 70160. **PLEASE DO NOT SEND CASH.** IF NO RECORD IS FOUND, YOU WILL BE NOTIFIED AND FEES WILL BE RETAINED FOR THE SEARCH.

MARRIAGE RECORD OF: FEE: $5.00 ea

_____
Groom (First, Middle, Last)

_____
Bride (First, Middle, Maiden Name)

_____
Parish where License was Purchased

_____
Date of Marriage

PLEASE NOTE: A MARRIAGE RECORD IS AVAILABLE FROM THE VITAL RECORDS REGISTRY ONLY IF THE MARRIAGE LICENSE WAS PURCHASED IN ORLEANS PARISH. OTHERWISE YOU MUST CONTACT THE CLERK OF COURT IN THE PARISH WHERE THE LICENSE WAS PURCHASED.

PRINT YOUR ADDRESS

Name _____

Street or
Route No. _____

City and
State _____
                                    Zip Code

Home   Office
Phone No. _____ Phone No. _____

Number of Copies
Requested   _____

Total Fees Due $_____

- -

Certificate to be mailed to:

Name _____

Street or
Route No. _____

City
and State _____
                                    Zip Code

MAINE

Send your requests for records from 1923 to the present to:

Maine Department of Human Services
Office of Vital Statistics
221 State Street
State House Station 11
Augusta, Maine 04333-0011

(207) 287-3181

For earlier vital records write to:

Maine State Archives
State House Station 84
Augusta, Maine 04333-0084

(207) 287-5795

or to:

County Clerk
County Courthouse
(County Seat), Maine

Cost for a certified Birth Certificate	$10.00
Cost for a certified Marriage or Divorce Certificate	$10.00
Cost for a certified Death Certificate	$10.00
Cost for a duplicate copy, when ordered at the same time	$4.00

The Maine Office of Vital Statistics has records from January 1, 1923 to the present.

If your request is urgent you may call and charge your certificates to your Visa, Discover, or MasterCard. There is a $5.00 fee for this service. If you need overnight service there is a $15.50 delivery charge.

The Maine State Archives also has Maine vital records on microfilm from the 1600s to 1955.

The Family History Library of The Church of Jesus Christ of Latter-day Saints in Salt Lake City, Utah has microfilmed many of the original and published vital records of Maine. They have microfilm copies of births, marriages and deaths from 1670 to 1922. They also have a bride's marriage index from 1895 to 1953. For details on their holdings please consult your nearest Family History Center.

MAINE DEPARTMENT OF HUMAN SERVICES
OFFICE OF VITAL STATISTICS

APPLICATION FOR A SEARCH AND CERTIFIED COPY OF A VITAL RECORD

Applicant:

Please fill in the information in the appropriate box for
the record you are requesting, the reason for requesting
the record, and the name and address for mailing the
certified copy. Enclose a check or money order payable
to TREASURER, STATE OF MAINE and mail application to:

DEPARTMENT OF HUMAN SERVICES
OFFICE OF VITAL STATISTICS
STATE HOUSE STATION 11
AUGUSTA, MAINE 04333-0011

**BIRTH
RECORD**

| Full Name of Child |
| Date of Birth |
| Place of Birth |
| Farther's Full Name |
| Mother's Maiden Name |

**DEATH
RECORD**

| Full Name of Decendent |
| Date of Death |
| Place of Death |

**MARRIAGE
RECORD**

| Full Name of Groom |
| Full Maiden Name of Bride |
| Date of Marriage |
| Place of Marriage |

**DIVORCE
RECORD**

| Full Name of Husband |
| Full Maiden Name of Wife |
| Date of Divorce or Annulment |
| Place Superior Court, County or District(Division) |

Reason for requesting <u>Record:</u>

Print or type name and
address to whom the
record is to be sent.

Applicant signature: _____ _____

VS-107 R1/92

Applicant address: _____

Send your requests to:

Maryland Department of Health & Mental Hygiene
Division of Vital Records
4201 Patterson Avenue, First Floor
P.O. Box 68760
Baltimore, Maryland 21215-0020

(410) 225-5988, (410) 764-3038, (800) 832-3277 (inside Maryland)

For records before January 1, 1969 write to:

Maryland State Archives
350 Rowe Boulevard
Annapolis, Maryland 21401-1602

(410) 974-3914

Cost for a certified Birth Certificate	$4.00
Cost for a commemorative Birth Certificate	$25.00
Cost for a certified Marriage Certificate	$4.00
Cost for verification of a Divorce	Free
Cost for a certified Death Certificate	$4.00

The Division of Vital Records has birth and death records for Maryland counties from August 1, 1898, marriage records from June 1, 1951 and divorce records from July 1, 1961. They also hold birth and death records for Baltimore City from January 1, 1875. For marriage records before June 1, 1951 write to the Clerk of the Circuit Court in the county where the marriage license was issued.

The Maryland State Archives has restrictions on birth records for 100 years and death records for 20 years. They will, however, provide an abstract of the record for a fee of $5.00.

If your request is urgent you may call and charge your certificates to your Visa or MasterCard. There is a $5.00 fee for this service, plus the postal charges.

The Family History Library of The Church of Jesus Christ of Latter-day Saints in Salt Lake City, Utah has microfilmed many of the original and published vital records and church registers of Maryland. For details on their holdings please consult your nearest Family History Center.

STATE OF MARYLAND
DEPARTMENT OF HEALTH & MENTAL HYGIENE
DIVISION OF VITAL RECORDS
P.O. BOX 68760
BALTIMORE, MARYLAND 21215-0020

Send Check or Money Order Payable to:
DIVISION OF VITAL RECORDS

APPLICATION FOR A COPY OR ABSTRACT OF BIRTH CERTIFICATE

PLEASE PRINT   Date: _____ 19 _____

Full name at birth: _____
                    (First)   (Middle)   (Last)

Date of birth: _____ Sex: _____
               (Month)   (Day)   (Year)

Age last birthday: _____ Certificate No. (If known): _____

Place of birth: _____ County: _____

Name of hospital (If known): _____

Full name of father: _____

Full maiden name of mother: _____

Your relationship to person on the certificate: _____

NOTE: A non-refundable $4.00 fee is required for each certificate requested.
You may apply in person or by mail. **DO NOT SEND CASH OR STAMPS.** Birth
records are on file beginning 1875 for Baltimore City and 1898 for
Maryland Counties. For County birth records prior to 1898, contact the
Maryland State Archives.

<u>**IMPORTANT:**</u> **PLEASE INDICATE IN THE BOX BELOW THE NUMBER OF CERTIFICATES REQUESTED**
CERTIFIED COPY: This certificate can be used for all purposes.

┌─────────┐
│   │   APPLICANT'S NAME (Print): _____
└─────────┘
                APPLICANT'S SIGNATURE: _____

                MAILING ADDRESS: _____

                CITY AND STATE: _____

                ZIP CODE: _____

                TELEPHONE NUMBER: _____

"Any person who willfully uses or attempts to use the requested certificate(s)
for fraudulent or deceptive purposes is guilty of a misdemeanor and on
conviction is subject to a fine not exceeding $500.00 in accordance with MD
Health-General Article, Annotated Code, Section 4-227"

STATE OF MARYLAND
DEPARTMENT OF HEALTH & MENTAL HYGIENE
DIVISION OF VITAL RECORDS
P.O. BOX 68760
BALTIMORE, MARYLAND 21215-0020

Send Check or Money Order Payable to:
DIVISION OF VITAL RECORDS

DO NOT WRITE IN ABOVE SPACE

APPLICATION FOR A COPY OF MARRIAGE CERTIFICATE

Date: _____ 19 _____

Groom's name: _____
                 (First)   (Middle)   (Last)

Bride's maiden name: _____
                 (First)   (Middle)   (Last)

Date of marriage: _____
                 (Month)   (Day)   (Year)

Place of marriage: _____
                 (Town)   (County)

Reason for request: _____

Whom do you represent: _____

NOTE: A non-refundable $4.00 fee is required for each certificate requested. If the search provides no record, the $4.00 fee is not returned, and a certificate of no record will be issued. You may apply in person or by mail. When applying by mail, please enclose a self-addressed, stamped envelope. DO NOT SEND CASH OR STAMPS. For marriages performed PRIOR TO JUNE, 1951, certified copies of certificates are available only from the Circuit Court of the County in which the marriage took place.

IMPORTANT: PLEASE INDICATE BELOW THE NUMBER OF COPIES REQUESTED.

[ ] CERTIFIED PHOTOCOPY

APPLICANT'S NAME (Print): _____

APPLICANT'S SIGNATURE: _____

MAILING ADDRESS: _____

CITY AND STATE: _____

ZIP CODE: _____

VR C-80
DHMH 1937
REV. 7/89

STATE OF MARYLAND
DEPARTMENT OF HEALTH & MENTAL HYGIENE
DIVISION OF VITAL RECORDS
P.O. BOX 68760
BALTIMORE, MARYLAND 21215-0020

Send check or money order payable to:
_____**DIVISION OF VITAL RECORDS**_____

APPLICATION FOR A COPY OF A DEATH CERTIFICATE

DATE:_____

NOTE: A non-refundable 4.00 fee is required for each certificate requested. If the search provides no record, the $4.00 fee is not returned, and a certificate of No Record will be issued. You may apply in person or by mail. When applying by mail, please enclose a self-addressed, stamped envelope. DO NOT SEND CASH OR STAMPS. We do not issue records prior to 1969 for genealogical purposes. If you desire a death certificate for genealogical purposes, please contact the Maryland Hall of Records, 305 Rowe Boulevard, Annapolis, Maryland 21401.

Name of deceased:_____
(First)   (Middle)   (Last)

Date of death:_____
(Month)   (Day)   (Year)

Place of death **(regardless of residence):**_____
(Town)   (County)

Certificate number (if known)_____

Reason for request:_____

Your relation to deceased:_____

If Fetal Death (Stillborn) please indicate_____

IMPORTANT: PLEASE INDICATE BELOW THE NUMBER OF COPIES REQUESTED.

☐   CERTIFIED PHOTOCOPY

APPLICANT'S NAME (Print):_____

APPLICANT'S SIGNATURE:_____

MAILING ADDRESS:_____

CITY, STATE AND ZIP CODE:_____

PHONE NUMBER (   )_____
                area code (required if added Information is necessary).

"Any person who willfully uses or attempts to use the requested certificate(s) for fraudulent or deceptive purposes is guilty of a fine not exceeding $500.00 in accordance with **MD.** Health-General Article, Code Ann., Section 4-227."

CR C-34
DHMH 4326
REV 4/90

MASSACHUSETTS

Send your requests to:

Massachusetts Department of Public Health
Registry of Vital Records and Statistics
150 Tremont Street, Room B-3
Boston, Massachusetts 02111

(617) 727-0036

For records from 1841 to 1895 write to:

Massachusetts State Archives
220 Morrissey Boulevard
Boston, Massachusetts 02125

(617) 727-2816, (617) 727-9150

For Divorce Records write to:

County Clerk
County Courthouse
(County Seat), Massachusetts

Cost for a certified Birth Certificate ordered by mail	$11.00
Cost for an heirloom Birth Certificate ordered in person	$25.00
Cost for an heirloom Birth Certificate ordered by mail	$30.00
Cost for a certified Marriage Certificate ordered by mail	$11.00
Cost for a certified Death Certificate ordered by mail	$11.00
Cost for certificates ordered in person	$6.00

The Massachusetts Registry of Vital Records and Statistics has birth, marriage, and death records from January 1, 1901 to the present. They do not have divorce records but do have an index to divorces from 1952. The State Archives has records from January 1, 1841 to the end of 1895. For earlier records write to the Town Clerk of the town where the event occurred.

If your request is urgent you may call and charge only your birth certificate to your Visa, Discover, or MasterCard. There is a $19.00 charge for the first certificate and a $14.00 fee for each duplicate certificate ordered at the same time. There is a an additional charge of $34.50 for next-day delivery service.

The Family History Library of The Church of Jesus Christ of Latter-day Saints in Salt Lake City, Utah has microfilmed many of the original and published vital records of Massachusetts, including vital records from 1841 to 1899, corrections of the vital records made from 1893 to 1970, and indexes from 1891 to 1971. For details on their holdings please consult your nearest Family History Center.

MASSACHUSETTS DEPARTMENT OF PUBLIC HEALTH
REGISTRY OF VITAL RECORDS AND STATISTICS
150 TREMONT STREET, ROOM B-3
BOSTON, MA 02111

APPLICATION FOR VITAL RECORD
(Please print legibly.)

Please fill out and return this form to the address above, along with a stamped, self-addressed, business-letter-sized envelope and a personal check or money order for $11.00 for each record. Make checks payable to the Commonwealth of Massachusetts. Do not submit more than 5 requests per letter. *DO NOT SEND CASH THROUGH THE MAIL.*

BIRTH RECORD   Number of copies:_____

Name of Subject:_____			
	(first)	*(middle)*	*(last)*
Date of Birth:		City or Town of Birth:	
Mother's Name:_____			
	(first)	*(middle)*	*(maiden)*	*(last)*
Father's Name:_____			
	(first)	*(middle)*	*(last)*

MARRIAGE RECORD   Number of copies:_____

Name of Groom:_____			
	(first)	*(middle)*	*(last)*
Name of Bride:_____			
	(first)	*(middle)*	*(maiden)*
Date of Marriage:		City or Town of Marriage:	

DEATH RECORD   Number of copies:_____

Name of Deceased:_____			
	(first)	*(middle)*	*(last)*	*(maiden, if applicable)*
Spouse's Name:_____			
	(first)	*(middle)*	*(last)*	*(maiden, if applicable)*
Social Security Number (if known):			
Date of Death:		City or Town of Death:	
Father's Name:_____			
	(first)	*(middle)*	*(last)*
Mother's Name:_____			
	(first)	*(middle)*	*(maiden)*	*(last)*

Relationship of requestor to subject(s) named on record:_____

Mail record to:	
Address:	
City/State/ZIP Code:	
Your signature:	
Date of request:_____	
	month/day/year

PLEASE NOTE: The earliest records available from this office are for calendar year 1901.

Send your requests to:

Michigan Department of Public Health
Office of the State Registrar
   and Center for Health Statistics
3423 North Logan Street
P.O. Box 30195
Lansing, Michigan 48909

(517) 335-8656

Vital records are also kept by the:

County Clerk
County Courthouse
(County Seat), Michigan

Cost for a certified Birth Certificate	$13.00
Cost for a wallet-size Birth Certificate	$13.00
Cost for a certified Marriage Certificate	$13.00
Cost for a certified Divorce Record	$13.00
Cost for a certified Death Certificate	$13.00
Cost for a duplicate copy, when ordered at the same time	$4.00

The Office of the State Registrar has birth and death records from January 1, 1867, marriage records from April 1867, and divorce records from January 1, 1897.

If your request is urgent you may call and charge your certificates to your Visa or MasterCard. There is a $32.00 fee for this service, which includes the cost of the certificate and the Federal Express delivery charge.

The Family History Library of The Church of Jesus Christ of Latter-day Saints in Salt Lake City, Utah has microfilmed many of the original and published vital records of Michigan. For details on their holdings please consult your nearest Family History Center.

PLEASE USE ONE FORM PER RECORD REQUEST
APPLICATION FOR A CERTIFICATE OF REGISTRATION OR A
CERTIFIED COPY OF A BIRTH RECORD

PRINT CLEARLY

1. Name at Birth_____ Date of
   Or adopted name: First   Middle   Last   Birth: _____
                                                              Mo   Day   Year

2. Place of Birth: _____
                        Hospital (if known)   City   County

3. Mother's Maiden Name: _____
                              First   Middle   Last

4. Father's Name: _____
                        First   Middle   Last

5. Is the individual named in No. 1 adopted? ☐ yes   ☐ no   ☐ maybe
   If the information is available and you are the individual named in No. 1, or if the record is being sent to the individual named in No. 1, do you wish to receive the name and location of the court where the adoption took place? ☐ yes   ☐ no

   ┌───┐
   │ PLEASE PROVIDE IN THIS SPACE ANY ADDITIONAL INFORMATION THAT WOULD HELP US LOCATE THE RECORD. FOR EXAMPLE, A LEGAL CHANGE OF NAME │
   │   │
   │   │
   │   │
6. └───┘

RECORDS CAN BE PROVIDED ONLY TO ELIGIBLE PERSONS

7. Please place an "X" in the appropriate area and follow additional instructions.
   My Relationship To The Person In Line 1 Is:

   ☐ INDIVIDUAL NAMED IN   ☐ PARENT NAMED   ☐ LEGAL   │ IF YOU STATE YOUR RELATIONSHIP
      LINE 1   ON RECORD   GUARDIAN   │ AS AN HEIR PLEASE PROVIDE THE
   ☐ LEGAL REPRESENTATIVE — Whom Are You Representing?_____ │ DATE AND PLACE OF DEATH OF THE
   ☐ HEIR — Specify Your Relationship To The Person In Line 1?_____ ►│ PERSON NAMED IN LINE 1.
                                                                 │
8. Applicant's   │ _____
   Signature:_____   │   DATE
               Signature of Applicant   Date   │
                                                                 │ _____
                                                                 │   PLACE
   Applicant's
   Address:_____
              Street   City   State   Zip   Area Code   Phone
            (APPLICATION MUST BE SIGNED TO PROCESS YOUR REQUEST)

   ┌───┬───────────────────────────┐
   │ THIS BOX FOR INTERNAL USE ONLY   │ DP INFORMATION   │
   │   │   │
   │   │ YEAR _____   │
   │   │   │
   │   │ REGISTRATION NUMBER   │
   │   │   │
   │   │ _____   │
   └───┴───────────────────────────┘

- -

(PLEASE DO NOT REMOVE THIS STUB)   PLEASE SEND THE FOLLOWING
                                                                          Fee
PRINT THE NAME AND MAILING ADDRESS OF THE PERSON   ☐ Certified Photocopy   @ $ 13.00 _____ *
TO WHOM THE RECORD(S) ARE TO BE SENT   _____ Additional Copies   @ $ 4.00 _____
                                                        _____ Additional years   @ $ 4.00 _____
THIS IS A MAILING INSERT AND WILL BE USED   Searched   Per Year
TO MAIL THE RECORDS   (See instructions)

                                                        ☐ Certificate of
                                                           Registration (wallet size) @ $ 13.00 _____ *
                                                        _____ Additional Certificates
9. Name: _____   of Registration   @ $ 4.00 _____
   Street: _____
   City: _____   TOTAL _____
   State: _____ Zip: _____
                                                        MAKE CHECK OR MONEY ORDER
                                                                PAYABLE TO
                                                        STATE OF MICHIGAN

APPLICATION FOR A CERTIFIED COPY OF A MARRIAGE CERTIFICATE

We are required by Act 368 of 1978 as amended, to collect the statutory fee before a search may be made for any record. Fee schedule is itemized below. Please make check or money order payable to the STATE OF MICHIGAN.

Minimum fee for **ONE CERTIFIED COPY** — **$13.00** Minimum fee includes a 3 year search	
ADDITIONAL CERTIFIED COPIES of the same record ordered at the same time — **$4.00 each**	
ADDITIONAL YEARS searched over 3 years — **$4.00 each** (when exact year is not known and more than a 3 year search is required, remit — $4.00 FOR EACH additional year over the minimum 3 years searched)	
TOTAL	

FEES PAID TO SEARCH THE FILES ARE NOT REFUNDABLE.

When a record is not found, the applicant will receive notification that the record as requested is not on file in this office.

PLEASE PRINT

Please send me a certified copy of the marriage certificate of:

Name of groom _____

Name of bride at time of
application for marriage license _____

Date of marriage _____
                          (Month)   (Day)   (Year)

If exact year is unknown: _____
                                        (Years to be searched)

Place where license was obtained _____
                                                      (County)

_____   _____
        (Applicant's Signature)   (Date)

(PLEASE DO NOT REMOVE THIS STUB)   ADDITIONAL INFORMATION

PRINT THE NAME AND MAILING ADDRESS OF THE PERSON TO
WHOM THE RECORD(S) ARE TO BE SENT. THIS IS A MAILING
INSERT AND WILL BE USED TO MAIL THE RECORDS.

NAME: _____

STREET: _____

CITY: _____

STATE: _____ ZIP: _____

MICHIGAN DEPARTMENT OF PUBLIC HEALTH
Office of the State Registrar and Center for Health Statistics
3423 North Logan Street
P.O. Box 30195
Lansing, MI 48909

APPLICATION FOR A CERTIFIED COPY OF A DIVORCE OR ANNULMENT RECORD

We are required by Act 368 of 1978 as amended, to collect the statutory fee before a search may be made for any record. Fee schedule is itemized below. Please make check or money order payable to the STATE OF MICHIGAN.

Minimum fee for **ONE CERTIFIED COPY** — $13.00 Minimum fee includes a 3 year search	
ADDITIONAL CERTIFIED COPIES of the same record ordered at the same time — **$4.00 each**	
ADDITIONAL YEARS searched over 3 years — **$4.00 each** (when exact year is not known and more than a 3 year search is required, remit — $4.00 FOR EACH additional year over the minimum 3 years searched)	
TOTAL	

FEES PAID TO SEARCH THE FILES ARE NOT REFUNDABLE.

When a record is not found, the applicant will receive notification that the record as requested is not on file in this office.

PLEASE PRINT

Please send me a certified copy of the divorce or annulment decree of:

Name of man _____

Name of woman _____

Date of decree _____
              (Month)   (Day)   (Year)

If exact year is unknown: _____
                   (Years to be searched)

Place where divorce or annulment was granted _____
                   (County)

_____   _____
(Applicant's Signature)   (Date)

(PLEASE DO NOT REMOVE THIS STUB)

PRINT THE NAME AND MAILING ADDRESS OF THE PERSON TO WHOM THE RECORD(S) ARE TO BE SENT. THIS IS A MAILING INSERT AND WILL BE USED TO MAIL THE RECORDS.

ADDITIONAL INFORMATION

NAME: _____

STREET: _____

CITY: _____

STATE: _____ ZIP: _____

B-225-D 5/92

MICHIGAN DEPARTMENT OF PUBLIC HEALTH
Office of the State Registrar and Center for Health Statistics
3423 North Logan Street
P.O. Box 30195
Lansing, MI 48909

APPLICATION FOR A CERTIFIED COPY OF A DEATH CERTIFICATE

We are required by Act 368 of 1978 as amended, to collect the statutory fee before a search may be made for any record. Fee schedule is itemized below. Please make check or money order payable to the STATE OF MICHIGAN.

Minimum fee for ONE CERTIFIED COPY — $13.00 Minimum fee includes a 3 year search	
ADDITIONAL CERTIFIED COPIES of the same record ordered at the same time — $4.00 each	
ADDITIONAL YEARS searched over 3 years — $4.00 each (when exact year is not known and more than a 3 year search is required, remit — $4.00 FOR EACH additional year over the minimum 3 years searched	
TOTAL	

FEES PAID TO SEARCH THE FILES ARE NOT REFUNDABLE

WHEN A RECORD IS NOT FOUND, THE APPLICANT WILL RECEIVE NOTIFICATION THAT THE RECORD AS REQUESTED IS NOT ON FILE IN THIS OFFICE.

PLEASE PRINT

Please send me a certified copy of the death certificate of:

Name of deceased: _____
                        (First)   (Middle)   (Last)

Date of death: _____
                    (Month)   (Day)   (Year)

If exact year is unknown: _____
                                    (Years to be searched)

Place of death _____
                    (Township, Village, or City)   (County)

_____   _____
        Applicant's Signature   Date

IF THE INFORMATION REQUESTED ABOVE IS NOT KNOWN, please indicate in the box below any data which may be used for identifying the record, such as marital status, name of husband or wife if married, parents' names, age or birthplace.

(PLEASE DO NOT REMOVE THIS STUB)

ADDITIONAL INFORMATION

PRINT THE NAME AND MAILING ADDRESS OF THE PERSON TO WHOM THE RECORD(S) ARE TO BE SENT.
THIS IS A MAILING INSERT AND WILL BE USED TO MAIL THE RECORDS

NAME: _____

STREET: _____

CITY: _____

STATE: _____ ZIP: _____

B-225B 5/92

MINNESOTA

Send your requests to:

Minnesota Department of Health
Section of Vital Statistics Registration
717 Delaware Street, S.E.
P.O. Box 9441
Minneapolis, Minnesota 55440-9441

(612) 623-5121

Send your requests for Marriage and Divorce Certificates and early vital records to:

Court Administrator
County District Court
(County Seat), Minnesota

Cost for a certified Birth Certificate	$11.00
Cost for a duplicate Birth Certificate	$5.00
Cost for a certified Marriage Certificate	$8.00
Cost for a copy of the Divorce Decree	Varies
Cost for a certified Death Certificate	$8.00
Cost for a duplicate Death Certificate when ordered at the same time	$2.00

The Section of Vital Statistics Registration has birth records from January 1, 1900 and death records from January 1, 1908. Although they do not issue marriage and divorce certificates they do have an index of marriages from 1958 and divorces from 1970.

If your request is urgent you may call and charge your certificates to your Visa or MasterCard. There is a $5.00 fee for this service.

The Minnesota Historical Society (Minnesota History Center, 345 Kellogg Boulevard West, St. Paul, MN 55102-1906; Tel. 612-296-2143) has an extensive collection. For more information on their collection see *Genealogical Resources of the Minnesota Historical Society: A Guide,* published by the Society in 1989.

The Family History Library of The Church of Jesus Christ of Latter-day Saints in Salt Lake City, Utah has microfilmed many of the original and published vital records and church registers of Minnesota. For details on their holdings please consult your nearest Family History Center.

MINNESOTA DEPARTMENT OF HEALTH
Section of Vital Statistics Registration
717 Delaware Street S. E.
P.O. Box 9441
Minneapolis, Minnesota 55440

1. Our files include <u>birth records since 1900</u> and <u>death records since 1908</u> for the entire State of Minnesota.
    Some records prior to these years are on file with the Court Administrator or County Recorder in the
    county of occurrence.

2. If payment is made by check or money order, please make it payable to "Treasurer, State of Minnesota".
    PLEASE NOTE: We cannot accept third party checks, Canadian checks or Canadian currency.

NAME & ADDRESS OF PERSON COMPLETING THIS FORM	FOR OFFICE USE ONLY
Signature: _____	Fee # _____
Street or Route: _____	# of Copies: ____+___
City, State & Zip Code: _____	Amount: _____

(A)   BIRTH RECORD $11.00 for one copy.
    $ 5.00 for each additional copy of the same record requested at the same time
        as the first copy.

Name: _____

Date of Birth: _____

City, Town or Township of Birth: _____

County of Birth: _____

Father's Full Name: _____

Mother's Full Maiden Name: _____

(B)   DEATH RECORD $8.00 for one copy.
    $2.00 for each additional copy of the same record requested at the same time
        as the first copy.

Name: _____

Date of Death: _____
        (or year last known to be alive)

City, Town or Township of Death: _____

County of Death: _____

Age at the time of Death: _____

Occupation: _____

Spouse's Full Name: _____

F 117

MISSISSIPPI

Send your requests to:

Mississippi State Department of Health
Vital Records Office
2423 North State Street
P.O. Box 1700
Jackson, Mississippi 39215-1700

(601) 960-7981, FAX (601) 352-0013

For Marriage Records (July 1, 1938 to December 31, 1941) and Divorce Records write to:

Circuit Court Clerk
County Circuit Courthouse
(County Seat), Mississippi

Cost for a certified Birth Certificate	$12.00
Cost for a short form Birth Certificate	$7.00
Cost for a duplicate Birth Certificate, when ordered at the same time	$3.00
Cost for a certified Marriage Certificate	$10.00
Cost for a certified Death Certificate	$10.00
Cost for duplicate Marriage and Death Certificates, when ordered at the same time	$2.00

The Vital Records Office has birth and death records from November 1, 1912. Marriage records are on file from January 1, 1926 to June 30, 1938. Marriage records from July 1, 1938 to December 31, 1941, as well as divorce records, are on file with the Circuit Court Clerk in the county where the marriage license (or divorce decree) was issued. The Vital Records Office will conduct genealogical research for a charge of $20 per hour.

The Mississippi Department of Archives and History (100 South State Street, Capitol Green, P.O. Box 571, Jackson, MS 39205; Tel. 601-359-6876) has early marriage records in with the county records (dates vary by county) and Mississippi death records from November 1912 to December 1937.

If your request is urgent you may call and charge your order for birth certificates to your Visa, Discover, or MasterCard. There is a $5.00 fee for this service.

The Family History Library of The Church of Jesus Christ of Latter-day Saints in Salt Lake City, Utah has microfilmed many of the original and published vital records of Mississippi. For details on their holdings please consult your nearest Family History Center.

MISSISSIPPI STATE DEPARTMENT OF HEALTH
Vital Records
P.O. Box 1700
Jackson, Mississippi 39215-1700
APPLICATION FOR CERTIFIED COPY OF BIRTH CERTIFICATE

INFORMATION

1. Only births recorded after November 1, 1912, are on file.
2. We recommend that the certified ABSTRACT (Short Form) be ordered. This is a certified transcript showing child's name, date and county of birth, state file number, filing and issue dates, and is sufficient for proof of birth. These may be obtained for $7.00* each, and $3.00* for each additional copy ordered at the same time.
3. There are some instances where, for family, historical or legal reasons, additional information is required. A certified COPY of the birth certificate (Long Form) is available for $12.00* for the first copy and $3.00* for each additional copy ordered at the same time.
4. A five year search of our records will be made. If no record is on file a certification of the NOT—ON—FILE will be issued and a search fee of $6.00 will be retained.

* Fee includes $1.00 to be collected for each copy and deposited in the Children's Trust Fund to fund programs to prevent child abuse and neglect.

INSTRUCTIONS

1. Complete ALL the information sections of the form. PLEASE PRINT.
2. The application must be signed.
3. PAYMENT:

Out-of-state: Remit a bank or postal money order or a bank cashier's check in the correct amount made payable to Mississippi State Department of Health.

Mississippi Resident: In addition to the above methods of payment, personal checks are acceptable if drawn on a Mississippi bank; make payable to Mississippi State Department of Health.

We accept no responsibility for cash sent through the mail.

4. Send completed application, appropriate fee and self-addressed stamped legal size envelope to the address at the top of this form.

BASIC INFORMATION: DOUBLE CHECK SPELLING AND DATE

DO NOT WRITE IN THIS SPACE

1. FULL NAME AT BIRTH	FIRST NAME	MIDDLE NAME	LAST NAME	STATE FILING NUMBER
2. DATE OF BIRTH	MONTH	DAY	YEAR	
3. PLACE OF BIRTH	COUNTY	CITY OR TOWN	STATE	FILING DATE

4. Has name ever been changed other than by marriage? If so, what was original name?
   ☐ Yes ☐ No

ADDITIONAL INFORMATION REQUIRED

`12 — 36`

5. SEX		6. RACE		`37 — 66`
7. FULL NAME OF FATHER	FIRST NAME	MIDDLE NAME	LAST NAME	S.C.
8. FULL MAIDEN NAME OF MOTHER	FIRST NAME	MIDDLE NAME	LAST NAME	S.C.

ABOUT THE APPLICANT

S.C.

9. FEE
   I AM ENCLOSING FEE OF $ _____ FOR _____ SHORT FORMS.

   S.C.

   I AM ENCLOSING FEE OF $ _____ FOR _____ LONG FORMS.

   C.D.

10. RELATIONSHIP OF APPLICANT TO PERSON NAMED IN ITEM 1.

    SUP.

11. PURPOSE FOR WHICH THIS COPY IS REQUESTED

    P.

Pursuant to Section 41-57-2 of the Mississippi Code of 1972, Annotated, and as defined by Mississippi State Board of Health Rules and Regulations, I hereby certify that I have a legitimate and tangible interest in the birth record requested. I understand that obtaining a record under false pretenses may subject me to the penalty as described in Section 41-57-27 of the Mississippi Code of 1972, Annotated.

CWA.

12. SIGNATURE OF APPLICANT   DATE SIGNED

PRINT YOUR MAILING ADDRESS HERE

13.		Name
14.	Apt. No.	Street or Route
15.		City or Town State, ZIP Code

MISSISSIPPI STATE DEPARTMENT OF HEALTH
Vital Records
Jackson, Mississippi 39215-1700

APPLICATION FOR CERTIFIED COPY OF STATISTICAL RECORD OF MARRIAGE

INFORMATION

1. Marriage records have been kept by state and county officials since January 1, 1926. From July 1, 1938, to December 31, 1941, records were kept only by the circuit court clerk in the county in which the marriage license was issued.
2. The fee for a search of the records and a certified copy is $10.00. Additional copies ordered at the same time are $2.00 each.
3. A five year search of our records will be made. If the record is not on file, a search fee of $6.00 will be retained.

INSTRUCTIONS

1. Complete the required section of this form. PLEASE PRINT.
2. The application must be signed.
3. PAYMENT:
   Out-of-state: Remit a bank or postal money order or a bank cashier's check in the correct amount made payable to Mississippi State Department of Health.
   Mississippi Resident: In addition to the above methods of payment, personal checks are acceptable if drawn on a Mississippi bank; make payable to Mississippi State Department of Health.
   We accept no responsibility for cash sent through the mail.
4. Send completed application, appropriate fee and self-addressed stamped legal size envelope to the address at the top of this form.

INFORMATION ABOUT BRIDE AND GROOM WHOSE STATISTICAL RECORD OF MARRIAGE IS REQUESTED (Please Print)			
1. FULL NAME OF GROOM	FIRST NAME	MIDDLE NAME	LAST NAME
2. FULL NAME OF BRIDE	FIRST NAME	MIDDLE NAME	LAST NAME
3. DATE OF MARRIAGE	MONTH	DAY	YEAR
4. PLACE OF MARRIAGE	COUNTY	CITY OR TOWN	STATE
5. WHERE LICENSE WAS BOUGHT	COUNTY	CITY OR TOWN	STATE
PERSON REQUESTING CERTIFIED COPY			
6. PURPOSE FOR WHICH COPY IS TO BE USED			
7. RELATIONSHIP OR INTEREST OF PERSON REQUESTING CERTIFICATE			
8. FEE I AM ENCLOSING A FEE OF $ _____ FOR _____ CERTIFIED COPIES.			
9. SIGNATURE OF APPLICANT		10. DATE SIGNED	

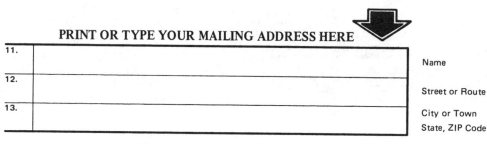

PRINT OR TYPE YOUR MAILING ADDRESS HERE

11.		Name
12.		Street or Route
13.		City or Town
		State, ZIP Code

MISSISSIPPI STATE DEPARTMENT OF HEALTH
Vital Records
P.O. Box 1700
Jackson, Mississippi 39215-1700

APPLICATION FOR CERTIFIED COPY OF DEATH CERTIFICATE

INFORMATION

1. Only deaths recorded after November 1, 1912 are on file.
2. The death certificate is the most important legal document in the settlement of the estate and insurance. It is important that the information on the certificate is correct. When you receive copies of the death certificate, check particularly spelling of names and that dates are correct.
3. If there are incorrect items on the certificate and the death occurred less than one year ago, please notify the funeral director who filed the certificate.
4. If there are incorrect items on the certificate and the death occurred more than one year ago, a court order may be required. Please contact Vital Records at the above address for additional information.
5. The fee for a certified copy of a death certificate is $10.00. Each additional copy ordered at the same time is $2.00.
6. A five year search of our records will be made. If the record is not on file, a search fee of $6.00 will be retained.

INSTRUCTIONS

1. Complete the information sections of this form. PLEASE PRINT.
2. The application must be signed.
3. PAYMENT:
   Out-of-state: Remit a bank or postal money order or a bank cashier's check in the correct amount made payable to Mississippi State Department of Health.
   Mississippi Resident: In addition to the above methods of payment, personal checks are acceptable if drawn on a Mississippi bank; make payable to Mississippi State Department of Health.
   We accept no responsibility for cash sent through the mail.
4. Send completed application, appropriate fee and self-addressed stamped legal size envelope to the address at the top of this form.

INFORMATION ABOUT PERSON WHOSE DEATH CERTIFICATE IS REQUESTED (Type or Print)		
1. FULL NAME OF DECEASED — First Name	Middle Name	Last Name
2. DATE OF DEATH — Month	Day	Year
3. PLACE OF DEATH — County	City or Town	State
4. Sex	5. Race — 6. Age at Death	7. State File Number if known
8. Name of Father	9. Name of Mother	
10. FUNERAL DIRECTOR — Name	Address	

11. PURPOSE FOR WHICH CERTIFIED COPY IS TO BE USED	NO. OF COPIES . . . . ————
12. RELATIONSHIP OR INTEREST OF PERSON REQUESTING CERTIFICATE	VETERAN'S SERVICE OR VA CLAIM NO:
Pursuant to Section 41-57-2 of the Mississippi Code of 1972, Annotated, and as defined by Mississippi State Board of Health Rules and Regulations, I hereby certify that I have a legitimate and tangible interest in the birth record requested. I understand that obtaining a record under false pretenses may subject me to the penalty as described in Section 41-57-27 of the Mississippi Code of 1972, Annontated.	————————
13. SIGNATURE OF APPLICANT	TOTAL . . . . ————
14. DATE SIGNED	FEE SUBMITTED . . . . $ ————

PRINT OR TYPE YOUR MAILING ADDRESS HERE

15.		Name
16.		Street or Route
17.		City or Town / State, ZIP Code

MISSOURI

Send your requests to:

Missouri Department of Health
Bureau of Vital Records
P.O. Box 570
Jefferson City, Missouri 65102-0570

(314) 751-6400

Send your requests for Marriage Certificates to:

Recorder of Deeds
County Courthouse
(County Seat), Missouri

Send your requests for Divorce Records to:

Clerk of the Circuit Court
(County Seat), Missouri

Cost for a certified Birth Certificate	$10.00
Cost for a wallet-size Birth Certificate	$10.00
Cost for verification of a Marriage or Divorce	Free
Cost for a certified Death Certificate	$10.00

The Bureau of Vital Records has birth and death records from January 1, 1910. They also have an index to marriages and divorces from July 1, 1948 and will search this index for free; however, marriage certificates and divorce records must be obtained from the county courts.

The Missouri State Archives (600 West Main Street, P.O. Box 778, Jefferson City, MO 65102; Tel. 314-751-3280) has microfilm copies of the records of the County Recorders. Some of these records date from the early 1800s.

If your request is urgent you may call and charge your birth certificates to your Visa, Discover, or MasterCard. There is a $22.95 fee for this service, which includes overnight delivery and one copy of the certificate.

The Family History Library of The Church of Jesus Christ of Latter-day Saints in Salt Lake City, Utah has microfilmed many of the original and published vital records and church registers of Missouri. For details on their holdings please consult your nearest Family History Center.

MISSOURI DEPARTMENT OF HEALTH
BUREAU OF VITAL RECORDS

APPLICATION FOR CERTIFIED COPY OF BIRTH CERTIFICATION

INSTRUCTIONS	COPIES REQUESTED	

INSTRUCTIONS

Recording of births began in this office January 1, 1910. The law requires a fee of $10 for a search of the files. This fee entitles you to a certified copy, if available. Additional copies are $10 each. **Fee must accompany application.**

NO CASH BY MAIL PLEASE. Make check or money order payable to *Missouri Department of Health.*

Mail this application to:

Missouri Department of Health
Bureau of Vital Records
P.O. Box 570
Jefferson City, Missouri 65102-0570

COPIES REQUESTED

Birth Certification   How Many ☐
Certification of facts of birth contained in original record.

Birth Card   How Many ☐
A nonlaminated wallet-size card that includes only information shown in sample.

Amount of Money Enclosed $

MISSOURI DEPARTMENT OF HEALTH
BIRTH CERTIFICATION
DATE FILED **June 22, 1955**   STATE FILE NUMBER **124-41-42355**
CHILD NAME **John Henry Dow**
BIRTH DATE **Feb. 31, 1984**   SEX **M**
COUNTY OF BIRTH **Butler**
DATE ISSUED **March 9, 1999**

**ALL FORMS OF CERTIFICATE
$10.00 EACH**

INFORMATION ABOUT PERSON WHOSE BIRTH CERTIFICATE IS REQUESTED   (TYPE OR PRINT ALL ITEMS EXCEPT SIGNATURE)

1. FULL NAME OF PERSON*	FIRST NAME	MIDDLE NAME	LAST NAME (MAIDEN NAME)
	IF THIS BIRTH COULD BE RECORDED UNDER ANOTHER NAME, PLEASE INDICATE THE NAME		

2. DATE OF BIRTH	MONTH	DAY	YEAR	3. SEX	4. RACE

5. PLACE OF BIRTH	CITY OR TOWN	COUNTY	STATE
	HOSPITAL OR STREET NO.	ATTENDING PHYSICIAN	☐ PHYSICIAN ☐ MIDWIFE ☐ OTHER

6. FULL NAME OF FATHER	FIRST NAME	MIDDLE NAME	LAST NAME

7. FULL MAIDEN NAME OF MOTHER	FIRST NAME	MIDDLE NAME	LAST NAME (MAIDEN)

*IF NEWBORN, PLEASE WAIT 6 TO 8 WEEKS BEFORE REQUESTING.

PERSON REQUESTING CERTIFIED COPY   (IF LEGAL GUARDIAN OF REGISTRANT, SEND ALONG GUARDIANSHIP PAPERS.)

8. PURPOSE FOR WHICH CERTIFIED COPY IS TO BE USED	9. RELATIONSHIP (MUST BE REGISTRANT, MEMBER OF IMMEDIATE FAMILY, LEGAL GUARDIAN, OR LEGAL REPRESENTATIVE)

10. SIGNATURE OF APPLICANT ▶	DATE SIGNED

12. ADDRESS OF APPLICANT (TYPE OR PRINT)	STREET ADDRESS		
	CITY OR TOWN	STATE	ZIP CODE

THIS COUPON MUST BE COMPLETED AND WILL BE USED TO ADDRESS OUR REPLY

NAME OF PERSON CERTIFICATION IS REQUESTED FOR

PLEASE PRINT OR TYPE THE NAME AND ADDRESS OF THE PERSON TO WHOM THE RECORD IS TO BE RETURNED.

▶ NAME

ADDRESS (NUMBER AND STREET)

CITY   STATE   ZIP CODE

MO 580-0641 (8-92)   VS-151 (R8-92)

MISSOURI DEPARTMENT OF HEALTH
BUREAU OF VITAL RECORDS

APPLICATION FOR SEARCH OF MARRIAGE INDEXES

P.O. BOX 570
JEFFERSON CITY, MO 65102

THE BUREAU OF VITAL RECORDS IS AUTHORIZED NO FEE FOR THIS SERVICE

FULL NAME OF GROOM (FIRST, MIDDLE, LAST)

FULL MAIDEN NAME OF BRIDE (FIRST, MIDDLE, LAST) | PREVIOUS MARRIED NAME

COUNTY ISSUING THE LICENSE

DATE OR APPROXIMATE DATE THE MARRIAGE OCCURRED

NOTE:

THESE INDEXES BEGIN ON JULY 1, 1948.

MARRIAGE INFORMATION PRIOR TO THAT DATE MAY BE OBTAINED ONLY FROM THE RECORDER OF DEEDS OF THE COUNTY THAT ISSUED THE LICENSE.

MO 580-0692 (3-92)　　　　　　　　　　　　　　　　　　　　　　　　　　VS-705 (R3-92)

MISSOURI DEPARTMENT OF HEALTH
BUREAU OF VITAL RECORDS

APPLICATION FOR SEARCH OF DIVORCE
OR DISSOLUTION OF MARRIAGE INDEXES

P O BOX 570
JEFFERSON CITY MO 65102

THE BUREAU OF VITAL RECORDS IS AUTHORIZED NO FEE FOR THIS SERVICE.

HUSBAND'S NAME

WIFE'S MAIDEN NAME

COUNTY ISSUING THE DECREE

DATE OR APPROPRIATE DATE DEGREE WAS ISSUED

NOTE: THESE INDEXES BEGIN ON JULY 1, 1948.

INFORMATION PRIOR TO THAT DATE MAY BE OBTAINED ONLY FROM THE CIRCUIT CLERK OF THE COUNTY THAT ISSUED THE DECREE.

MO 580-0693 (2-91)　　　　　　　　　　　　　　　　　　　　　　　　　　VS 803 (R2-91)

MISSOURI DEPARTMENT OF HEALTH
BUREAU OF VITAL RECORDS

APPLICATION FOR CERTIFIED COPY OF DEATH CERTIFICATION

INSTRUCTIONS	COPIES REQUESTED	THE RECORDING OF DEATHS BEGAN IN THIS OFFICE ON JAN. 1, 1910. RECORDS ARE FILED BY YEAR OF DEATH AND ALPHABETICALLY BY THE NAME OF THE DECEASED AT THE TIME OF DEATH. THEREFORE, AT LEAST THE APPROXIMATE YEAR OF DEATH OR LAST YEAR IN WHICH THE DECEASED WAS KNOWN TO BE ALIVE MUST BE GIVEN.
The law requires a $10.00 fee for a search of the files. This search fee also entitles you to one certification copy of the death record if it is available. Additional copies are $10.00 each. **The fee must accompany this application.** **No Cash Please.** Make check or money order payable to: Missouri Department of Health Mail this application to: Missouri Department of Health Bureau of Vital Records P.O. Box 570 Jefferson City, Missouri 65102-0570	Death Certification How Many (Certification of facts of death contained in original record) **$10.00 EACH** Amount of Money Enclosed	

INFORMATION ABOUT PERSON WHOSE DEATH CERTIFICATE IS REQUESTED *(TYPE or PRINT all items EXCEPT SIGNATURE)*

1. FULL NAME OF DECEASED	FIRST NAME	MIDDLE NAME		LAST NAME AT TIME OF DEATH		
2. DATE OF DEATH	MONTH	DAY	YEAR	3. SEX	RACE	AGE
4. PLACE OF DEATH	CITY OR TOWN	COUNTY		STATE		
5. FULL NAME OF SPOUSE	FIRST NAME	MIDDLE NAME		LAST NAME		
6. FULL NAME OF FATHER	FIRST NAME	MIDDLE NAME		LAST NAME		
7. FULL MAIDEN NAME OF MOTHER	FIRST NAME	MIDDLE NAME		LAST NAME (MAIDEN)		

PERSON REQUESTING CERTIFIED COPY OF DEATH RECORD

8. PURPOSE FOR WHICH CERTIFIED COPY IS TO BE USED (PLEASE CHECK)	9. RELATIONSHIP TO REGISTRANT OR INTEREST OF PERSON REQUESTING CERTIFICATION
☐ INSURANCE CLAIM ON POLICY ISSUED WITHIN 2 YEARS OF DEATH ☐ OTHER INSURANCE CLAIMS ☐ OTHER (SPECIFY) ▶	

10. SIGNATURE OF APPLICANT ▶	DATE SIGNED

11. NAME AND ADDRESS WHERE COPIES ARE TO BE MAILED (TYPE OR PRINT)	NAME AND ADDRESS OF FUNERAL HOME	
	NAME OF INDIVIDUAL TO RECEIVE COPIES	STREET ADDRESS
	CITY OR TOWN	STATE / ZIP CODE

THIS COUPON MUST BE COMPLETED AND WILL BE USED TO ADDRESS OUR REPLY

NAME OF PERSON CERTIFICATION IS REQUESTED FOR

PLEASE PRINT OR TYPE THE NAME AND ADDRESS OF THE PERSON TO WHOM THE RECORD IS TO BE RETURNED.

▶ NAME

ADDRESS (NUMBER AND STREET)

CITY   STATE   ZIP CODE

MO 580-0640 (8-92)   VS-351 (R8-92)

MONTANA

Send your requests to:

Montana Department of Health and Environmental Sciences
Vital Records and Statistics Bureau
1400 Broadway
P.O. Box 200901
Helena, Montana 59620-0001

(406) 444-4228

Send your requests for Marriage Certificates and early vital records to:

Clerk
County District Court
(County Seat), Montana

Cost for a certified Birth Certificate	$10.00
Cost for searching the Marriage and Divorce Indexes	$10.00
Cost for a certified Death Certificate	$10.00

The Montana Vital Records and Statistics Bureau has birth and death records from late 1907. They have an index to marriage and divorce records from January 1, 1945 to the present, which they will search for a fee of $10.00 per hour. Copies of the marriage certificate must be obtained from the County Clerk.

If your request is urgent you may call and charge your certificates to your Visa, Discover, or MasterCard. There is a $5.00 charge for this service, plus an additional $10.50 charge for express delivery.

The Montana Historical Society (225 North Roberts Street, Helena, MT 59620-9990; Tel. 406-444-2694; toll-free 800-243-9900; FAX 406-444-2696) has an extensive collection.

The Family History Library of The Church of Jesus Christ of Latter-day Saints in Salt Lake City, Utah has microfilmed many of the original and published vital records of Montana. For details on their holdings please consult your nearest Family History Center.

INSTRUCTIONS AND FEES FOR VITAL STATISTICS RECORDS SERVICE
(Effective January 30, 1992)

The Vital Records and Statistics Bureau maintains permanent storage of original certificates of birth, deaths dating back to 1907. The bureau also maintains indexes of marriage and divorce records for Montana dating back to 1945. The bureau is authorized to perform legal amendments to filed certificates and to create substitute birth certificates and to file delayed certificates of birth. The bureau issues certified copies of certificates through an application process and provides record location services for marriage and divorce records.

Our address is   **VITAL RECORDS AND STATISTICS BUREAU**
MONTANA DEPARTMENT OF HEALTH & ENVIRONMENTAL SCIENCES
1400 BROADWAY
HELENA, MT 59620

Telephone: (406) 444-4228

CERTIFIED COPIES OF BIRTH/DEATH CERTIFICATES . . . . . . .Fee: $10.00
1. Requestor should complete an application form and submit it to the bureau along with the appropriate fee. Checks should be made payable to the MONTANA DEPARTMENT OF HEALTH. CANADIAN requests must be made by Money Order with U. S. Funds.
2. Applications are subject to approval/disapproval under provisions of Montana laws and Department of Health regulations.

SEARCHES OF MARRIAGE AND DIVORCE INDEXES . . . . .Fee $10.00 PER HOUR
1. Names and appropriate dates should be submitted to the bureau, in writing, along with the appropriate fees. Checks should be made payable To MONTANA DEPARTMENT OF HEALTH.
2. There are some searches the bureau is not able to conduct. In these cases, the fees will be refunded.
3. If the requested record is located, the requestor will be provided the name of the county in which the record is on file. If a certified copy of The record is needed the Clerk of the District Court in the County of occurrence needs to be contacted.
4. Response time by the bureau to these requests may be as long as 60 working days.

GENEALOGICAL USE OF VITAL RECORDS is available under limited conditions. Certified copies of death certificates may be requested provided the death occurred at least (20) years prior the date of application. Certified copies of birth certificates may be requested provided the requestor submits proof of death and provided that the death occurred at least thirty (30) years prior to the date of the request.
1. Requestor should submit a completed application to the Bureau along with the appropriate fees (non-refundable). Checks should be made payable to the MONTANA DEPARTMENT OF HEALTH.
2. RESPONSE TIME BY THE BUREAU TO THESE REQUESTS MAY BE AS LONG AS 60 WORKING DAYS.

APPLICATION FOR A CERTIFIED COPY OF A BIRTH CERTIFICATE
(Please Print)

Applicant's Name_____

Mailing Address_____

City_____State_____Zip Code_____

Telephone Number(_____)_____ Relationship to Individual Named on Certificate (Check one only):

Self_____Mother_____Father_____Spouse_____Relative (specify) _____

Legal Guardian or Custodian (proof required)_____ Purpose for which record is needed_____
. . . .
Name on Certificate_____
             First   Middle   Last

Date of Birth_____-_____-_____ Place of Birth_____
                                                        City   County

Mother's MAIDEN Name _____
             First   Middle   Last

Father's Name_____
             First   Middle   Last

Number of Copies Requested_____ Adopted? Yes_____No_____ If known, state original name_____

GENEOLOGISTS: IS THIS INDIVIDUAL DECEASED? IF DECEASED HOW LONG_____
. . . .
FOR STATE USE ONLY

EXP_____ #_____

Date Received_____ Receipt #_____ Index #_____

Cert # Issued_____ Mailed _____

Comments_____
_____
_____

The Vital Records and Statistics Bureau maintains permanent storage of original certificates of birth, deaths dating back to 1907. The bureau also maintains index of marriage and divorce records for Montana dating back to 1945. The bureau is authorized to perform legal amendments to filed certificates and to create substitute birth certificates and to file delayed certificates of birth. The bureau issues certified copies of certificates through an application process and provides record location services for marriage and divorce records.

Our address is
    VITAL RECORDS AND STATISTICS BUREAU
    MONTANA DEPARTMENT OF HEALTH & ENVIRONMENTAL SCIENCES
    1400 BROADWAY
    HELENA, MT 59620

Telephone: (406) 444-4228

CERTIFIED COPIES OF BIRTH/DEATH CERTIFICATES . . . . Fee: $10.00
    1. Requestor should complete an application form and submit it to the bureau along with the appropriate fee. Checks should be made payable to the MONTANA DEPARTMENT OF HEALTH. CANADIAN requests must be made by Money Order with U. S. Funds.
    2. Applications are subject to approval/disapproval under provisions of Montana laws and Department of Health regulations.

SEARCHES OF MARRIAGE AND DIVORCE INDEXES . . . . Fee: $10.00
    1. Names and appropriate dates should be submitted to the bureau, in writing, along with the appropriate fees. Checks should be made payable to MONTANA DEPARTMENT OF HEALTH.
    2. There are some searches the bureau is not able to conduct. In these cases, the fees will be refunded.
    3. If the requested record is located, the requestor will be provided the name of the county in which the record is on file. If a certified copy of the record is needed the Clerk of the District Court in the County of occurrence needs to be contacted.
    4. Response time by the bureau to these requests may be as long as 60 working days.

GENEALOGICAL USE OF VITAL RECORDS is available under limited conditions. Certified copies of death certificates may be requested provided the death occurred at least (30) years prior the date of application. Certified copies of birth certificates may be requested provided the requestor submits proof of death and provided that the death occurred at least thirty (30) years prior to the date of the request.
    1. Requestor should submit a completed application to the Bureau along with the appropriate fees (non-refundable). Checks should be made payable to the MONTANA DEPARTMENT OF HEALTH.
    2. RESPONSE TIME BY THE BUREAU TO THESE REQUESTS MAY BE AS LONG AS 60 WORKING DAYS.

APPLICATION FOR SEARCH OF MARRIAGE/DIVORCE INDEXES

Applicant's Name:_____

Mailing Address:_____

City:_____ State:_____ Zip Code:_____

BRIDE:

    Complete maiden name:_____

    Date of birth:_____ Place of birth:_____

    Fathers name:_____

    Mothers full maiden name:_____

    Previous marriage?_____ If so what surname?_____ Date to be searched:_____
        City/county to be searched:_____

GROOM:
    Complete name:_____

    Date of birth:_____ Place of birth:_____

    Fathers name:_____

    Mothers full maiden name:_____

    Previous marriage:_____Date to be searched:_____ City or county to be searched:_____

(FOR STATE USE ONLY)

Exp_____/____(____)#_____ coll#(____)_____

Date received_____ Rct#_____

Amount recieved_____ Index#_____ Mailed_____

INSTRUCTIONS AND FEES FOR VITAL STATISTICS RECORDS SERVICE
(Effective January 30, 1992)

The Vital Records and Statistics Bureau maintains permanent storage of original certificates of birth, deaths dating back to 1907. The bureau also maintains indexes of marriage and divorce records for Montana dating back to 1945. The bureau is authorized to perform legal amendments to filed certificates and to create substitute birth certificates and to file delayed certificates of birth. The bureau issues certified copies of certificates through an application process and provides record location services for marriage and divorce records.

Our address is   **VITAL RECORDS AND STATISTICS BUREAU**
MONTANA DEPARTMENT OF HEALTH & ENVIRONMENTAL SCIENCES
1400 BROADWAY
HELENA, MT 59620

Telephone: **(406) 444-4228**

___

CERTIFIED COPIES OF BIRTH/DEATH CERTIFICATES . . . . . . .Fee: $10.00
1. Requestor should complete an application form and submit it to the bureau along with the appropriate fee. Checks should be made payable to the **MONTANA DEPARTMENT OF HEALTH. CANADIAN** requests must be made by Money Order with U. S. Funds.
2. Applications are subject to approval/disapproval under provisions of Montana laws and Department of Health regulations.

___

SEARCHES OF MARRIAGE AND DIVORCE INDEXES . . . . .Fee $10.00 PER HOUR
1. Names and appropriate dates should be submitted to the bureau, in writing, along with the appropriate fees. Checks should be made payable to **MONTANA DEPARTMENT OF HEALTH.** Searches consist of 5 years searched for each $10.00.
2. There are some searches the bureau is not able to conduct. In these cases, the fees will be refunded.
3. If the requested record is located, the requestor will be provided the name of the county in which the record is on file. If a certified copy of the record is needed the Clerk of the District Court in the County of occurrence needs to be contacted.
4. Response time by the bureau to these requests may be as long as **60 working days.**

___

GENEALOGICAL USE OF VITAL RECORDS is available under limited conditions. Certified copies of death certificates may be requested provided the death occurred at least (20) years prior the date of application. Certified copies of birth certificates may be requested provided the requestor submits proof of death and provided that the death occurred at least thirty (30) years prior to the date of the request.
1. Requestor should submit a completed application to the Bureau along with the appropriate fees (non-refundable). Checks should be made payable to the **MONTANA DEPARTMENT OF HEALTH.**
2. RESPONSE TIME BY THE BUREAU TO THESE REQUESTS MAY BE AS LONG AS **60 WORKING DAYS.**

___

APPLICATION FOR A CERTIFIED COPY OF A DEATH CERTIFICATE
(Please Print)

Applicant's Name _____

Mailing Address _____

City _____ State _____ Zip Code _____

Telephone Number (_____)_____ Relationship to Individual Named on Certificate (Check one only):

Self _____ Mother _____ Father _____ Spouse _____ Relative (specify) _____

Legal Guardian or Custodian (proof required) _____ Purpose for which record is needed _____
****

NAME OF DECEDENT_____

DATE OF DEATH_____ PLACE OF DEATH_____
(Need at least a starting date)

OCCUPATION_____ MARRIED?_____ SPOUSE NAME_____

AGE AT TIME OF DEATH_____ PLACE OF BIRTH_____

PARENTS_____

HOW LONG DECEASED_____
****

FOR STATE USE ONLY

EXP_____ # _____

Date Received _____ Receipt # _____ Index # _____

Cert # Issued _____ Mailed _____

Comments _____

_____

_____

NEBRASKA

Send your requests to:

Bureau of Vital Statistics
Nebraska State Department of Health
P.O. Box 95007
Lincoln, Nebraska 68509-5007

(402) 471-2872

For earlier vital records contact:

County Clerk
County Courthouse
(County Seat), Nebraska

Cost for a certified Birth Certificate	$8.00
Cost for a wallet-size Birth Certificate	$8.00
Cost for a certified Marriage or Divorce Certificate	$7.00
Cost for a certified Death Certificate	$7.00

The Nebraska Bureau of Vital Statistics has birth and death records from 1904 and marriage and divorce records from January 1, 1909.

The Nebraska State Historical Society (1500 R Street, P.O. Box 82554, Lincoln, NE 68501; Tel. 402-471-4771) has a large collection of county marriage and divorce records.

The Family History Library of The Church of Jesus Christ of Latter-day Saints in Salt Lake City, Utah has microfilmed many of the original and published vital records of Nebraska. For details on their holdings please consult your nearest Family History Center.

APPLICATION FOR CERTIFIED COPY OF
BIRTH CERTIFICATE

Nebraska has been registering births with this office since <u>1904</u>.

PLEASE TYPE OR PRINT LEGIBLY

Full name at birth_____
    (If adopted, list adoptive name)

Month, day, and year of birth_____

City or town of birth_____ County of birth_____

Father's full name_____
    (If adopted, list adoptive father's name)

Mother's full maiden name_____
    (If adopted, list adoptive mother's name)

Is this the record of an adopted person?   Yes_____   No_____

For what purpose is this record to be used?_____

If this is not your record, how are you related?_____

<u>Delayed Birth Certificate</u>--Legislation passed in 1941 provides for the filing of delayed birth certificates for persons who were born prior to 1904 **or** for persons whose births were not recorded at the time of birth.

Is this a delayed birth certificate?   Yes_____   No_____

****
WARNING: Section 71-649, Nebraska Revised Statutes: It is a felony to obtain, possess, use, sell, furnish, or attempt to obtain any vital record for purposes of deception.
****

SIGNATURE_____ | **FOR OFFICE USE ONLY**

Type or print name_____ | ____Check   ____MO   ____Cash

Street Address_____ | Amount Received_____

City, State, Zip_____ | Date Received_____

Phone Number_____ | By Whom Received_____

Today's Date_____ | PROOF OF IDENTIFICATION:

Please indicate type and number of copies desired:
(Fees are subject to change without notice)

_____ x $8.00 each = _____ Certified Copy

_____ x $8.00 each = _____ Birth Registration Card
    (Plastic billfold size card--Not always
    acceptable for passport or school purposes
    as it does not list parentage)

<u>Mail to:</u>

Bureau of Vital Statistics
P.O. Box 95007
Lincoln, NE 68509-5007
PH: (402) 471-2872

**Please enclose a stamped, self-addressed,
business-size envelope.**

Rev.07/92   printed on recycled paper

APPLICATION FOR CERTIFIED COPY OF
MARRIAGE CERTIFICATE

Nebraska has been registering marriages in this office since <u>1909</u>.

(For records occurring prior to 1909, contact the county clerk of the county in which the marriage license was issued or the State Historical Society, P.O. Box 82554, Lincoln, NE 68501. They both will require a file search fee.)

PLEASE TYPE OR PRINT LEGIBLY

Full name of groom_____

Full maiden name of bride_____
   (Please list any other name bride may have used)

County in which license was issued_____

Month, day, and year of marriage_____

For what purpose is this record to be used?_____

If this is not your marriage record,
how are you related to these persons?_____

****
WARNING: Section 71-649, Nebraska Revised Statutes: It is a felony to obtain, possess, use, sell, furnish, or attempt to obtain any vital record for purposes of deception.
****

SIGNATURE_____	**FOR OFFICE USE ONLY**
Type or print name_____	____Check ____MO ____Cash
Street Address_____	Amount Received_____
City, State, Zip_____	Date Received_____
Today's Date_____	By Whom Received_____
	PROOF OF IDENTIFICATION:
Number of certified copies ____ x $7.00 each = ____	_____

<u>Mail to:</u>

Bureau of Vital Statistics
P.O. Box 95007
Lincoln, NE 68509-5007
PH: (402) 471-2872

Please enclose a stamped, self-addressed, business-size envelope.

Rev.07/92

     printed on recycled paper

APPLICATION FOR CERTIFIED COPY OF DISSOLUTION OF MARRIAGE (DIVORCE) CERTIFICATE

Nebraska has been registering certificates of dissolution of marriage (divorces) in this office since **1909**.

(For records occurring prior to 1909 or if you wish to obtain the divorce decree, contact the district court in the county where the divorce was granted.)

PLEASE TYPE OR PRINT LEGIBLY

Full name of husband_____

Full name of wife_____

City or county where granted_____

Month, day, and year granted_____

For what purpose is this record to be used?_____

If this is not your divorce certificate,
how are you related to these persons?_____

****

WARNING: Section 71-649, Nebraska Revised Statutes: It is a felony to obtain, possess, use, sell, furnish, or attempt to obtain any vital record for purposes of deception.

****

SIGNATURE_____

Type or print name_____

Street Address_____

City, State, Zip_____

Today's Date_____

Number of certified copies _____ x $7.00 each = _____

Mail to:

Bureau of Vital Statistics
P.O. Box 95007
Lincoln, NE 68509-5007
PH: (402) 471-2872

Please enclose a stamped, self-addressed, business-size envelope.

```
------------------------------------
|        FOR OFFICE USE ONLY        |
|                                   |
| Proof of Identification:          |
|                                   |
| _____  |
|                                   |
| _____  |
------------------------------------
```

Rev.04/10/92

APPLICATION FOR CERTIFIED COPY OF
DEATH CERTIFICATE

Nebraska has been registering deaths with this office since <u>1904</u>.

PLEASE TYPE OR PRINT LEGIBLY

Full name of deceased_____
   (If female, list married name or any other name decedent may have used)

City or town of death_____ County of death_____
   (If exact place of death is not known, list last known address)

Month, day, and year of death_____
     (If exact date of death is not known, list date decedent was last known to be alive
     or indicate a span of years to search.)

For what purpose is this record to be used?_____
****

The information in this section is **optional** information which will assist our office in locating and identifying the requested record:

Year of birth_____ Birthplace_____

Spouse's full name_____ Home address_____

Father's full name_____

Mother's full maiden name_____

Funeral Director_____ City_____

****
WARNING: Section 71-649, Nebraska Revised Statutes: It is a felony to obtain, possess, use, sell, furnish, or attempt to obtain any vital record for purposes of deception.
****

SIGNATURE_____ | **FOR OFFICE USE ONLY**

Type or print name_____ | ____Check ____MO ____Cash
   (If funeral director, print name of firm) |

   Street Address_____ | Amount Received_____

   City, State, Zip_____ | Date Received_____

   Today's date_____ | By Whom Received_____

Number of certified copies _____ x $7.00 each = _____ | PROOF OF IDENTIFICATION:

If copies are to be sent to another address, enter that mailing address below:

Name_____

Street Address_____

City, State, Zip_____

<u>Mail completed application and fee to:</u>

Bureau of Vital Statistics
P.O. Box 95007
Lincoln, NE 68509-5007
PH: (402) 471-2872

Please enclose a stamped, self-addressed, business-size envelope.

Rev.07/92   ♻ *printed on recycled paper*

Send your requests to:

Nevada State Department of Human Resources
State Health Division
Section of Vital Statistics
505 East King Street, Room 102
Carson City, Nevada 89710-4761

(702) 687-4480

Send your requests for Marriage Certificates and Divorce Records to:

County Recorder
County Courthouse
(County Seat), Nevada

Cost for a certified Birth Certificate	$11.00
Cost for a wallet-size Birth Certificate	$11.00
Cost to search the Marriage Index (1968-)	$2.00
Cost for a certified Marriage Certificate	$5.00
Cost for a copy of the Marriage Application	$3.00
Cost for Divorce Record ($1.00 per page and the following fee)	$4.00
Cost for a certified Death Certificate	$8.00

The Nevada Section of Vital Statistics has birth and death records from July 1, 1911. They also have an index to marriage certificates from 1968 to date; however, the marriage certificate must be requested from the County Recorder.

If your request is urgent you may call (702) 687-4481 and charge your certificates to your Visa, Discover, or MasterCard. There is a $5.00 fee for this service, plus the postal charges.

The Nevada State Library (100 North Stewart Street, Carson City, NV 89710; Tel. 702-687-5160) has an index to marriages and divorces from January 1968 to June 1991.

The Family History Library of The Church of Jesus Christ of Latter-day Saints in Salt Lake City, Utah has microfilmed many of the original and published vital records and registers of Nevada. For details on their holdings please consult your nearest Family History Center.

NEVADA STATE HEALTH DIVISION
Section of Vital Statistics
505 E. King Street., Room 102
Carson City, Nevada 89710
(702)687-4480

DEATH CERTIFICATE APPLICATION   No. of Copies _____

$8.00 per Certified Certificate
Search fee when no record is found......$4.00 per name

FULL NAME OF DECEDENT _____

DATE OF DEATH _____

PLACE OF DEATH _____
                        (City or County)

DECENDENT'S FATHER _____

DECENDENT'S MOTHER'S MAIDEN NAME _____
                                        (First, Middle & Last)

MORTUARY IN CHARGE OF ARRANGEMENTS _____

ADDRESS _____

Purpose for which certificate is to be used _____

Mailing Address _____   (THIS SECTION **MUST** BE COMPLETED)

Signature of Applicant _____

Relationship to Decedent _____
            (Parent, Spouse, Child, Executor, Attorney, etc.)

XXXXXXXXXXXXXXXXXXXXXXXXXXXXXXXXXXXXXXXXXXXXXXXX
For Office Use Only:

Amount Received _____   Receipt No. _____

Copies Ordered _____   Date _____

NEVADA STATE HEALTH DIVISION
Section of Vital Statistics
505 E. King St., Rm. 102
Carson City, Nevada 89710
(702)687-4480

BIRTH CERTIFICATE APPLICATION   No. of Copies _____

$11.00 per Certified Copy
$11.00 per Certified Card

Search fee when no record is found....$4.00 per name

FULL NAME AT BIRTH _____

DATE OF BIRTH _____

PLACE OF BIRTH _____
                        (City or County)

FATHER'S NAME _____

MOTHER'S MAIDEN NAME _____
                            (First, Middle & Last)

ATTENDING PHYSICIAN OR MIDWIFE _____

Purpose for which certificate is to be used _____

Mailing Address _____   (This section MUST be completed)

_____

_____

Signature of Applicant _____

Relationship _____   (Mother, Father, Self, etc.)

XXXXXXXXXXXXXXXXXXXXXXXXXXXXXXXXXXXXXXXXXXXXXXXX

For Office Use Only:

Amount Received _____   Receipt No. _____

Copies Ordered _____   Date _____

FOR LEGAL COPIES OF MARRIAGE OR DIVORCES

COMPLETE THE FOLLOWING FOR CERTIFIED, LEGAL COPIES OF THESE DOCUMENTS

( ) Marriage Certificates - Order from County Recorder
( ) Marriage Application - Order from County Clerk
( ) Divorce Decree   - Order from County Clerk

COST OF COPIES

Marriage Certificates.......$5.00 per copy
Marriage Applications....... 3.00 per copy
Divorce Decree.............. 1.00 per page + $4.00 for certification

INFORMATION REQUIRED TO FILL ORDER

Date of Event (Month/Day/Year)   Location of Event (City-County)

Name of Male   Name of Female (Maiden Name)

ADDRESS YOUR REQUEST TO THE COUNTY COURTHOUSE IN THE COUNTY WHERE THE
LICENSE WAS PURCHASED OR THE DIVORCE WAS GRANTED.

ADDRESSES:

CARSON CITY COUNTY
Courthouse
Carson City, NV 89701
(702) 887-2260

CHURCHILL COUNTY
Courthouse
Fallon, NV 89406
(702) 423-6001

CLARK COUNTY
309 South Third Street
Las Vegas, NV 89155
(702) 455-4340

DOUGLAS COUNTY
Courthouse
Minden, NV 89423
(702) 782-9029

ELKO COUNTY
Courthouse, Rm. 103
Elko, NV 89801
(702) 738-6526

ESMERALDA COUNTY
Courthouse
Goldfield, NV 89013
(702) 485-6337

EUREKA COUNTY
Courthouse
Eureka, NV 89316
(702) 237-5263

HUMBOLDT COUNTY
Courthouse
Winnemucca, NV 89445
(702) 623-5081

LANDER COUNTY
Courthouse
Battle Mtn. 89820
(702) 635-5127

LINCOLN COUNTY
P.O. Box 218
Pioche, NV 89043
(702) 962-3390

LYON COUNTY
Courthouse
Yerington, NV 89447
(702) 463-3341

MINERAL COUNTY
Courthouse
Hawthorne, NV 89415
(702) 945-3676

NYE COUNTY
Courthouse
Tonopah, NV 89049
(702) 482-8127

PERSHING COUNTY
Courthouse
Lovelock, NV 89419
(702) 273-2408

STOREY COUNTY
Courthouse
Virginia City, NV 89440
(702) 847-0244

WASHOE COUNTY *
P.O. Box 11130
Reno, NV 89520
(702) 328-3660

WHITE PINE COUNTY
Courthouse
Ely, NV 89301
(702) 289-4567

3/15/91

* NO PERSONAL CHECKS

NEW HAMPSHIRE

Send your requests to:

New Hampshire Division of Public Health Services
Bureau of Vital Records and Health Statistics
6 Hazen Drive
Concord, New Hampshire 03301-6527

(603) 271-4650

Vital records are also available from:

Town Clerk
Town Hall
(Town), New Hampshire

Cost for a certified Birth Certificate by mail	$10.00
Cost for a certified Marriage Certificate by mail	$10.00
Cost for a copy of the Divorce Record	$10.00
Cost for a certified Death Certificate by mail	$10.00
Cost for a duplicate certificate	$6.00

The New Hampshire Bureau of Vital Records has copies of vital records from 1640 to the present. There are restrictions on birth records after 1901 and on marriage, divorce, and death records after 1938. Make your payment payable to "Treasurer, State of New Hampshire." The Bureau has a research room with birth records from the mid-1600s through 1900 and marriage and death records from the mid-1600s through 1937. You can do your own search and obtain copies of the records for $.50 a copy.

If your request is urgent you may call and charge your certificates to your Visa, Discover, or MasterCard. There is a $6.00 fee for this service.

The Family History Library of The Church of Jesus Christ of Latter-day Saints in Salt Lake City, Utah has microfilmed many of the original and published vital records and church registers of New Hampshire. They have microfilm of birth, marriage, and death records from 1640 to 1900 and the index to early town records from 1639 to 1910. For details on their holdings please consult your nearest Family History Center.

BIRTHS

New Hampshire Division of Public Health Services
Bureau of Vital Records & Health Statistics
Health & Welfare Building, 6 Hazen Drive
Concord, New Hampshire 03301

NUMBER: _____

REQUESTED: _____

ISSUED: _____

APPLICATION FOR COPY OF BIRTH CERTIFICATE

PLEASE PRINT

Name
at Birth: _____
       FIRST   MIDDLE   LAST

Date   Place
of Birth: _____   of Birth: _____
    MONTH   DAY   YEAR

Father's
Name: _____
          FIRST   LAST

Mother's
Maiden Name: _____
         FIRST   LAST

Purpose for which
certificate is requested? _____

Your   Your Relationship
Signature: _____   to Registrant? _____

A FEE OF $10 IS REQUIRED BY LAW FOR THE SEARCH OF THE FILE FOR ANY ONE RECORD.

A FEE OF $6 IS REQUIRED BY LAW FOR EACH SUBSEQUENT COPY ISSUED AT THE SAME TIME AS THE INITIAL COPY.

Notice: *Any person shall be guilty of a Class B Felony if he/she willfully and knowingly makes any false statement in an application for a certified copy of a vital record. (RSA 126:24)*

DEATHS

DIVISION OF PUBLIC HEALTH SERVICES
BUREAU OF VITAL RECORDS & HEALTH STATISTICS
H&W BUILDING, HAZEN DRIVE
CONCORD, NEW HAMPSHIRE 03301

NUMBER _____

REQUESTED _____

ISSUED _____

APPLICATION FOR COPY OF DEATH RETURN

PLEASE PRINT PLAINLY

NAME OF
DECEASED _____
      (FIRST NAME)   (MIDDLE NAME)   (LAST NAME)

DATE OF
DEATH _____
    (MONTH)   (DAY)   (YEAR)

PLACE OF
DEATH _____
               (COUNTY)

PURPOSE FOR WHICH CERTIFICATE IS REQUESTED _____

BY WHOM _____ RELATIONSHIP TO REGISTRANT _____

☐ ISSUED WITH CAUSE OF DEATH   ☐ ISSUED WITHOUT CAUSE OF DEATH

A FEE OF TEN DOLLARS IS REQUIRED BY LAW FOR THE SEARCH OF THE FILE FOR ANY ONE RECORD

NOTICE: ANY PERSON SHALL BE GUILTY OF A CLASS B FELONY IF HE/SHE WILLFULLY AND KNOW-
INGLY MAKE ANY FALSE STATEMENT IN AN APPLICATION FOR A CERTIFIED COPY OF A VITAL
RECORD.
(RSA 126:24)

MARRIAGES

DIVISION OF PUBLIC HEALTH SERVICES
BUREAU OF VITAL RECORDS & HEALTH STATISTICS
H&W BUILDING, HAZEN DRIVE
CONCORD, NEW HAMPSHIRE 03301

NUMBER	
REQUESTED	
ISSUED	

APPLICATION FOR COPY OF MARRIAGE RETURN

PLEASE PRINT PLAINLY

GROOM'S
NAME . . . .
                                    (FIRST NAME)   (LAST NAME)

BRIDE'S
NAME . . . .
                                    (FIRST NAME)   (LAST NAME)

DATE OF
MARRIAGE . . . .
                                    (MONTH)   (DAY)   (YEAR)

PLACE OF
MARRIAGE . . . .
                                                        (COUNTY)

PURPOSE FOR WHICH CERTIFICATE IS REQUESTED . . . .

BY WHOM . . . . . . *ten* . . . . RELATIONSHIP TO REGISTRANT . . . .

A FEE OF ~~THREE~~ DOLLARS IS REQUIRED BY LAW FOR THE SEARCH OF THE FILE FOR ANY ONE RECORD

NOTICE: ANY PERSON SHALL BE GUILTY OF A CLASS B FELONY IF HE/SHE WILLFULLY AND KNOWINGLY MAKE ANY FALSE STATEMENT IN AN APPLICATION FOR A CERTIFIED COPY OF A VITAL RECORD. (RSA 126:24)

VS B-1

The State of New Hampshire
DEPARTMENT OF HEALTH AND WELFARE
BUREAU OF VITAL RECORDS

NUMBER	
REQUESTED	
ISSUED	

APPLICATION FOR COPY OF DIVORCE, LEGAL SEPARATION
OR ANNULMENT RECORD

PLEASE PRINT PLAINLY

HUSBAND'S
NAME ....
                                    (FIRST NAME)   (LAST NAME)

WIFE'S
NAME ....
                                    (FIRST NAME)   (LAST NAME)

DATE OF
DECREE ....
                                    (MONTH)   (DAY)   (YEAR)

PLACE OF
DECREE ....
                                                        (COUNTY)

PURPOSE FOR WHICH CERTIFICATE IS REQUESTED: ....

BY WHOM .... RELATIONSHIP ....

A FEE OF ~~THREE~~ DOLLARS IS REQUIRED BY LAW
FOR THE SEARCH OF THE FILE FOR ANY ONE RECORD.

FORM V.S. L-1

For Birth, Marriage, and Death Records from June 1878 to date write to:

New Jersey Department of Health
State Registrar
Bureau of Vital Statistics
CN 370
Trenton, New Jersey 08625-0370

(609) 292-4087, FAX (609) 392-4292

For Birth, Marriage, and Death Records from May 1848 to May 1878 write to:

New Jersey State Archives
Division of Archives and Records Management
Department of State
185 West State Street
CN-307
Trenton, New Jersey 08625-0307

(609) 292-6260

For Divorce Records write to:

Superior Court of New Jersey
Records Management Center
171 Jersey Street
CN-967
Trenton, New Jersey 08611

Cost for a certified Birth Certificate	$4.00
Cost for a certified Marriage Certificate	$4.00
Cost for a certified Death Certificate	$4.00
Cost for a duplicate copy, when ordered at the same time	$2.00

The State Registrar has birth, marriage, and death records from June 1878. They have an index to the records from June 1878 to December 31, 1900 and annual indexes for each year thereafter. At the time of publication, they were not honoring any genealogical requests.

If your request is urgent you may call (609) 633-2860 and charge your certificates to your Visa, Discover, or MasterCard. There is a $5.00 fee for this service.

The New Jersey State Archives has a statewide index to the May 1848-May 1878 records in their custody. They also have incomplete marriage records back to 1665, and indexes to the 1665-1800 and 1848-1878 marriage records. The index and abstract of marriages from 1665 to 1800 was published under the title *New Jersey Archives*, volume 22. The Archives also has divorce records from 1743 to 1850.

The Family History Library of The Church of Jesus Christ of Latter-day Saints in Salt Lake City, Utah has microfilmed the original and published vital records of New Jersey from 1670 to 1900. For details on their holdings please consult your nearest Family History Center.

New Jersey State Department of Health

**APPLICATION FOR CERTIFIED COPY
OF VITAL RECORD**

1. *VITAL RECORDS - JUNE, 1878 TO PRESENT*
   When the correct year of the event is supplied, the total fee (payable in advance) for a search is four dollars for each name for which a search must be made. Searches for more than one year cost one dollar for each additional year per name. If found, a certified copy will be forwarded at no additional cost. If not found, the fee will not be refunded. Additional copies may be ordered at this time at a charge of two dollars per copy. Specify the total number of copies requested.

2. *VITAL RECORDS - MAY, 1848 THROUGH MAY, 1878*
   These records have been transferred to the Archives Section, Division of Archives and Records Management, Department of State, CN 307, Trenton, NJ 08625. Information as to fee schedules and how to obtain records from the Archives can be obtained from that Section.

Name of Applicant	Date of Application	**FOR STATE USE ONLY**	
Street Address	Telephone No.		
City State	Zip Code	Certified Copy Completed	

**MAKE CHECK OR MONEY ORDER PAYABLE TO "STATE REGISTRAR."
DO NOT MAIL CASH OR STAMPS. PLEASE PRINT OR TYPE**

Amount Received

Why is a Certified Copy being requested?

☐ School/Sports ☐ Genealogy ☐ Medicare
☐ Social Security ID Card ☐ Welfare ☐ Veteran Benefits
☐ Passport ☐ Soc. Sec. Disability ☐ Other (specify)
☐ Driver License ☐ Other Soc. Sec. Benefits _____

Method of Payment
☐ Check ☐ Cash
☐ Money Order

Fee Due

FILL IN ONLY IF YOU WANT A BIRTH RECORD	No. Copies Requested	Amount Refunded	Date Refunded
Full Name of Child at Time of Birth		Received By	
Place of Birth (City, Town or Township)	County	Enclosures	
Date of Birth	Name of Hospital, If Any	☐ REG-34 ☐ REG-36 ☐ REG-37 ☐ REG-38 ☐ X ☐ REG-30 ☐ REG-40 ☐ REG-41 ☐ C	
Father's Name		**SEARCH UNIT**	
Mother's Maiden Name		First Search	
If Child's Name was Changed, Indicate New Name and How it was changed		REG-30	
		Alphabetical Second Check	

FILL IN ONLY IF YOU WANT A MARRIAGE RECORD	No. Copies Requested	File Date on Record	
Name of Husband		**PROCESSING UNIT**	
Maiden Name of Wife		Places	
Place of Marriage (City, Township)	County	W.W.	
Date of Marriage or Close Approximation		Late Months	
		Second Check	

FOR ANY DEATH RECORD BEFORE 1901, A SEARCH CANNOT
BE MADE UNLESS YOU CAN NAME THE COUNTY WHERE THE
EVENT TOOK PLACE.

CORRESPONDENCE/RECEPTION UNIT

FILL IN ONLY IF YOU WANT A DEATH RECORD	No. Copies Requested	REG-L7	
Name of Deceased	Date of Death	Hospital Records	
Place of Death (City, Town, Township, County)	Age at Death	REG-28	
Residence if Different from Place of Death		Comments	
Father's Name			
Mother's Maiden Name			

Address your envelope to:

STATE REGISTRAR — SEARCH UNIT:
NEW JERSEY STATE DEPARTMENT OF HEALTH
CN 370, TRENTON, N.J. 08625-0370
COMPLETE SECTION BELOW - TYPE OR PRINT CLEARLY!
This will be used as a mailing label when we send the results of the search.

Name

Street Address

City   State   Zip Code

Dear Applicant:

The fee you paid is correct unless either block below is checked.

☐ An additional fee of $ _____ is due, since
either additional years or another name was involved.
Send it with this form.

☐ You are entitled to a refund check of $ _____
which will be forwarded within 45 days of _____
If you have occasion to write about this matter, return this
form with your letter.

— STATE REGISTRAR —

REG-3
Nov 89

G2363

Send your requests to:

Public Health Division
Office of Vital Records and Health Statistics
1190 St. Francis Drive
P.O. Box 26110
Santa Fe, New Mexico 87502-6110

(505) 827-2321

For Marriage Certificates and Divorce Records contact:

County Clerk
County Courthouse
(County Seat), New Mexico

Cost for a certified Birth Certificate	$10.00
Cost for a certified Marriage Certificate	$1.50
Cost for a certified Death Certificate	$5.00

The New Mexico Office of Vital Records and Health Statistics has birth and death records from 1889. Contact the County Clerk in the county where the event occurred for earlier records, as well as for marriage and divorce records.

If your request is urgent you may call (505) 827-0598 and charge your certificates to your Visa or MasterCard. There is a $6.00 fee for this service.

The Family History Library of The Church of Jesus Christ of Latter-day Saints in Salt Lake City, Utah has microfilmed many of the original and published vital records and church registers of New Mexico. For details on their holdings please consult your nearest Family History Center.

Search Application for BIRTH Record

Mail request with fee or bring to:
Department of Health/P.H.D.
Office of Vital Records and Health Statistics
1190 St. Francis Drive
P.O. Box 26110
Santa Fe, NM 87502-6110

ID. No. _____

Request No.· _____

PUBLIC HEALTH DIVISION

PLEASE PRINT or TYPE

I.   BIRTH CERTIFICATE OF

FULL NAME at BIRTH		
DATE of BIRTH		SEX
PLACE of BIRTH *(city, county, state)*		

II.   PARENTS OF PERSON NAMED ON BIRTH CERTIFICATE

FATHER'S FULL NAME

MOTHER'S FULL MAIDEN NAME

ABOVE NAMED PARENTS ARE:

FATHER: ☐ Natural ☐ Adoptive   ☐ MOTHER: ☐ Natural ☐ Adoptive

III.   PERSON MAKING THIS REQUEST

YOUR NAME:	Last	First	Initial
	No. and Street		
YOUR ADDRESS:	Mailing Address/P.O. Box		
	Town/City	State	Zip

IV.   NUMBER OF COPIES WANTED and FEE(S)

I am requesting:

_____ certified copy(ies)   _____
Number   *Date of Request*

I am enclosing the Fee(s) of: **$**
($10.00 for each certified copy)

LEGAL NOTICE: For the protection of the individual, certificates of birth are NOT open to public inspection. In order to comply with this request, State Regulations require Section V below to be completed.

WARNING: False application for a birth certificate is a criminal offense and punishable by fine and/or imprisonment. Requests submitted without street address will not be processed.

V.   STATEMENT OF REQUESTOR

Your relationship to person named in Certificate *(e.g., parent, attorney, etc.)*	For what purpose(s) do you need the copy(ies)?	Your signature
		Daytime telephone number ( )

OVRHS 913   Revised 3/92

Search Application for DEATH Record

Mail request with fee or bring to:
Department of Health/P.H.D.
Office of Vital Records and Health Statistics
1190 St. Francis Drive
P.O. Box 26110
Santa Fe, NM 87502-6110

ID. No. _____

PUBLIC HEALTH DIVISION

PLEASE PRINT or TYPE

I.   DEATH CERTIFICATE OF

FULL NAME of DECEASED			FULL NAME of SPOUSE *(Maiden name, if wife)*
DATE of DEATH		SEX	DECEASED's DATE of BIRTH or AGE at TIME of DEATH
PLACE of DEATH *(city, county, state)*			MORTUARY in CHARGE of FINAL ARRANGEMENTS

II.   PERSON MAKING THIS REQUEST

YOUR NAME:	Last	First	Initial
	No. and Street		
YOUR ADDRESS:	Mailing Address/P.O. Box		
	Town/City	State	Zip

III.   NUMBER OF COPIES WANTED and FEE(S)

I am requesting:

_____ certified copy(ies)   _____
Number   *Date of Request*

I am enclosing the Fee(s) of: **$**
($5.00 for each certified copy)

LEGAL NOTICE: For the protection of the individual, whose name appears on the death certificate, and surviving family members, certificates of death are NOT open to public inspection.

WARNING: False application for a death certificate is a criminal offense and punishable by fine and/or imprisonment.

IV.   STATEMENT OF REQUESTOR

Your relationship to person named in Certificate *(e.g., spouse, attorney, etc.)*	For what purpose(s) do you need the copy(ies)?	Your signature
		Daytime telephone number ( )

OVRHS 914   Revised 3/92

NEW YORK—NEW YORK CITY

Send your requests to:

Municipal Archives
Department of Records and Information Services
31 Chambers Street, Room 103
New York, New York 10007-1288

(212) 788-8580

Cost for a certified Birth Certificate	$10.00
Cost for a certified Marriage Certificate	$10.00
Cost for a certified Death Certificate	$10.00
Cost for a duplicate copy, when ordered at the same time	$5.00

The Municipal Archives has records of:

Manhattan births from July 1847-1848 and July 1853-1909; marriages from June 1847-1848 and July 1853-1937; deaths from 1795, 1802-1804, 1808, and 1812-1948.

Brooklyn births from 1866-1909; marriages from 1866-1937; deaths from 1847-1853 and 1857-1948.

Bronx births from 1898-1909; deaths from 1898-1948.

Queens births from 1898-1909; deaths from 1898-1948.

Richmond (Staten Island) births from 1898-1909; marriages from 1898-1937; deaths from 1898-1948.

The Family History Library of The Church of Jesus Christ of Latter-day Saints in Salt Lake City, Utah has microfilmed many of the original and published vital records and church registers of New York City. For details on their holdings please consult your nearest Family History Center.

NEW YORK CITY
DEPARTMENT OF RECORDS AND INFORMATION SERVICES
MUNICIPAL ARCHIVES
31 Chambers Street
New York, N.Y. 10007
(212) 566-5292

BIRTH

APPLICATION FOR A SEARCH AND/OR CERTIFIED COPY
OF A BIRTH RECORD:

FEES

$10.00	Search of birth records in one year and one City/Borough for one name and issuance of one certified copy or "not found" statement.
$ 2.00	Per additional year to be searched in one City/Borough for same name.
$ 2.00	Per additional City/Borough to be searched in one year for same name.
$ 5.00	Per additional copy of record.
$ 5.00	Issuance of certified copy, when certificate number is provided.

Enclose stamped, self-addressed envelope.

Make check or money order payable to: NYC Department of Records.

PLEASE PRINT OR TYPE:

Last name on birth record	First name	Female/Male

Date of birth

Month   Day   Year

Place of birth – if at home, house number and street	City/Borough

Father's name, if known	Mother's name, if known

Your relationship to person named above	Certificate no., if known

Purpose for which this record will be used	Number of copies requested

Your name, please print	Signature

Address

City	State	Zip Code

MA-22 (9-90)

NEW YORK CITY
DEPARTMENT OF RECORDS AND INFORMATION SERVICES
MUNICIPAL ARCHIVES
31 Chambers Street
New York, N.Y. 10007
(212) 566-5292

MARRIAGE

APPLICATION FOR A SEARCH AND/OR CERTIFIED COPY
OF A MARRIAGE RECORD:

FEES

$10.00	Search of marriage records in one year and one City/Borough for one Groom and/or Bride and issuance of one certified copy or "not found" statement.
$ 2.00	Per additional year to be searched in one City/Borough for same name.
$ 2.00	Per additional City/Borough to be searched in one year for same name.
$ 5.00	Per additional copy of record.
$ 5.00	Issuance of certified copy, when certificate number is provided.

Enclose stamped, self-addressed envelope.

Make check or money order payable to: NYC Department of Records.

PLEASE PRINT OR TYPE:

Last name of Groom	First name of Groom
Last name of Bride (Maiden name)	First name of Bride

Date of Marriage

Month   Day   Year(s)

Place of Marriage	City/Borough

Your relationship to people named above	Certificate no., if known
Purpose for which this record will be used	Number of copies requested

Your name, please print	Signature

Address

City	State	Zip Code

MA-25 (9-90)

NEW YORK CITY
DEPARTMENT OF RECORDS AND INFORMATION SERVICES
MUNICIPAL ARCHIVES
31 Chambers Street
New York, N.Y. 10007
(212) 566-5292

DEATH

APPLICATION FOR A SEARCH AND/OR CERTIFIED COPY
OF A DEATH RECORD:

FEES

$10.00	Search of death records in one year and one City/Borough for one name and issuance of one certified copy or "not found" statement.
$ 2.00	Per additional year to be searched in one City/Borough for same name.
$ 2.00	Per additional City/Borough to be searched in one year for same name.
$ 5.00	Per additional copy of record.
$ 5.00	Issuance of certified copy, when certificate number is provided.

Enclose stamped, self-addressed envelope.

Make check or money order payable to: NYC Department of Records.

PLEASE PRINT OR TYPE:

Last name at time of death	First name	Middle name

Date of death	Cemetery, if known	
Month Day Year		

Place of death	City/Borough	Age

Father's name, if known	Mother's name, if known

Your relationship to decedent	Certificate no., if known

Purpose for which this record will be used	Number of copies requested

Your name, please print	Signature

Address

City	State	Zip Code

MA-23 (9-90)

NEW YORK—NEW YORK CITY

Send your requests to:

Division of Vital Records
New York City Department of Health
125 Worth Street
P.O. Box 3776, Church Street Station
New York, New York 10007

(212) 619-4530

Send your requests for Marriage or Divorce Certificates to:

City Clerk
Marriage License Bureau
(Borough where the marriage license or divorce decree was issued), New York

Cost for a certified Birth Certificate	$15.00
Cost for a search of Marriage Records	$5.00
Cost for a certified Death Certificate	$15.00

The Division of Vital Records has birth records from 1910 and death records from 1949. Please include a self-addressed stamped envelope with your request.

The Municipal Archives, Department of Records and Information Services (31 Chambers Street, New York, NY 10007; Tel. 212-788-8580) has birth records prior to 1909, marriage records prior to 1938, and death records prior to 1949.

If your request is urgent you may call (212) 788-4507 or FAX (212) 962-6105 and charge your certificates to your Visa, Discover, or MasterCard. There is a $5.00 fee for this service.

The Family History Library of The Church of Jesus Christ of Latter-day Saints in Salt Lake City, Utah has microfilmed many of the original and published vital records and church registers of New York City. For details on their holdings please consult your nearest Family History Center.

THE CITY OF NEW YORK – DEPARTMENT OF HEALTH

DIVISION OF VITAL RECORDS
P.O. Box 3776
Church Street Station
New York, N.Y. 10007

APPLICATION FOR A BIRTH RECORD
(Print All Items Clearly)

LAST NAME ON BIRTH RECORD	FIRST NAME	☐ FEMALE ☐ MALE

DATE OF BIRTH	PLACE OF BIRTH (NAME OF HOSPITAL, OR IF AT HOME, NO. AND STREET)	BOROUGH OF BIRTH
Month Day Year		

MOTHER'S MAIDEN NAME (Name Before Marriage)	CERTIFICATE NUMBER IF KNOWN
FIRST LAST	

FATHER'S NAME	*For Office Use Only*
FIRST LAST	

NO. OF COPIES	YOUR RELATIONSHIP TO PERSON NAMED ON BIRTH RECORD, IF SELF, STATE "SELF"	

FOR WHAT PURPOSE ARE YOU GOING TO USE THIS BIRTH RECORD

NOTE: Copy of a birth record can be issued only to persons to whom the record of birth relates, if of age, or a parent or other lawful representative. IF THIS REQUEST IS NOT FOR YOUR OWN BIRTH RECORD OR THAT OF YOUR CHILD, NOTARIZED AUTHORIZATION FROM THE PARENT OR THE PERSON NAMED ON THE CERTIFICATE MUST BE PRESENTED WITH THIS APPLICATION.

Section 3.19, New York City Health Code provides, in part: ". . . no person shall make a false, untrue or misleading statement or forge the signature of another on a certificate, application, registration, report or other document required to be prepared pursuant to this Code." Section 558 (d) of the New York City Charter provides that any violation of the Health Code shall be treated and punished as a misdemeanor.

SIGN YOUR NAME AND ADDRESS BELOW

NAME
ADDRESS
CITY   STATE   ZIP CODE

NOTE: PLEASE ATTACH A STAMPED SELF-ADDRESSED ENVELOPE

FEES

SEARCH FOR TWO CONSECUTIVE YEARS AND ONE COPY OR A CERTIFIED "NOT FOUND STATEMENT" ·········· $15.00
EACH ADDITIONAL COPY REQUESTED ································ $15.00
EACH EXTRA YEAR SEARCHED (WITH THIS APPLICATION) ································ $ 3.00
    1. Make certified check or money order payable to: Department of Health, N.Y.C.
    2. If from a foreign country, send an international money order or a certified check drawn on a U.S. Bank.
    3. Stamps or foreign currency will not be accepted. **CASH NOT ACCEPTED BY MAIL.**

FOR OFFICE USE ONLY

SEARCH → RESULTS	REPORTED BY ☐ CRT ☐ MANUAL →	CERTIFICATE NUMBER	LAST NAME - 4 LETTERS	DATE OF BIRTH		
				Month	Day	Year
READING DATE		DATE ISSUED: BY MAIL		DATE ISSUED: IN PERSON		

VR-67 (REV. 6/91)

PLEASE TYPE OR PRINT CLEARLY ALL INFORMATION BELOW
PLEASE ENCLOSE THE PROPER FEE FOR YOUR REQUEST

Today's Date: _____

Date of Marriage Ceremony: MONTH- DAY- YEAR-	Borough where the license was issued
If uncertain, specify other years you want searched:	
GROOM (man) Full name:	
BRIDE (woman) Full MAIDEN name:	
If woman was previously married, give LAST NAME of former husband(s):	

		How Many
Reason search & copy are needed:		

Name of person requesting search:	Your relationship to Bride & Groom:

Your Address	City	State	Zip

DO NOT WRITE BELOW - THIS SPACE FOR OFFICE USE

License
Number:_____/_____   Microfilm Cart No.   _____/_____/_____

Searched by:_____ Type of Cert_____

Receipt No._____ Amount-$_____ Typist_____

Date Mailed_____ Cert No.(s)_____

Date Request
was received_____ Amount of Money Received - $_____

NO RECORD ( ) Amount Refunded-$_____ Receipt No._____ Mailed_____

This is to certify that_____

residing at_____ _____ Born_____

at_____ AND _____

Residing at_____ Born_____

at_____ Were married on _____

at_____ By _____

Groom's Parents_____

Bride's Parents_____

Witnesses_____

Previous Marriages_____

REMARKS _____

B-1

NO PERSONAL CHECKS

THE CITY OF NEW YORK – DEPARTMENT OF HEALTH

DIVISION OF VITAL RECORDS
P.O. Box 3776
Church Street Station
New York, N.Y. 10007

APPLICATION FOR A COPY OF A DEATH RECORD

(Print All Items Clearly)

1. LAST NAME AT TIME OF DEATH	2. FIRST NAME	2.A ☐ FEMALE ☐ MALE

3. DATE OF DEATH Month Day Year	4. PLACE OF DEATH	5. BOROUGH	6. AGE

7. NO OF COPIES	8. SPOUSE'S NAME	9. OCCUPATION OF DECEASED

10. FATHER'S NAME	11. SOCIAL SECURITY NUMBER

12. MOTHER'S NAME (Name Before Marriage)	13. BURIAL PERMIT NUMBER (IF KNOWN)

14. FOR WHAT PURPOSE ARE YOU GOING TO USE THIS CERTIFICATE	15. YOUR RELATIONSHIP TO DECEDENT

NOTE: Section 205.07 of the Health Code provides, in part:" . . . The confidential medical report of death shall not be subject to subpoena or to inspection." Therefore, copies of the medical report of death cannot be issued.

SIGN YOUR NAME AND ADDRESS BELOW

NAME
ADDRESS
CITY   STATE   ZIP CODE

INFORMATION: APPLICATION SHOULD BE MADE IN PERSON AT 125 WORTH STREET OR BY MAIL TO THE ABOVE DIVISION.

NOTE: 1. CASH NOT ACCEPTED BY MAIL
2. PLEASE ATTACH A STAMPED SELF-ADDRESSED ENVELOPE

FEES

(FOR OFFICE USE ONLY)

SEARCH FOR TWO CONSECUTIVE YEARS AND ONE COPY $15.00
EACH ADDITIONAL COPY REQUESTED $15.00
EACH EXTRA YEAR SEARCHED (WITH THIS APPLICATION) .... $ 3.00
IF RECORD IS NOT ON FILE, A CERTIFIED "NOT FOUND STATEMENT" WILL BE ISSUED.

1. Make certified check or money order payable to: Department of Health, N.Y.C.
2. If from a foreign country, send an international money order or a certified check drawn on a U.S. Bank.
3. Stamps or foreign currency will not be accepted.

MAIL REQUESTS TO:
Department of Health, Division of Vital Records
P.O. Box 3776, Church Street Station, New York City, N.Y. 10007

VR-66 (REV. 6/91)

NEW YORK—NEW YORK STATE

Send your requests to:

New York State Department of Health
Vital Records Section
Corning Tower
Empire State Plaza
Albany, New York 12237-0023

(518) 474-3077, (518) 486-1863

For earlier records send your request to:

Registrar of Vital Statistics
(Town or Township), New York

Cost for a certified Birth Certificate	$15.00
Cost for a certified Marriage Certificate	$5.00
Cost for a certified Divorce Certificate	$15.00
Cost for a certified Death Certificate	$15.00
Cost for a duplicate copy, when ordered at the same time	$5.00

The Vital Records Section has records of births, marriages, and deaths from 1881 to the present and divorces from 1963, except those that occurred in New York City (SEE: NEW YORK—NEW YORK CITY) or those that occurred in Albany, Buffalo, or Yonkers prior to 1914. For these three cities write to the City Clerk in the City Hall of the respective city. The Vital Records Section has a 14-month wait before a genealogical request is filled. The Registrar of Vital Statistics in each town or township generally has records from the early 1800s to the present.

If your request is urgent you may call and charge your certificates to your Visa or MasterCard. This service costs $35.50, including the charge for the certificate.

The New York State Archives (11th Floor, Cultural Education Center, Empire State Plaza, Albany, NY 12220; Tel. 518-474-8955) has a microfilm copy of the indexes to these records.

The fee for a birth or death certificate from the New York State Vital Records Section is $15.00. The fee for the same certificate from a City Registrar of Vital Statistics is $5.00. The fee for marriage certificates is $5.00 from both offices.

The Family History Library of The Church of Jesus Christ of Latter-day Saints in Salt Lake City, Utah has microfilmed many of the original and published vital records and church registers of New York. For details on their holdings please consult your nearest Family History Center.

NEW YORK STATE DEPARTMENT OF HEALTH
Vital Records Section

Application to Department of Health for Copy of Birth Record

PLEASE COMPLETE FORM AND ENCLOSE FEE

FEE: $15.00 per copy or No Record Certification.

Make money order or check payable to New York State Department of Health. Please do not send cash or stamps.
Send to:

New York State Department of Health
Vital Records Section
Corning Tower, Empire State Plaza
Albany, NY 12237-0023

PLEASE PRINT OR TYPE

	First	Middle	Last	Date of Birth or Period Covered By Search
Name				

Place of Birth	Hospital (If not hospital, give street & number)	(Village, town or city)	(County)

	First	Middle	Last	Maiden Name of Mother	First	Middle	Last
Father							

Number of Copies Requested

Standard Size _____
Wallet Size _____

Enter Birth No. if Known

Enter Local Registration No. if known

Purpose for Which Record is Required (Check One)

- ☐ Passport
- ☐ Social Security
- ☐ Retirement
- ☐ Employment
- ☐ Working Papers
- ☐ School Entrance
- ☐ Driver's License
- ☐ Marriage License
- ☐ Welfare Assistance
- ☐ Veteran's Benefits
- ☐ Court Proceeding
- ☐ Entrance Into Armed Forces
- ☐ Other (specify) _____

What is your relationship to person whose record is required? If self, state "self"

_____

If attorney, give name and relationship of your client to person whose record is required

_____
(name of client)

_____
(relationship)

This office requires written authorization of the person/parents whose record is requested before a search is processed.

Signature of Applicant

Date ⎵⎵ ⎵⎵ ⎵⎵
m   d   y

Address of Applicant

_____
(street)

_____
(city)   (state)   (zip)

Please print name and address where record should be sent.

_____
(name)

_____
(street)

_____
(city)   (state)   (zip)

DOH-296B (5/91)

VS-34B

Application for Search of Marriage Records

TYPE OF RECORD DESIRED (Check One)

Search and
Certification

☐ Fee $5.00 per copy

A Certification, an abstract from the marriage record issued under the seal of the Health Department, includes the names of the contracting parties, their residence at the time the license was issued as well as date and place of birth of the bride and groom.

A Certification may be used as proof that a marriage occurred.

Search and
Certified Copy

☐ Fee $5.00 per copy

A Certified Transcript includes all of the items of information occurring on the original record of the marriage.

A Certified Transcript may be needed where proof of parentage and certain other detailed information may be required such as: passports, veterans' benefits, court proceedings, or settlement of an estate.

PLEASE COMPLETE FORM AND REMIT FEE

FEES: Make money order or check payable to New York State Department of Health. Please do not send cash or stamps.
There is no fee for a record to be used for eligibility determination for social welfare or veterans' benefits.

PLEASE PRINT OR TYPE

Name Of Groom	(First)	(Middle)	(Last)	Maiden Name Of Bride	(First)	(Middle)	(Last)
Groom's Age Or Date Of Birth				Bride's Age Or Date Of Birth			
Residence Of Groom	(County)		(State)	Residence Of Bride	(County)		(State)
Date Of Marriage Or Period Covered By Search				If Bride Previously Married State Name Used At That Time			
Place Where License Was Issued				Place Where Marriage Was Performed			

For what purpose is information required?

What is your relationship to person whose record is requested? If self, state "self"

In what capacity are you acting?

If attorney: Name and relationship of your client to persons whose marriage record is required

Signature of Applicant

Date

Address of Applicant

Please print name and address where record is to be sent.

NEW YORK STATE DEPARTMENT OF HEALTH
Vital Records Section
Albany, N.Y. 12237-0023

Application to Department of Health
for Copy of Death Record

PLEASE COMPLETE FORM AND ENCLOSE FEE

FEE: $15.00 per copy or No Record Certification. Make money order or check payable to New York State Department of Health. Please do not send cash or stamps.

PLEASE PRINT OR TYPE

Name of Deceased

First   Middle   Last

Date of Death or Period to be Covered by Search

Name of Father of Deceased

First   Middle   Last

Social Security Number of Deceased

Maiden Name of Mother of Deceased

First   Middle   Last

Date of Birth of Deceased

Month   Day   Year

Age at Death

Place of Death

Name of Hospital or Street Address   Village, Town or City   County

Purpose for Which Record is Required

What was your relationship to deceased?_____

In what capacity are you acting?_____

If attorney, name and relationship of your client to deceased_____

Signature of Applicant_____ Date_____

Address of Applicant_____

PLEASE PRINT NAME AND ADDRESS WHERE RECORD SHOULD BE SENT

Name_____

Address_____

City_____ State_____ Zip Code_____

DOH-294 B (2/91)

`VS-34D

NORTH CAROLINA

Send your requests to:

North Carolina Department of Environment, Health and Natural Resources
Vital Records Section
225 North McDowell Street
P.O. Box 29537
Raleigh, North Carolina 27626-0537

(919) 733-3526, FAX (919) 733-1511

Vital records are also maintained by the:

County Clerk
County Courthouse
(County Seat), North Carolina

Cost for a certified Birth Certificate	$10.00
Cost for a certified Marriage or Divorce Certificate	$10.00
Cost for a certified Death Certificate	$10.00
Cost for a duplicate copy, when ordered at the same time	$5.00

The North Carolina Division of Health Services has birth records from October 1, 1913, marriage records from January 1, 1962, divorce records from January 1, 1958, and death records from January 1, 1930. County Clerks often have much earlier records.

If your request is urgent you may call and charge your certificates to your Visa or MasterCard. There is a charge of $20.00 plus the cost of shipping.

The North Carolina Division of Archives and History (109 East Jones Street, Raleigh, NC 27601-2807; Tel. 919-733-7442; FAX 919-733-1439) has extensive records, including a marriage bond index from 1741 to 1868 and death records from 1910 to 1929.

The Family History Library of The Church of Jesus Christ of Latter-day Saints in Salt Lake City, Utah has microfilmed many of the original and published vital records and church registers of North Carolina. They have a microfiche copy of the statewide marriage index. For details on their holdings please consult your nearest Family History Center.

REQUEST FOR CERTIFICATE OF BIRTH

	First	Middle	Last
NAME AT BIRTH:			

	Month	Day	Year	AGE:	RACE:
DATE OF BIRTH:					

	City	County	State
PLACE OF BIRTH:			

FATHER'S
FULL NAME:

MOTHER'S FULL
MAIDEN NAME:

SIGNATURE: _____

MAILING ADDRESS: _____

_____ Zip: _____

YOUR RELATIONSHIP
TO PERSON NAMED:

CERTIFICATE
NEEDED FOR:

The fee for each copy or for conducting a search when no record is found is **$10.00**. Each additional copy is $5.00. Please make check or money order payable to N.C. Vital Records.

No. Copies: _____

Amount: $_____

FORWARD APPLICATION AND FEES TO: N. C. Vital Records
P.O. Box 29537
Raleigh, N.C. 27626-0537

**Section Below
for Office Use Only**

No. Copies _____

1st Search _____

2nd Search _____

Delays _____

Date Mailed _____

Vol. & Page _____

DEHNR 1215 (Revised 7/91)
Vital Records

N.C. Department of Environment, Health, and Natural Resources
Division of Epidemiology

- -

REQUEST FOR CERTIFICATE OF DEATH

Name of Deceased _____

Date of Death _____

Place of Death _____

Race _____ Age _____ SS No. (if known) _____

Name of Husband or Wife _____

Your relationship to person named _____

Signature:

Address:

City & State: Zip Code:

Telephone No.:

$10.00 The fee for each copy or for conducting a search when no record is found is ~~$5.00~~. Please make check or money order payable to VITAL RECORDS SECTION.

Forward application and fees to:

Vital Records Section
P.O. Box 29537
Raleigh, NC 27626-0537

REQUEST FOR CERTIFICATE OF MARRIAGE

Full Name of Groom _____

Full Name of Bride
(including maiden name)_____

Date of Marriage _____

Place of Marriage_____

Your relationship to person named_____

Signature:

Address:

City & State: Zip Code:

Telephone No.:

The fee for each copy or for conducting a search when no record is found is $10.00. Please make check or money order payable to Vital Records Section.

Forward application and fees to:

> Vital Records Section
> PO Box 29537
> Raleigh, NC 27626-0537

- -

REQUEST FOR CERTIFICATE OF DIVORCE

Name of Plaintiff _____

Name of Defendant _____

Date of Divorce _____

Place of Divorce _____

Your relationship to person named _____

Signature:

Address:

City & State: Zip Code:

Telephone No.:

The fee for each copy or for conducting a search when no record is found is $5.00. Please make check or money order payable to VITAL RECORDS SECTION.
$10.00

Forward application and fees to:

> Vital Records Section
> P.O. Box 29537
> Raleigh, NC 27626-0537

NORTH DAKOTA

Send your requests to:

North Dakota State Department of Health and Consolidated Laboratories
Division of Vital Records
State Capitol
600 East Boulevard Avenue
Bismarck, North Dakota 58505-0200

(701) 224-2360

Send your requests for Divorce Records and pre-July 1, 1925 Marriage Certificates to:

County Judge
County Court
(County Seat), North Dakota

Cost for a certified Birth Certificate	$7.00
Additional copy of Birth Certificate	$4.00
Cost for a certified Marriage Certificate	$5.00
Cost for a certified Death Certificate	$5.00
Additional copy of Death Certificate	$2.00

The North Dakota State Department of Health has birth and death records from July 1, 1893 and marriage records from July 1, 1925. Vital records are also filed in the office of the County Judge in the county where the event occurred. The County Judge also has divorce records as well as some earlier vital records.

If your request is urgent you may call and charge your certificates to your Visa or MasterCard. There is a $5.00 fee for this service.

The State Historical Society of North Dakota (North Dakota Heritage Center, Bismarck, ND 58505; Tel. 701-224-2666) also has records. For further information see their publication written by David P. Gray, *Guide to the North Dakota State Archives*, published in 1985.

The Family History Library of The Church of Jesus Christ of Latter-day Saints in Salt Lake City, Utah has microfilmed many of the original and published vital records and church registers of North Dakota. For details on their holdings please consult your nearest Family History Center.

REQUEST FOR COPY OF BIRTH CERTIFICATE
NORTH DAKOTA STATE DEPARTMENT OF HEALTH AND CONSOLIDATED LABORATORIES
SFN 8140 (5-92)

PLEASE PRINT - ALL ITEMS MUST BE COMPLETED

1. Full Name at Birth	2. Sex ☐ Male ☐ Female

3. Date of Birth (Month, Day, Year)	4. Place of Birth (City or Township)	County

5. Residence of Parents at Time of this Birth (City & State)	6. Order of Birth (1st Child, 2nd, etc.)

7. Full Name of Father (First, Middle, Last)

8. Full Name of Mother (First, Middle, <u>Maiden</u>)

9. Certificate for An Adopted Child ☐ Yes ☐ No	10. Purpose of Requested Copy

11. Type of Copy Desired
☐ Paper Copy   ☐ Plastic Birth Card - (Birth card <u>may not</u> be acceptable for travel outside the U.S.)

12. Your Relationship to Person on Line 1	13. Fee Enclosed (see schedule) $	No. of Copies

This Section Is To Be Completed By Person Making Request

Signature	
Printed Name	Daytime Telephone Number ( )
Address	Apartment No.	City	State	Zip Code

If Copy Is To Be Mailed Elsewhere

Name	
Address	Apartment No.	City	State	Zip Code

The above information is necessary to properly identify and locate the correct birth certificate. Please enter full information.

Birth certificates are by law confidential. Copies or information are to be furnished only to persons having a direct and tangible interest - the registrant, parent or guardian, legal representative, or on court order.

FEE SCHEDULE

<u>The fee for one certified copy is $7.00.</u> Additional copies of the same certificate issued at the same time are $4.00 each. (Two dollars of this fee is used to support the Children's Trust Fund, a state fund for aiding in the prevention of child abuse and neglect.)

NOTE: Make all checks or money orders payable to "NORTH DAKOTA STATE DEPARTMENT OF HEALTH". Stamps are not accepted. Cash is sent at your own risk!

Mail Request with fee to:
NORTH DAKOTA STATE DEPARTMENT OF HEALTH AND
CONSOLIDATED LABORATORES
VITAL RECORDS
STATE CAPITOL
600 EAST BOULEVARD AVENUE
BISMARCK, ND 58505-0200

THIS PORTION FOR VITAL RECORDS
OFFICE USE ONLY

REQUEST FOR COPY OF MARRIAGE RECORD

Please Print

FULL NAME OF GROOM	FULL MAIDEN NAME OF BRIDE
RESIDENCE OF GROOM AT MARRIAGE	RESIDENCE OF BRIDE AT MARRIAGE
DATE OF MARRIAGE (Month) (Day) (Year)	COUNTY WHERE LICENSE ISSUED
PLACE WHERE MARRIED (City)	(County)
FOR WHAT PURPOSE IS COPY NEEDED	YOUR RELATIONSHIP TO GROOM/BRIDE (e.g. self, parent, attorney — specify)
SIGNATURE OF APPLICANT	
STREET ADDRESS OR BOX NUMBER	
CITY AND STATE ZIP CODE	Enclosed is $_____ for _____ certified copies. (See fee schedule below)

Original Licenses and Certificates of Marriage are filed in the office of the **COUNTY JUDGE** of the **COUNTY WHERE THE LICENSE WAS ISSUED.** It is recommended that requests for certified copies be directed to the custodian of the <u>original</u> record as follows:

County Judge
County Where License Was Issued
County Seat

• •

Since July 1, 1925, copies of Licenses and Certificates of Marriage have been forwarded to the State Registrar for statistical purposes and for maintaining a state-wide index. The state office is also authorized to issue certified copies. For marriages which have occurred <u>since July 1, 1925,</u> you may secure copies from the County Judge (as noted above) or from address listed below!

<u>The fee is $5 for one copy</u> and $2 for each additional copy issued of the same certificate at the same time.

THIS PORTION FOR VITAL RECORD'S OFFICE USE ONLY

Date:_____

Telephone____ Client____ Mail____

Searcher:_____

State File No. 133—_____

Number/Type Copies Issued_____

REMARKS:

Mail request with fee to:

NORTH DAKOTA STATE DEPARTMENT OF HEALTH
VITAL RECORDS
STATE CAPITOL
BISMARCK, ND 58505

REQUEST FOR COPY OF DEATH CERTIFICATE

Please Print

FULL NAME OF DECEASED					SEX
DATE OF DEATH (Month)		(Day)	(Year)	SPOUSE'S NAME	
PLACE OF DEATH (Hospital)			(City)	(County)	
WHAT IS YOUR RELATIONSHIP TO THE DECEASED?				FUNERAL HOME	
FOR WHAT PURPOSE IS THIS COPY REQUESTED?				Enclosed is $_____ for _____ certified copies. (See fee schedule below)	

SIGNATURE OF PERSON MAKING THIS REQUEST			
PRINTED NAME			
ADDRESS	CITY	STATE	-ZIP CODE
TELEPHONE NO. (area code and seven digits)			

IF COPY TO BE MAILED ELSEWHERE

NAME			
ADDRESS	CITY	STATE	ZIP CODE

The above information is necessary to properly identify and locate the correct death certificate. Please enter full information.

Death certificates are by law confidential, and copies or information are to be furnished only to persons having a direct and tangible interest –– a parent, a member of the immediate family, a legal representative, or on court order. Be sure to state your relationship to the deceased and the purpose for which the copy is needed.

The fee for a search of the files is $5; one search fee pays for one certified copy. Additional copies of the same certificate issued at the same time are $2 each.

NOTE: Make all checks or money orders payable to the "NORTH DAKOTA STATE DEPARTMENT OF HEALTH." Cash is sent at your own risk!

THIS PORTION FOR VITAL RECORD'S OFFICE USE ONLY

Date: _____

Telephone____ Client____ Mail____

Searcher:_____

State File No. 133–_____

Number/Type Copies Issued_____

REMARKS:

Mail request with fee to:

**NORTH DAKOTA STATE DEPARTMENT OF HEALTH AND CONSOLIDATED LABORATORIES
DIVISION OF VITAL RECORDS
STATE CAPITOL, 600 EAST BOULEVARD AVENUE
BISMARCK, NORTH DAKOTA 58505-0200**

OHIO

Ohio State Department of Health
Bureau of Vital Statistics
246 North High Street
P.O. Box 15098
Columbus, Ohio 43215-0098

(614) 466-2531

For Marriage Certificates and earlier vital records write to:

Probate Judge
County Probate Court
(County Seat), Ohio

For Divorce Records write to:

Clerk
Court of Common Pleas
(County Seat), Ohio

Cost for a certified Birth Certificate	$7.00
Cost for a non-certified Birth Certificate	$1.10
Cost for a certified Marriage Certificate	$7.00
Cost for a certified Death Certificate	$7.00

The Ohio State Department of Health has birth records from December 20, 1908 and death records from January 1, 1937. They also have marriage and divorce records from September 7, 1949, but do not issue copies.

Ohio death records from December 20, 1908 through December 1936 are available at the Ohio Historical Society (1985 Velma Avenue, Columbus, OH 43211-2497; Tel. 614-297-2525).

County Probate Judges also have vital records on file, often much earlier than the records on file with the Bureau of Vital Statistics.

The Family History Library of The Church of Jesus Christ of Latter-day Saints in Salt Lake City, Utah has microfilmed many of the original and published vital records and church registers of Ohio. For details on their holdings please consult your nearest Family History Center.

APPLICATION FOR COPY OF BIRTH CERTIFICATE

STATE OF OHIO
DEPARTMENT OF HEALTH
BUREAU OF VITAL STATISTICS
P.O. Box 15098
Columbus, Ohio 43215-0098

Check the Appropriate Box for Proper
Processing of the Application
Type of Birth Copy Requested

☐ Certified Copy - $ 7.00 Each
(Required for Passport, etc.)

☐ Plain Copy - $ 1.10 Each
(Not for legal Purposes)

DO NOT WRITE IN THIS SPACE	
DATE	
AMOUNT	NO. OF COPIES
VOLUME NO.	
CERTIFICATE NO.	

IMPORTANT

EACH COPY REQUESTED MUST HAVE REQUIRED FEE
ENCLOSED CHECK OR MONEY ORDER MUST BE MADE PAYABLE TO "STATE TREASURY" - DO NOT SEND CASH
NOTICE: FEE OVERPAYMENTS OF $ 2.00 OR LESS WILL NOT BE REFUNDED - O.R.C. 3705.24

TO BE PRINTED ● INFORMATION ABOUT PERSON WHOSE BIRTH CERTIFICATE IS REQUESTED ● TO BE PRINTED

FULL NAME AT BIRTH	FIRST	MIDDLE	LAST	
DATE OF BIRTH	MONTH	DAY	YEAR	AGE (AT LAST BIRTHDAY)
PLACE OF BIRTH	COUNTY	CITY, VILLAGE OR TOWNSHIP		STATE OHIO
FULL NAME OF FATHER	FIRST	MIDDLE	LAST	
MOTHER'S MAIDEN NAME (NAME BEFORE MARRIAGE)	FIRST	MIDDLE	LAST (MAIDEN)	
APPLICANT'S SIGNATURE			PHONE NO. ( )	
PRESENT ADDRESS	NUMBER AND STREET	CITY, VILLAGE OR TOWNSHIP	STATE	ZIP

AMOUNT ENCLOSED $	☐ CHECK ☐ MONEY ORDER	DATE	TO YOUR KNOWLEDGE HAS A COPY OF THIS RECORD BEEN OBTAINED BEFORE?	☐ YES ☐ NO ☐ UNKNOWN
TO YOUR KNOWLEDGE HAVE ANY CORRECTIONS OR CHANGES BEEN MADE TO THIS CERTIFICATE?				☐ YES ☐ NO ☐ UNKNOWN

DO NOT DETACH

- -

PRINT NAME AND ADDRESS OF PERSON TO WHOM CERTIFICATES(S) IS (ARE) TO BE MAILED IN THE SPACE
BELOW -- THIS IS MAILING INSERT AND WILL BE USED TO MAIL THE CERTIFIED COPY WHICH YOU HAVE
REQUESTED. WHEN THE ABOVE APPLICATION AND THE NAME AND ADDRESS IN THE SECTION BELOW
HAVE BEEN COMPLETED PLEASE SEND THE ENTIRE FORM TO:

OHIO DEPARTMENT OF HEALTH
BUREAU OF VITAL STATISTICS
P.O. Box 15098
Columbus, Ohio 43215-0098

NAME
ADDRESS NUMBER AND STREET
CITY   STATE   ZIP

HEA 2709 (Rev. 3/92)

5132.06

APPLICATION FOR COPY OF DEATH CERTIFICATE

DO NOT WRITE IN THIS SPACE	
DATE	
AMOUNT	NO. OF COPIES
VOLUME NO.	
CERTIFICATE NO.	

STATE OF OHIO
DEPARTMENT OF HEALTH
BUREAU OF VITAL STATISTICS
P.O. BOX 15098
COLUMBUS, OHIO 43215-0098

Check the Appropriate Box for Proper
Processing of the Application
Type of Death Copy Requested
☐ **Certified Copy -** $ 7.00 Each
☐ **Plain Copy -** $ 1.10 Each

IMPORTANT

EACH COPY REQUESTED MUST HAVE REQUIRED FEE

ENCLOSE CHECK OR MONEY ORDER. MUST BE MADE PAYABLE TO "STATE TREASURY" - DO NOT SEND CASH

NOTICE: FEE OVERPAYMENTS OF $2.00 OR LESS WILL NOT BE REFUNDED - O.R.C. 2705.24

TO BE PRINTED • INFORMATION ABOUT PERSON WHOSE DEATH CERTIFICATE IS REQUESTED • TO BE PRINTED

FULL NAME OF DECEASED	FIRST	MIDDLE	LAST

DATE OF DEATH	MONTH	DAY	YEAR	AGE (AT LAST BIRTHDAY)

PLACE OF DEATH	COUNTY	CITY, VILLAGE OR TOWNSHIP	STATE **OHIO**

FUNERAL DIRECTOR

ADDRESS OF FUNERAL DIRECTOR NUMBER AND STREET	CITY	STATE	ZIP

APPLICANTS SIGNATURE	PHONE NO. ( )

PRESENT ADDRESS	NUMBER AND STREET	CITY, VILLAGE OR TOWNSHIP	STATE	ZIP

AMOUNT ENCLOSED	☐ CHECK ☐ MONEY ORDER	DATE	TO YOUR KNOWLEDGE HAS A COPY OF THIS RECORD BEEN OBTAINED BEFORE?	☐ YES ☐ NO ☐ UNKNOWN

TO YOUR KNOWLEDGE HAVE ANY CORRECTIONS OR CHANGES BEEN MADE TO THIS CERTIFICATE?   ☐ YES ☐ NO ☐ UNKNOWN

DO NOT DETACH

- -

PRINT NAME AND ADDRESS OF PERSON TO WHOM CERTIFICATE(S) IS (ARE) TO BE MAILED IN THE SPACE
BELOW -- THIS IS A MAILING INSERT AND WILL BE USED TO MAIL THE CERTIFIED COPY WHICH YOU HAVE
REQUESTED . WHEN THE ABOVE APPLICATION AND THE NAME AND ADDRESS IN THE SECTION BELOW HAVE
BEEN COMPLETED PLEASE SEND THE ENTIRE FORM TO:

NAME
ADDRESS NUMBER AND STREET
CITY   STATE   ZIP

OHIO DEPARTMENT OF HEALTH
BUREAU OF VITAL STATISTICS
P.O. Box 15098
Columbus, Ohio 43215-0098

HEA 2720 (Rev. 3/92)

5161.06

Send your requests to:

Division of Vital Records
Oklahoma State Department of Health
1000 Northeast 10th Street
P.O. Box 53551
Oklahoma City, Oklahoma 73152-3551

(405) 271-4040

Send your requests for Marriage Certificates to:

County Clerk
County Courthouse
(County Seat), Oklahoma

Send your requests for Divorce Records to:

Clerk
District Court
(County Seat), Oklahoma

Cost for a certified Birth Certificate	$5.00
Cost for a certified Marriage Certificate	$5.00
Cost for a certified Death Certificate	$10.00

The Oklahoma State Department of Health has birth and death records from October 1908. Please enclose a self-addressed stamped envelope with your request. The County Clerks also maintain vital records, including many records from the 1800s.

The Family History Library of The Church of Jesus Christ of Latter-day Saints in Salt Lake City, Utah has microfilmed many of the original and published vital records and church registers of Oklahoma. For details on their holdings please consult your nearest Family History Center.

Division of Vital Records, Oklahoma State Department of Health
1000 Northeast 10th Street, Post Office Box 53551
Oklahoma City, Oklahoma 73152-3551

APPLICATION FOR SEARCH AND CERTIFIED COPY OF BIRTH CERTIFICATE

Facts Concerning This Birth

Full name of child _____

Date of
birth _____ Place of birth _____ , OKLAHOMA
    (Mo.)   (Day)   (Year)   (County)   (City)

Full name of father _____

Full Maiden name of mother _____

Signature of person
making this application _____ Date of this application _____

If both parents names are not indicated on the original certificate of birth and a "full copy" is desired it will be necessary to have the signature of the mother, or the registrant if of legal age, or if certificate is required for "adoption purposes" the signature of the attorney of record and a statement from him to that effect.

The above signature is by ( ) person himself-herself ( ) next-of-kin ( ) authorized agent

Purpose for which this copy is needed
( ) School   ( ) Passport   ( ) Employment   ( ) Adoption   ( ) Other (Please state)_____

Has copy of this person's birth certificate been received before? ( )   ( )   ( )
                                        Yes   No   Unknown

PLEASE PRINT CORRECT MAILING ADDRESS BELOW:

_____
                (Name)

_____
         (Street address)

_____
    (City)   (State)   (Zip Code)

Number of copies
wanted @ $5.00 _____

Fee enclosed $_____

ENCLOSE A STAMPED, SELF-ADDRESSED ENVELOPE WITH THIS APPLICATION

Request for a search of the records for a birth certificate of any person born in Oklahoma should be submitted on this blank along with the required fee of $5.00 If the birth record is on file, a certified copy will be mailed. If no record of the birth is found, then blanks and instructions for filing a "delayed" birth certificate will be sent. This fee will be credited on the $10.00 fee required for the first certified copy from the delayed record after it has been placed on file.

The information requested above should be filled in carefully and accurately. It is the minimum needed in the Vital Records office to make a thorough search for any birth record.

Send five dollars ($5.00) in cash, money order or check for each copy desired. Cash is sent at sender's risk. Make checks or money orders payable to the State Department of Health.

A copy required to be submitted to the Veterans Administration or U.S. Commissioner of Pensions, in connection with a claim for military-service-connected benefits may be obtained without fee provided a signed statement is attached which sets forth these facts and requests that the copy be issued without fee. Members of the armed forces and veterans must pay regular fees for copies to be used for all other purposes.

recycled paper

VS 151 R8-91

Division of Vital Records, Oklahoma State Department of Health
1000 Northeast 10th Street, Post Office Box 53551
Oklahoma City, Oklahoma 73152-3551

APPLICATION FOR SEARCH AND CERTIFIED COPY OF DEATH CERTIFICATE

Facts Concerning This Death

Full name of deceased _____ Race _____

Date of
death _____ Place of
death _____ ,OKLAHOMA
    (Mo.)   (Day)   (Year)   (County)   (City)

Check box if death was stillbirth or fetal death ☐

Funeral director
in charge _____ Address _____

Purpose for which this copy is needed _____

Signature of person
making this application _____ Date of
application _____

PLEASE PRINT CORRECT MAILING ADDRESS BELOW: Number of copies
                                                    wanted @ $10.00 _____

_____   Fee enclosed $ _____
            (Name)

_____   ENCLOSE A STAMPED,
        (Street address)   SELF-ADDRESSED
                                                    ENVELOPE WITH THIS
_____   APPLICATION
    (City)   (State)   (Zip)

Request for a search of the records for a death certificate of any person who died in the State of Oklahoma should be submitted on this blank along with the required fee of $10.00. If the death certificate is on file a certified copy will be mailed.

The information requested above should be filled in carefully and accurately. It is the minimum needed to make a thorough search for a death record.

Send ten dollars ($10.00) in cash, money order or check for each copy desired. Cash is sent at sender's risk. Make checks or money orders payable to the State Department of Health.

A copy required to be submitted to the Veterans Administration or U.S. Commissioner of Pensions, in connection with a claim for military-service-connected benefits may be obtained without fee provided a signed statement is attached which sets forth these facts and requests that the copy be issued without fee. Members of the armed forces and veterans must pay regular fees for copies to be used for all other purposes.

VS150 R8-93

OREGON

Send your requests to:

Oregon State Department of Human Resources
Health Division
Vital Records
800 N.E. Oregon Street, Suite 205
P.O. Box 14050
Portland, Oregon 97214-0050

(503) 731-4095

Vital records are also maintained by the:

County Clerk
County Courthouse
(County Seat), Oregon

Cost for a certified Birth Certificate	$14.00
Cost for a wallet-size Birth Certificate	$14.00
Cost for a certified Marriage or Divorce Certificate	$14.00
Cost for a certified Death Certificate	$14.00

The Oregon Department of Human Resources has birth and death records from January 1, 1903, marriage records from January 1, 1906 and divorce records from 1925. Earlier records are also maintained by the County Clerks.

You may call (503) 731-4108 and charge the certificates to your Visa, Discover, or MasterCard for an additional $10.00 fee.

The Oregon State Archives (800 Summer Street, N.E., Salem, OR 97310; Tel. 503-373-0701) has marriage indexes for 1906-1924 and 1946-1990; a divorce index for 1946-1990; death records for 1903-1942 and a death index for 1903-1990.

The Family History Library of The Church of Jesus Christ of Latter-day Saints in Salt Lake City, Utah has microfilmed many of the original and published vital records and church registers of Oregon. They have a microfilm copy of the index to death records from 1903 to 1970. For details on their holdings please consult your nearest Family History Center.

VITAL RECORDS ORDER FORM
Complete the appropriate Block for desired document

BIRTH
$~~~~~~$ Birth in Oregon since 1903

$13.00 EACH
14.00

QUANTITY $~~~~~~$ CERTIFIED COPY — Suitable for any purpose

QUANTITY $~~~~~~$ BIRTH CARD — Not accepted by some agencies

1. Name on Record _____
(First) $~~~~~~$ (Middle) $~~~~~~$ (Last) $~~~~~~$ SEX

2. Date of Birth _____
(Month) $~~~~~~$ (Day) $~~~~~~$ (Year)

3. Place of Birth _____ **OREGON**
(City) $~~~~~~$ (County)

4. Father's Name _____

5. Mother's Full Maiden Name _____

6. Name of Person Ordering Record _____

7. Your Relationship to Line 1 _____

* In accordance with law — ORS 432.120, in addition to having one's own record, a birth record can be furnished to the parents, guardian or respective representative. If you do not fall into one of the above categories, we will need written permission with a notarized signature from one of the above eligible persons. The written consent must accompany this form.

DEATH
$~~~~~~$ Death in Oregon since 1903

$13.00 EACH
14.00

QUANTITY $~~~~~~$ Certified Copy

1. Name of Deceased _____

2. Spouse of Decedent _____

3. Date of Death _____
(Month) $~~~~~~$ (Day) $~~~~~~$ (Year)

4. Place of Death _____ **OREGON**
(City) $~~~~~~$ (County)

5. Name of Person Ordering Record _____

6. Your Relationship to Line 1 _____

MARRIAGE
$~~~~~~$ Marriage in Oregon since 1906

$13.00 EACH
14.00

QUANTITY $~~~~~~$ Certified Copy

1. Name of Groom _____

2. Bride's Full Maiden Name _____

3. Date of Marriage _____
(Month) $~~~~~~$ (Day) $~~~~~~$ (Year)

4. Place License Issued _____ **OREGON**
(City) $~~~~~~$ (County)

DIVORCE
$~~~~~~$ Divorce in Oregon since 1925

$13.00 EACH
14.00

QUANTITY $~~~~~~$ Certified Copy

1. Name of Husband _____

2. Maiden Name Of Wife _____

3. Date of Divorce _____
(Month) $~~~~~~$ (Day) $~~~~~~$ (Year)

4. County Divorce Granted _____ **OREGON**
(City) $~~~~~~$ (County)

PHONE/ ADDRESS
(FOR FOLLOW UP TO YOUR ORDER)

DAYTIME PHONE NUMBER: ( )

NAME _____

STREET ADDRESS _____

CITY $~~~~~~$ STATE $~~~~~~$ ZIP

DO NOT WRITE IN THIS SPACE

ATTENTION:

CERTIFICATE #:

	1	2
FILM		
FILM (P)		
COMPUTER		
INDEXES		
INDEX (P)		
DF/CO		

OFFICE USE ONLY

REFUND: $

Excess Fee: $~~~~~~$ Out/State:

No Rec: $~~~~~~$ Uncompltd:

CHECK: #

Date _____

OFFICE USE ONLY

File Date	Amendment Fee
NRL/Ref. Issued	Full Issued
Follow Up	Card Issued

Send To:

OREGON VITAL RECORDS
P.O. Box 14050
PORTLAND, OR 97214-0050

ALL RECORDS ARE $14.00 EACH

If the requested record cannot be found the fee must be retained as prescribed by Administrative Rule 333-11-106.

Make money orders payable to:
OREGON HEALTH DIVISION
Please Do Not Send Cash

CALL (503) 731-4095 for
CURRENT FEE INFORMATION

Your Mailing Address Must Be Entered Above and Below:

THIS SECTION WILL BE DETACHED AND USED TO MAIL
THE CERTIFIED COPY OF THE CERTIFICATE TO:

NAME _____

STREET _____

CITY, STATE _____ ZIP

← YOUR MAILING ADDRESS

Thank you for your order.

This is not a bill.

In case yours was an order for more than one person's record, the other parts of your order may be handled and sent separately.

Produced by STATE PRINTING

45-13 (R 8/92)

PENNSYLVANIA

Send your requests to:

Pennsylvania Department of Health
Division of Vital Records
101 South Mercer Street
P.O. Box 1528
New Castle, Pennsylvania 16103-1528

(412) 656-3100

Send your requests for Marriage Certificates to:

Marriage License Clerk
County Courthouse
(County Seat), Pennsylvania

Send your requests for Divorce Certificates to:

Prothonotary
County Courthouse
(County Seat), Pennsylvania

Cost for a certified Birth Certificate	$4.00
Cost for a certified Death Certificate	$3.00

The Pennsylvania Department of Health has birth and death records from January 1906. The County Clerks also maintain vital records. Please note the special addresses on the application form if the birth or death occurred in Erie, Philadelphia, Pittsburgh, or Scranton. For marriage or divorce records you must contact the county where the event occurred.

If your request is urgent you may call and charge your certificates to your Visa, Discover, or MasterCard. There is a $5.00 fee for this service.

The Historical Society of Pennsylvania (1300 Locust Street, Philadelphia, PA 19107; Tel. 215-732-6201) has a large microfilm collection of Pennsylvania vital, county, and church records.

The Family History Library of The Church of Jesus Christ of Latter-day Saints in Salt Lake City, Utah has microfilmed many of the original and published vital records and church registers of Pennsylvania. They have microfilm copies of births from 1852 to 1854, marriages from 1852 to 1854 and 1885 to 1889, and deaths from 1774 to 1873. For details on their holdings please consult your nearest Family History Center.

H105.102 REV 6-91

PENNSYLVANIA DEPARTMENT OF HEALTH
VITAL RECORDS

APPLICATION FOR CERTIFIED COPY OF BIRTH OR DEATH RECORD
RECORDS AVAILABLE FROM 1906 TO THE PRESENT

PRINT OR TYPE ALL ITEMS MUST BE COMPLETED OFFICE USE ONLY

INDICATE NUMBER OF COPIES IN BOX	☐ BIRTH $4.00	☐ DEATH $3.00 If social security number is known of deceased ___ ___ ___	

1. Date of Birth **OR** Date of Death	2. Place of Birth **OR** Place of Death	County	Boro/City/Twp.	File No.
3. Name at Birth **OR** Name at Death			4. Sex 5. Age Now	Searched By
6. Father's Full Name First Middle Last				Typed By
7. Mother's Maiden Name First Middle Last				File Date
8. Hospital	Funeral Director			Refund Ck. No.

9. **REASON FOR REQUEST.** **THIS ITEM MUST BE COMPLETED** Date Amt.

10. **HOW** ARE YOU RELATED TO PERSON IN NUMBER 3?

11. In accordance with §4904, Unsworn Falsification to Authorities, I state that the above information is accurate. (If subject is under 18, parent must sign.) Signature Required: Please sign here.

12. Mailing Address

13. City, State, Zip Code

14. Daytime Phone Number Area Code: Number:

FEE FOR CERTIFIED COPIES ARE: BIRTHS $4.00 DEATHS $3.00
NOT REFUNDABLE
DO NOT SEND CASH
Make Check or Money Order Payable to VITAL RECORDS

PLEASE ENCLOSE A LEGAL-SIZE SELF-ADDRESSED STAMPED ENVELOPE FOR RETURN OF COPIES

IF ALL ITEMS ARE NOT COMPLETED, APPLICATION MAY BE REJECTED

☐ Prev. Amend. ☐ Adopt ☐ Affidavit
☐ Usage ☐ Court Order ☐ Issue Affidavit

- -

DO NOT REMOVE THIS STUB

If birth or death occured in: Mail application to:

1) Philadelphia — Division of Vital Records, 1400 W. Spring Garden St., Room 1009, Philadelphia, Pa. 19130-4090
2) Pittsburgh — Division of Vital Records, 300 Liberty Ave., Room 512, Pittsburgh, Pa. 15222
3) Erie — Division of Vital Records, 1910 West 26th St., Erie, Pa. 16508
4) Scranton — Division of Vital Records, 100 Lackawanna Ave., Scranton, Pa. 18503

Print or type your name and address in the space below.

Name
Street
City, State, Zip Code

**FOR ALL OTHER AREAS
MAIL COMPLETED APPLICATION TO:**

**PENNSYLVANIA DEPARTMENT OF HEALTH
DIVISION OF VITAL RECORDS
P.O. BOX 1528
NEW CASTLE, PA. 16103**
or visit our public offices at
101 South Mercer Street, New Castle or
Room 516, Health & Welfare Bldg., Harrisburg

RHODE ISLAND

Send your requests to:

Division of Vital Records
Rhode Island Department of Health
3 Capitol Hill, Room 101
Providence, Rhode Island 02908-5097

(401) 277-2811, (401) 277-2812, TDD (401) 277-2506

Vital records are also maintained by:

Town Clerk
Town Hall
(Town), Rhode Island

For Divorce Records write to:

Rhode Island Family Court
Dorrance Street
Providence, Rhode Island 02903

(401) 277-3040

Cost for a certified Birth Certificate	$12.00
Cost for a certified Marriage Certificate	$12.00
Cost for a certified Death Certificate	$12.00
Cost for a duplicate copy, when ordered at the same time	$7.00

The Rhode Island Division of Vital Records has birth and marriage records from January 1, 1894 and death records from January 1, 1944. For earlier records contact the Rhode Island State Archives (State House, Room 43, 82 Smith Street, Providence, RI 02903; Tel. 401-277-2353). See also James Newell Arnold's *Vital Records of Rhode Island 1636-1850* (Providence, RI: Narragansett Historical Publishing Co., 1891-1912. 20 vols.).

If your request is urgent you may call (401) 277-2812 and charge your certificates to your Visa card for an additional charge of $8.95 plus $15.50 if you want it shipped by Federal Express.

The Family History Library of The Church of Jesus Christ of Latter-day Saints in Salt Lake City, Utah has microfilmed many of the original and published vital records and church registers of Rhode Island. For details on their holdings please consult your nearest Family History Center.

R.I. DEPT. OF HEALTH, DIV. OF VITAL RECORDS, 3 CAPITOL HILL, PROVIDENCE, R.I. 02908-5097

APPLICATION FOR A CERTIFIED COPY OF A BIRTH RECORD

PLEASE COMPLETE ALL QUESTIONS 1-5

1. Please fill in the information below for the person whose birth record you are requesting.

FULL NAME AT BIRTH _____ AGE _____

DATE OF BIRTH _____ CITY/TOWN OF BIRTH _____ HOSPITAL _____

MOTHER'S FULL MAIDEN NAME _____

FATHER'S FULL NAME _____ (if listed on record)

2. Please complete one of the following:

I am applying for the birth record of: _____ MYSELF _____ MY CHILD

_____ MY MOTHER/FATHER _____ MY GRANDPARENT _____ MY BROTHER/SISTER

_____ MY CLIENT. I'M AN ATTORNEY REPRESENTING: _____

_____ OTHER PERSON (SPECIFY HOW YOU ARE RELATED): _____

3. Copies cost $12.00 for the first copy and $7.00 for additional copies of the same record.

FULL COPY _____. How many do you want? _____

WALLET SIZE _____. How many do you want? _____
(A wallet size is not accepted by all offices)

4. Why do you need this record? (We ask this question so that we can supply you with a certified copy which will be suitable for your needs.)

SCHOOL _____ WIC _____ PASSPORT _____ SOCIAL SECURITY _____ LICENSE _____

WORK _____ WELFARE _____ OTHER SPECIFY _____

5. I hereby state that the information supplied above is true to the best of my knowledge, and that the signature on this application is my own.

PLEASE SIGN _____ _____
(Signature of person completing this form) Date signed

YOUR ADDRESS _____
Street or mailing address   City/Town   State   Zip Code

******************** BELOW THIS LINE FOR STATE USE ONLY ********************

State File Number _____ Amount Received _____ Receipt Number _____ Date Sent _____ Initials _____

	Birth	Death	Marriage
Number of First Copies	_____	_____	_____
Number of Add'l Copies	_____	_____	_____

Number of Searches _____ Add'l Yrs Searched _____ Del.Fil. Corr. Pat. Adop. Legit.

VS 82B REV 5/93

R.I. DEPT. OF HEALTH, DIV. OF VITAL RECORDS, 3 CAPITOL HILL, PROVIDENCE, R.I. 02908-5097

APPLICATION FOR A CERTIFIED COPY OF A MARRIAGE RECORD

1. Please fill in the information below for the persons whose marriage record you are requesting:

   FULL NAME OF GROOM _____

   FULL NAME OF BRIDE _____

   FULL MAIDEN NAME OF BRIDE (IF DIFFERENT)_____

   DATE OF MARRIAGE _____ PLACE OF MARRIAGE _____

2. What is your relationship to the Bride or Groom?

   ____ BRIDE OR GROOM   ____ GRANDPARENT

   ____ MOTHER OR FATHER   ____ BROTHER OR SISTER

   ____ MY CLIENT. I'M AN ATTORNEY REPRESENTING: _____

   ____ OTHER PERSON (SPECIFY HOW YOU ARE RELATED) _____

3. Why do you need this record?

   _____

4. Copies cost $12.00 for the first copy and $7.00 for additional copies of the same record. How many copies do you want? _____

5. PLEASE SIGN _____ _____
              (Signature of person completing this form)   Date signed

   YOUR ADDRESS _____
              Street or mailing address   City/Town   State Zip Code

***************************BELOW THIS LINE FOR STATE USE ONLY************************
State File   Amount   Receipt   Date   Initials
Number _____ Received _____ Number _____ Sent _____   _____

                 Birth   Death   Marriage
Number of First Copies _____   _____   _____

Number of Add'l Copies _____   _____   _____

Number of Searches _____ Add'l Yrs Searched _____ Del.Fil. Corr. Pat. Adop. Legit.

VS 82M REV 5/93

R.I. DEPT. OF HEALTH, DIV. OF VITAL RECORDS, 3 CAPITOL HILL,
PROVIDENCE, R.I. 02908-5097

APPLICATION FOR A CERTIFIED COPY OF A DEATH RECORD

1. Please fill in the information below for the individual whose death record you are requesting:

FULL NAME _____

DATE OF DEATH _____ PLACE OF DEATH _____

NAME OF SPOUSE (IF MARRIED) _____

MOTHER'S FULL MAIDEN NAME _____

FATHER'S FULL NAME _____

2. How are you related to the person whose death record is being requested?

_____

3. Why do you need this record?

_____

4. Copies cost $12.00 for the first copy and $7.00 for additional copies of the same record. How many copies do you want? _____

5. PLEASE SIGN _____   _____
                (Signature of person completing this form)   Date signed

YOUR
ADDRESS _____
        Street or mailing address   City/Town   State   Zip Code

************************BELOW THIS LINE FOR STATE USE ONLY************************

VS 82D REV 5/93

SOUTH CAROLINA

Send your requests to:

> South Carolina Department of Health and Environmental Control
> Office of Vital Records and Public Health Statistics
> 2600 Bull Street
> Columbia, South Carolina 29201-1797

(803) 734-4830, (803) 734-4810

For pre-July 1, 1950 Marriage Certificates write to:

> Probate Judge
> Probate Court
> (County Seat), South Carolina

For Divorce Decrees write to:

> Clerk of Court
> County Courthouse
> (County Seat), South Carolina

Cost for a certified Birth Certificate	$8.00
Cost for a wallet-size Birth Certificate	$8.00
Cost for a certified Marriage or Divorce Certificate	$8.00
Cost for a certified Death Certificate	$8.00
Cost for a duplicate copy, when ordered at the same time	$3.00

The Office of Vital Records has birth and death records from January 1, 1915, marriage records from July 1, 1950, and divorce records from January 1, 1962.

If your request is urgent you may call and charge your certificates to your Visa or MasterCard. There is a charge of $5.00 for this service plus postage. County health departments also issue certificates.

The South Carolina Department of Archives and History (P.O. Box 11669, Columbia, SC 29211-1669; Tel. 803-734-8577) has death records from 1915 to 1941. See *A Guide to Local Government Records in the South Carolina Archives* (Columbia, SC: University of South Carolina Press, 1988. 315p.).

The Family History Library of The Church of Jesus Christ of Latter-day Saints in Salt Lake City, Utah has microfilmed many vital records, including state marriage records from 1785 to 1889. For details on their holdings please consult your nearest Family History Center.

SOUTH CAROLINA DEPARTMENT OF HEALTH AND ENVIRONMENTAL CONTROL

OFFICE OF VITAL RECORDS & PUBLIC HEALTH STATISTICS
2600 BULL STREET
COLUMBIA, SC 29201

APPLICATION FOR CERTIFIED COPY OF BIRTH CERTIFICATE

PLEASE READ BEFORE COMPLETING THIS APPLICATION

A. Only births recorded after January 1, 1915 in South Carolina are on file.
B. The application must be signed by the registrant, parent, guardian, or their legal representative.
C. **WARNING: FALSE APPLICATION IS PUNISHABLE BY LAW.** (Section 44-63-161; S.C. Code of Laws, 1976, amended Feb. 24, 1988.)
D. S.C. Law requires a $8.00 fee for the search of the records. If located, the search fee includes issuance of one copy. If not located, search fee is not refundable. Checks and money orders should be made payable to DHEC.
E. Complete all of the information sections required on this form. **PLEASE PRINT.**

				OFFICE USE ONLY
1. FULL NAME	First Name	Middle Name	Last Name (If married woman, please enter maiden surname)	
2. DATE OF BIRTH	Month	Day	Year	Year - Cert. No.
3. PLACE OF BIRTH	County	Hospital/and or city/town	State SOUTH CAROLINA	Search 1st Date
4. SEX		5. RACE		2nd Date
6. FULL NAME OF FATHER	First Name	Middle Name	Last Name Living ☐ Deceased ☐	Pending Sect. Date C
7. FULL MAIDEN NAME OF MOTHER	First Name	Middle Name	LAST NAME BEFORE MARRIAGE Living ☐ Deceased ☐	D

8. WERE PARENTS MARRIED?   Yes ☐   No ☐

9. NUMBER OF OLDER CHILDREN BORN TO THIS MOTHER _____
   NUMBER OF YOUNGER CHILDREN BORN TO THIS MOTHER _____

A

10. NAME OF NEXT OLDER BROTHER OR SISTER, LIVING OR DEAD		DATE OF BIRTH		L
11. NAME OF NEXT YOUNGER BROTHER OR SISTER LIVING OR DEAD		DATE OF BIRTH		PR

12. HAS NAME EVER BEEN CHANGED OTHER THAN MARRIAGE?   Yes ☐   No ☐   If so, what was the original name?   LOC

13. PURPOSE FOR WHICH THIS COPY IS REQUESTED?   Final Disposition

Issue Date

FEE
14. I am enclosing $ _____ for _____ certificates as follows: Specify Number and Type Certification
   _____ Wallet size, short form certification - Accepted for all purposes except to establish relationship of parent to child. Does not include parents' names. Initial certification - $8.00. Additional short form certification ordered at same time - $3.00 each.
   _____ Photocopy certification - Issued only by the state office and only to registrant if legal age (18 yrs.) parent/guardian or their legal representative. Initial certification - $8.00. Additional photocopy certifications ordered at same time - $3.00 each.

Control Number(s)

☐ Refund
Refunded
Amount $ _____

15. WRITTEN SIGNATURE OF registrant, parent/guardian or legal representative
DO NOT PRINT _____

OFFICE USE ONLY
IDENTIFICATION

Your relationship to registrant: Self ____ Parent ____ Guardian ____
Other (specify) _____

SYS/36

NAME & ADDRESS OF APPLICANT (MUST BE COMPLETED)	PLEASE PRINT	CERTIFICATE TO BE MAILED TO:
PLEASE PRINT 16. NAME		PLEASE PRINT (If other than applicant) 19. NAME
17. NUMBER, P.O. BOX AND STREET		20. NUMBER, P.O. BOX AND STREET
18. CITY, STATE, AND ZIP CODE		21. CITY, STATE, AND ZIP CODE

SC DHEC 612 (Rev. 12/91)

SOUTH CAROLINA DEPARTMENT OF HEALTH AND ENVIRONMENTAL CONTROL

OFFICE OF VITAL RECORDS & PUBLIC HEALTH STATISTICS
2600 BULL STREET
COLUMBIA, S.C. 29201

APPLICATION FOR CERTIFIED COPY OF MARRIAGE RECORD

INFORMATION	INSTRUCTIONS
1. Only marriage licenses issued after July, 1950, in South Carolina are on file.	1. Complete all the information sections of the form. **PLEASE PRINT.**
2. S.C. Law requires a $8.00 fee for the search of a marriage record. If located, a certified copy of the marriage record will be issued to those entitled. Verification of the date and place of marriage will be provided if the applicant is not entitled to a copy of the record. Additional copies of the same record ordered at the same time are $3.00 each. If not located, search fee is not refundable.	2. An application for a certified copy of a marriage record must be signed by one of the married parties, their adult children, a present or former spouse, or the legal representative of one of these persons. Relationship must be stated.
3. S.C. Law (Section 44-63-86) provides that "Copies of marriage certificates . . . may be issued to the parties married . . . , their adult children, a present or former spouse of either party married, . . . or their respective legal representative."	3. Send completed application and appropriate fee to the address at the top of this form. Checks and money orders should be made payable to ~~the Office of Vital Records~~ *SCDHEC.*
4. If the marriage occurred prior to July, 1950, or if a copy of the application is required contact the probate judge of the county where the marriage license was issued.	
5. WARNING: FALSE APPLICATION FOR A MARRIAGE CERTIFICATE IS PUNISHABLE BY LAW. (Section 44-63-161, S.C. Code of Laws, 1976, Amended.)	

					OFFICE USE ONLY
1. FULL NAME OF GROOM	First	Middle	Last		
2. DATE OF BIRTH	Month	Day	Year	Race	YEAR - CERT. NO.
3. FULL NAME OF BRIDE	First	Middle	Last		DNL. DATE
4. DATE OF OF BIRTH	Month	Day	Year	Race	PROC. DATE
5. HAS BRIDE EVER USED ANY OTHER NAME? ☐ Yes ☐ No	If so, please list:				ISSUE DATE
6. DATE OF MARRIAGE	Month	Day	Year		CONTROL NO.
7. PLACE LICENSE ISSUED	City	County	State South Carolina		

8. FEE   I am enclosing a Fee of $ _____ for _____ CERTIFIED COPIES.

☐ Refund
Refunded Amount
$ _____

9a. WRITTEN SIGNATURE OF APPLICANT

IDENTIFICATION

9b. RELATIONSHIP:

Self ☐ Adult Child ☐ Present/Former Spouse ☐ Legal Representative of: _____ Not Related ☐

SYS/36

NAME & ADDRESS OF APPLICANT (MUST BE COMPLETED)   **PLEASE PRINT**   **CERTIFICATE TO BE MAILED TO:**

PLEASE PRINT 10. NAME	PLEASE PRINT (If other than applicant) 13. NAME
11. NUMBER, P.O. BOX AND STREET	14. NUMBER, P.O. BOX AND STREET
12. CITY, STATE, AND ZIP CODE	15. CITY, STATE, AND ZIP CODE

SC DHEC 678 (Rev. 12/91)

SOUTH CAROLINA DEPARTMENT OF HEALTH AND ENVIRONMENTAL CONTROL

OFFICE OF VITAL RECORDS & PUBLIC HEALTH STATISTICS
2600 BULL STREET
COLUMBIA, S.C. 29201

APPLICATION FOR CERTIFIED COPY OF A DIVORCE OR ANNULMENT

INFORMATION	INSTRUCTIONS
1. Reports of divorces or annulments granted after July 1, 1962, in South Carolina are on file.	1. Complete all of the information sections of the form. **PLEASE PRINT.**
2. S.C. Law requires a $8.00 fee for the search of a report of a divorce or annulment. If located, a certified copy of the report will be issued to those entitled. Verification of the date and place of divorce will be provided if the applicant is not entitled to a copy of the record. Additional copies of the same record ordered at the same time are $3.00 each. If not located, search fee is not refundable.	2. An application for a certified copy of a report of a divorce or annulment must be signed by one of the parties to the divorce or annulment, their adult children, a present or former spouse, or their respective legal representatives. Relationship must be stated.
3. S.C. Law (Section 44-63-86) provides that "Copies of . . . reports of divorce . . . may be issued to the parties . . . divorced, their adult children, a present or former spouse of either party . . . divorced, or their respective legal representative."	3. Send completed application and appropriate fee to the address at the top of this form. Checks and money orders should be made payable to the Office of Vital Records.
4. If a copy of the decree of divorce or annulment is required, or if the event occurred prior to July 1, 1962, a complete record can be obtained from the Clerk of Court of the county in which the decree was granted	
5. WARNING: FALSE APPLICATION FOR A REPORT OF DIVORCE OR ANNULMENT IS PUNISHABLE BY LAW. (Section 44-63-161, S.C. Code of Laws, 1976, Amended.)	

					OFFICE USE ONLY
1. FULL NAME OF HUSBAND	First	Middle	Last	Race	
2. MAIDEN NAME OF WIFE	First	Middle	Last	Race	YEAR - CERT. NO.
3. DATE OF DIVORCE OR ANNULMENT	Month	Day	Year		DNL. DATE
4. PLACE DIVORCE GRANTED	City	County	State SOUTH CAROLINA		PROC. DATE

5. FEE   I am enclosing a Fee of $ _____ for _____ CERTIFIED COPIES.

ISSUE DATE

6a. WRITTEN SIGNATURE OF APPLICANT

CONTROL NO.

6b. RELATIONSHIP:

Self ☐ Adult Child ☐ Present/Former Spouse ☐ Legal Representative of: _____ ☐ Not Related ☐

☐ Refund
Refunded Amount
$ _____
IDENTIFICATION

SYS/36

NAME & ADDRESS OF APPLICANT (MUST BE COMPLETED)	PLEASE PRINT CERTIFICATE TO BE MAILED TO:
PLEASE PRINT 7. NAME	PLEASE PRINT (If other than applicant) 10. NAME
8. NUMBER, P.O. BOX AND STREET	11. NUMBER, P.O. BOX AND STREET
9. CITY, STATE, AND ZIP CODE	12. CITY, STATE, AND ZIP CODE

SC DHEC 679 (Rev. 12/91)

SOUTH CAROLINA DEPARTMENT OF HEALTH AND ENVIRONMENTAL CONTROL

OFFICE OF VITAL RECORDS & PUBLIC HEALTH STATISTICS
2600 BULL STREET
COLUMBIA, S.C. 29201

APPLICATION FOR CERTIFIED COPY OF A DEATH RECORD

INFORMATION	INSTRUCTIONS
1. Only deaths recorded after January 1, 1915, are on file.	1. Complete all of the information sections required on this form. **PLEASE PRINT.**
2. S.C. Law requires a $8.00 fee for the search of a death record. If located, a certified copy will be issued to those entitled. Verification of the date and place of death will be provided if the applicant is not entitled to a copy of the record. Additional copies of the same record ordered at the same time are $3.00 each. If not located, search fee is not refundable.	2. Application must be signed by the applicant. Relationship to the deceased must be stated. If applicant is not a family member or is not the legal representative of a family member, the applicant's interest in the record must be stated to determine entitlement to the record. Proof of entitlement may be required by the registrar.
3. S.C. Law (Section 44-63-84) provides that "Copies of death certificates may be issued to members of the deceased's family or their respective legal representatives. Others who demonstrate a direct and tangible interest may be issued copies when information is needed for the determination of a personal or property right . . ."	3. Send completed application and appropriate fee to the address at the top of this form. Checks and money orders should be made payable to the SC DHEC.
4. WARNING: FALSE APPLICATION FOR A DEATH CERTIFICATE IS PUNISHABLE BY LAW. (Section 44-63-161, S.C. Code of Laws, 1976, Amended.)	

1. FULL NAME OF DECEASED	First Name	Middle Name and/or Maiden	Last Name	OFFICE USE ONLY
2. DATE OF DEATH	Month	Day	Year	YEAR - CERT. NO.
3. PLACE OF DEATH	Hospital/City	County	State SOUTH CAROLINA	DNL. DATE
4. SEX		5. RACE	6. AGE AT TIME OF DEATH	PROC. DATE
7. SOCIAL SECURITY NO. OF DECEASED (IF KNOWN)				
8. NAME OF FUNERAL DIRECTOR				ISSUE DATE
9. IF THE DECEASED WAS MARRIED, PLEASE LIST HUSBAND/WIFE			Living ☐ Dead ☐	CONTROL NO.
10. FATHER OF THE DECEASED	Last Name	First Name	Middle Name	
11. MOTHER OF THE DECEASED	Last Name	First Name	Middle Name	☐ Refund Refunded Amount

12. FEE   I am enclosing a Fee of $ _____ for _____ CERTIFIED COPIES. $ _____

13a. WRITTEN SIGNATURE OF APPLICANT:

13b. Relation of Applicant to the Deceased: Family Member ☐ ; Legal Rep. of a Family Member ☐ ; Not Related ☐

13c. If not a family member or the legal representative of a family member, state need for record.

IDENTIFICATION

SYS/36

NAME & ADDRESS OF APPLICANT (MUST BE COMPLETED)	(PLEASE PRINT)	CERTIFICATE TO BE MAILED TO:
PLEASE PRINT 14. NAME	PLEASE PRINT 17. NAME	(If other than applicant)
15. NUMBER, P.O. BOX AND STREET	18. NUMBER, P.O. BOX AND STREET	
16. CITY, STATE, AND ZIP CODE	19. CITY, STATE, AND ZIP CODE	

SC DHEC 677 (Rev. 2/92)

SOUTH DAKOTA

Send your requests to:

South Dakota Department of Health
Center for Health Statistics
445 East Capitol
Pierre, South Dakota 57501-3185

(605) 773-4961

For copies of pre-1905 Marriage Certificates write to:

County Treasurer
County Courthouse
(County Seat), South Dakota

Cost for a certified Birth Certificate	$5.00
Cost for a certified Marriage or Divorce Certificate	$5.00
Cost for a certified Death Certificate	$5.00

The South Dakota Department of Health has records from July 1, 1905, with some earlier birth records. The County Clerks also maintain vital records and often have records much earlier than the records at the Center for Health Statistics.

If your request is urgent you may call and charge your certificates to your Visa or MasterCard. There is a $5.00 fee for this service.

The South Dakota State Library (800 Governors Drive, Pierre, SD 57501-2294; Tel. 605-773-3131, toll-free 800-592-1841) has an extensive collection of records.

The Family History Library of The Church of Jesus Christ of Latter-day Saints in Salt Lake City, Utah has microfilmed many of the original and published vital records and church registers of South Dakota, including indexes to birth and death records from 1880 to 1990. For details on their holdings please consult your nearest Family History Center.

South Dakota

Department of Health

Center For Health Statistics
445 East Capitol
Pierre, South Dakota 57501-3185
605/773-4961

RECEIPT # _____

DATE _____

We have received your request and fee of $_____ for a certified copy of a vital record.
We require an additional fee of $_____ before we can process your request. THE ADDITIONAL
FEE AND THIS COMPLETED FORM MUST BE RETURNED WITHIN 30 DAYS.

BIRTH	FULL NAME AT BIRTH OR ADOPTIVE NAME _____
	DATE OF BIRTH (Month, Day & Year) _____
	PLACE OF BIRTH (City & County) _____
	FATHER'S FULL NAME _____
	MOTHER'S FULL MAIDEN NAME _____
	STATE REASON RECORD IS NEEDED _____
	(Must be beneficial to person (Applies only to out of wedlock births)
	named on the birth record)
	_____
	(Signature of person requesting record)
DEATH	FULL NAME AT TIME OF DEATH _____
	DATE OF DEATH (Month, Day & Year) _____
	PLACE OF DEATH (City & County) _____
MARRIAGE	FULL NAME OF GROOM _____
	FULL NAME OF BRIDE _____
	DATE OF MARRIAGE (Month, Day & Year) _____
	WHERE LICENSE WAS OBTAINED
DIVORCE	FULL NAME OF HUSBAND _____
	FULL NAME OF WIFE _____
	DATE OF DIVORCE (Month, Day & Year) _____

PRINT OR TYPE NAME AND ADDRESS OF PERSON TO WHOM CERTIFICATE IS TO BE SENT

_____
(Name)

_____
(Street or Box)

_____
(City and State)   ZIP +

HAS-0252 REV. 5/91

TENNESSEE

Send your requests to:

Tennessee Department of Health
Vital Records Office
C3-324 Cordell Hull Building
Nashville, Tennessee 37247-0350

(615) 741-1763, FAX (615) 726-2559

For earlier Birth, Marriage, and Death Records write to:

County Clerk
County Courthouse
(County Seat), Tennessee

Cost for a certified Birth Certificate	$10.00
Cost for a short form Birth Certificate (1949-present only)	$5.00
Cost for a certified Marriage or Divorce Certificate	$10.00
Cost for a certified Death Certificate	$5.00
Cost for a duplicate copy, when ordered at the same time	$2.00

The Tennessee Vital Records Office has birth and death records from January 1, 1914 and marriage and divorce records from July 1, 1945. The County Clerks also maintain vital records, many of which are much earlier than the records in the Vital Records Office.

If your request is urgent you may call and charge your certificates to your Visa, Discover, or MasterCard. There is a $10.00 fee for this service.

The Tennessee State Library and Archives (403 Seventh Avenue North, Nashville, TN 37243-0312; Tel. 615-741-2764) has birth records from 1908 to 1912, death records from 1908 to 1945, and a large collection of marriage and divorce records for various years among its county records.

The Family History Library of The Church of Jesus Christ of Latter-day Saints in Salt Lake City, Utah has microfilmed many of the original and published vital records and church registers of Tennessee. They have microfilm copies of births from 1908 to 1912 and deaths from 1908 to 1912, and 1914 to 1925. For details on their holdings please consult your nearest Family History Center.

IT IS UNLAWFUL TO WILLFULLY AND KNOWINGLY MAKE ANY FALSE STATEMENT ON THIS APPLICATION. VIOLATORS WILL BE PROSECUTED.

TENNESSEE DEPARTMENT OF HEALTH
Tennessee Vital Records

APPLICATION FOR CERTIFIED COPY OF CERTIFICATE OF BIRTH
DO NOT SEND CASH. Send check or money order.

DATE: _____

Full Name on Birth Certificate_____
   First   Middle   Last

Has name ever been changed other than by marriage?_____

If yes, what was original name? _____

Date of Birth_____ Sex_____
   Month   Day   Year

Place of Birth_____
   City   County   State

Full Name of Father_____

Full Maiden Name of Mother_____

Last Name of Mother at Time of Birth_____

Hospital Where Birth Occurred _____

Next Older Brother or Sister_____Younger_____

Signature of Person Making Request _____

Relationship_____

Purpose of Copy_____

Telephone number where you may be reached for additional information_____

Indicate number of each type of certificate desired and enclose appropriate fee:

For years 1950—Current:

__ Short form—$5.00 first copy
Additional copies of same record purchased at same time—$2.00 each

Short form is a certified transcript showing child's name, birthdate, sex, county of birth, certificate number and file date (1976—current year also shows parents' names)

__ Long form—$10.00 first copy
Additional copies of same record purchased at same time—$2.00 each

Long form is a copy showing all information.

For births before 1950:
(No short form available)

__ First copy—$10.00
Additional copies of same record purchased at same time—$2.00 each

The above fees for the first copy are charged for the search for the record even if no record is on file in this office. A 3 year search is provided for the initial fee.

Fees subject to change without notice.

PH-1654
VR (Rev. 8-91)

All items must be completed and appropriate fees attached to process this request. If you have not received a response within 45 days, please write or call Tennessee Vital Records at (615) 741-1763.

DO NOT DETACH

PRINT name and address of person to whom the certified copy is to be mailed.
ADDRESS MUST BE COMPLETED ON <u>ALL</u> APPLICATIONS

SEND TO:

Tennessee Vital Records
C3-324 Cordell Hull Building
Nashville, Tennessee 37247-0350

Name: _____

Street or
Route: _____

City or
Town: _____ State: _____ Zip: _____

PH-1654
VR (Rev. 8-91)

TENNESSEE DEPARTMENT OF HEALTH AND ENVIRONMENT
Office of Vital Records

APPLICATION FOR A CERTIFIED COPY OF A CERTIFICATE OF MARRIAGE

(It is unlawful to willfully and knowingly make any false statement on this application.)

_____ First copy $10.00

Date _____   _____ Each additional copy $2.00

Name of Groom _____
                    First   Middle   Last

Name of Bride at Birth _____
                           First   Middle   Last

Place This License Was Issued _____
                                        County   State

Date of Marriage _____
                      Month   Day   Year

Place of Marriage _____
                       City   County   State

Signature of Person Making Request _____

Relationship of Requester _____

Purpose of Copy _____

Records filed in this office July 1945 thru current date. Records prior to this date are filed in the county of occurrence.

DO NOT DETACH

PH-1670
VR (Rev. 7/87)

IMPORTANT

Make check or money order payable to the TENNESSEE DEPARTMENT OF HEALTH AND ENVIRONMENT
Fee Will Be Charged For Search And Cannot Be Refunded
(Fees are subject to change without notice)

PRINT name and address of person to whom the certified copy is to be mailed. (Address must be completed on all applications)

_____

Name _____

Street or
Route _____

City or
Town _____ Zip _____

SEND TO
Office of Vital Records
Tennessee Department of
   Health and Environment
Cordell Hull Building
Nashville, Tennessee 37219-5402

PH-1670
VR (Rev. 7/87)

TENNESSEE DEPARTMENT OF HEALTH AND ENVIRONMENT
Office of Vital Records

APPLICATION FOR CERTIFIED COPY OF CERTIFICATE OF DIVORCE OR ANNULMENT

Date _____

_____ First copy $10.00

_____ Each additional copy $2.00

Name of Husband_____
　　　　　　　　　First　　　　　　　　　　Middle　　　　　　　　　　Last

Name of Wife _____
　　　　　　　　　First　　　　　　　　　　Middle　　　　　　　　　　Last

Date of Divorce _____
　　　　　　　　　Month　　　　　　　　　　Day　　　　　　　　　　Year

Place of Divorce _____
　　　　　　　　　City　　　　　　　　　　County　　　　　　　　　　State

Signature of Person Making Request _____

Relationship of Requestor _____

Purpose of Copy_____

(It is unlawful to willfully and knowingly make any false statement on this application.)

Records filed in this office July 1945 thru current. Records prior to this date are filed in the county of occurrence.

DO NOT DETACH

PH-1671
VR (Rev. 7/87)

IMPORTANT

Make check or money order payable to the TENNESSEE DEPARTMENT OF HEALTH AND ENVIRONMENT
Fee Will Be Charged For Search And Cannot Be Refunded
(Fees are subject to change without notice)

PRINT name and address of person to whom the certified copy is to be mailed. (Address must be completed on all applications)

SEND TO:

_____

NAME

Street or
Route

_____

City or
Town　　　　　　　　Zip

Office of Vital Records
Tennessee Department of
　　Health and Environment
Cordell Hull Building
Nashville, Tennessee 37219-5402

PH-1671
VR (Rev. 7/87)

TENNESSEE DEPARTMENT OF HEALTH
Vital Records
APPLICATION FOR CERTIFIED COPY OF CERTIFICATE OF DEATH
Make check or money order payable to the TENNESSEE DEPARTMENT OF HEALTH
Do Not Send Cash. Check or Money Order Preferred.

DATE _____

_____ $5.00 per copy requested

Name of Deceased _____
  first   middle   last

Date of Death _____
          month   day   year

Sex _____ Race _____ Age _____

Place of Death_____
          city   county   state

Name of Funeral Home _____

Location of Funeral Home _____
                              city   state

Signature of Person Making Request: _____

Relationship to Deceased: _____

Purpose of Copy: _____

Telephone Number Where You May Be Reached:_____

A fee of $5.00 is charged for the search of our records even if no record is found, and includes one copy if a record is on file in this office.

PH-1663
VR (Rev. 1-92)   **(It is unlawful to willfully and knowingly make any false statement on this application.)**

DO NOT DETACH

Mail Copy To:

PRINT name and address of person to whom the certified copy
is to be mailed. (Address to be completed on all applications)

_____

NAME _____
Street or
Route _____
City or
Town _____ State _____ Zip _____

SEND TO:

VITAL RECORDS
C3-324 Cordell Hull Building
Tennessee Department of Health
Nashville, Tennessee 37247-0350

PH-1663
VR (Rev. 1-92)

TEXAS

Send your requests to:

> Texas Department of Health
> Bureau of Vital Statistics
> 1100 West 49th Street
> Austin, Texas 78756-3191

(512) 458-7111

Send your requests for Marriage or Divorce Certificates to:

> County Clerk
> County Courthouse
> (County Seat), Texas

Cost for a certified Birth Certificate	$11.00
Cost for a wallet-size Birth Certificate	$11.00
Cost for the verification of a Marriage or Divorce Certificate	$9.00
Cost for a certified Death Certificate	$9.00
Cost for a duplicate copy of a death record, when ordered at the same time	$3.00

The Texas Department of Health has birth and death records from January 1, 1903. They also have marriage applications from January 1, 1966 and reports of divorce from January 1, 1968. They will verify marriage and divorce information only if you present your request in person, not by mail; however, certificates must be issued by the County Clerk. '

If your request is urgent you may call (512) 458-7364 and charge your certificates to your Visa or MasterCard. There is a $10.00 fee for this service.

The Local Records Division of the Texas State Library (1201 Brazos Street, P.O. Box 12927, Austin, TX 78711-2927; Tel. 512-463-5465) has an extensive collection of Texas county vital records.

The Family History Library of The Church of Jesus Christ of Latter-day Saints in Salt Lake City, Utah has microfilmed many of the original and published vital records and church registers of Texas. For details on their holdings please consult your nearest Family History Center.

TEXAS DEPARTMENT OF HEALTH
BUREAU OF VITAL STATISTICS
1100 WEST 49TH STREET
AUSTIN, TEXAS 78756-3191
PHONE (512) 458-7111

APPLICATION FOR CERTIFIED COPY OF BIRTH OR DEATH CERTIFICATE

BIRTH ☐   ## DEATH ☐

REQUESTED   # REQUESTED
_____ CERTIFIED COPIES X $11.00= _____   _____ CERTIFIED COPY X $9.00 =_____
_____ WALLET-SIZE X $11.00   = _____   _____ EXTRA COPIES X $3.00   =_____
                TOTAL ENCLOSED = _____   **TOTAL ENCLOSED = _____**

PLEASE PRINT

1. NAME ON
   RECORD _____
                    FIRST   MIDDLE   LAST

2. DATE OF
   EVENT_____
            MONTH   DAY   YEAR

3. PLACE OF
   EVENT_____
            CITY   or   COUNTY

4. FATHER'S
   NAME _____
                    FIRST   MIDDLE   LAST

5. MOTHER'S
   MAIDEN NAME _____
                    FIRST   MIDDLE   LAST

6. ADDITIONAL IDENTIFYING INFORMATION FOR DEATH CERTIFICATE.

   SOCIAL SECURITY NUMBER OF DECEASED _____

   BIRTH DATE _____

   BIRTH PLACE, ETC. _____

7. APPLICANT'S NAME: _____ 8. TELEPHONE #: (_____)_____
                                                                    (MON-FRI 8:00-5:00)

9. MAILING ADDRESS: _____
                    STREET ADDRESS   CITY   STATE   ZIP

10. RELATIONSHIP TO PERSON NAMED IN ITEM 1: _____

11. PURPOSE FOR OBTAINING THIS RECORD: _____

WARNING: THE PENALTY FOR KNOWINGLY MAKING A FALSE STATEMENT IN THIS FORM CAN BE 2-10 YEARS IN PRISON AND A FINE OF UP TO $10,000. (HEALTH AND SAFETY CODE, CHAPTER 678, SEC.195.003)

_____   _____
SIGNATURE OF APPLICANT   DATE

IDENTIFICATION TYPE_____   NUMBER_____
             Drivers License, I.D. Card, etc.   on Drivers License, I.D. Card, etc

FEES ARE SUBJECT TO CHANGE WITHOUT NOTICE (CALL 512-458-7111 FOR FEE VERIFICATION). THE SEARCHING OR INDEXING FEE IS NON-REFUNDABLE EVEN IF A RECORD IS NOT FOUND.

BIRTH RECORDS ARE CONFIDENTIAL FOR 50 YEARS AND DEATH RECORDS ARE CONFIDENTIAL FOR 25 YEARS; THEREFORE, ISSUANCE IS RESTRICTED. OTHER RECORDS MAY BE OBTAINED WHEN SUFFICIENT INFORMATION FOR IDENTIFICATION IS PROVIDED.

ADMINISTRATIVE RULES REQUIRE THA˙   ˙L IDENTIFYING INFORMATION (ITEMS 1-5), RELATIONSHIP (ITEM 10), AND PURPOSE (ITEᎥ   ) ISSUE THE RECORD.

VS-141 REV. 11/91

UTAH

Cost for a certified Birth Certificate	$12.00
Cost for a certified Death Certificate	$9.00
Cost for a duplicate copy, when ordered at the same time	$5.00

The Bureau of Vital Records and Health Statistics has birth and death records from January 1, 1905. They keep marriage and divorce records from January 1, 1978, but these are not always available to the public. If you do not know the exact date that the birth or death occurred there is a $50.00 fee for a search of their files. Contact the County Clerk in the county where the event occurred for divorce and marriage certificates.

If your request is urgent you may call and charge your certificates to your Visa, Discover, or MasterCard. There is a $15.00 fee for this service.

The Family History Library of The Church of Jesus Christ of Latter-day Saints in Salt Lake City, Utah has microfilmed many of the original and published vital records and church registers of Utah. For details on their holdings please consult your nearest Family History Center.

INFORMATION

Certificates for births that occurred in Utah since 1905 are on file in this office. Persons who were born in Utah and have no birth certificate on file may make application to file a Delayed Registration of Birth. Application forms for Delayed Registration of Birth must be obtained from this office. It is a violation of Utah State law for any person to obtain, possess, use, sell or furnish for any purpose of deception, a birth certificate or certified copy thereof.

INSTRUCTIONS—FEES ARE EFFECTIVE JULY 1. 1990

1. An application must be completed for each birth certificate requested.

2. If the applicant is not the person whose birth certificate is being requested, the reason for requesting the record must be provided.

3. There is a fee of $12.00 for each search of our files. This includes $3.00 to be used for Child Abuse Prevention programs. The search includes the year the event is reported to have occurred and two years on either side of that year. Each additional five years to be searched requires an additional fee of $12.00. The entire file of birth certificates from 1905 to the present will be searched for the fee of $50.00. One certified copy of the record is issued, or a certificate of search if the record is not found. Additional certified copies of this record ordered at the same time are $5.00 each.

4. Send the completed application and required fee to the Bureau of Vital Records and Health Statistics, 288 North 1460 West, P.O. Box 16700, Salt Lake City, Utah 84116-0700.

INDENTIFYING   INFORMATION

FULL NAME OF CHILD AT BIRTH _____

DATE OF BIRTH _____

PLACE OF BIRTH (City) _____ (County) _____

FULL NAME OF FATHER _____

BIRTHPLACE OF FATHER _____

FULL MAIDEN NAME OF MOTHER _____

BIRTHPLACE OF MOTHER _____

APPLICANT

Please state your relationship and/or the reason for requesting certified copy(s).

_____

Signature of Applicant _____ Date _____

Address of Applicant _____ Telephone Number _____

Number of copies requested   Birth certificate copy ____)
  and amount of fee: or   ) $12.00 for first copy
                                    Laminated birth card   ____)

                                    Number of extra copies ____ $ 5.00 each after first copy

If copies are to be mailed to address other than above, specify name and mailing address:

_____
              Name   Address

UDH-BVR-1 Revised 6/90

UTAH DEPARTMENT OF HEALTH
APPLICATION FOR CERTIFIED COPY OF A DEATH CERTIFICATE

INFORMATION

Death certificates for deaths that occurred in
Utah since 1905 are on file in this office.

INSTRUCTIONS—FEES ARE EFFECTIVE JULY 1, 1990

1. An application must be completed for each death certificate requested.

2. If the applicant is not a member of the immediate family of the deceased person, the reason for requesting the record must be provided.

3. There is a fee of $9.00 for each search of our files. The search includes the year the event is reported to have occurred and two years on either side of that year. Each additional five years to be searched requires an additional fee of $9.00. The entire file of death certificates from 1905 to the present will be searched for the fee of $50.00. One certified copy of the record is issued, or a certificate of search if the record is not found. Additional certified copies of the same record at the same time are $5.00 each.

4. Send the completed application and required fee to the Bureau of Vital Records and Health Statistics, 288 North 1460 West, P.O. Box 16700, Salt Lake City, Utah 84116-0700.

INDENTIFYING INFORMATION

FULL NAME OF DECEASED _____ SOCIAL SECURITY NO. _____

DATE OF DEATH _____(If not known, specify years to be searched)_____

PLACE OF DEATH (City) _____ (County) _____

BIRTHPLACE OF DECEDENT (State or County) _____DATE OF BIRTH OF DECEDENT _____

USUAL RESIDENCE OF DECEDENT (City & State) _____

FULL NAME OF FATHER _____

FULL MAIDEN NAME OF MOTHER _____

IF DECEASED WAS MARRIED, NAME OF SPOUSE _____

APPLICANT

Reason for Requesting Certified Copy (include your relationship to the person whose certificate is being requested).

_____

Signature of Applicant _____ Date _____

Address of Applicant _____ Telephone Number _____

Number of copies requested _____Amount of Fee Attached _____

If copies are to be mailed to address other than above, specify name and mailing address:

_____

               Name   **Address**

Send your requests for records up to ten years old to:

Vermont Department of Health
Vital Records Unit
108 Cherry Street
P.O. Box 70
Burlington, Vermont 05402-0070

(802) 863-7275; (800) 642-3323, ext. 7275 (inside Vermont)

Send your request for records more than ten years old to:

General Services Center
Public Records Division
U.S. Route 2, Middlesex
Drawer 33
Montpelier, Vermont 05633-7601

(802) 828-3286

Cost for a certified Birth Certificate	$5.00
Cost for a certified Marriage or Divorce Certificate	$5.00
Cost for a certified Death Certificate	$5.00

The Vermont Department of Health keeps birth, marriage, divorce, and death records for the past 10 years. They do not charge for a verification of a birth, marriage, divorce, or death record.

The Vermont Historical Society (Pavilion Building, 109 State Street, Montpelier, VT 05609-0901; Tel. 802-828-2291) has an extensive collection of records.

The Family History Library of The Church of Jesus Christ of Latter-day Saints in Salt Lake City, Utah has microfilmed many of the original and published vital records and church registers of Vermont. They have microfilm copies of the vital records from 1760 to 1908. For details on their holdings please consult your nearest Family History Center.

Application for Vital Record
BIRTH CERTIFICATE

REQUEST FOR (Check one): _____ Certified Copy _____Verification _____ Record Search

INSTRUCTIONS

Public Records, US Rte 2 - Middlesex, 133 State Street, Montpelier, VT 05 633-7601
(802) 828-3286

Type or print all information clearly.
Sign and date application and return it with your check or money order (made payable to the Vermont Department of Health) to the address shown below. **Do not mail cash.**

Fees:
Certified Copy $5.00
Verification   no charge
Record Search   no charge

Amount enclosed _____

BIRTH INFORMATION

Name on birth certificate _____ Sex _____

Date of birth _____ Town or city of birth _____

Name of father _____

Maiden name of mother _____

APPLICANT INFORMATION

Your name _____

Address _____

_____

Town _____ State _____ Zip _____

Phone number (_____) _____

Your relationship to person on birth certificate _____

Intended use of certificate:

_____ Social Security   _____ School Enrollment

_____ Passport   _____ Driver's License

_____ Family History   _____ Other: Specify:

Signature _____ Date _____

Return to: Vermont Department of Health, Vital Records Unit
Box 70, Burlington, VT 05402
(telephone 863-7275 or 1-800-642-3323, ext. 7275)

Application for Vital Record
MARRIAGE CERTIFICATE

REQUEST FOR (Check one): ____ Certified Copy ____ Verification ____ Record Search

MARRIAGE INFORMATION

Date of Marriage _____   Town of Marriage _____

Groom: **Bride:**
Name _____   Name _____

Date of Birth: _____   Date of Birth: _____

Name of Father _____   Name of Father _____

Name of Mother _____   Name of Mother _____

APPLICANT INFORMATION

Your name _____

Address _____

_____

Town _____   State _____   Zip _____

Phone number (_____) _____

Your relationship to couple on certificate _____

Intended use of certificate:

_____ Proof of Marriage

_____ Family History

_____ Other: Specify: _____

Signature _____   Date _____

Application for Vital Record
DIVORCE CERTIFICATE

FOR OFFICE USE ONLY:
ID# _____
CPA# _____
REC# _____

REQUEST FOR (Check one): ____ Certified Copy ____ Verification ____ Record Search

INSTRUCTIONS

Type or print all information clearly.
Sign and date application and return it with your check or money order (made payable to the Vermont Department of Health) to the address shown below. **Do not mall cash.**

Fees:
Certified Copy $5.00
Verification no charge
Record Search no charge

Amount enclosed _____

DIVORCE INFORMATION

Husband's Name _____

Wife's Name _____

Date Divorce became final _____

County of Divorce _____

Date of Marriage _____

APPLICANT INFORMATION

Your name _____

Address _____

_____

Town _____ State _____ Zip _____

Phone number (_____) _____

Your relationship to people on certificate_____

Intended use of certificate:

____ Proof of Divorce

____ Personal Use

____ Other: Specify: _____

Signature _____ Date _____

Return to: Vermont Department of Health, Vital Records Unit
Box 70, Burlington, VT 05402
(telephone 863-7275 or 1-800-642-3323, ext. 7275)

Application for Vital Record
DEATH CERTIFICATE

REQUEST FOR (Check one): ____ Certified Copy ____ Verification ____ Record Search

DEATH INFORMATION

Name on death certificate _____ Sex _____

Date of death _____ Town or city of death _____

Date of birth _____ City and state of birth _____

Age at death _____ Name of spouse _____

APPLICANT INFORMATION

Your name _____

Address _____

_____

Town _____ State _____ Zip _____

Phone number (_____) _____

Your relationship to person on death certificate _____

Intended use of certificate:

____ Benefits   ____ Family History

____ Settlement of Estate   ____ Other: Specify

Signature _____ Date _____

Return to: Vermont Department of Health, Vital Records Unit
Box 70, Burlington, VT 05402
(telephone 863-7275 or 1-800-642-3323, ext. 7275)

VIRGINIA

Cost for a certified Birth Certificate	$5.00
Cost for a short form plastic Birth Card	$5.00
Cost for a certified Marriage or Divorce Certificate	$5.00
Cost for a certified Death Certificate	$5.00

The Virginia Division of Vital Records has records from January 1, 1853. Birth and death records were not routinely filed between 1896 and 1912. County Clerks have vital records that are much earlier than the records of the Division of Vital Records.

The Virginia State Library and Archives (11th Street, Richmond, VA 23219-3491; Tel. 804-786-2306) has birth and death records from 1853 to 1896 and marriage records from 1853 to 1935.

The Family History Library of The Church of Jesus Christ of Latter-day Saints in Salt Lake City, Utah has microfilmed original and published vital records and church registers of Virginia. For details on their holdings please consult your nearest Family History Center.

VS6-2/91

COMMONWEALTH OF VIRGINIA
APPLICATION FOR A CERTIFICATION OF A BIRTH RECORD

1 FULL NAME AT BIRTH			**DO NOT WRITE IN THIS SPACE**
2 DATE OF BIRTH	SEX	COLOR OR RACE	
3 PLACE OF BIRTH	**VIRGINIA**		
4 FULL NAME OF FATHER	ENCLOSED IS $ _____		SEARCHED BY _____
5 FULL MAIDEN NAME OF MOTHER	FOR _____ PAPER CERTIFICATIONS ($5.00 EACH)		☐ INDEX ☐ DF ☐ BOOK ☐ HOS
6 NAME OF PHYSICIAN OR MIDWIFE AT BIRTH (IF KNOWN)	**NOTE:** IF SHORT FORM PLASTIC BIRTH CARD DESIRED, CHECK HERE ☐ ($5.00 EACH)		RECHECKED BY _____
7 NAME OF HOSPITAL (IF ANY) WHERE BIRTH OCCURRED			
8 HAS ORIGINAL NAME EVER BEEN CHANGED OTHER THAN BY MARRIAGE? YES ☐ NO ☐	IF SO, WHAT WAS ORIGINAL NAME?		I.N.
9 ARE YOU THE PERSON NAMED IN LINE 1? YES ☐ NO ☐	IF NOT, WHAT IS YOUR RELATIONSHIP?		
10 SPECIFIC PURPOSE FOR WHICH THIS CERTIFICATION IS REQUESTED			
11 SIGNATURE OF APPLICANT ▶			
12 STREET ADDRESS			
13 CITY, STATE AND ZIP CODE			ISSUED

DO NOT REMOVE THIS STUB

IMPORTANT

Virginia statutes require a fee of $5.00 be charged for each certification of a vital record or for a search of the files when no certification is made. Make check or money order payable to STATE HEALTH DEPARTMENT. **THERE IS A $15.00 SERVICE CHARGE FOR RETURNED CHECKS.**

Birth records were not routinely filed during the period 1896-1912. If birth occurred then, or if no record is on file, other types of evidence may be acceptable to using agencies.

Birth records are, by statute, confidential. Certifications may be issued to the individual registrant, members of the registrant's immediate family, the registrant's guardian, their respective legal representative, or by court order.

Warning: Making a false application for a vital record is a felony under state as well as federal law.

PLEASE NOTE!
PRINT YOUR NAME AND COMPLETE MAILING ADDRESS IN THIS SPACE— THIS IS A MAILING INSERT AND WILL BE USED TO MAIL THE CERTIFICATION TO YOU.

THANK YOU!

Send To:
Division of Vital Records
P. O. Box 1000
Richmond, Virginia 23208-1000

NAME	
STREET OR ROUTE	
CITY OR TOWN, STATE, ZIP CODE	

COMMONWEALTH OF VIRGINIA
APPLICATION FOR A CERTIFIED COPY OF A MARRIAGE RECORD

	DO NOT WRITE IN THIS SPACE
1 FULL NAME OF HUSBAND	
2 FULL MAIDEN NAME OF WIFE	
3 DATE OF MARRIAGE　　　　　COLOR OR RACE	**1st SEARCH BY** ☐ INDEX　☐ BOOK _____
4 CITY OR COUNTY IN WHICH MARRIAGE LICENSE WAS ISSUED　　VIRGINIA	**2nd SEARCH BY** ☐ INDEX　☐ BOOK _____
5 SPECIFIC PURPOSE FOR WHICH THIS CERTIFIED COPY IS REQUESTED	**CERTIFICATE NUMBER**
6 SIGNATURE OF ➤ APPLICANT	
7 STREET ADDRESS	
8 CITY, STATE AND ZIP CODE	ISSUED

ENCLOSED IS $_____ FOR _____ CERTIFIED COPIES ($5.00 EACH)

DO NOT REMOVE THIS STUB

IMPORTANT

As required by statute, a fee of $5.00 is charged for each certification of a vital record or for a search of the files when no certification is made. Make check or money order payable to the STATE HEALTH DEPARTMENT. Give all information possible in above application for record. If exact date is unknown, give approximate year of marriage. **THERE IS A $15.00 SERVICE CHARGE FOR RETURNED CHECKS.**

Certifications of marriage records may also be obtained from Clerk of Court in city or county in which marriage license was issued.

NAME
STREET OR ROUTE
CITY OR TOWN, STATE, ZIP CODE

PLEASE NOTE!

PRINT YOUR NAME AND COMPLETE MAILING ADDRESS IN THIS SPACE—

THIS IS A MAILING INSERT AND WILL BE USED TO MAIL THE CERTIFIED COPY TO YOU.

THANK YOU!

Send To:

Division of Vital Records
P.O. Box 1000
Richmond, Virginia 23208-1000

COMMONWEALTH OF VIRGINIA
APPLICATION FOR A CERTIFIED COPY OF A DIVORCE RECORD

	DO NOT WRITE IN THIS SPACE
1 FULL NAME OF HUSBAND	
2 FULL MAIDEN NAME OF WIFE	**1st SEARCH BY** ☐ INDEX ☐ BOOK _____
3 DATE OF DIVORCE · COLOR OR RACE	**2nd SEARCH BY** ☐ INDEX ☐ BOOK _____
4 PLACE OF DIVORCE · VIRGINIA	CERTIFICATE NUMBER
5 SPECIFIC PURPOSE FOR WHICH THIS CERTIFIED COPY IS REQUESTED	
6 SIGNATURE OF APPLICANT ▶	
7 STREET ADDRESS	
8 CITY, STATE AND ZIP CODE	
ENCLOSED IS $ _____ FOR _____ CERTIFIED COPIES ($5.00 EACH)	ISSUED

DO NOT REMOVE THIS STUB

IMPORTANT

As required by statute, a fee of $5.00 is charged for each certification of a vital record or for a search of the files when no certification is made. Make check or money order payable to the STATE HEALTH DEPARTMENT. Give all information possible in above application for a record. If exact date is unknown, give approximate year. **THERE IS A $15.00 SERVICE CHARGE FOR RETURNED CHECKS.**

Divorce records were not routinely filed with Division of Vital Records prior to 1918. If divorce occurred prior to that time, or if you desire a full copy of decree, apply to Clerk of Court in city or county where decree granted.

NAME
STREET OR ROUTE
CITY OR TOWN, STATE, ZIP CODE

PLEASE NOTE!

PRINT YOUR NAME AND COMPLETE MAILING ADDRESS IN THIS SPACE— THIS IS A MAILING INSERT AND WILL BE USED TO MAIL THE CERTIFIED COPY TO YOU.

THANK YOU!

Send To:

DIVISION OF VITAL RECORDS
P.O. Box 1000
Richmond, Virginia 23208-1000

COMMONWEALTH OF VIRGINIA
APPLICATION FOR A CERTIFIED COPY OF A DEATH RECORD

1 FULL NAME OF DECEASED	**DO NOT WRITE IN THIS SPACE**
2 DATE OF DEATH SEX COLOR OR RACE	
3 PLACE OF DEATH VIRGINIA	
4 NAME OF HOSPITAL (IF ANY, WHERE DEATH OCCURRED)	1st SEARCH BY _____ ☐ INDEX ☐ BOOK ☐ HOSP.
5 IF MARRIED, NAME OF HUSBAND OR WIFE	2nd SEARCH BY _____ ☐ INDEX ☐ BOOK ☐ HOSP.
6 NAME OF FUNERAL DIRECTOR (IF KNOWN)	
7 ADDRESS OF FUNERAL DIRECTOR	CERTIFICATE NUMBER
8 HOW ARE YOU RELATED TO THE PERSON NAMED ON LINE 1?	
9 SPECIFIC PURPOSE FOR WHICH THIS CERTIFIED COPY IS REQUESTED	
10 SIGNATURE OF APPLICANT ➤	
11 STREET ADDRESS	
12 CITY STATE AND ZIP CODE	
ENCLOSED IS $ _____ FOR _____ CERTIFIED COPIES	ISSUED

DO NOT REMOVE THIS STUB

IMPORTANT

Virginia statutes require a fee of $5.00 for a certification of a death record or for a search of the files when no certification is issued. Make check or money order payable to STATE HEALTH DEPARTMENT. **THERE IS A $15.00 SERVICE CHARGE FOR RETURNED CHECKS.**

Death records were not routinely filed during the period 1896-1912. However, some records are available in the health departments of a few of the larger cities.

Death records are, by statute, confidential. Certifications may be issued to surviving relatives, their legal representatives, an authorized agency acting in their behalf, or by court order.

Warning: Making a false application for a vital record is a felony under state as well as federal law.

PLEASE NOTE!
PRINT YOUR NAME AND COMPLETE MAILING ADDRESS IN THIS SPACE— THIS IS A MAILING INSERT

THANK YOU!

Send To:
Division of Vital Records
P. O. Box 1000
Richmond, Virginia 23208-1000

NAME
STREET OR ROUTE
CITY OR TOWN, STATE, ZIP CODE

Send your requests to:

Washington State Department of Health
Center for Health Statistics
P.O. Box 9709
Olympia, Washington 98507-9709

(206) 753-5936

Send your requests for pre-1968 Marriage Certificates to:

County Auditor
County Courthouse
(County Seat), Washington

Cost for a certified Birth Certificate	$11.00
Cost for an heirloom Birth Certificate	$25.00
Cost for a certified Marriage Certificate or Divorce Record	$11.00
Cost for a certified Death Certificate	$11.00

The Washington Center for Health Statistics has birth and death records from July 1, 1907 and marriage and divorce records from January 1, 1968. The Center does not have printed application forms for marriage, divorce, and death records. If no record is found $3.00 of the fee will be returned to you. The County Clerks also maintain vital records and have records much earlier than those at the State Office.

If your request is urgent you may call (206) 753-5842 and charge your certificates to your Visa, Discover, or MasterCard. There is a $21.00 fee for the first certificate and $16.00 for the second certificate.

The Washington State Archives and Records Center (12th and Washington Streets, P.O. Box 9000, Olympia, WA 98504; Tel. 206-586-1492) has an index to death records from 1907 to 1986.

The Family History Library of The Church of Jesus Christ of Latter-day Saints in Salt Lake City, Utah has microfilmed many of the original and published vital records and church registers of Washington. They have microfilm copies of birth records and indexes from 1907 to 1959 and death records from 1907 to 1952, with indexes from 1907 to 1949. For details on their holdings please consult your nearest Family History Center.

This is your mailing label. It is required to send the certified copy to the address you specify.

NAME _____

MAILING ADDRESS _____

CITY _____ STATE _____ ZIP _____

WASHINGTON STATE BIRTH APPLICATION

QTY _____ CERTIFIED COPY @ $11 EACH (28 0005)   QTY _____ ADOPTION SEALED FILE @ $15 EACH (31 0007)

QTY _____ HEIRLOOM COPY @ $25 EACH (30 0006)   QTY _____ PATERNITY SEALED FILE @ $15 EACH (32 0008)

WAS THIS PERSON ADOPTED? _____

HAVE YOU RECEIVED A COPY BEFORE? _____

NAME ON RECORD _____
First   Middle   Last

DATE OF BIRTH _____
Month   Day   Year (or 10 year period)

PLACE OF BIRTH _____
City   County   Hospital

FATHER'S FULL NAME _____
First   Middle   Last

MOTHER'S FULL MAIDEN NAME _____
First   Middle   Last

REQUESTOR'S NAME AND ADDRESS REQUIRED

NAME _____ PHONE _____

MAILING ADDRESS _____

CITY _____ STATE _____ ZIP _____

MAKE CHECK/MONEY ORDER PAYABLE TO DEPARTMENT OF HEALTH

FOR OFFICE USE ONLY

REFUND AMT $ _____

☐ SIE   001 04 41 28 X 8
         02K 04 21 03 X 3

☐ OP   001 04 41 28

☐ H   001 04 41 30 X 17
         04 41 28 X 8

☐ AS   001 04 41 31 X 15

☐ PS   001 04 41 32 X 15

☐ NR   02K 04 21 03 X 3

DOH 110-011A Front (Rev. 6/92)

⌐ 04414 ⌐

WEST VIRGINIA

Send your requests to:

West Virginia Department of Health
Division of Vital Statistics
Capitol Complex
Charleston, West Virginia 25305

(304) 558-2931

Certificates are also issued by:

County Clerk
County Courthouse
(County Seat), West Virginia

Send your requests for Divorce Records to:

Clerk
Circuit Court
(County Seat), West Virginia

Cost for a certified Birth Certificate	$5.00
Cost for a certified Marriage Certificate	$5.00
Cost for a certified Death Certificate	$5.00

The West Virginia Division of Vital Statistics has birth and death records from January 1, 1920 and marriage records from January 1, 1964. They do not have a separate form for requesting a copy of a marriage certificate. For marriages before 1964 write to the County Clerk in the county where the marriage took place. The Division of Vital Statistics can obtain records as early as the 1880s if you write to them with a request. They have an index of divorces from 1968 but do not issue divorce certificates. The County Clerks have much earlier vital records on file than those kept at the Division of Vital Statistics.

If your request is urgent you may call and charge your certificates to your Visa, Discover, or MasterCard. There is a $10.00 fee for this service, $15.00 if you want express service.

The Family History Library of The Church of Jesus Christ of Latter-day Saints in Salt Lake City, Utah has microfilmed many of the original and published vital records and church registers of West Virginia. They have microfilm copies of vital records from 1853 to 1860. For details on their holdings please consult your nearest Family History Center.

APPLICATION FOR CERTIFIED COPY OF CERTIFICATE OF BIRTH OR DEATH

WEST VIRGINIA DEPARTMENT OF HEALTH — DIVISION OF VITAL STATISTICS

CHARLESTON, WEST VIRGINIA 25305

NOTE: FEE OF $5.00 FOR EACH COPY
MUST ACCOMPANY THIS APPLICATION
CASH IS SENT AT SENDERS RISK.
PLEASE SEND ME _____ COPIES.

FOR OFFICE USE ONLY

WHEN STAMPED PAID
THIS IS YOUR RECEIPT

CASH	
CHECK	
MONEY ORD.	
NO. COPIES	
AMOUNT	

CHECK ONE

| BIRTH CERTIF. | | DEATH CERTIF. | |

BIRTH OR DEATH

NAME— FIRST   MIDDLE   LAST

DATE— MONTH   DAY   YEAR

PLACE— CITY OR POST OFFICE   COUNTY   STATE

ONLY BIRTH

FATHER'S NAME— FIRST   MIDDLE   LAST

MAIDEN NAME OF MOTHER— FIRST   MIDDLE   LAST

ONLY DEATH

NAME OF FUNERAL DIRECTOR—

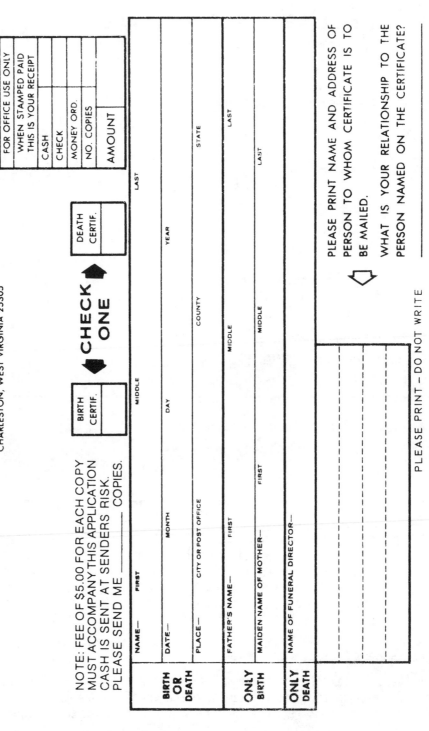

PLEASE PRINT NAME AND ADDRESS OF
PERSON TO WHOM CERTIFICATE IS TO
BE MAILED.

WHAT IS YOUR RELATIONSHIP TO THE
PERSON NAMED ON THE CERTIFICATE? _____

PLEASE PRINT – DO NOT WRITE

HAVE COUNTY RECORDS BEEN SEARCHED?   YES ☐   NO ☐

WISCONSIN

Send your requests to:

Wisconsin Department of Health and Social Services
Section of Vital Statistics
1 West Wilson Street
P.O. Box 309
Madison, Wisconsin 53701-0309

(608) 266-0330, (608) 266-1371, (608) 266-1372

Vital records are also kept by the:
County Clerk
County Courthouse
(County Seat), Wisconsin

Cost for a certified Birth Certificate	$10.00
Cost for a certified Marriage or Divorce Certificate	$7.00
Cost for a certified Death Certificate	$7.00
Cost for a duplicate copy, when ordered at the same time	$2.00

The Wisconsin Department of Health has birth, marriage, and death records as early as 1814, but they are sparse; between 1865 and 1907 less than half of the records were ever filed. The Department has a list of the earliest records on file arranged by county. Complete birth, marriage, divorce, and death records begin January 1, 1907.

If your request is urgent you may call and charge your certificates to your Visa or MasterCard. There is a $5.00 for this service.

The Family History Library of The Church of Jesus Christ of Latter-day Saints in Salt Lake City, Utah has microfilmed many of the original and published vital records and church registers of Wisconsin. They have microfilm copies of birth records from 1852 to 1907 and delayed birth records from 1937 to 1941; an index to marriage records from 1852 to 1907; and death records from 1862 to 1907. For details on their holdings please consult your nearest Family History Center.

Department of Health and Social Services
Division of Health
DOH 5291 (Rev. 07/91)

STATE OF WISCONSIN
Chap. 69, Wis Stats.

WISCONSIN **BIRTH** CERTIFICATE APPLICATION

Please complete this form and return it to the following address with a self-addressed stamped envelope and appropriate fee. Please make check or money order payable to "CENTER FOR HEALTH STATISTICS"

Division of Health
Section of Vital Statistics
P.O. Box 309
Madison, WI 53701-0309

PENALTIES: Any person who wilfully and knowingly makes false application for a birth certificate shall be fined not more than $10,000, or imprisoned not more than 2 years or both.

APPLICANT INFORMATION

THE FOLLOWING INFORMATION IS ABOUT THE PERSON **COMPLETING THIS APPLICATION:**

YOUR Name: (Please Print) _____

YOUR Signature: _____ TODAY'S DATE: _____

YOUR Daytime Phone Number: (___) ___ - ___

YOUR Address: _____
Street: _____

Mail To:
(If Different)

City: _____ State: _____ Zip: _____

RELATIONSHIP TO PERSON NAMED ON CERTIFICATE

According to Wisconsin State Statute, a **CERTIFIED** copy of a **BIRTH** record is only available to persons with a "Direct and Tangible Interest".

Please complete the box which indicates YOUR RELATIONSHIP to the PERSON NAMED on the record:

☐ A. I AM the PERSON NAMED on the record.

☐ B. I AM the PARENT of the PERSON NAMED on the record, and my parental rights have not been terminated. **NOTE:** In the case of an out-of-wedlock child, the father's rights must have been established by a court or by a paternity affidavit before he may obtain a copy of the record.

☐ C. I AM the Legal Custodian or Guardian of the PERSON NAMED on the record.

☐ D. I AM a member of the immediate family of the PERSON NAMED on the record. *PLEASE CIRCLE ONE:* (Only those listed below qualify as Immediate Family)

Spouse   Child   Brother   Sister   Grandparent

☐ E. I AM a representative authorized, in writing, by any of the before mentioned (A through D), including an attorney:
Specify who you represent: _____

☐ F. I can demonstrate that the information from the record is necessary for the determination or protection of a personal or property right for myself/my agency/my client.
Specify Interest: _____

☐ G. Other: Non-certified copy only. **NOTE:** Out-of-wedlock births are only available to any of the before mentioned (A through F).

FEES

☐ $10.00   First Copy
☐ $ 2.00   Each additional copy of the same record issued at the same time.
The fee is for a search and first copy. In the event the record is not found, the fee is not refundable.

BIRTH INFORMATION

FIRST	MIDDLE	LAST (MAIDEN)

SEX	MONTH	DAY	YEAR	CITY	COUNTY

MOTHER'S MAIDEN LAST NAME	FIRST NAME	MIDDLE NAME

FATHER'S LAST NAME	FIRST NAME	MIDDLE NAME

CERTIFICATE NUMBER IF KNOWN _____

FOR OFFICE USE ONLY

FILE DATE _____   MOTHER'S CO. _____

Printed on
Recycled Paper

WISCONSIN **MARRIAGE** CERTIFICATE APPLICATION

Please complete this form and return it to the following address with a self-addressed stamped envelope and appropriate fee. Please make check or money order payable to "CENTER FOR HEALTH STATISTICS".

Division of Health
Section of Vital Statistics
P.O. Box 309
Madison, WI 53701-0309

PENALTIES: Any person who wilfully and knowingly makes false application for a marriage certificate shall be fined not more than $10,000, or imprisoned not more than 90 days or both.

APPLICANT INFORMATION

THE FOLLOWING INFORMATION IS ABOUT THE PERSON **COMPLETING THIS APPLICATION:**

YOUR Name: (Please Print) _____

YOUR Signature: _____ TODAY'S DATE: _____

YOUR Daytime Phone Number: ( ) - _____

YOUR Address: _____
Street:

Mail To:
(If Different)

City: _____ State: _____ Zip: _____

RELATIONSHIP TO PERSON NAMED ON CERTIFICATE

According to Wisconsin State Statute, a **CERTIFIED** copy of a **MARRIAGE** record is only available to persons with a "Direct and Tangible Interest".

Please complete the box which indicates YOUR RELATIONSHIP to either of the PERSONS NAMED on the record:

☐ A. I AM one of the people NAMED on the record.
☐ B. I AM the PARENT of one of the people NAMED on the record.
☐ C. I AM the Legal Custodian or Guardian of one of the people NAMED on the record.
☐ D. I AM a member of the immediate family of one of the people NAMED on the record. *PLEASE CIRCLE ONE:* (Only those listed below qualify as Immediate Family)
    Spouse   Child   Brother   Sister   Grandparent
☐ E. I AM a representative authorized, in writing, by any of the before mentioned (A through D), including an attorney:
    Specify who you represent: _____
☐ F. I can demonstrate that the information from the record is necessary for the determination or protection of a personal or property right for myself/my agency/my client.
    Specify Interest: _____
☐ G. Other: Non-certified copy only.

FEES

☐ $7.00 First Copy
☐ $2.00 Each additional copy of the same record issued at the same time.
    NOTE: The fee is for a search and first copy. In the event the record is not found, the fee is not refundable.

MARRIAGE INFORMATION

FULL NAME OF GROOM

FULL MAIDEN NAME OF BRIDE

PLACE OF MARRIAGE:	CITY, VILLAGE, TOWNSHIP	COUNTY

DATE OF MARRIAGE:

WISCONSIN **DIVORCE** CERTIFICATE APPLICATION

Please complete this form and return it to the following address with a self-addressed stamped envelope and appropriate fee. Please make check or money order payable to "CENTER FOR HEALTH STATISTICS".

Division of Health
Section of Vital Statistics
P.O. Box 309
Madison, WI 53701-0309

PENALTIES: Any person who wilfully and knowingly makes false application for a divorce certificate shall be fined not more than $10,000, or imprisoned not more than 90 days or both.

APPLICANT INFORMATION

THE FOLLOWING INFORMATION IS ABOUT THE PERSON **COMPLETING THIS APPLICATION:**

YOUR Name: (Please Print) _____

YOUR Signature: _____ TODAY'S DATE: _____

YOUR Daytime Phone Number: (___) ___ - ___

YOUR Address: _____ Mail To:
Street: _____   (If Different)

City: _____ State: ___ Zip: ___

RELATIONSHIP TO PERSON NAMED ON CERTIFICATE

According to Wisconsin State Statute, a **CERTIFIED** copy of a **DIVORCE** record is only available to persons with a "Direct and Tangible Interest".

Please complete the box which indicates YOUR RELATIONSHIP to either of the PERSONS NAMED on the record:

☐ A. I AM one of the people NAMED on the record.
☐ B. I AM the PARENT of one of the people NAMED on the record.
☐ C. I AM the Legal Custodian or Guardian of one of the people NAMED on the record.
☐ D. I AM a member of the immediate family of one of the people NAMED on the record. *PLEASE CIRCLE ONE:* (Only those listed below qualify as Immediate Family.)
     Spouse   Child   Brother   Sister   Grandparent
☐ E. I AM a representative authorized, in writing, by any of the before mentioned (A through D), including an attorney:
     Specify who you represent: _____
☐ F. I can demonstrate that the information from the record is necessary for the determination or protection of a personal or property right for myself/my agency/my client.
     Specify Interest: _____
☐ G. Other: Non-certified copy only.

FEES

☐ $7.00 First Copy
☐ $2.00 Each additional copy of the same record issued at the same time.
     NOTE: The fee is for a search and first copy. In the event the record is not found, the fee is not refundable.

DIVORCE INFORMATION

FULL NAME OF HUSBAND

FULL MAIDEN NAME OF WIFE

PLACE OF DIVORCE:	CITY, VILLAGE, TOWNSHIP	COUNTY

DATE OF DIVORCE:	DIVORCE GRANTED TO: (Check One)
	☐ Husband ☐ Wife

Department of Health and Social Services
Division of Health
DH 5280 (Rev. 07/91)

State of Wisconsin
Chap. 69. Wis. Stat.
Section of Vital Statistics
P.O. Box 309
Madison, WI 53701-0309

APPLICATION FOR WISCONSIN **DEATH** CERTIFICATE

Please complete this form and return it to the above address with a self-addressed stamped envelope and appropriate fee. Please make check or money order payable to "CENTER FOR HEALTH STATISTICS"

PENALTIES: Any person who wilfully and knowingly makes false application for a death certificate shall be fined not more than $10,000, or imprisoned not more than 2 years or both.

APPLICANT INFORMATION

THE FOLLOWING INFORMATION IS ABOUT THE PERSON **COMPLETING THIS APPLICATION:**

YOUR Name: (Please Print) _____

YOUR Signature: _____ TODAY'S DATE: _____

YOUR Daytime Phone Number: ( ) - _____

YOUR Address: _____

Mail To:
(If Different)

RELATIONSHIP TO PERSON NAMED ON CERTIFICATE

According to Wisconsin State Statute, a **CERTIFIED** copy of a **DEATH** record is only available to persons with a "Direct and Tangible Interest".

Please complete the box which indicates YOUR RELATIONSHIP to the PERSON NAMED on the record:

☐ A. I AM the PARENT of the PERSON NAMED on the record.

☐ B. I AM the Legal Custodian or Guardian of the PERSON NAMED on the record.

☐ C. I AM a member of the immediate family of the PERSON NAMED on the record. *PLEASE CIRCLE ONE:* (Only those listed below qualify as Immediate Family)

    Spouse   Child   Brother   Sister   Grandparent

☐ D. I AM a representative authorized, in writing, by any of the before mentioned (A through D), including an attorney:
    Specify who you represent: _____

☐ E. I can demonstrate that the information from the record is necessary for the determination or protection of a personal or property right for myself/my agency/my client.
    Specify Interest: _____

☐ F. Other: Non-certified copy only.

FEES

☐ $7.00 First Copy
☐ $2.00 Each additional copy of the same record issued at the same time.
    NOTE: The fee is for a search and first copy. In the event the record is not found, the fee is not refundable.

DEATH INFORMATION

FULL NAME OF DECEDENT

PLACE OF DEATH:	CITY, VILLAGE, TOWNSHIP	COUNTY

DATE OF DEATH	DECEDENT'S SOCIAL SECURITY NUMBER

DECEDENT'S AGE/BIRTHDATE	DECEDENT'S OCCUPATION

DECEDENT'S SPOUSE	DECEDENT'S PARENTS

WYOMING

Send your requests to:

Wyoming State Vital Records Services
Hathaway Building
Cheyenne, Wyoming 82002

(307) 777-7591

Vital records are also kept by the:

County Clerk
County Courthouse
(County Seat), Wyoming

Cost for a certified Birth Certificate	$11.00
Cost for a certified Marriage or Divorce Certificate	$11.00
Cost for a certified Death Certificate	$ 9.00

The Wyoming State Vital Records Services has birth and death records from July 1909 and marriage and divorce records from May 1941. The records kept by the County Clerks are much earlier than those held by the State.

There are also records of interest at the Wyoming State Library (Supreme Court Building, Cheyenne, WY 82002-0600; Tel. 307-777-6333; FAX 307-777-6289).

The Family History Library of The Church of Jesus Christ of Latter-day Saints in Salt Lake City, Utah has microfilmed many of the original and published vital records and church registers of Wyoming. For details on their holdings please consult your nearest Family History Center.

STATE OF WYOMING
APPLICATION FOR CERTIFIED COPY OF BIRTH CERTIFICATE

A request for a certified copy of a birth certificate should be submitted on this form along with the fee of $11.00 per copy. Money orders or a personalized check from the person making the request should be made payable to VITAL RECORDS SERVICES. Please enclose a self-addressed, stamped envelope with the application.

Send to:
Vital Records Services
Hathaway Building
Cheyenne, WY 82002
(307) 777-7591

If you do not have a birth record on file, you will be sent instructions for filing a Delayed Birth Certificate, and your $11.00 fee will be retained as a searching fee.

Enclosed is $ _____ for _____ certified copy(s).

Full Name at Birth	First Name	Middle Name	Last Name (Maiden Name)
	If this birth could be recorded under another name, please list that name here:		
Sex	Date of Birth (Month, Day and Year)		City or County of Birth
Full Maiden Name of Mother	First Name	Middle Name	Last Name (Maiden Name)
Full Name of Father	First Name	Middle Name	Last Name
Signature of person whose certificate is being requested or parent named on certificate. (If under 18 years of age, signature of parent or legal guardian required. Legal guardian must submit a copy of guardianship papers.) ▶ _____			

Address to which copy is to be mailed: _____

_____

_____

W.S. 35-1-428 as amended by the 52nd Legislature requires Vital Records Services to collect a $5.00 surcharge on all certified copies and searches of the files to be deposited in the Wyoming Children's Trust Fund. This surcharge is included in the fee listed above. The fund is used to establish programs for the prevention of child abuse and neglect.

STATE OF WYOMING
APPLICATION FOR CERTIFIED COPY OF MARRIAGE OR DIVORCE CERTIFICATE

A request for a certified copy of a marriage or divorce certificate should be submitted on this form along with the fee of $11.00 per copy. A money order or a personalized check from the person making the request should be made payable to VITAL RECORDS SERVICES. Please enclose a self-addressed, stamped envelope with the application.

Send to:
Vital Records Services
Hathaway Building
Cheyenne, WY 82002
(307) 777-7591

If a record is not located, your $11.00 fee will be retained as a searching fee.

Type of record requested: (check one) Marriage _____ Divorce _____

Enclosed is $ _____ for _____ certified copy(s).

Name of Husband - First	Middle	Last
Name of Wife - First	Middle	Surname at time of Marriage
Date of occurrence (month, day, year)	Place of Occurrence - City or County	
Signature of Husband or Wife Named on Certificate ▶ _____		

Address to which copy is to be mailed: _____

_____

_____

W.S. 35-1-428 as amended by the 52nd Legislature requires Vital Records Services to collect a $5.00 surcharge on all certified copies and searches of the files to be deposited in the Wyoming Children's Trust Fund. This surcharge is included in the fee listed above. The fund is used to establish programs for the prevention of child abuse and neglect.

STATE OF WYOMING
APPLICATION FOR CERTIFIED COPY OF DEATH CERTIFICATE

A request for a certified copy of a death certificate should be submitted on this form along with the fee of $9.00 per copy. If the date of death is unknown, a searching fee of $11.00 for every five years searched is charged, which includes either a certified copy or verification of the record if one is found. A money order or a personalized check from the person making the request should be made payable to VITAL RECORDS SERVICES. Please enclose a self-addressed, stamped envelope with the application.

Send to: Vital Records Services
                                Hathaway Building
                                Cheyenne, WY 82002
                                (307) 777-7591

If a death record is not located, your fee will be retained as a searching fee.

Enclosed is $ _____ for _____ certified copy(s).

Full Name of Deceased - First	Middle Name	Last Name
Date of Death	Place of Death - City or County	
Name of Surviving Spouse		
Signature of person requesting certificate ▶ _____		
Relationship to Deceased (If funeral director, state the relationship of the person for whom you are obtaining the copies. Ex: Funeral director for spouse)		Purpose for Which Copy is Needed

Address of applicant: _____

_____

Address to which copy is to be mailed: _____
  (if different)

_____

_____

W.S. 35-1-428 as amended by the 52nd Legislature requires Vital Records Services to collect a $5.00 surcharge on all certified copies and searches of the files to be deposited in the Wyoming Children's Trust Fund. This surcharge is included in the fee listed above. The fund is used to establish programs for the prevention of child abuse and neglect.

AMERICAN SAMOA

Send your requests to:

> Registrar of Vital Statistics
> Vital Statistics Section
> Health Services Department
> LBJ Tropical Medical Center
> Pago Pago, American Samoa 96799

(011) (684) 633-1222

Cost for a certified Birth Certificate	$2.00
Cost for a certified Marriage Certificate	$2.00
Cost for a certified Death Certificate	$2.00

The Registrar of Vital Statistics has records from 1900. The Registrar only issues an application form for birth certificates.

The Family History Library of The Church of Jesus Christ of Latter-day Saints in Salt Lake City, Utah has microfilmed original and published vital records and church registers of American Samoa. For details on their holdings please consult your nearest Family History Center.

TO: _____

_____

_____

REFERENCE: _____

I REQUEST A CERTIFIED COPY OF MY BIRTH CERTIFICATE BE SENT TO THE
ABOVE ADDRESS TO ESTABLISH BIRTH IN THE UNITED STATES. THIS BIRTH
CERTIFICATE MUST HAVE A RAISED OR MULTI-COLORED STATE SEAL ON IT.
THE FOLLOWING INFORMATION IS PROVIDED TO ASSIST YOUR OFFICE IN
LOCATING MY BIRTH CERTIFICATE.

_____
SIGNATURE

NAME I WAS BORN UNDER:_____
FIRST   MIDDLE   MAIDEN   LAST

PLACE OF BIRTH:_____
CITY OR TOWN   COUNTY   STATE

DATE OF BIRTH:_____
MONTH   DAY   YEAR

SEX:_____   RACE:_____

FATHER'S NAME:_____
FIRST   MIDDLE   LAST

MOTHER'S MAIDEN NAME:_____
FIRST   MIDDLE   LAST

NAME OF HOSPITAL:_____

ENCLOSED FIND A MONEY ORDER IN THE AMMOUNT OF $_____

GUAM

Send your requests to:

> Office of Vital Statistics
> Department of Public Health and Social Services
> P.O. Box 2816
> Agana, Guam 96910

(011) (671) 734-2931

Cost for a certified Birth Certificate	$2.00
Cost for a certified Marriage Certificate	$2.00
Cost for a certified Death Certificate	$2.00

The Office of Vital Statistics has birth, marriage, and death records from October 26, 1901.

The Family History Library of The Church of Jesus Christ of Latter-day Saints in Salt Lake City, Utah has microfilmed original and published records of Guam. For details on their holdings please consult your nearest Family History Center.

OFFICE OF VITAL STATISTICS
Department of Public Health and Social Services
P.O. Box 2816
Agana, Guam 96910

APPLICATION FOR A COPY OF Birth /_/ Death /_/ Marriage /_/

INFORMATION FOR APPLICANT: It is absolutely essential that the name be accurately spelled and that the exact date - month, day and year - the exact place of birth, name of hospital be fully given in every application.

PRINT ALL ITEMS CLEARLY

1. NAME _____
            (First name)   (Middle)   (Last name at time of birth)

2. DATE OF BIRTH _____   DATE OF DEATH _____
                   (Month)   (Day)   (Year)   DATE OF MARRIAGE _____

3. PLACE OF BIRTH _____   PLACE OF DEATH _____
                   (Name of Hospital or village)

4. FATHER'S NAME _____
                      (First)   (Middle)   (Last)

5. MOTHER'S MAIDEN NAME _____
                              (First)   (Middle)   (Last)

6. NUMBER OF COPIES DESIRED _____Certificate. NUMBER, IF KNOWN _____

7. _____
        Relationship to person named in Item one above. If self, state "SELF"

NOTE: Copy of a birth or death record can be issued only to persons to whom the record relates, if of age, or a parent or other lawful representative.

IF THIS REQUEST IS NOT FOR YOUR OWN BIRTH RECORD OR THAT OF YOUR CHILD, PROPER WRITTEN AUTHORIZATION FROM THE PERSON MUST BE PRESENTED WITH THIS APPLICATION.

SIGN YOUR NAME AND ADDRESS BELOW

NAME _____

ADDRESS _____

CITY _____ STATE _____ ZIP CODE _____

FEE

PURSUANT TO PUBLIC LAW 10-44, Section 9324, a fee of $2.00 is now being charged for each certified copy issued.

APPLICANTS ARE ADVISED NOT TO SEND CASH BY MAIL. Fees must be paid at time application is made.   Money order should be made payable to the Treasurer of Guam. Stamps and foreign currency cannot be accepted.

PANAMA CANAL ZONE

Send your requests to:

Panama Canal Commission
Vital Statistics Unit
Unit 2300
APO AA 34011-5000

(011) (507) 52-7854, FAX (011) (507) 52-2122

Cost for a certified Birth Certificate	$2.00
Cost for a certified Marriage or Divorce Certificate	$2.00
Cost for a certified Death Certificate	$2.00

The Panama Canal Commission maintains and issues certificates for births, marriages, and deaths that occurred in the former Canal Zone from 1904 to September 30, 1979, when the Panama Canal Treaty became effective and the Canal Zone Government ceased to exist.

The United States District Court for the District of the Canal Zone was closed on March 31, 1982. All records of the court are at the National Archives Records Center in Suitland, Maryland. For divorce information write to the Panama Canal Commission, which will send you the information needed by the Records Center to process the request. All certified copies are provided only by the National Archives.

The Family History Library of The Church of Jesus Christ of Latter-day Saints in Salt Lake City, Utah has microfilmed original and published records about the Panama Canal Zone. For details on their holdings please consult your nearest Family History Center.

COMISION DEL CANAL DE PANAMA

La Comisión del Canal de Panamá cobra $2 por cada copia entregada de certificado de nacimiento, defunción o matrimonio. Sírvase llenar esta solicitud y enviarla junto con la suma correspondiente a la dirección que aparece en la parte de abajo. Se girará todo giro postal a favor del TESORERO, Comisión del Canal de Panamá.

Solamente los certificados de nacimiento, defunción o matrimonio ocurridos en la antigua Zona del Canal reposan en los archivos de esta oficina. Para los casos de nacimientos, defunciones o matrimonios ocurridos en la República de Panamá, diríjase al Registro Civil, Apartado 5281, Panamá 5, República de Panamá.

_____

....
(Fecha)

COMISION DEL CANAL DE PANAMA
División Administrativa
Oficina de Estadística Demográfica
Unit 2300
APO AA 34011

REGISTRADOR:

Por favor entregue ....copia(s) en ☐ inglés ☐ español del certificado de ☐ nacimiento ☐ defunción ☐ matrimonio, solicitado a continuación. Adjunto $.......................... (giro postal).

_____

Certificado de Nacimiento:

Nombre en el Certificado............................

Fecha de Nacimiento ....

Lugar de Nacimiento ....

Nombre completo del Padre ....

Nombre de soltera de la Madre ....

Certificado de Defunción:

Nombre del Difunto ....

Fecha de Defunción ....

Lugar de Defunción ....

Certificado de Matrimonio:

Nombre de los Contrayentes: Masculino .... Femenino............................

Fecha de Matrimonio........................... Nº de la Licencia...........................

Lugar de Matrimonio .... Balboa........................... Cristóbal.

....
Firma del solicitante

....
Parentesco

Motivo de la solicitud...

....
Dirección—Llénese solamente si el certificado se ha de enviar por correo.

PUERTO RICO

Send your requests to:

Puerto Rico Department of Health
Demographic Registry
P.O. Box 9342
San Juan, Puerto Rico 00908

(809) 728-7980

Cost for a certified Birth Certificate	$2.00
Cost for a certified Marriage Certificate or Divorce Record	$2.00
Cost for a certified Death Certificate	$2.00

The Puerto Rico Department of Health has birth, marriage, and death records from June 22, 1931 and divorce records from 1962. For records from 1885 to June 21, 1931, write to the municipality where the event occurred.

The Family History Library of The Church of Jesus Christ of Latter-day Saints in Salt Lake City, Utah has microfilmed original and published vital records and church registers of Puerto Rico. For details on their holdings please consult your nearest Family History Center.

DEMOGRAPHIC REGISTRY AREA

BIRTH CERTIFICATE APPLICATION

Name at Birth: _____

   Father's last name   Mother's last name   Name

Date of Birth: _____

   Month   Day   Year

Place of Birth: _____

                              Town

Father's Name: _____

Mother's maiden Name: _____

Name of the Hospital: _____

Are you the person named in line #1? _____Yes _____No. If not,

what is your relationship with her or him _____.

Specific purpose for which this certification is requested: _____

_____

Signature of Applicant: _____

Address where you want the certificate to be sent: _____

_____

Address of Applicant: _____

_____

Number of copies: _____.

Applicant IDENTIFICATION: _____Driving License _____Work

_____Passport _____Other DATE: _____

IMPORTANT:

If event occurred from June 22, 1931 to present, you can apply with us to
the following address: Department of Health, Demographic Registry, P.O.
Box 9342, San Juan, Puerto Rico 00908.

If event occurred from 1885 to June 21, 1931 you must write to the municipality where the event occurred.

Please send a photocopy of an IDENTIFICATION with photography of applicant.

Applicant in Puerto Rico, please send a $2.00 Internal Revenue Stamp for
each copy requested.

Applicant out of Puerto Rico, please send a $2.00 money order for each
copy you need payable to "SECRETARY OF THE TREASURY" for each copy requested.

Please send us a pre-addressed envelope to mail your certificate.

_____

Direct Interest-Registrant, parents, their sons or legal representatives.

DEMOGRAPHIC REGISTRY AREA

MARRIAGE CERTIFICATE APPLICATION

Husband's Name: _____

        Father's last name   Mother's last name   Name

Spouse's maiden Name: _____

        Father's last name   Mother's last name   Name

Date of Marriage: _____

        Month   Day   Year

Place of Marriage: _____

               Town

Are you the person named in line #1? _____Yes _____No. If not,

what is your relationship with this person: _____.

Specific purpose for which this certification is requested: _____

_____.

Signature of Applicant: _____.

Applicant's address: _____

_____.

Address you want the certificate to be sent: _____

_____.

Number of copies: _____.

Applicant's IDENTIFICATION: _____Driving License _____Work

_____Passport _____Other DATE: _____

IMPORTANT:

If event occurred from June 22, 1931 to present you can apply with us to
the following address: Department of Health, Demographic Registry, P.O.
Box 9342, San Juan, Puerto Rico 00908.

If event occurred from 1885 to June 21, 1931 you must write to the municipality where the event occurred.

Please send a photocopy of an IDENTIFICATION with photography of applicant.

Applicant in Puerto Rico, please send $2.00 Internal Revenue Stamp for
each copy requested.

Applicant out of state, please send a $2.00 money order payable to "SE-
CRETARY OF THE TREASURY" for each copy requested.

Please send us a self addressed envelope to mail your certificate.

_____

Applicant's definition-contracting parties, parents, child or legal
representative.

_____

COPY EXPEDITION'S

DEPARTMENT OF HEALTH
DEMOGRAPHIC REGISTRY AREA

DEATH CERTIFICATED APPLICATION

Deceased Name: _____

            Father's last name   Mother's last name   Name

Date of Death: _____

            Month   Day   Year

Place of Death: _____

                        Town

Name of the Hospital: _____

Relationship with deceased: _____

Specific purpose for which this certification is requested: _____

_____

Applicant's signature: _____

Aplicant's address: _____

_____

Address where you want the certificate to be sent: _____

_____

Number of copies: _____

Applicant IDENTIFICATION: _____Driving License _____Work

_____Passport _____Other DATE: _____

IMPORTANT:

If event occurred from June 22, 1931 to present, you can apply with us to the following address: Department of Health, Demographic Registry, P.O. Box 9342, San Juan, Puerto Rico 00908.

If event occurred from 1885 to June 21, 1931 you must write to the municipality where the event occurred.

Please send a photocopy of an IDENTIFICATION with photography of applicant.

Applicant in Puerto Rico please send a $2.00 Internal Revenue Stamp for each copy requested.

Applicant out of Puerto Rico send a $2.00 money order payable to "SECRETARY OF THE TREASURY" for each copy requested.

Please send us a self addressed envelope to mail your certificate

_____

Applicant's definition-The funeral home, parents, child or legal representative of the deceased.

_____

COPY EXPEDITION'S

VIRGIN ISLANDS—
St. Croix

Send your requests to:

> Virgin Islands Department of Health
> Office of the Registrar of Vital Statistics
> Charles Harwood Memorial Hospital
> P.O. Box 520
> Christiansted, St. Croix, Virgin Islands 00820

(809) 773-4050

Send your requests for Marriage Certificates and Divorce Records to:

> Chief Deputy Clerk
> Territorial Court of the Virgin Islands
> P.O. Box 9000
> St. Croix, Virgin Islands 00859

(809) 778-3350

Cost for a certified Birth Certificate	$10.00
Cost for a short form Birth Certificate	$5.00
Cost for a certified Marriage Certificate	$10.00
Cost for a certified Divorce Record	Varies
Cost for a certified Death Certificate	$10.00
Cost for a verification of Death	$5.00

The Office has birth and death records from 1919. Current registration is considered to be complete.

The Family History Library of The Church of Jesus Christ of Latter-day Saints in Salt Lake City, Utah has microfilmed original and published records of the Virgin Islands and the region. For details on their holdings please consult your nearest Family History Center.

VIRGIN ISLANDS —
St. Thomas and St. John

Send your requests to:

Virgin Islands Department of Health
Office of the Registrar of Vital Statistics
St. Thomas, Virgin Islands 00802

(809) 774-1734

Send your requests for Marriage Certificates and Divorce Records to:

Chief Deputy Clerk
Territorial Court of the Virgin Islands
P.O. Box 70
Charlotte Amalie, St. Thomas, Virgin Islands 00801

(809) 774-6680

Cost for a certified Birth Certificate	$10.00
Cost for a short form Birth Certificate	$5.00
Cost for a certified Marriage Certificate	$10.00
Cost for a certified Divorce Record	Varies
Cost for a certified Death Certificate	$10.00
Cost for verification of a Death	$5.00

The Office has birth records from July 1, 1906 and death records from January 1, 1906. Current registration is considered to be complete. The Registrar will do genealogical research for a base charge of $50.00.

The Family History Library of The Church of Jesus Christ of Latter-day Saints in Salt Lake City, Utah has microfilmed original and published records of the Virgin Islands and the region. For details on their holdings please consult your nearest Family History Center.

VIRGIN ISLANDS OF THE UNITED STATES

DEPARTMENT OF HEALTH
OFFICE OF THE REGISTRAR OF VITAL STATISTICS

HD-ve   St. — — — — — — — — — — — — —, Virgin Islands

APPLICATION FOR BIRTH RECORD

PLEASE PRINT OR TYPE: FAILURE TO COMPLETE THIS FORM PROPERLY MAY DELAY SERVICE TO YOU.

TYPE OF RECORD DESIRED (Check one)

VERIFICATION

A verification is a statement as to the date of birth and name of the child. A verification is used when it is necessary to prove age only.

CERTIFIED COPY

A certified copy is an abstract from the original birth certificate. It gives the name, sex, date and place of birth, certificate number, as well as the names of the parents.

An application for a certified copy of birth must be signed by the person named in the original certificate if 18 years or more or by a parent or legal representative of that person.

FEES: Send money order or check payable to the VIRGIN ISLANDS DEPARTMENT OF HEALTH.
(Please do not send cash)

FULL NAME	DATE OF BIRTH Or period to be searched.
PLACE OF BIRTH (City and Island)	
NAME FATHER	MAIDEN NAME MOTHER
AGE AT BIRTH	AGE AT BIRTH
BIRTHPLACE	BIRTHPLACE
ADDRESS (At time of birth)	ADDRESS (At time of birth)
PURPOSE FOR WHICH RECORD IS REQUIRED	SOCIAL SECURITY NUMBER

Your relationship to person whose record is required? If self, state "SELF". _____

If attorney give name and relationship of your client to person whose record is required. _____

TO WHOM SHALL RECORD BE SENT?	
Name _____	Signature of Applicant _____
Address _____	Address of Applicant _____
City _____ State _____	_____ Date _____

Sworn to and subscribed before me this _____ day of _____ 19 _____ .

_____

(Signature and Seal of Notary Public)

VIRGIN ISLANDS OF THE UNITED STATES

DEPARTMENT OF HEALTH

OFFICE OF THE REGISTRAR OF VITAL STATISTICS

St. ————————————, Virgin Islands

HD-vf

●

APPLICATION FOR DEATH RECORD

PLEASE PRINT OR TYPE: FAILURE TO COMPLETE THIS FORM PROPERLY MAY DELAY SERVICE TO YOU.

TYPE OF RECORD DESIRED (Check one)

VERIFICATION	CERTIFIED COPY ☐ Fee
A verification is a statement as to the date of death and name of decedent. A verification is used as proof that the event occurred. Anyone may apply for a verification of death.	A certified copy is a replica of the original death certificate. Anyone who can establish that the record is needed for proof of parentage, social security and other benefits, settlement of estate, or for judicial or other proper purpose may apply for a certified copy.

FEES: Send money order or check payable to the VIRGIN ISLANDS DEPARTMENT OF HEALTH. **(PLEASE DO NOT SEND CASH)**

No fee is charged when the certificate is required by a local, state or federal government agency.

NAME OF DECEDENT	DATE OF DEATH OR PERIOD TO BE SEARCHED
PLACE OF DEATH (CITY AND ISLAND)	
NAME OF FATHER OF DECEDENT	MAIDEN NAME OF MOTHER OF DECEDENT
NUMBER OF COPIES DESIRED	CERTIFICATE NUMBER, IF KNOWN
PURPOSE FOR WHICH RECORD IS REQUIRED	

What is your relationship to decedent? _____

In what capacity are you acting? _____

If attorney, give name and relationship of your client to decedent. _____

TO WHOM SHALL RECORD BE SENT?	
Name _____	Signature of Applicant _____
Address _____	Address of Applicant _____
City _____ State _____	_____ Date _____

2. International

AFGHANISTAN

Department of Population
Registration and Vital Statistics
Ministry of the Interior
Sharinow, Kabul, Afghanistan

Afghanistan has required all males to register for identification cards since 1952. Efforts to strengthen the registration of vital records in Afghanistan have been of limited success. Documents are provided for free.

ALBANIA

Drejtoria Qendore e Statistikave
Keshili i Ministrave (Kryemistrial)
Bulevardi Deshmoret e Kombit
Tirane, Albania

Registration is required of all residents. Documents are provided for free.

ALGERIA

Service d'Etat Civil des Communes
Ministere de l'Interieur
Alger, Algeria

Vital registration began in Algeria in 1882 and included principally Muslims in the North. By 1905 coverage also included Muslims in the South. Today the registration of vital records is considered to be incomplete.

ANGOLA

Direccao Nacional dos Registos
Notariado e Identificacao
Ministerio de Justicia
Luanda, Angola

Vital registration began for Europeans earlier in this century and efforts have been made to expand registration throughout the country. The civil strife there has made this an impractical goal for the nation.

ANTIGUA and BARBUDA

Registrar General's Office
High Court
High Street
St. John's, Antigua

(809) 462-0609

Cost for a certified Birth Certificate	US $1.20	EC $3.00
Cost for a certified Marriage Certificate	US $3.80	EC $10.00
Cost for a certified Death Certificate	US $1.20	EC $3.00

Antigua was discovered by Columbus in 1493 and became independent in 1967. The Registrar General has records from August 1, 1856.

ARGENTINA

Director of Civil Registration
Office of Civil Registration
(Capitol, Province), Argentina

Additional information is available from the National Registry of Persons in Buenos Aires. Each state maintains its own vital records and issues the national identification card for the National Registry of Persons. Vital registration began on August 1, 1886 in Argentina. The current registration is considered to be 90 percent complete. The fee for documents varies from state to state.

ARMENIA

Russian-American Genealogical
  Archival Service (RAGAS)
P.O. Box 236
Glen Echo, Maryland 20812

(202) 501-5206

Cost for a Birth, Marriage, or Death Certificate	$20.00

By an agreement between the United States National Archives Volunteer Association and the Archives of Russia Society RAGAS receives and processes requests for vital records in some of the former Soviet republics. Although at this time RAGAS is able to deal mainly with Russia, Belarus, and Ukraine they might be able to help you with your inquiries regarding Armenia. There is a $2.00 shipping fee. The service also is available at an hourly rate. (See Russia for application forms.) The National Library of Armenia also has records. Contact them at Terian 72, Yerevan 375009, Armenia; Tel. (011) (7) (8852) 56-45-74.

AUSTRALIA — AUSTRALIAN CAPITAL TERRITORY

Send your requests to:

Office of the Registrar General of Births, Deaths and Marriages
Allara House
Allara Street
P.O. Box 788
Canberra City, A.C.T. 2601
Australia

(011) (61) (6) 207-0460, FAX (011) (61) (6) 207-0455

Cost for a certified Birth Certificate	Au $20.00
Cost for a short form Birth Certificate	Au $16.00
Cost for a certified Marriage Certificate	Au $20.00
Cost for a certified Death Certificate	Au $20.00

The Registrar General holds records from January 1, 1930.

Records of interest are also available at the National Library of Australia, Parkes Place, Canberra, A.C.T. 2600; Tel. (011) (61) (62) 621-111.

Australian Capital Territory

OFFICE OF THE REGISTRAR BIRTHS, DEATHS, AND MARRIAGES

APPLICATION FOR BIRTH CERTIFICATE

RECORD OF FEES PAID

FEES — to be prepaid:

Full Certificate ... ...

Extract ... ...

PARTICULARS OF BIRTH
(Please use block letters)

Given (Christian) Names

Surname

Date of Birth

Age last Birthday (if applicable)

Place of Birth   A.C.T.

Father's full Given (Christian) Names

Mother's full Given (Christian) Names

Mother's full MAIDEN Surname

FOR OFFICE USE ONLY

Reg. No. ....

No. of Certified Copies ....

No. of Extracts ....

Total No. of Certificates ....

No. to be posted ....

No. to be collected ....

Date for Collection ....

Date Posted ....

Date Collected ....

Purpose for which certificate is required ....

Name of Applicant (Block Letters) Mr / Mrs / Miss ....

....

Relationship to person registered ....

Address in full ....

.... Postcode ....

Telephone No. .... Date of Application ....

Signature ....

Post to — The Registrar,
Births, Deaths & Marriages,
P.O. Box 788
CANBERRA CITY. 2601

Deliver to — Births, Deaths & Marriages Office.
Allara House.
Allara Street.
CANBERRA CITY. A.C.T.

Australian Capital Territory

OFFICE OF THE REGISTRAR BIRTHS, DEATHS, AND MARRIAGES

APPLICATION FOR MARRIAGE CERTIFICATE

RECORD OF FEES PAID

FEES — to be prepaid:
    Full Certificate   ... ...,
    Extract   ... ...

APPLICANT TO FURNISH PARTICULARS OF MARRIAGE
(Please use block letters)

Bridegroom's given names	
Surname	
Bride's given names	
Surname before Marriage	
Date of Marriage	/ /19
Place of Marriage	A.C.T.

FOR OFFICE USE ONLY

Reg. No. ....

No. of Certified Copies ....

No. of Extracts ....

Total No. of Certificates ....

No. to be posted ....

No. to be collected ....

Date for Collection ....

Date Posted ....

Date Collected ....

Purpose for which certificate is required ....

Name of Applicant (Block Letters) Mr
Mrs ....
Miss

....

Relationship to bride/groom ....

Address in full ....

.... Postcode ....

Telephone No. .... Date of Application ....

Signature ....

Post to — The Registrar,
    Births, Deaths & Marriages,
    P.O. Box 788
    CANBERRA CITY. 2601

Deliver to — Births. Deaths & Marriages Office,
    Allara House.
    Allara Street.
    CANBERRA A.C.T.

Australian Capital Territory

OFFICE OF THE REGISTRAR BIRTHS, DEATHS, AND MARRIAGES

APPLICATION FOR DEATH CERTIFICATE

FEES— to be prepaid:
Full Certificate · · · ·
Extract · · · ·

RECORD OF FEES PAID

APPLICANT TO FURNISH PARTICULARS OF DECEASED
(Please use block letters)

		FOR OFFICE USE ONLY
Given (Christian) Names		
Surname		
Husband/Wife of		Reg. No. . . . .
Date of Death		No. of Certified Copies . . . .
		No. of Extracts . . . .
Place of Death	A.C.T.	Total No. of Certificates . . . .
		No. to be posted . . . .
		No. to be collected . . . .
Age last Birthday	years	Date for Collection . . . .
Father's full Names (Including surname)		
Mother's full Given (Christian) Names and Maiden Surname		Date posted . . . .
		Date Collected . . . .

Purpose for which certificate is required . . . .

Name of Applicant (*Block Letters*) Mr Mrs Miss . . . .

. . . .

Relationship to deceased . . . .

Address in full . . . .

. . . . Postcode . . . .

Telephone No. . . . . Date of Application . . . .

Signature . . . .

Post to— The Registrar
Births, Deaths & Marriages,
P.O. Box 788
CANBERRA CITY

Deliver to— Births, Deaths & Marriages Office,
Allara House,
Allara Street
CANBERRA CITY A C T

Australian Capital Territory

OFFICE OF THE REGISTRAR BIRTHS, DEATHS, AND MARRIAGES

APPLICATION FOR SEARCH

BIRTH	PARTICULARS OF SEARCH (Please use block letters)

Given (Christian) Names

Surname

Date of Birth	Place of Birth
	A.C.T.

Father's Given (Christian) Names	Surname

Mother's Given (Christian) Names

Mother's full MAIDEN Surname

FOR OFFICE USE ONLY

Reg. No.(if any) ....

No. of Searches ....

No. to be collected ....

Date for Collection   /   /

Date Posted   /   /

Date Collected   /   /

Searched by ....

Verified by ....

Result ☐ Yes   ☐ No

DEATH	PARTICULARS OF SEARCH (Please use block letters)

Given (Christian) Names

Surname

Date of Death (or year)	Place of Death
	A.C.T.

MARRIAGE	PARTICULARS OF SEARCH (Please use block letters)

Bridegroom's Given (Christian) Names

Surname

Bride's Given (Christian) Names

Bride's full MAIDEN Surname

Date of Marriage (or year)	Place of Marriage
	A.C.T.

NOTES

1. Applications for searches must comply with section 51 of the Registration of Births, Deaths and Marriages Ordinance 1963.
2. The Registrar has authority to refuse a search in certain circumstances.
3. Registration of events in the A.C.T. commenced on 1.1.1930. Events before that date are registered in Queanbeyan, N.S.W.
4. The Registrar will issue written notification of the result of a search in all cases.

Reason for which search is required (in full) ....

....

Name of Applicant (Block letters) Mr
Mrs ....
Miss

Relationship to person registered ....

Address in full ....

.... Postcode ....

Telephone .... Date of Application ....

Signature

Post to — The Registrar,
Births, Deaths, & Marriages,
P.O. Box 788
CANBERRA CITY, 2601

Deliver to — Births, Deaths & Marriages Office,
Allara House,
Allara Street,
CANBERRA CITY, A.C.T.

AUSTRALIA — NEW SOUTH WALES

Send your requests to:

Registry of Births, Deaths and Marriages
191 Thomas Street
P.O. Box 30 G.P.O.
Sydney, New South Wales 2001
Australia

(011) (61) (2) 228-8511

Cost for a certified Birth Certificate	Au $20.00
Cost for a certified Marriage Certificate	Au $20.00
Cost for a certified Death Certificate	Au $20.00

The Registry has records from March 1, 1856. Payment must be made in Australian dollars using an international money order or bank draft made payable to the Registry of Births, Deaths and Marriages.

If your request is urgent you may call them at (011) (61) (2) 228-7777. There is an additional charge of Au $20.00.

The Family History Library of The Church of Jesus Christ of Latter-day Saints in Salt Lake City, Utah has microfilmed original and published vital records and church registers of New South Wales. For further details on their holdings please consult your nearest Family History Center.

Records of interest are also available at the National Library of Australia, Parkes Place, Canberra, A.C.T. 2600; Tel. (011) (61) (62) 621-111.

PR188

N.S.W. BIRTH CERTIFICATE APPLICATION

Please print using block letters and complete all sections.
Personal cheques will not be accepted for Urgent Applications.
Counter Applications: Documents will not be issued at counter unless this receipt is produced.
For information on Certificate Applications please phone: 228 7777

If this application relates to a person other than yourself written authority may be required.	FEE

☐ NON URGENT   ☐ URGENT   ☐ COLLECT   ☐ POST

Applicants Name:	Signature:	
Address:	Postcode:	Daytime Phone:
Reason Certificate is Required:	Relationship to Person Registered:	
Information for Posting – Name:		
Address:	Postcode:	

DETAILS OF BIRTH REQUIRED

Family Name at Birth:	Number in Register:	
Given Names:	Date Searched	
Date of Birth:	Present Age:	Date Examined
If date unknown, years to be searched – From: To:	Extra Fees	
Place of Birth in N.S.W.:	Date Issued	
Fathers Full Name:	Date Posted	
Mothers Full Name before Marriage:		
Any other Family Name used:		

IF MORE DETAILS TO ASSIST SEARCH ARE KNOWN PLEASE USE BACK OF FORM.

PLEASE COMPLETE YOUR POSTAL ADDRESS IN BLOCK LETTERS

Name

Address
and
Postcode

Your Office Reference ....

Registry of Births, Deaths and Marriages 191 Thomas Street, Sydney (Box 30 GPO, Sydney 2001)

Please print using block letters and complete all sections.
Personal cheques will not be accepted for Urgent Applications.
Counter Applications: Documents will not be issued at counter unless this receipt is produced.
For information on Certificate Applications please phone: 228 7777

If this application relates to a marriage other than your own written authority may be required.	FEE

☐ **NON URGENT**   ☐ **URGENT**   ☐ **COLLECT**   ☐ **POST**

Applicants Name:		Signature:	
Address:		Postcode:	Daytime Phone:
Reason Certificate is Required:		Relationship to Person Registered:	
Information for Posting – Name:			
Address:			Postcode:

Family Name of Bridegroom:	Number in Register	
Given Names:	Date Searched	
Family Name of Bride before Marriage:	Date Examined	
Given Names:	Extra Fees	
Date of Marriage:	Date Issued	
Place of Marriage in N.S.W.:	Date Posted	
If date unknown, years to be searched – From: To:		

IF MORE DETAILS TO ASSIST SEARCH ARE KNOWN PLEASE USE BACK OF FORM.

PLEASE COMPLETE YOUR POSTAL ADDRESS IN BLOCK LETTERS

Name _____

Address
and
Postcode _____

Your Office Reference ....

Registry of Births, Deaths and Marriages 191 Thomas Street, Sydney (Box 30 GPO, Sydney 2001)

N.S.W. DEATH CERTIFICATE APPLICATION

Please print using block letters and complete all sections.
Personal cheques will not be accepted for Urgent Applications.
Counter Applications: Documents will not be issued at counter unless this receipt is produced.
For information on Certificate Applications please phone: 228 7777

Written authority may be required in some circumstances				FEE
☐ NON URGENT	☐ URGENT	☐ COLLECT	☐ POST	

Applicants Name:		Signature:	
Address:		Postcode:	Daytime Phone:
Reason Certificate is Required:	Relationship to Person Registered:		
Information for Posting – Name:			
Address:		Postcode:	

DETAILS OF DEATH REQUIRED

Family Name at Death:		Number in Register:	
Given Names:		Date Searched	
Date of Death:	Age at Death:	Date Examined	
If date unknown, years to be searched – From:	To:	Extra Fees	
Place of Death in N.S.W.:		Date Issued	
Fathers Full Name:		Date Posted	
Mothers Full Name before Marriage:			
Name of Spouse:			

IF MORE DETAILS TO ASSIST SEARCH ARE KNOWN PLEASE USE BACK OF FORM.

PLEASE COMPLETE YOUR POSTAL ADDRESS IN BLOCK LETTERS

Name	_____
Address and Postcode	_____
	_____
	_____

Your Office Reference ....

AUSTRALIA — NORTHERN TERRITORY

Send your requests to:

> Office of the Registrar of Births, Deaths and Marriages
> Department of Law
> Nichols Place
> G.P.O. Box 3021
> Darwin, Northern Territory 0801
> Australia

(011) (61) (89) 6119, FAX (011) (61) (89) 6239

Cost for a certified Birth Certificate	Au $20.00
Cost for a certified Marriage Certificate	Au $20.00
Cost for a certified Death Certificate	Au $20.00

The Office of the Registrar has birth records from August 24, 1870, marriage records from 1871, and death records from 1872. If your request is urgent there is an additional fee of Au $10.00.

The Family History Library of The Church of Jesus Christ of Latter-day Saints in Salt Lake City, Utah has microfilmed original and published vital records and church registers of the Northern Territory. For further details on their holdings please consult your nearest Family History Center.

Records of interest are also available at the National Library of Australia, Parkes Place, Canberra, A.C.T. 2600; Tel. (011) (61) (62) 621-111.

NORTHERN TERRITORY OF AUSTRALIA
OFFICE OF THE REGISTRAR OF BIRTHS, DEATHS, AND MARRIAGES

APPLICATION FOR BIRTH CERTIFICATE

Certificate Required: Certified Copy ☐ (specify if more than one)

Extract ☐

Note: A certified copy contains all particulars of birth.
: An extract contains name, date and place of birth.

FEES — to be prepaid.

APPLICANT TO FURNISH PARTICULARS OF BIRTH (Please use block letters)	FOR OFFICE USE ONLY
(Registered) SURNAME	Fee Paid:
Given (Christian) Names	Receipt No:
Date of Birth	Reg No:
Age last Birthday Yrs. Newborn ☐	Certificate Nos.:
	Date Posted:
Place of Birth N.T.	Date Collected:
Father's full name	(Signature) Received ....
Mother's full given names (Christian Names)	Date for Collection:
Mother's full MAIDEN SURNAME	Refund Action (if any):

Purpose for which Certificate is required (e.g. school, passport, family records, etc.) ....
(Registration of Births, Deaths & Marriages Act-S.50)

Name of Applicant
(Block Letters)   Mr/Mrs/Ms/Miss ....

Relationship to above person (e.g. mother, father, self, etc.) ....

Postal Address in full ....

.... Postcode:.................

COLLECT: ☐   POST: ☐   TOTAL NUMBER OF CERTIFICATES ORDERED ☐

Signature .... Telephone No. ....

Date of Application ....

Post to: The Registrar,
            Births, Deaths & Marriages,
            G.P.O. Box 3021,
            DARWIN, N.T. 0801
            Telephone: 89 6119

or for Alice Springs District:
            District Registrar,
            P.O. Box 8043,
            ALICE SPRINGS, N.T. 0871
            Telephone: 50 3339

Deliver to Births, Deaths & Marriages Office,
            Nichols Place,
            Cnr Cavenagh & Bennett Streets
            DARWIN, N.T.

or: Ground Floor
            Greatorex Building,
            Parsons Street,
            ALICE SPRINGS, N.T.

36/727   Government Printer of the Northern Territory

NORTHERN TERRITORY OF AUSTRALIA

RG 2/5

OFFICE OF THE REGISTRAR OF BIRTHS, DEATHS AND MARRIAGES

APPLICATION FOR MARRIAGE CERTIFICATE

FEES — to be prepaid:

Certificate Required: Certified Copy ☐ (specify if more than one)

Extract ☐

For further information contact offices listed below.

Official receipts to be produced when taking delivery of documents.

APPLICANT TO FURNISH PARTICULARS OF MARRIAGE **(Please use Block letters)**		FOR OFFICE USE ONLY
Bridegroom's Given Names		Fee Paid: Receipt No:
Surname		Reg No:
		Date to be Collected:
Bride's Given Names		Refund Action (if any):
Surname before Marriage		Certificate Nos.:
		Date Posted:
Date of Marriage		Date Collected:
Place of Marriage	N.T.	(Signature) Received ....

Purpose for which certificate is required ....
(Registration of Births, Deaths and Marriages Act-S.50)

Name of Applicant
(Block Letters)   Mr/Mrs/Ms/Miss ....

Relationship to above persons ....

Postal Address in full ....

.... Postcode: ....

COLLECT: ☐   POST: ☐   Total Number of Certificates to be collected: ☐

Signature .... Telephone No. ....   Date of Application ....

Post to: The Registrar, Births, Deaths and Marriages, G.P.O. Box 3021, DARWIN, N.T. 5794 Telephone: 89 6119

or for Alice Springs District: District Registrar, P.O. Box 8043, ALICE SPRINGS, N.T. 5750 Telephone: 50 3339

Deliver to: Births, Deaths and Marriages Office, Nichols Place, Cnr Cavenagh and Bennett Streets, DARWIN, N.T.

or: Ground Floor, Greatorex Building, Parsons Street, ALICE SPRINGS, N.T.

36-20   Government Printer of the Northern Territory

NORTHERN TERRITORY OF AUSTRALIA
OFFICE OF THE REGISTRAR OF BIRTHS, DEATHS, AND MARRIAGES

APPLICATION FOR DEATH CERTIFICATE

FEES — to be prepaid.   Certificate Required: Certified Copy ☐ (specify if more than one)

Extract ☐

For further information contact offices listed below.

Official receipts to be.produced when taking delivery of documents.

APPLICANT TO FURNISH PARTICULARS OF DECEASED (Please use block letters)	FOR OFFICE USE ONLY
Given (Christian) Name	Fee Paid: Receipt No:
Surname	Reg No:
Husband/Wife of	No. of Copies:
	No. of Extracts:
Date of Death	Certificate Nos.:
Place of Death N.T.	Date Posted:
Age last Birthday YEARS	Date Collected:
	(Signature) Received ....
Father's full names	Date for Collection:
Mother's full MAIDEN name	Refund Action (if any):

Purpose for which certificate is required ....
(Registration of Births, Deaths & Marriages Act-S.50)

Name of Applicant
(Block Letters)   Mr/Mrs/Ms/Miss ....

Relationship to above person ....

Postal Address in full ....

....Postcode:.................

COLLECT: ☐   POST: ☐

Signature .... Telephone No. ....

Date of
Application ....

Post to: The Registrar,   or for Alice Springs District: Deliver to Births, Deaths & Marriages Office,   or: Ground Floor
           Births, Deaths & Marriages,   District Registrar,   Nichols Place,   Greatorex Building,
           G.P.O. Box 3021,   P.O. Box 8043,   Cnr Cavenagh & Bennett Streets   Parsons Street,
           DARWIN, N.T. 5794   ALICE SPRINGS, N.T. 5750   DARWIN, N.T.   ALICE SPRINGS, N.T.
           Telephone: 89 6119   Telephone: 50 3339

36-53   G. L. DUFFIELD, Government Printer of the Northern Territory

AUSTRALIA — QUEENSLAND

Send your requests to:

Office of the Registrar General of Births, Deaths and Marriages
Old Treasury Building
P.O. Box 188
Brisbane, North Quay
Queensland 4002
Australia

(011) (61) (7) 224-6222, FAX (011) (61) (7) 224-5415

Cost for a certified Birth Certificate	Au $17.00
Cost for a certified Marriage Certificate	Au $17.00
Cost for a certified Death Certificate	Au $17.00
Cost for a certified short form for the above	Au $10.50

The Office of the Registrar General has records from March 1, 1856. When writing please make the international bank draft in Australian dollars and made payable to the Registrar General. If your request is urgent there is an additional charge of Au $10.50.

The Family History Library of The Church of Jesus Christ of Latter-day Saints in Salt Lake City, Utah has microfilmed many of the original and published vital records and church registers of Queensland. For further details on their holdings please consult your nearest Family History Center.

Records of interest are also available at the National Library of Australia, Parkes Place, Canberra, A.C.T. 2600; Tel. (011) (61) (62) 621-111.

REGISTRAR-GENERAL'S OFFICE, BRISBANE

TO: REGISTRAR-GENERAL
P.O. BOX 188
BRISBANE
NORTH QUAY 4002

BIRTH

OFFICE USE ONLY

(Office Use Only)

Entry No.:

Certified Copy:

Extract:

Priority:

Search:

Change of Name:

Alterations:

Misc.:

Late Fee:

Short:

Cheque Refund:

Amount Received:

Assessor

Number of cheque/bank/money order and name of drawer of cheque if different from applicant.

Copy No.(s):

Date Copy Produced:

Application for Search and/or Certified Copy or Extract

I hereby apply for a search for and/or of the Registration of the undermentioned Birth.

☐ Certified Copy
☐ Short Extract

Name of Applicant:_____

Signature of Applicant:_____

Address:_____

_____

Date of Application:_____19____

PARTICULARS OF BIRTH REGISTERED IN QUEENSLAND

1	Surname	
	First Names in Full	
2	Date and Year of Birth or Period of Years to be searched If Date of Birth is unknown		Present Age
3	Place of Birth	
4	Father's Name in Full	
5	Mother's First Names and Maiden Surname	
6	Applicant's Relationship to person described in Item 1	
7	Reason for which Certificate is Required	

TICK APPROPRIATE BOX/BOXES

☐ PRIORITY SERVICE (Additional Fee Required)

☐ COLLECT

☐ POST (Complete section below

(Office Use Only)

Entry No.

Surname & Initials_____

REGISTRAR-GENERAL'S OFFICE, BRISBANE

BIRTH

Please Print Name and Postal Address of Person to whom Document is to be Posted.

N.B. This document will not be available for collection prior to

_____

_____

_____Postcode_____

Official receipts must be produced when taking delivery of documents.

104619—W 267—Govt. Printer, Qld.

REGISTRAR-GENERAL'S OFFICE, BRISBANE

MARRIAGE

OFFICE USE ONLY

(Office Use Only)

Entry No.:

Certified Copy:

Extract:

Priority:

Search:

Change of Name:

Alterations:

Misc.:

Late Fee:

Short:

Cheque Refund:

Amount Received:

Assessor:

Number of cheque/bank/money order and name of drawer of cheque if different from applicant.

Copy No.(s):

Date Copy Produced:

Application for Search and/or Certified Copy or Extract

I hereby apply for a search for and/or of the Registration of the undermentioned Marriage.

☐ Certified Copy
☐ Short Extract

Name of Applicant:_____

Signature of Applicant:_____

Address:_____

_____

Date of Application:_____ 19____

PARTICULARS OF MARRIAGE REGISTERED IN QUEENSLAND

1	BRIDE GROOM	Surname	
		First Names in Full	
2	BRIDE	Surname before Marriage	
		First Names in Full	
3		Date and Year of Marriage or Period of Years to be searched if Date of Marriage is unknown.	
4		Place of Marriage	
5		Relationship to person described in Items 1 and 2	
6		Reason for which Certificate is Required	

TICK APPROPRIATE BOX/BOXES

☐ PRIORITY SERVICE (Additional Fee Required)
☐ COLLECT
☐ POST (Complete section below)

REGISTRAR-GENERAL'S OFFICE, BRISBANE

(Office Use Only)

Entry No.

Surname

MARRIAGE

N.B. This document will not be available for collection prior to ⟶

Please Print Name and Postal Address of Person to whom Document is to be Posted.

_____

_____

_____Postcode_____

Official receipts must be produced when taking delivery of documents.

REGISTRAR-GENERAL'S OFFICE, BRISBANE

TO: REGISTRAR-GENERAL
P.O. BOX 188
BRISBANE
NORTH QUAY 4002

DEATH

OFFICE USE ONLY

Application for Search and/or Certified Copy or Extract

I hereby apply for a search for and/or of the Registration of the undermentioned Death.

☐ Certified Copy
☐ Short Extract

Name of Applicant:_____

Signature of Applicant:_____

Address:_____

_____

Date of Application:_____ 19____

PARTICULARS OF DEATH REGISTERED IN QUEENSLAND

1	Surname	
	First Names in Full	
2	Date and Year of Death or Period of Years to be searched If Date of Death is unknown	
3	Place of Death	
4	Father's Name in Full	
5	Mother's First Names and Maiden Surname	
6	Applicant's Relationship to person described in Item 1	
7	Is the applied for Certificate (or information) required for the purpose of locating a person? If 'NO', state reason for applying	YES ☐ NO ☐

TICK APPROPRIATE BOX/BOXES

☐ PRIORITY SERVICE (Additional Fee Required)

☐ COLLECT

☐ POST (Complete section below)

(Office Use Only)

Entry No.:

Certified Copy:

Extract:

Priority:

Search:

Change of Name:

Alterations:

Misc.:

Late Fee:

Short:

Cheque Refund:

Amount Received:

Assessor_____

Number of cheque/bank/money order and name of drawer of cheque if different from applicant.

Copy No.(s):

_____

Date Copy Produced:

(Office Use Only)

Entry No.

Surname & Initials_____

REGISTRAR-GENERAL'S OFFICE, BRISBANE

DEATH

Please Print Name and Postal Address of Person to whom Document is to be Posted.

➡

N.B. This document will not be available for collection prior to➡

_____

_____

_____Postcode_____

Official receipts must be produced when taking delivery of documents.

W 267—GOPRINT

AUSTRALIA — SOUTH AUSTRALIA

Send your requests to:

> Principal Registrar of Births, Deaths and Marriages
> Department of Public and Consumer Affairs
> Edmund Wright House
> 59 King William Street
> G.P.O. Box 1351
> Adelaide, South Australia 5001
> Australia

(011) (61) (8) 226-8561

Cost for a certified Birth Certificate	Au $21.00
Cost for a certified Marriage Certificate	Au $21.00
Cost for a certified Death Certificate	Au $21.00

The Registrar has records from July 1, 1842. Enclose an additional Au $1.00 per certificate for airmail postage. If your request is urgent there is an additional charge of Au $15.00. Please make your international bank draft in Australian dollars payable to the Principal Registrar.

The Family History Library of The Church of Jesus Christ of Latter-day Saints in Salt Lake City, Utah has microfilmed original and published vital records and church registers of South Australia. For further details on their holdings please consult your nearest Family History Center.

Records of interest are also available at the National Library of Australia, Parkes Place, Canberra, A.C.T. 2600; Tel. (011) (61) (62) 621-111.

Births Deaths and Marriages Registration Office
59 King William Street
ADELAIDE 5000

BIRTH

G.P.O. Box 1351
ADELAIDE 5001
This Receipt MUST be produced when collecting documents

BIRTH OF ....

Received amount printed by cash register

You are advised that a certified copy includes **any former married name(s) of the mother.** A copy MAY be supplied omitting this information. Please indicate if you wish this information to be omitted.

☐   place tick in box

NOTE:—If Birth occurred within 6 months of application, state at which hospital

....

Reg. No.

Book........................ Page........................

(Tick appropriate boxes)

☐ **EXTRACT**

☐ **CERTIFICATE**   ☐ **PRIORITY SERVICE**

COMPLETE IN BLOCK LETTERS. Incorrect information may result in a No-Record Result. Additional Fee Payable for a further search.

SURNAME (1.)........................ (2.)........................
            (At Birth)   (At Present)

Given Names........................

Date of Birth........................ Age Last Birthday .... Sex ....

Place of Birth........................
            (Suburb/Town/City)

Father's Name (in full)........................

Mother's Name (in full)........................
            (Include any previous surnames)

1. Name and address of person completing this form

   ....

   Contact Telephone........................

2. Relationship to person named above (e.g. self, mother, brother, etc.)

   ....

3. Purpose for which document is required (e.g. passport, pension, employment, etc.)........................

4. Signed........................

OFFICE USE ONLY

PLEASE COMPLETE THIS SECTION IF DOCUMENT IS TO BE POSTED.

Name
Address and
Postcode

....

....

....

H6550

Births Deaths & Marriages Registration Office
59 King William Street
ADELAIDE 5000

SURNAMES OF PARTIES

..................................**AND**..................................

MARRIAGE

G.P.O. Box 1351
ADELAIDE 5001
This Receipt MUST be produced when collecting documents

Received amount printed by cash register

(Tick appropriate boxes)

☐ **EXTRACT**

☐ **CERTIFICATE**   ☐ **PRIORITY SERVICE**

COMPLETE IN BLOCK LETTERS. Incorrect information may result in a No-Record result. Additional fee payable for a further search.

Groom

SURNAME..

Given Names...

Bride

SURNAME (Prior to Marriage)....................................

Given Names...

Place of Marriage...

Date of Marriage...

Note:—If Marriage occurred within 6 months of application, state name of celebrant

....

Reg. No.

Book ....Page...............................

OFFICE USE ONLY

1. Name and address of person completing this form

....

....

Telephone:..

2. Relationship to person named above (e.g. bride, groom, broker, etc.)..

3. Purpose for which document is required (e.g. passport, real estate, legal, etc.)..................................

4. Signed..

PLEASE COMPLETE THIS SECTION IF DOCUMENT IS TO BE POSTED.

Name
Address and
Postcode

....

....

....

H6536

Births Deaths & Marriages Registration Office
59 King William Street
ADELAIDE 5000

DEATH

G.P.O. Box 1351
ADELAIDE 5001
This Receipt MUST be produced when collecting documents

Received amount printed by cash register

(Tick appropriate boxes)

☐ **EXTRACT**

☐ **CERTIFICATE**

☐ **PRIORITY SERVICE**

Note:—If Death occurred within last 6 months, state name of funeral director

....

COMPLETE IN BLOCK LETTERS. Incorrect information may result in a No-Record result. Additional fee payable for a further search.

SURNAME...

Given Names...

Date of Death...

Place of Death...

Age at Death...

Usual Residence...

Reg. No.

Book ....Page................................

OFFICE USE ONLY

1. Name and address of person completing this form

....

....

2. Relationship to person named above (e.g. widow, solicitor, son, etc.)...

3. Purpose for which document is required (e.g. estate purposes, pension, etc.)...

4. Signed...

PLEASE COMPLETE THIS SECTION IF DOCUMENT IS TO BE POSTED.

Name
Address and
Postcode

....

....

....

STATE PRINT R1073

AUSTRALIA — TASMANIA

Send your requests to:

Registrar General of Births, Deaths and Marriages
15 Murray Street
G.P.O. Box 198
Hobart, Tasmania 7001
Australia

(011) (61) (2) 30-3793

Cost for a certified Birth Certificate	Au $20.00
Cost for a certified Marriage Certificate	Au $20.00
Cost for a certified Death Certificate	Au $20.00
Cost for an extract of the above Certificates	Au $15.00

The Registrar General has records from 1803 now that church registers from 1803 to 1838 have been added to the Registrar's records. If your request is urgent there is a Au $20.00 fee per document.

The Family History Library of The Church of Jesus Christ of Latter-day Saints in Salt Lake City, Utah has microfilmed original and published vital records and church registers of Tasmania. For further details on their holdings please consult your nearest Family History Center.

Records of interest are also available at the National Library of Australia, Parkes Place, Canberra, A.C.T. 2600; Tel. (011) (61) (62) 621-111.

Application for Search

BIRTH — TASMANIA

To: Registrar General,
    Registrar.

I hereby apply for:- (Tick appropriate box)

EXTRACT search ☐   CERTIFICATE search ☐   EXTENDED search ☐

of birth on the following information:—

    Christian names...

    Surname at birth (Maiden name) ....

    Birthplace (City or Town) ....

    Date of birth ..../ .... / .... (Age ....) OR if not known

        years to be searched..................to................. inclusive.

    Full names natural parents: (delete as necessary)
               adoptive

    Father: ....

    Mother: ....(Maiden name ....)

    Purpose for which Extract or Certificate is required ....

Name of Applicant   Mr
  (Block Letters)   Mrs ....
                  Ms
                  Miss

Relationship to person registered ....

    Address in full ....

                   .... Postcode ....

    Telephone No. .... Date ....

I enclose the amount of $ .... as payment for search.

PLEASE POST THE RESULT OF SEARCH TO ME.

                (Tick One)

I WILL COLLECT THE RESULT OF SEARCH.

Signature ....

FOR OFFICE USE ONLY
Collected ....
Posted ....

K4781

Application for Search

MARRIAGE — TASMANIA

To: Registrar-General, GPO Box 198, Hobart TAS 7001

I hereby apply for:— (Tick appropriate box)

EXTRACT search ☐   CERTIFICATE search ☐   EXTENDED search ☐

of marriage on the following information:—

Full names of parties:—

Bridegroom: ....

Bride (prior to marriage): ....

Date of marriage ..../ ..../ .... OR if not known

years to be searched..................to................. inclusive.

Place of Marriage: ....in Tasmania.

Purpose for which Extract or Certificate is required ....

....

Name of Applicant   Mr
(Block Letters)   Mrs ....
   Ms
   Miss

Relationship to person registered ....

Address in full ....

.... Postcode ....

Telephone No. .... Date ....

I enclose the amount of $ .... as payment for search.

PLEASE POST THE RESULT OF SEARCH TO ME.

(Tick One)

I WILL COLLECT THE RESULT OF SEARCH.

Signature ....

FOR OFFICE USE ONLY
Collected ....
Posted ....

K2772

Application for Search

DEATH — TASMANIA

To: Registrar General,
Registrar.

I hereby apply for:— (Tick appropriate box)

EXTRACT search ☐   CERTIFICATE search ☐   EXTENDED search ☐

of death on the following information:—

Full Names: ....

Place of Death: ....in Tasmania.

Date of Death ..../...................../...................... OR if not known

years to be searched .... to .... inclusive.

Purpose for which Extract or Certificate is required: ....

_____

Name of Applicant
(Block Letters)

Mr
Mrs ....
Ms
Miss

Relationship to person registered ....

Address in full ....

.... Postcode ....

Telephone No. .... Date ....

I enclose the amount of $ .... as payment for search.

PLEASE POST THE RESULT OF SEARCH TO ME.

(Tick One)

I WILL COLLECT THE RESULT OF SEARCH.

Signature ....

FOR OFFICE USE ONLY
Collected ....
Posted ....

K3995

AUSTRALIA — VICTORIA

Send your requests to:

Registry of Births, Deaths, and Marriages
295 Queen Street
P.O. Box 4332
Melbourne, Victoria 3001
Australia

(011) (61) (3) 603-5800

Cost for a certified Birth Certificate	Au $30.00
Cost for an heirloom Birth Certificate	Au $32.00
Cost for a certified Marriage Certificate	Au $30.00
Cost for a certified Death Certificate	Au $30.00

With the incorporation of early church records, the Registry now has records from 1837. Vital registration began on July 1, 1853. If your request is urgent there is a charge of Au $26.00.

The Family History Library of The Church of Jesus Christ of Latter-day Saints in Salt Lake City, Utah has microfilmed many of the original and published vital records and church registers of Victoria. For further details on their holdings please consult your nearest Family History Center.

Records of interest are also available at the National Library of Australia, Parkes Place, Canberra, A.C.T. 2600; Tel. (011) (61) (62) 621-111.

PLEASE USE BLOCK LETTERS

APPLICATION FOR CERTIFICATE OF

BIRTHS IN VICTORIA

Registration of Births, Deaths & Marriages Regulations Form 4

THIS RECEIPT MUST BE PRODUCED WHEN COLLECTING DOCUMENTS

Applications to be made to:

Registry of Births, Deaths & Marriages
P.O. Box 4332
Melbourne 3001

or delivered to

295 Queen Street
Melbourne
Telephone: 603 5800

Insert family name and initials of the birth		Year of birth	

Received amount printed by cash register

TICK APPROPRIATE BOXES

☐ **PRIORITY SERVICE (Additional Fee)**

☐ **POST (Complete section below)**

☐ **COLLECT**

FOR DETAILS CONCERNING FEES AND APPLICATION ENQUIRIES TELEPHONE RECORDED INFORMATION SERVICE ON (03) 603 5888

Enclosed is a cheque/money order/

for $..........................

DETAILS OF BIRTH REQUIRED

Official Entry No. If Known		Place of birth City/suburb/town Hospital	VICTORIA
Date of birth	Day Month Year / /	Or years to be searched 5 year period(s)	From.. to..
Family name (at birth)		Christian or given names	
Fathers name	Family name	Christian or given names	
Mothers name	Family name (Maiden)	Christian or given names	

APPLICANTS DETAILS

Applicants name		Signature of applicant	
Applicants address			Tel:
Reason document is required		Relationship of applicant	

Office hours for making applications—8.30 a.m. to 4 p.m. Monday to Friday

IF THIS APPLICATION RELATES TO A PERSON OTHER THAN YOURSELF WRITTEN AUTHORITY AND IDENTIFICATION MAY BE REQUIRED

PLEASE COMPLETE THIS SECTION IF DOCUMENT IS TO BE POSTED

PLEASE USE BLOCK LETTERS

Name	
Address and Postcode	

Printed by Corporate Image—Telephone 416 3211

PLEASE USE BLOCK LETTERS

APPLICATION FOR CERTIFICATE OF

MARRIAGES IN VICTORIA

Registration of Births, Deaths & Marriages Regulations Form 9

THIS RECEIPT MUST BE PRODUCED WHEN COLLECTING DOCUMENTS

Applications to be made to:

Registry of Births, Deaths & Marriages
P.O. Box 4332
Melbourne 3001

or delivered to

295 Queen Street
Melbourne
Telephone: 603 5800

Insert family name of marriage party(ies)		Year of marriage	Received amount printed by cash register

TICK APPROPRIATE BOXES

☐ **PRIORITY SERVICE (Additional Fee)**

☐ **POST (Complete section below)**

☐ **COLLECT**

FOR DETAILS CONCERNING FEES AND APPLICATION ENQUIRIES TELEPHONE RECORDED INFORMATION SERVICE ON (03) 603 5888

Enclosed is a cheque/money order/

for $....................................

DETAILS OF MARRIAGE REQUIRED

Registration Number (if known)			Place of marriage City/suburb/town		Victoria
Date of marriage	Day Month Year / /		Or years to be searched 5 year period(s)	From........................ to........................	
Bridegroom	Family name			Christian or given names	
Bride	Family name at time of marriage			Christian or given names	

APPLICANTS DETAILS

Applicants name		Signature of applicant	
Applicants address			Tel:
Reason document is required		Applicants relationship to parties	

Office hours for making applications—8.30 a.m. to 4 p.m. Monday to Friday

IF THIS APPLICATION RELATES TO A PERSON OTHER THAN YOURSELF WRITTEN AUTHORITY AND IDENTIFICATION MAY BE REQUIRED

PLEASE COMPLETE THIS SECTION IF DOCUMENT IS TO BE POSTED

PLEASE USE BLOCK LETTERS

Name	
Address and Postcode	

Printed by Corporate Image—Telephone 416 3211

PLEASE USE BLOCK LETTERS

APPLICATION FOR CERTIFICATE OF

DEATHS IN VICTORIA

Registration of Births, Deaths & Marriages Regulations Form 8

THIS RECEIPT MUST BE PRODUCED WHEN COLLECTING DOCUMENTS

Applications to be made to:

Registry of Births, Deaths & Marriages
P.O. Box 4332
Melbourne 3001

or delivered to

295 Queen Street
Melbourne
Telephone: 603 5800

Insert family name of deceased and initials		Year of death	

Received amount printed by cash register

TICK APPROPRIATE BOXES

☐ **PRIORITY SERVICE (Additional Fee)**

☐ **POST (Complete section below)**

☐ **COLLECT**

FOR DETAILS CONCERNING FEES AND APPLICATION ENQUIRIES TELEPHONE RECORDED INFORMATION SERVICE ON (03) 603 5888

Enclosed is a cheque/money order/

for $....................................

DETAILS OF DEATH REQUIRED

Registration Number (if known)		Place of death City/suburb/town	, Victoria
Date of death	Day Month Year / /	Search period if date unknown	From...................................... to......................................

Full name of deceased			Age at death
	(Surname)	(Christian or given Names)	, years
Fathers full name		Mothers full name (maiden)	
Name of spouse (if applicable)		Other information e.g. birthplace, children, etc.	

APPLICANTS DETAILS

Applicants name		Signature of applicant	
Applicants address			Tel:
Reason document is required			

Office hours for making applications—8.30 a.m. to 4 p.m. Monday to Friday

PLEASE COMPLETE THIS SECTION IF DOCUMENT IS TO BE POSTED

PLEASE USE BLOCK LETTERS

Name	
Address and Postcode	

AUSTRALIA — WESTERN AUSTRALIA

Send your requests to:

> Registrar General of Births, Deaths and Marriages
> Westralia Square, Level 10
> 38 Mounts Bay Road
> P.O. Box 7720, Cloisters Square
> Perth, Western Australia 6850
> Australia
>
> (011) (61) (9) 264-1555, FAX (011) (61) (9) 264-1599

Cost for a certified Birth Certificate	Au $20.00
Cost for a certified Marriage Certificate	Au $20.00
Cost for a certified Death Certificate	Au $20.00

The Registrar General has records from September 9, 1841. Genealogists may obtain birth records more than 80 years old, marriage records more than 40 years old, and death records before 1980. If your request is urgent there is an additional charge of Au $12.00.

The Family History Library of The Church of Jesus Christ of Latter-day Saints in Salt Lake City, Utah has microfilmed original and published vital records and church registers of Western Australia. For further details on their holdings please consult your nearest Family History Center.

Records of interest are also available at the National Library of Australia, Parkes Place, Canberra, A.C.T. 2600; Tel. (011) (61) (62) 621-111.

Registrar General's Office, Westralia Square, 38 Mounts Bay Road, Perth W.A.

RG 284

BIRTH CERTIFICATE APPLICATION

PLEASE COMPLETE ALL ITEMS

USE BLOCK LETTERS

APPLICANTS NAME & POSTAL ADDRESS

....

....

.... Postcode ....

Please indicate Number of Documents required

| Extract | Number |
| Certified Copy | Number |

TO BE

Collected ☐   Posted ☐   Priority Service ☐
(additional Fee Payable)

038601

REGISTRATION DETAILS (USING BLOCK LETTERS)

SURNAME (at birth)	
GIVEN NAMES	
DATE OF BIRTH	
PLACE OF BIRTH	
FATHERS NAME (in full)	
MOTHERS MAIDEN NAME (in full)	

APPLICANT DETAILS

APPLICANTS NAME		
APPLICANTS ADDRESS		
PURPOSE DOCUMENT REQUIRED		**RELATIONSHIP OF APPLICANT**

APPLICANTS SURNAME (BLOCK LETTERS)

REGN No.
DUE ON
DUE ON
REGN No.
Receipt

THIS INTERIM RECEIPT MUST BE PRODUCED WHEN COLLECTING DOCUMENT

Registrar General's Office, Westralia Square, 38 Mounts Bay Road Perth W.A.
Telephone: 264 1555

05278/1/92–200 Pds–S/7816

038601

RG 473

№ 6101

OFFICE USE ONLY

MARRIAGE CERTIFICATE APPLICATION

PLEASE COMPLETE ALL ITEMS
USE BLOCK LETTERS

Received the amount as printed by Cash Register

APPLICANTS NAME & POSTAL ADDRESS

....
....
.... Postcode ....

Please indicate Number of Documents required

Extract	Number

Certified Copy	Number

TO BE | Collected ☐ | Posted ☐ | Priority Service ☐
(additional Fee Payable)

№ 6101

REGISTRATION DETAILS (USING BLOCK LETTERS)

BRIDEGROOM'S NAME (in full)	
BRIDE'S MAIDEN NAME (in full)	
IF BRIDE PREVIOUSLY MARRIED NAME OF FORMER HUSBAND	
DATE OF MARRIAGE	
PLACE OF MARRIAGE	

APPLICANT DETAILS

APPLICANTS NAME	
APPLICANTS ADDRESS	
PURPOSE DOCUMENT REQUIRED	RELATIONSHIP OF APPLICANT

REGN No.

DUE ON

APPLICANTS SURNAME (BLOCK LETTERS)

DUE ON

REGN No.

Receipt

THIS INTERIM RECEIPT MUST BE PRODUCED WHEN COLLECTING DOCUMENT

№ 6101

RG 365

N⁰ 2904

OFFICE USE ONLY

DEATH CERTIFICATE APPLICATION

PLEASE COMPLETE ALL ITEMS

USE BLOCK LETTERS

APPLICANTS NAME & POSTAL ADDRESS

....
....
.... Postcode ....

Received the amount as printed by Cash Register

Please indicate Number of Documents required

Extract	Number

Certified Copy	Number

N⁰ 2904

TO BE   Collected ☐   Posted ☐   Priority Service ☐
(additional Fee Payable)

REGISTRATION DETAILS (USING BLOCK LETTERS)

SURNAME	
GIVEN NAMES	
DATE OF DEATH	
PLACE OF DEATH	

APPLICANT DETAILS

APPLICANTS NAME		
APPLICANTS ADDRESS		
PURPOSE DOCUMENT REQUIRED	**RELATIONSHIP OF APPLICANT**	

REGN No.

DUE ON

APPLICANTS SURNAME (BLOCK LETTERS)

DUE ON

REGN No.

Receipt

THIS INTERIM RECEIPT MUST BE PRODUCED WHEN COLLECTING DOCUMENT

N⁰ 2904

AUSTRIA

Standesamt
(Town), Austria

Additional help is available from the Department for Personal Registration (Federal Ministry of the Interior, Herrengasse 7, A-1014 Vienna, Austria). There is no central office for vital records in Austria. To obtain copies of birth, marriage, and death certificates write to the Civil Registration District Office in the town where the event occurred. Vital records are on file from 1784. Current vital registration is considered to be complete.

AZERBAIJAN

Russian-American Genealogical
  Archival Service (RAGAS)
P.O. Box 236
Glen Echo, Maryland 20812

(202) 501-5206

Cost for a Birth, Marriage, or Death Certificate $20.00

By an agreement between the United States National Archives Volunteer Association and the Archives of Russia Society RAGAS receives and processes requests for vital records in some of the former Soviet republics. Although at this time RAGAS is able to deal mainly with Russia, Belarus, and Ukraine they might be able to help you with your inquiries regarding Azerbaijan. There is a $2.00 shipping fee. The service also is available at an hourly rate. (See Russia for application forms.)

BAHAMAS

Send your requests to:

Registrar General's Department
Office of the Attorney General
P.O. Box N 532
Nassau, NP, Bahamas

(809) 322-3316

Cost for a certified Birth Certificate	$2.50
Cost for a certified Marriage Certificate	$2.50
Cost for a certified Death Certificate	$2.50
Cost for a duplicate Certificate	$2.00

The Registrar General has birth and death records from January 1, 1850 and marriage records from January 1, 1799.

The Family History Library of The Church of Jesus Christ of Latter-day Saints in Salt Lake City, Utah has microfilmed original and published vital records and church registers of the Bahamas and the Caribbean. For further details on their holdings please consult your nearest Family History Center.

REGISTRAR GENERAL'S DEPARTMENT

P.O. Box N532   Nassau, Bahamas

To: Registrar General
Nassau, Bahamas

APPLICATION FOR BIRTH CERTIFICATE

I desire to have a search made for and* _____ copy/ies supplied
of the Register of Birth of

_____

(Enter All Names)

A.

Born at _____

on the Island of _____

Date of Birth _____

Father's full name _____

Mother's full name _____

Mother's maiden name _____

Signature of Applicant _____

*

Insert number of copies required.

OFFICE USE ONLY

B.

Period searched _____ By _____

Period checked _____ By _____

Certified copies made _____ By _____

Examined by _____

Copies received by _____

Registration found in year _____ At page _____

C.

_____ (a) No record of Birth can be found on file.

_____ (b) Birth Record shows information given above to be correct.

_____ (c) Birth of male/female child recorded without name.

_____ (d) Father's name not recorded.

Indicate with (   ) where appropriate at (a), (b), (c) or (d).

BAHRAIN

Registrar of Births and Deaths
Ministry of Health
Manama, Bahrain

Birth registrations are nearly comprehensive, however overall registration is incomplete.

BANGLADESH

Bangladesh Demographic Survey and
    Vital Registration System
Bangladesh Bureau of Statistics
Gana Bhavan Extension Block-1
Sher-A-Bangla Nagar
Dhaka 7, Bangladesh

Cost for a Birth, Marriage, or Death Certificate   Tk. 7.50/-

While some records exist from 1873, modern vital registration begins in 1960. Marriages and divorces are filed with the Ministry of Law and Parliamentary Affairs. The Directorate of Archives and Libraries, National Library of Bangladesh also has records; contact them at Sher-e-Banglanagar, Agargaon, Dhaka 7, Bangladesh.

BARBADOS

Send your requests to:

> Registration Office
> Supreme Court of Barbados
> Law Courts
> Coleridge Street
> Bridgetown, Barbados, WI

(809) 426-3461

Cost for a certified Birth Certificate	BD $5.00
Cost for a certified Marriage Certificate	BD $5.00
Cost for a certified Death Certificate	BD $5.00

The Registration Office has birth records from January 1, 1890, marriage records from 1637, and death records from January 1, 1925. There are also baptismal records before 1890 and burial records before 1925. These can be requested using the birth and death application forms, respectively.

For persons over 60 years of age the cost is BD $1.00. Make international bank draft payable in Barbados currency.

The Family History Library of The Church of Jesus Christ of Latter-day Saints in Salt Lake City, Utah has microfilmed original and published vital records and church registers of Barbados and the Caribbean. For further details on their holdings please consult your nearest Family History Center.

APPLICATION FOR BIRTH CERTIFICATE

SURNAME	CHRISTIAN NAMES

Date of Birth:	Day	Month	Year

Place of Birth:

Place of Baptism:

PARENTS NAMES

	SURNAME	CHRISTIAN NAMES
Father		
Mother		

OFFICE USE ONLY

References:

REGISTRATION OFFICE

APPLICATION FOR DEATH CERTIFICATE

SURNAME	CHRISTIAN NAMES

Date of Death:

Place of Death:

FOR OFFICE USE ONLY.

Reference

REGISTRATION OFFICE

APPLICATION FOR MARRIAGE CERTIFICATE

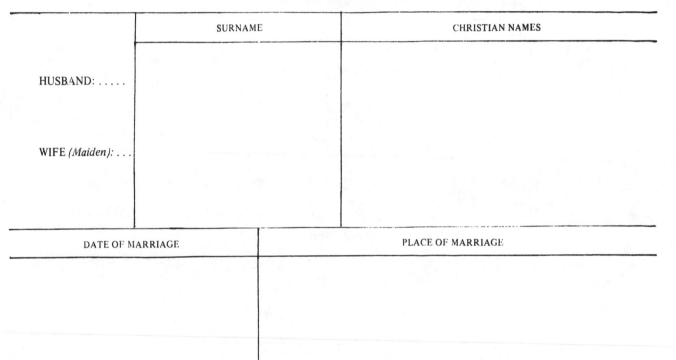

	SURNAME	CHRISTIAN NAMES
HUSBAND:		
WIFE *(Maiden)*: . . .		

DATE OF MARRIAGE	PLACE OF MARRIAGE

BELARUS

Russian-American Genealogical
  Archival Service (RAGAS)
P.O. Box 236
Glen Echo, Maryland 20812

(202) 501-5206

Cost for a Birth, Marriage, or Death Certificate $20.00

By an agreement between the United States National Archives Volunteer Association and the Archives of Russia Society this agency will receive and process requests for vital records in Belarus. There is a $2.00 shipping fee per document. The service also is available at an hourly rate. (See Russia for application forms.)

BELGIUM

Registres de l'Etat Civil
(Town), Belgium

There is no central office for vital records in Belgium. To obtain copies of birth, marriage, and death certificates write to the town where the event occurred. Vital records are on file from 1796 and the current registration is considered to be complete.

There are also records at the General State Archives; contact them at Archives Generales du Royaume (AGR), Algemeen Rijksarchief, rue de Ruysbroeck 2, B-1000 Brussels, Belgium; Tel. (011) (32) (2) 513-76-80; FAX (011) (32) (2) 513-76-81.

BELIZE

Send your requests to:

Registrar General
The General Registry
Judiciary Department
Court House Plaza
P.O. Box 87
Belize City, Belize

(011) (501) (2) 72-053

Cost for a certified Birth Certificate	B $4.00
Cost for a certified Marriage Certificate	B $5.00
Cost for a certified Death Certificate	B $4.00

The Registry has birth and death records from 1885 and marriage records from 1881 to the present.

The Family History Library of The Church of Jesus Christ of Latter-day Saints in Salt Lake City, Utah has microfilmed original and published records of Belize and South America. For further details on their holdings please consult your nearest Family History Center.

APPLICATION FOR BIRTH CERTIFICATE

A fee of $3.00 is payable for each certified copy and a $1.00 for a search in connection therewith.

I desire to have a search made for and if found .... copy/copies of the register of birth for:

NAME OF PERSON: ....

BORN AT: ....

ON THE .... DAY OF .... 19 ....

REGISTERED ON .... DAY OF .... 19 ....

AGE LAST BIRTHDAY ....

FATHER'S NAME ....

MOTHER'S NAME ....

MOTHER'S MAIDEN NAME ....

I enclose the sum of $ .... to cover cost.

APPLICANT'S NAME ....

ADDRESS ....

DATE ....

RECEIVED BY ....

DATE ....

_____

FOR OFFICIAL USE ONLY

REGIS. NO. ....

ENTRY NO. ....

TYPED BY ....

CHECKED BY ....

SIGNED BY ....

<u>APPLICATION FOR MARRIAGE CERTIFICATE</u>

A fee of $3.00 is payable for each certified copy and $2.00 for a search in connection therewith.

I desire to have a search made for, and if found ....copy/copies of the Register of Marriage for :

NME OF HUSBAND ....

MAIDEN NAME OF WIFE ....

MARRIED AT ....

IN THE DISTRICT OF ....

ON THE .... DAY OF .... 19 ....

BY REV. ....

        I enclose the sum of $ .... to cover cost.

                          NAME OF APPLICANT ....

                          ADDRESS ....

                          DATE ....

RECEIVED BY ....

DATE ....

_____

<u>FOR OFFICIAL USE ONLY</u>

R.C.R. NO. ....

ENTRY NO. ....

TYPED BY ....

EXAMINED BY ....

SIGNED BY ....

APPLICATION FOR DEATH CERTIFICATE

A fee of $3.00 is payable for each certified copy and a $1.00 for a search in connection therewith.

I desire to have a search made for and if found .... copy/copies of the Register of Death for:

NAME OF PERSON: ....

Died AT: ....

ON THE .... DAYOF .... 19 ....

REGISTERED ON .... DAY OF .... 19 ....

AGE LAST BIRTHDAY ....

I enclose the sum of $ .... to cover cost.

APPLICANT'S NAME ....

ADDRESS ....

DATE ....

RECEIVED BY ....

DATE ....

_____

FOR OFFICIAL USE ONLY

R.C.R. NO. ....

ENTRY NO. ....

TYPED BY ....

CHECKED BY ....

SIGNED BY ....

BENIN

Maire
(Town), Benin

Vital registration began in Benin, formerly known as Dahomey, in 1933 and included mostly French citizens and foreigners. By 1950 registration included most residents within 15 miles of a registration center.

BERMUDA

Registry General
Ministry of Labour and Home Affairs
Government Administration Building
30 Parliament Street
Hamilton 12, Bermuda

(809) 295-5151

Cost for a Birth or Death Certificate	US $23.00
Cost for a certified Marriage Certificate	US $25.00

The Registry General has birth and marriage records from 1866 and death records from 1865 to the present.

BHUTAN

Registration, Census and Immigration Division
Department of Registration
Ministry of Home Affairs
Thimphu, Bhutan

Cost for a Birth, Marriage, or Death Certificate	Nu. 2

Vital registration is considered to be 70 percent complete.

BOLIVIA

Dirección Nacional de Registro Civil
Ministerio del Interior, Migración,
  y Justicia
Av. Arce No. 2409
La Paz, Bolivia

The first laws authorizing vital registration were passed in 1898; modern vital registration in Bolivia begins July 1, 1940. Current vital registration is considered to be incomplete.

BOSNIA and HERZEGOVINA

Civil Registration Office
(Town), Bosnia and Herzegovina

Vital records are on file from 1946. Records before that were kept by the local churches.

BOTSWANA

Registrar, Civil Registration and Vital Events
Department of Culture, Registration and Social Welfare
Private Bag 00185
Gaborone, Botswana
(011) (267) 360-1000

Cost for a Birth or Death Certificate	50t
Cost for a Marriage Certificate	P 1.00

The Registrar has birth records from 1915, marriage records from 1895, and death records from 1904. In 1966 Botswana became independent, and vital registration became compulsory in 1969. The registration is not considered to be complete. Send your requests for divorce records to The High Court of Botswana, Private Bag 1, Lobatse, Botswana; FAX (011) (267) 332-317.

BRAZIL

State Archives
(Town, State), Brazil

Vital registration began on September 9, 1870. Records are kept by the Civil Registration Office in each town and are sent regularly to the State Archives of each of Brazil's states. Divorces are on file at the State Archives and at the court where the decree was issued.

BRUNEI

Registrar of Births and Deaths
Medical and Health Department
Ministry of Health
Bandar Seri Begawan 2062, Brunei

Vital registration began in 1923 for births and deaths and 1948 for marriages. Current registration is considered to be complete.

BULGARIA

Executive Committee
Town Council
(Town), Bulgaria

Registration began in 1881 and is more than 90 percent complete.

BURKINA FASO

Center for the Civil Status
(Town), Burkina Faso

Registration began in 1933 for French citizens and expanded in 1950 to include all residents living within 15 miles of the registration centers.

BURUNDI

Department de la Population
Ministere de l'Interieur
BP 160, Gitega
Bujumbura, Burundi

Vital registration began in 1922. Even though efforts have been made to include all areas the registration is not considered to be complete.

CAMBODIA

Cambodia has no organized system of vital registration.

CAMEROON

Ministere de l'Administration Territoriale
B.P. 7854
Yaounde, Cameroon

Registration began in 1917 for western Cameroon and in 1935 for the entire country. Divorces are recorded on the marriage and birth certificates of both parties.

CANADA—ALBERTA

Send your requests to:

> Health
> Division of Vital Statistics
> Texaco Building
> 10130, 112th Street
> Edmonton, Alberta
> Canada T5K 2P2
>
> (403) 427-2683, FAX (403) 422-9117

Cost for a certified Birth Certificate	Can $20.00
Cost for a certified Marriage Certificate	Can $20.00
Cost for a certified Death Certificate	Can $20.00

The Alberta Division of Vital Statistics has birth records from 1853, marriage records from 1898, and death records from 1893. Make payment payable to "Provincial Treasurer."

The Alberta Culture Center (Provincial Library, 16214 114th Avenue, Edmonton, Alberta T5M 2Z6) and the Provincial Archives of Alberta (12845 102nd Avenue, Edmonton, Alberta T5N 0M6) have materials of interest as well.

The National Archives of Canada (395 Wellington Street, Ottawa, K1A 0N3; Tel. 613-995-5138) and the National Library of Canada (same address; Tel. 613-995-9481; FAX 613-996-4424) have extensive holdings.

The Family History Library of The Church of Jesus Christ of Latter-day Saints in Salt Lake City, Utah has microfilmed original and published records of Alberta and Canada. For further details on their holdings please consult your nearest Family History Center.

Alberta

HEALTH
DIVISION OF VITAL STATISTICS
10130 - 112 STREET
EDMONTON, ALBERTA T5K 2P2
PHONE: 427-2683

APPLICATION FOR CERTIFICATE
(BIRTH, MARRIAGE, OR DEATH)
PLEASE PRINT ALL INFORMATION CLEARLY, ACCURATELY AND
IN FULL TO AVOID ANY DELAYS IN PROCESSING THIS APPLICATION

SHADED AREAS FOR
OFFICE USE ONLY!

Name:

If Company, Attention:

Your Reference No. (if applicable):

Apt. No.   Street Address:

City: Province: (Country)   Postal Code:

I require these certificates for the following purpose
(give date of departure if for passport):

State your Relationship to person named on certificate:

Signature of Applicant: Phone No. (During Office Hours)

Number of Certificates x _____   **= Total Fee Enclosed** _____

FOR OFFICE USE ONLY

☐ CHEQUE   Amount $ Mail Clerk: Cashier:
☐ CASH

Remarks:

Surname (if certificate is for a married woman surname required only):	(Given Names)	Sex: ☐ M ☐ F	Quantity	Size

Wallet

| Date of Birth: Month by Name   Day   Year | Place of Birth (city, town, or village): | Name of Hospital Where Birth Occurred: | | |

ALBERTA   Framing

| Surname of Father: | (Given Names) | Birthplace of Father: | | Certified Copy |

| Maiden Surname of Mother: | Any Other Surname Known By: | Given Names: | Birthplace of Mother: | Genealogical |

| Date of Registration: | Place of Registration: | Amendment Number: | Registration Number: | Searched: | Double Searched: | Verified: |

Surname of Groom:	(Given Names)	Birthplace of Groom:	Quantity	Size

Wallet

| Surname of Bride (prior to this marriage): | (Given Names) | Birthplace of Bride: | | Framing |

| Date of Marriage: Month by Name   Day   Year | Place of Marriage (city, town or village): | | Certified Copy |

ALBERTA   Genealogical

| Date of Registration: | Place of Registration: | Amendment Number: | Registration Number: | Searched: | Double Searched: | Verified: |

Surname of Deceased:	(Given Names)	Age:	Sex: ☐ M ☐ F	Quantity	Size

Framing

Date of Death: Month by Name Day Year	Place of Death (city, town or village):	Marital Status:
	ALBERTA	☐ Never married
		☐ Married

Certified Copy

| Usual Residence of Deceased Prior to Death (city, town or village): | Date of Birth: Month by Name   Day   Year | ☐ Widowed |
| | | ☐ Divorced |

Genealogical

| Date of Registration: | Place of Registration: | Amendment Number: | Registration Number: | Searched: | Double Searched: | Verified: |

DVS-32A (92/06)

CANADA—BRITISH COLUMBIA

Send your requests to:

Province of British Columbia
Ministry of Health
Division of Vital Statistics
818 Fort Street
Victoria, British Columbia
Canada V8W 1H8

(604) 952-2681, (800) 663-3528

Cost for a certified Birth Certificate	Can $25.00
Cost for a Genealogy Verification Abstract	Can $30.00
Cost for a certified Marriage Certificate	Can $25.00
Cost for a Genealogy Verification Abstract	Can $30.00
Cost for a certified Death Certificate	Can $25.00

The British Columbia Ministry of Health has vital records from 1872 and some baptismal registers from 1849. Birth certificates are issued only to the individual, parents of the child, or an authorized agent. Marriage certificates are issued only to the individuals married or to an authorized agent. Death certificates are issued to anyone who has a valid reason for the request. If your request is urgent there is a Can $50.00 charge for 24-hour service. Genealogists should request a genealogy verification extract for birth and marriage certificates. There is a Can $50.00 charge for an extended genealogical search.

Other repositories to contact are: The National Archives of Canada (395 Wellington Street, Ottawa, K1A 0N3; Tel. 613-995-5138), the National Library of Canada (same address; Tel. 613- 995-9481; FAX 613-996-4424), and the British Columbia Archives and Records Service (655 Belleville Street, Victoria, British Columbia V8V 1X4; Tel. 613-387-5885 or 387-1321).

The Family History Library of The Church of Jesus Christ of Latter-day Saints in Salt Lake City, Utah has microfilmed original and published records of British Columbia. For further details on their holdings please consult your nearest Family History Center.

APPLICATION FOR SERVICE

YOUR FILE _____

MAILING ADDRESS:
PLEASE **PRINT** YOUR NAME AND ADDRESS
CLEARLY INCLUDING POSTAL CODE

NAME _____

ADDRESS _____

CITY & PROVINCE _____

				–			

POSTAL CODE

IF COMPANY,
ATTENTION _____

HOME No. _____ BUSINESS No. _____

SHADED AREA FOR OFFICE USE ONLY

REFUND $

PLEASE INDICATE TYPE AND NUMBER
OF CERTIFICATE(S) REQUIRED _____

IF BIRTH CERTIFICATE(S) REQUIRED COMPLETE THIS SECTION (PLEASE PRINT)

SURNAME (IF FOR MARRIED WOMAN GIVEN MAIDEN SURNAME)   (GIVEN NAMES)   SEX

A   B Z

MONTH	DATE OF BIRTH DAY	YEAR	PLACE OF BIRTH (CITY, TOWN OR VILLAGE)
		C	

BRITISH
D COLUMBIA

SURNAME OF FATHER   (GIVEN NAMES)   BIRTHPLACE OF FATHER

E   F   G

MAIDEN SURNAME OF MOTHER   (GIVEN NAMES)   BIRTHPLACE OF MOTHER

H   I   J

REGISTRATION NUMBER   REGISTRATION DATE   AMENDMENT No.

S _____ D _____ V _____

SMALL 9.5 cm x 6.4 cm ☐
LARGE 21.6 cm x 17.8 cm ☐
Genealogy ☐

IF MARRIAGE CERTIFICATE(S) REQUIRED COMPLETE THIS SECTION (PLEASE PRINT)

SURNAME OF GROOM   (GIVEN NAMES)   BIRTHPLACE OF GROOM

K   L M

SURNAME OF BRIDE PRIOR TO MARRIAGE   (GIVEN NAMES)   BIRTHPLACE OF BRIDE

N   O P

MONTH	DATE OF MARRIAGE DAY	YEAR	PLACE OF MARRIAGE (CITY, TOWN OR VILLAGE)
		Q	

BRITISH
R COLUMBIA

REGISTRATION NUMBER   REGISTRATION DATE   AMENDMENT No.

SEARCHED _____ VERIFIED _____

SMALL 9.5 cm x 6.4 cm ☐
LARGE 21.6 cm x 17.8 cm ☐
CERTIFIED PHOTOCOPY SEE NOTE 3 ☐
Genealogy ☐

IF DEATH CERTIFICATE(S) REQUIRED COMPLETE THIS SECTION (PLEASE PRINT)

SURNAME OF DECEASED   (GIVEN NAMES)   AGE   SEX

S   T   U Z

MONTH	DATE OF DEATH DAY	YEAR	PLACE OF DEATH (CITY, TOWN OR VILLAGE)
		V	

BRITISH
W COLUMBIA

PERMANENT RESIDENCE OF DECEASED PRIOR TO DEATH   PLACE OF BIRTH

X   Y

REGISTRATION NUMBER   REGISTRATION DATE   AMENDMENT No.

SEARCHED _____ VERIFIED _____

LARGE 21.6 cm x 17.8 cm ☐
Genealogy ☐

STATE **YOUR** RELATIONSHIP TO THE PERSON NAMED IN APPLICATION

_____

STATE **SPECIFIC REASON** WHY CERTIFICATION IS REQUIRED

_____

X _____
(WRITTEN SIGNATURE OF APPLICANT) (DO NOT PRINT)

FEE ENCLOSED

$ _____

CANADA — MANITOBA

Send your requests to:

> Vital Statistics
> Department of Family Services
> 254 Portage Avenue
> Winnipeg, Manitoba
> Canada R3C 0B6

(204) 945-3701

Cost for a certified Birth Certificate	Can $20.00
Cost for a certified Marriage Certificate	Can $20.00
Cost for a certified Death Certificate	Can $20.00

The Manitoba Office of Vital Statistics has records from 1882. If your request is urgent there is a Can $50.00 fee for a 24-hour rush service.

The Manitoba Provincial Archives (200 Vaughan Street, Winnipeg, Manitoba R3C 1T5; Tel. 204-945-3971; FAX 204-948-2008) also has records.

The National Archives of Canada (395 Wellington Street, Ottawa, K1A 0N3; Tel. 613-995-5138) and the National Library of Canada (same address; Tel. 613-995-9481; FAX 613-996-4424) have extensive holdings.

The Family History Library of The Church of Jesus Christ of Latter-day Saints in Salt Lake City, Utah has microfilmed original and published records of Manitoba and Canada. For further details on their holdings please consult your nearest Family History Center.

Application Form/
Formule de demande

Manitoba
Family Services
Vital Statistics

Services à
la famille
Manitoba
État civil

File Number/
N° du
dossier

MAILING ADDRESS	ADRESSE POSTALE
PLEASE **PRINT** YOUR NAME AND ADDRESS CLEARLY. THIS PORTION WILL BE USED WHEN MAILING YOUR CERTIFICATE.	PRIÈRE D'ÉCRIRE VOTRE NOM ET ADRESSE CLAIREMENT **EN LETTRES MOULÉES.** CETTE PARTIE SERVIRA À L'ENVOI DE VOTRE CERTIFICAT.

Name/Nom

Address/Adresse   Apt. No./N° app.

City/Ville   Province   Postal Code/Code postal

ENGLISH/
ANGLAIS

FRENCH/
FRANÇAIS

INDICATE TYPE AND NUMBER OF
CERTIFICATES REQUIRED
INDIQUER LE GENRE ET LE NOMBRE
DE CERTIFICATS VOULUS

Please print all information clearly. / Prière d'écrire clairement en lettres moulées.

BIRTH / NAISSANCE

Surname (if married woman, maiden surname) Nom de famille (nom de jeune fille si vous êtes mariée)	Given Name(s)/Prénom(s)	Sex/Sexe	Wallet/Format portefeuille	☐
Date of Birth/Date de naissance month/mois day/jour year/année	Place of Birth/Lieu de naissance		Long/Format long	☐
Surname of Father/Nom de famille du père	Given Name(s)/Prénom(s)		CERTIFIED COPY/ COPIE CERTIFIÉE CONFORME	☐
Maiden Surname of Mother/Nom de jeune fille de la mère	Given Name(s)/Prénom(s)			

Date of Reg./Date d'enreg. :	Place of Reg./Lieu d'enreg. :	Am. No(s)./N° de mod. :	Reg. No./N° d'enreg. :	Checked/vérifié :

MARRIAGE / MARIAGE

Surname of groom/nom de famille du marié	Given Name(s)/Prénom(s)	Wallet/Format portefeuille	☐
Surname of bride at time of marriage/Nom de famille de l'épouse dès le mariage	Given Name(s)/Prénom(s)	Long/Format long	☐
Date of Marriage/Date du mariage month/mois day/jour year/année	Place of Marriage/Lieu du mariage	CERTIFIED COPY/ COPIE CERTIFIÉE CONFORME	☐

Date of Reg./Date d'enreg. :	Place of Reg./Lieu d'enreg. :	Am. No(s)./N° de mod. :	Reg. No./N° d'enreg.:	Checked/vérifié

DEATH / DÉCÈS

Surname of Deceased/Nom de famille du défunt	Given Name(s)/Prénom(s)	SEX/SEXE	Long/Format long	☐
Date of Death/Date du décès month/mois day/jour year/année	Place of Death/Lieu du décès	AGE/ÂGE	CERTIFIED COPY/ COPIE CERTIFIÉE CONFORME	☐

Date of Reg./Date d'enreg. :	Place of Reg./Lieu d'enreg. :	Am. No(s)./N° de mod. :	Reg. No./N° d'enreg. :	Checked/vérifié

Reason for Application/Raison de la demande	Relationship to Person Named/Liens de parenté avec la personne nommée	Telephone No.- Business/N° de téléphone - Bureau	FEE ENCLOSED/ MONTANT INCLUS
	SIGNATURE OF APPLICANT/SIGNATURE DU DEMANDEUR X	Telephone No - Home/N° de téléphone-Domicile	$

OFFICE USE ONLY/RÉSERVÉ À D'ADMINISTRATION

AMENDMENT FEE/FRAIS DE MODIFICATION

DATE MAILED/DATE D'ENVOI PAR LA POSTE	REFUND/REMBOURSEMENT $	CHEQUE NUMBER/N° DU CHÈQUE	CERTIFICATE NUMBER/N° DU CERTIFICAT

MG-1607 (Rev. 92)

NUMERICAL COPY/COPIE NUMÉRIQUE

RETURN ALL COPIES/ENVOYER TOUS LES EXEMPLAIRES

CANADA—NEW BRUNSWICK

Send your requests to:

Department of Health and Community Services
Division of Vital Statistics
P.O. Box 6000
Fredericton, New Brunswick
Canada E3B 5H1

(506) 453-2385, FAX (506) 453-3245

Cost for a certified Birth Certificate	Can $25.00
Cost for a wallet-size Birth Certificate	Can $20.00
Cost for a certified Marriage Certificate	Can $25.00
Cost for a wallet-size Marriage Certificate	Can $20.00
Cost for a certified Death Certificate	Can $25.00

The Division of Vital Statistics has records from January 1888. If your request is for genealogical purposes you may obtain a non-certified extract of the birth, marriage, or death record.

Records are also available at The Provincial Archives of New Brunswick, located at the Bonar Law-Bennett Building, Dineen Drive, University of New Brunswick, Fredericton (P.O. Box 6000, Fredericton, New Brunswick E3B 5H1; Tel. 506-453-3288; FAX 506-453-3288).

The National Archives of Canada (395 Wellington Street, Ottawa, K1A 0N3; Tel. 613-995-5138) and the National Library of Canada (same address; Tel. 613-995-9481; FAX 613-996-4424) have extensive holdings.

The Family History Library of The Church of Jesus Christ of Latter-day Saints in Salt Lake City, Utah has microfilmed original and published records of Manitoba and Canada. For further details on their holdings please consult your nearest Family History Center.

APPLICATION FOR CERTIFICATE OF BIRTH, MARRIAGE OR DEATH

**DEPARTMENT OF HEALTH
AND COMMUNITY SERVICES
VITAL STATISTICS
P.O. BOX 6000, FREDERICTON, N.B.
E3B 5H1**

New Nouveau
Brunswick

DEMANDE DE CERTIFICAT DE NAISSANCE, DE MARIAGE OU DE DÉCÈS

**MINISTÈRE DE LA SANTÉ
ET DES SERVICES COMMUNAUTAIRES
STATISTIQUES DE L'ÉTAT CIVIL
C.P. 6000, FREDERICTON (N.-B.)
E3B 5H1**

*Please print all information clearly.
Complete in full and return to the office above*

35-2262 (4/91)

*Prière d'écrire clairement en lettres moulées
Veuillez remplir en entier et renvoyer à l'adresse ci-dessus*

Name And Mailing Address of Applicant / Nom et l'adresse postale du demandeur	Name / Nom		Address / Adresse	
	City / Ville	Province	Postal Code postal	

If Birth Certificates Required, Complete This Section / Pour obtenir un (des) certificat(s) de naissance, veuillez remplir

Surname (if married woman, maiden surname) / Nom de famille ou nom de jeune fille si vous êtes mariée	Given Names / Prénoms	Medicare No. / N° d'assurance-maladie
Birth Date / Date de naissance — Yr. / Année — Month / Mois — Day / Jour — Sex / Sexe	Place of Birth / Lieu de naissance	County / Comté — NB
Surname of Father / Nom de famille du père		Given Names / Prénoms
Maiden Surname of Mother / Nom de jeune fille de la mère		Given Names / Prénoms

If Marriage Certificates Required, Complete This Section / Pour obtenir un (des) certificat(s) de mariage, veuillez remplir cette partie

Surname of Bridegroom / Nom de famille de l'époux	Given Names / Prénoms	Medicare No. / N° d'assurance-maladie
Maiden Surname of Bride / Nom de jeune fille de l'épouse	Given Names / Prénoms	Medicare No. / N° d'assurance-maladie
Date of Marriage / Date du mariage — Yr. / Année — Month / Mois — Day / Jour	Place of Marriage / Lieu du mariage	NB

If Death Certificates Required, Complete This Section / Pour obtenir un (des) certificat(s) de décès, veuillez remplir cette partie

Surname of Deceased / Nom de famille du défunt	Given Names / Prénoms	Sex / Sexe	Medicare No. / N° d'assurance-maladie
Date of Death / Date du décès — Yr. / Année — Month / Mois — Day / Jour	Place of Death / Lieu du décès		NB
If deceased was married give name of spouse / Si le défunt était marié, indiquez le nom du conjoint			
Name of Father of Deceased / Nom de famille du père du défunt		Maiden Name of Mother of Deceased / Nom de jeune fille de la mère du défunt	

Indicate the Type and Number of Certificates Required / Indiquez le genre et le nombre de certificats requis

	Certified / Certifié	Wallet Size / Format-poche	Photographic Print / Épreuve photographique	Genealogical Statement / Déclaration Généalogique
Birth / Naissance			////	
Marriage / Mariage				
Death / Décès		////	////	

Relationship to Person Named / Liens de parenté avec le personne nommée

Reason for Application / Raison de la demande

Telephone / Téléphone

☐ In English / en anglais
☐ In French / en français

Fee Enclosed
$ _____ Montant inclus

Signature of Applicant / Signature du demandeur

OFFICE USE ONLY / A L'USAGE DU BUREAU SEULEMENT	Registration Number / Numero d'enregistrement	Date Issued / By — Date d'émission / Par	Checked By / Verifié par

**APPLICATION FOR
GENEALOGICAL RESEARCH**
VITAL STATISTICS
P.O. BOX 6000, FREDERICTON, N.B.
E3B 5H1

New Nouveau
Brunswick
35-3723 (4/92)

**APPLICATION POUR RECHERCHE
GENEALOGIQUE**
STATISTIQUES DE L'ÉTAT CIVIL
C.P. 6000, FREDERICTON N.-B.
E3B 5H1

I,
Je soussigné, _____
(Name of Applicant / Nom du demandeur)

of
de _____
(Address / Adresse)

_____

DO HEREBY MAKE APPLICATION FOR INFORMATION / SEARCHES
OF THE REGISTRATION RECORD OF

FAIS APPLICATION POUR INFORMATION / RECHERCHE POUR
DOSSIER SUR L'ENREGISTREMENT DE

☐ Birth
Naissance

☐ Marriage
Mariage

☐ Death
Décès

of
de _____
(Complete Name of Person / Nom au complet de la personne)

who is my
qui est _____

and who was
et était

☐ Born
née

☐ Married
marié

☐ Deceased
décédé

on
le _____ 19 ___

at
à _____

, New Brunswick
, Nouveau-Brunswick

ADDITIONAL INFORMATION

INFORMATION ADDITIONNELLE

A) Name of Mother (Maiden Surname)
Nom de la mère, (jeune fille) _____

B) Name of Father
Nom du père _____

C) If a married woman give maiden surname
Si femme mariée, nom de jeune fille _____

D) If marriage record requested, give full name of Groom
Si un dossier de mariage, nom complet du marié _____

E) If marriage record requested, give full name used by Bride prior to marriage.
Si un dossier de mariage, nom complet de la mariée avant le mariage _____

_____

F) If request is for death record, give name of spouse, if married
Si dossier de décès demandé, donner le nom de l'époux ou l'épouse, si marié _____

Date _____ 19 ___

Signature of Applicant
Signature du demandeur _____

FOR OFFICE USE ONLY

POUR L'USAGE DU BUREAU SEULEMENT

INFORMATION WHICH MAY BE PROVIDED (If on Vital Statistics
Records) are:

INFORMATION QUI PEUT ÊTRE DÉVOILÉ (Si sur les dossiers des
Statistiques de l'état civil) est:

1. Registered name	10. Names of Father and Mother
2. Type of Event	11. Birthplace of Parents
3. Date of Event	12. Birthdate of Parents
4. Place of Event	13. Age of Parents
5. Date of Registration	14. Place of Disposition
6. Registration Number	15. Funeral Director
7. Sex	16. Occupation
8. Age	17. Attending Physician
9. Marital Status	18. Addresses

1. Nom enregistre	10. Nom du père et de la mère
2. Type d'événement	11. Lieu de naissance des parents
3. Date d'événement	12. Date de naissance des parents
4. Lieu d'événement	13. Âge des parents
5. Date d'enregistrement	14. Lieu de disposition
6. Numéro d'enregistrement	15. Directeur Funéraire
7. Sexe	16. Occupation
8. Âge	17. Médecin traitant
9. État matrimonial	18. Adresses

OFFICE USE ONLY	Registration Number Numéro d'enregistrement	Date Issued / By Date d'émission / Par	Checked By Verifié par
A L'USAGE DU BUREAU SEULEMENT			

CANADA—NEWFOUNDLAND

Send your requests to:

Vital Statistics Division
Department of Health
Confederation Building
P.O. Box 8700
St. John's, Newfoundland
Canada A1B 4J6

(709) 729-3308

Cost for a certified Birth Certificate	Can $10.00
Cost for a certified Marriage Certificate	No Charge
Cost for a certified Death Certificate	No Charge

The Newfoundland Department of Health has records from 1892. There is a Can $4.00 charge for each three-year period searched.

The Provincial Public Libraries Service (Provincial Reference and Resource Library, Arts and Culture Centre, St. John's, Newfoundland A1B 3A3; Tel. 709-737-3954; FAX 709-737-3009) and the Provincial Archives of Newfoundland (Colonial Building, Military Road, St. John's A1C 2C9; Tel. 709-733-9380) also have materials of interest.

The National Archives of Canada (395 Wellington Street, Ottawa, K1A 0N3; Tel. 613-995-5138) and the National Library of Canada (same address; Tel. 613-995-9481; FAX 613-996-4424) have extensive holdings.

The Family History Library of The Church of Jesus Christ of Latter-day Saints in Salt Lake City, Utah has microfilmed original and published records of Newfoundland and Canada. For further details on their holdings please consult your nearest Family History Center.

Vital Statistics Division, Department of Health

APPLICATION FOR BIRTH CERTIFICATE

Last Name . . . .

. . . .
              first name   middle name

Date of birth . . . .

Place of birth . . . .

Name of Parish or Mission . . . .

Names of parents . . . .

The fee is $10.00 for every certificate	Certificates required: PAPER . . . . or WALLET SIZE . . . .

Signature of Applicant . . . .

Address . . . .

Relationship to Applicant . . . .

This is an extract from the registration:

Name   Sex

Date   Father

Place   Mother

Record Number   Date of Registration

Baptized on   By Rev.

                                        Amt.   Cash Book No.

Search by   Date   rec'd.   Receipt No.

                                    Counter-
Certificate No.   signed by   Date

H-623
15-623-0515

H-703

Application for Search and Certificate — Marriage

TO: Department of Health
Vital Statistics Division
St. John's, Newfoundland

File No. _____

I hereby apply for Search of the Records and Certificate of Marriage of _____

_____ and _____
(Name of bridegroom)   (Name of bride)

Month, day and year of Marriage _____

Place of Marriage _____

Marriage was solemnized by the Rev. _____

in the _____ Church.
(Denomination)

I enclose $ _____ in payment fee for _____ certificates.

Signature of applicant _____

ADDRESS _____

Relationship to the above Named _____

The fee is $10.00 for every certificate

REPORT ON SEARCH

_____

_____

_____

_____

Bridegroom	Bride
Date of Marriage	
Place of Marriage	
Date of Registration	Record Number
Search by	Date	Amount Received
Certificate No.	Typed by	Cash Book

H-702

APPLICATION FOR SEARCH AND CERTIFICATE-DEATH

TO: Department of Health
    Vital Statistics Division
    St. John's, Newfoundland

File No. ....

I hereby apply for Search of the Records and Certificate of Death of.......................................

....
(name of deceased)

Month, day and year of death ....

Place of Death ....

Place of burial ....

I enclose $................. in payment of fee for .... certificates.

Signature of applicant ....

ADDRESS ....

The fee is $10.00 for every certificate

Report on Search

_____

_____

_____

_____

_____

Name of deceased

Age	Sex	Date of Death
Marital Status		Place of Death
Record Number		Date of Registration

Search by	Date	Amount Received
Certificate No.	Typed by	Cash Book

CANADA—NORTHWEST TERRITORIES

Send your requests to:

Registrar General
Vital Statistics
Government of the Northwest Territories
P.O. Box 1320
Yellowknife, Northwest Territories
Canada X1A 2L9

(403) 873-7404

Cost for a certified Birth Certificate	Can $10.00
Cost for a certified Marriage Certificate	Can $10.00
Cost for a certified Death Certificate	Can $10.00

The Northwest Territories Registrar General has records from 1925.

The Public Library Services of the Northwest Territories (P.O. Box 1100, Hay River, Northwest Territories X0E 0R0I) also has materials of interest.

The National Archives of Canada (395 Wellington Street, Ottawa, K1A 0N3; Tel. 613-995-5138) and the National Library of Canada (same address; Tel. 613-995-9481; FAX 613-996-4424) have extensive holdings.

The Family History Library of The Church of Jesus Christ of Latter-day Saints in Salt Lake City, Utah has microfilmed original and published records of the Northwest Territories and Canada. For further details on their holdings please consult your nearest Family History Center.

Northwest Territories

APPLICATION FOR CERTIFICATE OF
DEMANDE D'EXTRAIT D'ACTE DE

| ☐ BIRTH NAISSANCE | ☐ MARRIAGE MARIAGE | ☐ DEATH DECES |

CERTIFICATE TYPE – GENRE D'EXTRAIT   **QTY – QUANTITÉ**

BIRTH NAISSANCE	☐ PAPER PAPIER	☐ WALLET PORTEFEUILLE	☐ RESTRICTED PHOTOCOPY PHOTOCOPIE À USAGE RESTREINT	➤
MARRIAGE MARIAGE	☐ PAPER PAPIER	☐ WALLET PORTEFEUILLE	☐ RESTRICTED PHOTOCOPY PHOTOCOPIE À USAGE RESTREINT	➤
DEATH DÉCÈS	☐ PAPER ONLY (81/2" x 11") ☐ PAPIER SEULEMENT (81/2" x 11")			➤

BIRTH – NAISSANCE

SURNAME (if married woman, maiden surname) – NOM DE FAMILLE (si mariée, nom de jeune fille)   GIVEN NAME(S) – PRÉNOM(S)   SEX – SEXE ☐ MALE MASCULIN ☐ FEMALE FÉMININ

DATE OF BIRTH / DATE DE NAISSANCE   Y–A M–M D–J   PLACE OF BIRTH: (city, town or village) / LIEU DE NAISSANCE: (ville ou village)

CERTIFICATE TYPE - GENRE D'EXTRAIT
SPECIFY TYPE AND QUANTITY ABOVE.
SPÉCIFIER GENRE ET QUANTITÉ CI-DESSUS.

OFFICE USE ONLY / À L'USAGE DU BUREAU

FATHER SURNAME – NOM DE FAMILLE DU PÈRE   GIVEN NAME(S) – PRÉNOM(S)   REGISTR. DATE – DATE D'ENREGISTR.

MOTHER'S MAIDEN SURNAME – NOM DE JEUNE FILLE DE LA MÈRE   GIVEN NAME(S) – PRÉNOM(S)   REGISTRATION No. – N° D'ENREGISTR.

MARRIAGE – MARIAGE

BRIDEGROOM SURNAME – NOM DE FAMILLE DU MARIÉ   GIVEN NAME(S) – PRÉNOM(S)

OFFICE USE ONLY / À L'USAGE DU BUREAU

BRIDE'S MAIDEN SURNAME – NOM DE JEUNE FILLE DE LA MARIÉE   GIVEN NAME(S) – PRÉNOM(S)   REGISTR. DATE – DATE D'ENREGISTR.

DATE OF MARRIAGE: / DATE DU MARIAGE: Y–A M–M D–J   PLACE OF MARRIAGE: (city, town or village) / LIEU DU MARIAGE: (ville ou village)

CERTIFICATE TYPE - GENRE D'EXTRAIT
SPECIFY TYPE AND QUANTITY ABOVE.
SPÉCIFIER GENRE ET QUANTITÉ CI-DESSUS.

REGISTRATION No. – N° D'ENREGISTR.

DEATH – DÉCÈS

SURNAME OF DECEASED – NOM DE FAMILLE DE LA PERSONNE DÉCÉDÉE   GIVEN NAME(S) – PRÉNOM(S)   AGE–ÂGE   SEX – SEXE ☐ MALE MASCULIN ☐ FEMALE FÉMININ

DATE OF DEATH: / DATE DU DÉCÈS: Y–A M–M D–J   PLACE OF DEATH: (city, town or village) / LIEU DU DÉCÈS: (ville ou village)

CERTIFICATE - EXTRAIT
SPECIFY QUANTITY ABOVE (PAPER ONLY).
SPÉCIFIER QUANTITÉ CI-DESSUS (PAPIER SEULEM.)

OFFICE USE ONLY / À L'USAGE DU BUREAU

PERMANENT RESIDENCE OF DECEASED PRIOR TO DEATH – ADRESSE PERMANENTE DE LA PERSONNE DÉCÉDÉE   REGISTR. DATE – DATE D'ENREGISTR.

MARITAL STATUS – ÉTAT CIVIL   IF MARRIED, SPOUSE MAIDEN SURNAME – SI MARIÉ, NOM DE FAMILLE DU CONJOINT   GIVEN NAME(S) – PRÉNOM(S)   REGISTRATION No. – N° D'ENREGISTR.

NAME OF FATHER OF DECEASED – NOM DU PÈRE DE LA PERSONNE DÉCÉDÉE   MAIDEN NAME OF MOTHER OF DECEASED – NOM DE JEUNE FILLE DE LA MÈRE

RAISON(S) FOR REQUESTING CERTIFICATE(S) – RAISON(S) DE CETTE DEMANDE D'EXTRAIT(S) D'ACTE(S)

I require these certificate(s) for the following reason(s):
J'ai besoin de cet (ces) extrait(s) d'acte(s) pour les raisons suivantes:

X _____
APPLICANT'S SIGNATURE – SIGNATURE DU DEMANDEUR   DATE

RELATIONSHIP TO PERSON NAMED – LIEN AVEC LA PERSONNE CITÉE   PHONE No. (BUS.) – N° DE TÉLÉPHONE (TRAV.) (   )

NUMBER OF CERTIFICATE(S)
NOMBRE D'EXTRAITS D'ACTE(S)   ☐ (FEE NEEDED) **x $10.00 $** (MONTANT REQUIS)

FEE ENCLOSED:
MONTANT INCLUS: **$**

PHONE No. (RES.) – N° DE TÉLÉPHONE (DOM.) (   )

PRINT CLEARLY, THIS IS YOUR MAILING ADDRESS LABEL
IMPRIMER CLAIREMENT CAR CECI EST VOTRE ÉTIQUETTE POSTALE

NAME – NOM

MAILING ADDRESS – ADRESSE POSTALE

POSTAL CODE – CODE POSTAL

OFFICE USE ONLY / À L'USAGE DU BUREAU

AMOUNT RECEIVED: MONTANT REÇU: **$**

REFUND/RETURN: REMB./RETOUR: **$**

Return BOTH COPIES of form and PAYMENT to:

Registrar General, Vital Statistics
Government of the N.W.T.
P.O. Box 1320
Yellowknife, N.W.T.
X1A 2L9

Retourner les DEUX COPIES du formulaire avec votre PAIEMENT au:

Bureau de l'état civil
Gouvernement des T.N.–O.
C. P. 1320
Yellowknife, T.N.–O.
X1A 2L9

NOTES:

NWT 5243/0389

CANADA—NOVA SCOTIA

Send your requests for records after October 1, 1908 to:

Deputy Registrar General
Nova Scotia Department of Health
1723 Hollis Street
P.O. Box 157
Halifax, Nova Scotia
Canada B3J 2M9

(902) 424-8381

Send your requests for earlier records to:

Public Archives of Nova Scotia
6016 University Avenue
Halifax, Nova Scotia
Canada B3H 1W4

(902) 424-6060, FAX (902) 424-0516

Cost for a certified Birth Certificate	Can $15.00
Cost for a wallet-size Birth Certificate	Can $10.00
Cost for a certified Marriage Certificate	Can $15.00
Cost for a wallet-size Marriage Certificate	Can $10.00
Cost for a certified Death Certificate	Can $15.00
Cost for a short form Death Certificate	Can $10.00

The Department of Health has birth and death records from October 1, 1908 and marriage records from 1907 to 1918, depending on the county in which the marriage occurred.

Other sources are the Nova Scotia Provincial Library (3770 Kempt Road, Halifax B3K 4X8; Tel. 902-424-2460; FAX 902-424-0633), the National Archives of Canada (395 Wellington Street, Ottawa, K1A 0N3; Tel. 613-995-5138), and the National Library of Canada (same address; Tel. 613-995-9481; FAX 613-996-4424).

The Family History Library of The Church of Jesus Christ of Latter-day Saints in Salt Lake City, Utah has microfilmed original records of Nova Scotia. For further details on their holdings please consult your nearest Family History Center.

Department of Health

Applicant's Name:

Full Address:

Postal Code:

Signature of
Applicant: _____

Please address all communications to:

Deputy Registrar General
P.O. Box 157
Halifax, Nova Scotia   B3J 2M9

NOTE: Please complete full information under appropriate section below:

Have you written to this office regarding this request? Y ( ) N ( )

IF BIRTH CERTIFICATE (S) REQUIRED - COMPLETE THIS SECTION (Please Print)	Please (✓)
Full Name:	Wallet-size ☐
Full Date of Birth:	
Full Place of Birth:	Long form ☐ (Restricted)
Father's Full Name:	Subject to the Vital Statistics Act
Mother's Full Maiden Name:	
Specific Reason for Request:	
Relationship to Person Named	

IF MARRIAGE CERTIFICATE (S) REQUIRED - COMPLETE THIS SECTION (Please Print)	Please (✓)
Full Name of Groom:	Wallet-size ☐
Full Maiden Name of Bride:	
Full Date of Marriage:	Long form ☐ (Restricted)
Full Place of Marriage:	Subject to the Vital Statistics Act
Specific Reason for Request:	
Relationship to Person Named:	

IF DEATH CERTIFICATE (S) REQUIRED - COMPLETE THIS SECTION (Please Print)	Please (✓)
Full Name of Person Deceased:	Short Form ☐
Full Date of Death:	
Full Place of Death:	Long Form ☐ (Restricted)
Permanent Residence of Deceased Prior to Death:	Subject to the Vital Statistics Act
Specific Reason for Request:	
Relationship to Person Named:	

FEES: Payable in advance, **by personalized cheque or money order** to the **Deputy Registrar General**, P.O. Box 157, Halifax, Nova Scotia, B3J 2M9:

(a) Wallet-size – $10.00 each (search included)   (b) Long Form (Restricted) – **$15.00** (search included)

(c) Each search of records (confirmation of event only), without certificate issued – **$5.00**

Responsibility cannot be accepted by this Department for remittances by cash, or for remittances which are not received in this office. Payment requested in Canadian funds and foreign currency will be accepted at face value(where negotiable).

CANADA—ONTARIO

Send your requests to:

Office of the Registrar General
189 Red River Road
P.O. Box 4600
Thunder Bay, Ontario
Canada P7B 6L8

(807) 343-7459, (800) 461-2156

For births 1869-1896, marriages 1869-1911, or deaths 1869-1921 write to:

Archives of Ontario
77 Grenville Street
Toronto, Ontario
Canada M7A 2R9

(416) 327-1600, FAX (416) 324-3600

Cost for a Birth Certificate	Can $11.00
Cost for a wallet-size Birth Certificate	Can $11.00
Cost for a Marriage Certificate	Can $11.00
Cost for a wallet-size Marriage Certificate	Can $11.00
Cost for a Death Certificate	Can $11.00

The Office of the Registrar General has birth records from 1896, marriage records from 1911, and death records from 1921 to the present. They will issue certificates to the individual, the individual's parents or children, and to an attorney. These certificates cost Can $22.00. Any other requests are considered genealogical searches, and the charge is Can $22.00 per certificate.

Other sources include the Provincial Library (Ministry of Culture and Communications, 77 Bloor Street West, Toronto M7A 2R9; Tel 416-314-7627; FAX 416-314-7635), the National Archives of Canada (395 Wellington Street, Ottawa, K1A 0N3; Tel. 613-995-5138), and the National Library of Canada (same address; Tel. 613-995-9481; FAX 613-996-4424).

The Family History Library of The Church of Jesus Christ of Latter-day Saints in Salt Lake City, Utah has microfilmed original and published records of Ontario and Canada. For further details on their holdings please consult your nearest Family History Center.

Application for Certificate or Search
Ontario Events Only

Demande de certificat ou de recherche
Pour les événements ayant en lieu en Ontario seulement

For Office Use Only
Réservé au ministère

Language preference Langue de préférence

☐ English Anglais   ☐ French Français

Applicant's Address
Adresse de l'auteur(e) de la demande

Mail Certificate To: (Complete if different)
Poster le certificat at: (Si est une autre personne)

Name Nom	Name Nom

Street and No. N° et nom de rue — Apt. No. N° d'app.

Street and No. N° et nom de rue — Apt. No. N° d'app.

City Ville Zone Zone Prov. Prov. — Postal Code postal

City Ville Zone Zone Prov. Prov. — Postal Code postal

Todays Date Date d'aujourd'hui — Telephone No. - Home N° de téléphone - Domicile

Telephone No. - Business N° de téléphone - Bureau — Fee enclosed Droits inclus

State relationship to person named on certificate/solicitors
Lien de parenté avec la personne nommée sur le certificat/avocats

Signature of Applicant (Manatory)
Signature de l'auteur(e) de la demande

State reason certificate required
Motif de la demande de certificat

Complete this section for Birth Certificate — Remplir cette section pour un certificat de naissance

Last Name Nom de famille	First Name/Other Names Prénom(s)	Sex Sexe

Date of Birth Date de naissance (D/J, MM, Y/A) | Place of Birth (City, Town or Village) in Ontario Lieu de naissance (ville ou village) en Ontario | Hospital where event occured - if known Si connu, nom de l'hôpital

Last Name of Father Nom de famille du père | First Name Prénom | Fathers Birthplace Lieu de naissance du père | Age of father at child's birth Âge du père à la naissance de l'enfant

Birth Name of Mother (Last Name) Nom de jeune de la mère | First Name Prénom | Mothers Birthplace Lieu de naissance du mère | Age of mother at child's birth Âge de la mère à la naissance de l'enfant

Number and type of certificate: Le genre et le numbre de certificat(s) requis

☐ Wallet Size Format carte   ☐ File Size Format lettre   ☐ Extended Étoffé   ☐ Certified Certifte   ☐ Genealogical Généalogique

For Office Use Only Réservé au ministère | Registration Number Noméro d'enregistrement | Registration Date Date d'enregistrement

---

Complete this section for Marriage Certificate — Remplir cette section pour un certificat de mariage

Last Name of Groom Nom de famille du marié	First Name/Other Names Prénom(s)	Age at time of Marriage Âge le jour du mariage	Groom's Father's Name Nom du père du marié	Mother's Birth Name Nome de jeune fille de la mère
Last Name of Bride Nom de famille du marié	First Name Prénom	Age at time of Marriage Âge le jour du mariage	Bride's Father's Name Nom du père de la mariée	Mother's Birth Name Nome de jeune fille de la mère

Date of Marriage Date du mariage (D/J, MM, Y/A) | Place of Marriage (City, Town or Village) in Ontatio Lieu du mariage (ville ou village) en Ontario

Bridegroom's Place of Birth (City, Town or Village) Lieu de naissance (ville ou village) | Bride's Place of Birth (City, Town or Village) Lieu de naissance (ville ou village)

Number and type of certificate required: Le genre et le nombre de certificat(s) requis

☐ Wallet Size Format carte   ☐ File Size Format lettre   ☐ Certified Certifte   ☐ Genealogical Généalogique

For Office Use Only Réservé au ministère | Registration Number Noméro d'enregistrement | Registration Date Date d'enregistrement

---

Complete this section for Death Certificate — Remplir cette section pour un certificat de décès

Last Name of Deceased Nom de famille du défunt	First Name/Other Names Prénom(s)	Sex Sexe

Date of Death Date du décès (D/J, MM, Y/A) | Place of Death (City, Town or Village) in Ontario Lieu de décès (ville ou village) en Ontario | Hospital Hôpital | Marital Status État matrimonial | Occupation Profession

Permanent residence of deceased prior to death Domicile permanent du défunt avant le décès | Age upon death Âge au décès | Birthplace Lieu de naissance

Father's Name Nom du père | Father's Place of Birth Lieu de naissance du père | Mother's name Nom de la mère | Mother's Place of Birth Lieu de naissance de la mère

Spouses Full Name Nom complet du (de la) conjoint(e) | Informant's Name Nom de la personne fournissant les renseignements

Number and type of certificate required: Le genre et le nombre de certificat(s) requis

☐ File Size Format carte   ☐ Certified Certifte   ☐ Genealogical Généalogique

For Office Use Only Réservé au ministère | Registration Number Noméro d'enregistrement | Registration Date Date d'enregistrement

11076 (02/92)

NAME: _____

_____

MAILING: _____
ADDRESS   No. & Street

_____
City/town   Prov.   Country

| | | | | | | | |
___ ___ ___ ___ ___
Postal Code

I WANT A SEARCH FOR THE FOLLOWING REASON:

☐ LEGAL/MANDATORY   ☐ ALL OTHER
   PURPOSES   PURPOSES

FOR A LEGAL/MANDATORY SEARCH PLEASE ALSO SEND A WRITTEN EXPLANATION STATING WHY IT IS NEEDED AND A LETTER OF VERIFICATION FROM A SOLICITOR OR PERSON OF SIMILAR AUTHORITY.

▼ COMPLETE THIS SECTION FOR INFORMATION ON A BIRTH REGISTRATION ▼

NAME: _____   OTHER POSSIBLE   _____
      Last   (Search 1)   SPELLINGS OF   (Search 2)
                                 LAST NAME   _____
      _____   (if desired)   (Search 3)
      First   _____
                                                          (Search 4)

DATE OF _____   PLACE OF _____
BIRTH   Year/Month/Day   BIRTH   Town or City / Twsp. / Co.or Dist.
* You must provide at least a year *   * Please provide an approximate location *

IF KNOWN: NAME OF _____   MAIDEN NAME _____
           FATHER   OF MOTHER

▼ COMPLETE THIS SECTION FOR INFORMATION ON A MARRIAGE REGISTRATION ▼

GROOM'S NAME: _____   AGE WHEN MARRIED _____
              Last   First   * If known *

BRIDE'S NAME: _____   AGE WHEN MARRIED _____
(MAIDEN)   Last   First   * If known *

DATE OF _____   PLACE OF _____
MARRIAGE   Year/Month/Day   MARRIAGE   Town or City / Twsp. / Co.or Dist.
* You must provide at least a year *   * Please provide an approximate location *

IF KNOWN: RESIDENCE
           WHEN MARRIED GROOM _____   BRIDE _____

▼ COMPLETE THIS SECTION FOR INFORMATION ON A DEATH REGISTRATION ▼

NAME: _____   OTHER POSSIBLE   _____
      Last   (Search 1)   SPELLINGS OF   (Search 2)
                                 LAST NAME   _____
      _____   (if desired)   (Search 3)
      First   _____
                                                          (Search 4)

DATE OF _____   PLACE OF _____
DEATH   Year/Month/Day   DEATH   Town or City / Twsp. / Co. or Dist.
* You must provide at least a year *   * Please provide an approximate location *

IF   NAME OF   MAIDEN NAME OF   AGE AT TIME
KNOWN: FATHER _____   MOTHER _____   OF DEATH _____

YOUR SIGNATURE _____   DATE _____   Rev. 01/1992

CANADA—PRINCE EDWARD ISLAND

Send your requests to:

>Department of Health & Social Services
>Division of Vital Statistics
>P.O. Box 2000
>Charlottetown, Prince Edward Island
>Canada C1A 7N8

(902) 892-1001

Cost for a certified Birth Certificate	Can $20.00
Cost for a wallet-size Birth Certificate	Can $15.00
Cost for a short form Birth Certificate	Can $15.00
Cost for a certified Marriage Certificate	Can $20.00
Cost for a wallet-size Marriage Certificate	Can $15.00
Cost for a certified Death Certificate	Can $20.00

The Division of Vital Statistics has records from 1906. Make your fee payable to "The Minister of Finance."

Records are also available at The Public Archives and Records Office, located at the George Coles Building, Richmond Street, Charlottetown (P.O. Box 1000, Charlottetown, C1A 7M4; Tel. 902-368-4290).

The National Archives of Canada (395 Wellington Street, Ottawa, K1A 0N3; Tel. 613-995-5138) and the National Library of Canada (same address; Tel. 613-995-9481; FAX 613-996-4424) also have extensive holdings.

The Family History Library of The Church of Jesus Christ of Latter-day Saints in Salt Lake City, Utah has microfilmed original and published vital records and church registers of Prince Edward Island. For further details on their holdings please consult your nearest Family History Center.

V.S. 8 - **APPLICATION FORM (BIRTH)**   Regulations 28-1

TO:
Director of Vital Statistics
P.O. Box 2000
Charlottetown, P.E.I.
C1A 7N8
                                                        Date _____

Print Full   SURNAME _____
   Name
of Person   GIVEN NAMES _____

DATE OF BIRTH _____

PLACE OF BIRTH _____

FULL NAME OF FATHER _____ BIRTHPLACE _____

FULL NAME OF MOTHER _____ BIRTHPLACE _____
   (Before Marriage)

REGISTRATION NUMBER, IF KNOWN _____

I hereby make application for a search, if necessary, and the following:

                        _____ Wallet Size Certificate
Indicate what
  is required   _____ Short Form Certificate
  and number
                        _____ Framing Size or Long Form Certificate

                        _____ Search

STATE REASON CERTIFICATE REQUIRED _____

Relationship to person named on certificate _____

Signature of Applicant _____

Address _____

(Space Below This Line for Vital Statistics Only)

Full Name of Person _____ Sex _____

Date of Birth _____ Place of Birth _____

Name of Father _____ His Birthplace _____

Name of Mother _____ Her Birthplace _____
   before Marriage

Registration Date _____ Registration Number _____

Date Issued _____ Certificate typed by _____

Amendment _____ Fee _____

Certificate Number _____

Fee _____

Receipt Number _____

Form 8A   Province of Prince Edward Island   Reg. 28-1

DIVISION OF VITAL STATISTICS
THE VITAL STATISTICS ACT

MARRIAGE

Date _____   ☐ Wallet Size Certificate

I hereby make   ☐ Framing Size Certificate
    APPLICATION FOR SEARCH and _____
                                                 ☐ Certified Copy of Original Marriage

Full Name of Bridegroom _____

Birthplace of Bridegroom _____

Full Name of Bride _____

Birthplace of Bride _____

Date of Marriage _____

Place of Marriage _____

State Reason Certificate Required _____

Signature of Applicant _____

Address _____

_____

(Space Below This Line for Vital Statistics Office Use Only)

Full Name of Bridegroom _____

Birthplace of Bridegroom _____

Full Name of Bride _____

Birthplace of Bride _____

Date of Marriage _____

Place of Marriage _____

Registration Date _____   Registration No. _____

Date Issued _____   Certificate typed by _____

Fee _____ Receipt Number _____   Certificate Number _____

607

DIVISION OF VITAL STATISTICS

THE VITAL STATISTICS ACT

Date _____

I hereby make APPLICATION FOR SEARCH and _____ DEATH CERTIFICATE(S) of

Full Name of Person _____

Date of Death _____

Place of Death _____

Maritial Status _____ Sex _____ Age _____

Regular Residence _____

State Reason Certificate Required _____

Signature of Applicant _____

Address _____

(Space Below This Line for Vital Statistics Office Use Only)

Full Name of Deceased _____

Date of Death _____ Sex _____ Age _____

Place of Death _____

Marital Status _____

Regular Residence _____

Date of Registration _____ Registration No. _____

Date Issued _____ Certificate typed by _____

Certificate Number _____

Fee _____

Receipt Number _____

606

CANADA—QUEBEC

Send your requests to:

Registers of Civil Status
Civil Status Records Office
(Judicial District), Quebec

Send your requests for records before 1885 to:

Archives Nationales du Quebec
Regional Centre
1210 Ave de Seminaire
St. Foy, Quebec
Canada G1V 4N1

(418) 643-1322

Genealogy Department
Bibliotheque de la Ville de Montreal
1210 Sherbrooke East
Montreal, Quebec
Canada H2L 1L9

(514) 872-5923

Cost for a certified Birth Certificate	Can $8.00
Cost for a certified Marriage Certificate	Can $8.00
Cost for a certified Death Certificate	Can $8.00

Vital records are not kept in a central repository in Quebec. The Archives Nationales du Quebec and the Bibliotheque de la Ville de Montreal have extensive collections of vital records. To obtain copies of vital records you should contact them or write to the parish where the event took place.

The National Archives of Canada (395 Wellington Street; Ottawa, K1A 0N3; Tel. 613-995-5138) and the National Library of Canada (same address; Tel. 613-995-9481; FAX 613-996-4424) also have extensive holdings.

The Family History Library of The Church of Jesus Christ of Latter-day Saints in Salt Lake City, Utah has microfilmed original records of Quebec. For further details on their holdings please consult your nearest Family History Center.

Gouvernement du Québec
Ministère de la Justice
Archives de l'État civil
Civil Status Records

REQUEST FOR EXTRACT
OF REGISTERS OF CIVIL STATUS

Name	
Address	
City	Province
Country	Postal Code

INSTRUCTIONS
— COMPLETE IN BLOCK LETTERS
— ONLY ONE REQUEST PER FORM
— FILL IN THE SECTION CORRESPONDING
  TO YOUR REQUEST

☐ I WILL COME TO YOUR OFFICE FOR THE DOCUMENT

☐ PLEASE SEND THE DOCUMENT BY MAIL

NAME AND ADDRESS OF THE PERSON(S) TO WHOM THE DOCUMENT(S) WILL BE SENT — IN BLOCK LETTERS

THIS PART MUST BE COMPLETED BY THE PERSON MAKING THE REQUEST

Surname of requesting person	First Name(s)	Number of copies
Address (No., Street, Apt., Town, Province, Country)		

Postal Code	Home telephone No.	Work telephone No.

BIRTH

Surname at birth	First Name(s) (most frequently used)	Sex M F
Place of birth		Date of birth Year Month Day
Name of father		
Mother's maiden name		
Name of Church, Congregation and municipality where the person was baptized or registered		Religion
Municipality where birth was registered		☐ Plastic card ☐ Extract 21.5 cm X 35.5 cm

MARRIAGE

Surname of husband	First Name(s)	
Maiden name of wife	First Name(s)	Date of marriage Year Month Day
Name of Church, Congregation or Court-house where marriage was solemnized		Religion
Municipality where marriage was solemnized		☐ Plastic card ☐ Extract 21.5 cm X 35.5 cm

BURIAL

Surname of deceased person (in the case of a married woman, indicate her maiden name)	First Name(s)
Surname of husband or maiden name of wife	First Name(s)
Surname of father	First Name(s)
Mother's maiden name	First Name(s)
Name of cemetery or crematorium	Date of death Year Month Day
Name of Church or Congregation where this burial was registered	Religion
Municipality where burial was registered	

THERE IS A FEE OF $ 8 FOR EACH EXTRACT PAYABLE BY CERTIFIED CHEQUE OR MONEY ORDER MADE TO THE ORDER OF THE MINISTER OF FINANCE.

PLEASE SEND YOUR REQUEST TO THE BUREAU D'ARCHIVES DE L'ÉTAT CIVIL (CIVIL STATUS RECORDS OFFICE) WHERE THE BIRTH, MARRIAGE OR BURIAL TOOK PLACE.

SJ-365A (90-06)

CANADA—SASKATCHEWAN

Send your requests to:

Vital Statistics
Saskatchewan Health
1919 Rose Street
Regina, Saskatchewan
Canada S4P 3V7

(306) 787-3092

Cost for a certified Birth Certificate	Can $20.00
Cost for a wallet-size Birth Certificate	Can $20.00
Cost for a certified Marriage Certificate	Can $20.00
Cost for a wallet-size Marriage Certificate	Can $20.00
Cost for a certified Death Certificate	Can $20.00

The Saskatchewan Department of Health has records from 1878. Genealogical photocopies may be requested for birth, marriage, and death certificates.

The Provincial Library (1352 Winnipeg Street, Regina S4P 3V7; Tel. 306-787-2985; FAX 306-787-8866) also has materials of interest.

The National Archives of Canada (395 Wellington Street, Ottawa, K1A 0N3; Tel. 613-995-5138) and the National Library of Canada (same address; Tel. 613-995-9481; FAX 613-996-4424) also have extensive holdings.

The Family History Library of The Church of Jesus Christ of Latter-day Saints in Salt Lake City, Utah has microfilmed original and published vital records and church registers of Saskatchewan. For further details on their holdings please consult your nearest Family History Center.

Saskatchewan Health

Vital Statistics

1919 Rose Street
Regina, Saskatchewan
S4P 3V7   Phone (306) 787-3092

Birth Certificate(s)

Surname (If Married Woman, Maiden Surname)	Given Names		Sex	Quantity	Type
Birth Date (Month by Name, Day, Year)	Birthplace (City, Town or Village) _____, SASKATCHEWAN				Wallet
Father - Surname and Given Names					Intermediate
Mother - Maiden Surname and Given Names					Extended with Parental Information
		Birth Registration Number, If Known			Restricted Copy
					Genealogical Copy
For Office Use Only					

Marriage Certificate(s)

		Quantity	Type
Groom - Surname and Given Names	Date of Marriage (Month by Name, Day, Year)		Wallet
			Intermediate
Bride - Maiden Surname and Given Names	Place of Marriage (City, Town or Village)		Restricted Copy
	_____, SASKATCHEWAN		Genealogical Copy
For Office Use Only			

Death Certificate(s)

Surname and Given Names of Deceased	Date of Death (Month by Name, Day, Year)	Sex	Quantity	Type
Place of Death _____, SASKATCHEWAN	Age	Marital Status		Intermediate
Residence Prior to Death	Spouse's Name, If Applicable			Restricted Copy
Father - Surname and Given Names	Mother - Maiden Surname and Given Names			Genealogical Copy
For Office Use Only				

Please do not separate this form - this portion will be used as your mailing label and receipt ➤

Saskatchewan Health

Vital Statistics

Certificate(s) will be ☐ Picked Up, or ☐ Mailed

($20.00 Each) No GST

Date_____, 19____ Phone No. Work_____ Home_____

✕ Signature of Applicant _____

This is your mailing label. Please enter your name, address and postal code.
Please print clearly - include your postal code on the last line of your address.

Vital Statistics Reference No., If Any

Your Reference No., If Any

Reason for Requiring the Certificate(s) Ordered

Your Relationship to Person Named on Certificate(s) Requested

Place Of Residence, If Different From Mailing Address

For Office Use Only

V.S. 17 (2/91)

CANADA—YUKON

Send your requests to:

> Yukon Health and Human Resources
> Division of Vital Statistics
> P.O. Box 2703
> Whitehorse, Yukon
> Canada Y1A 2C6

(403) 667-5207

Cost for a certified Birth Certificate	Can $10.00
Cost for a wallet-size Birth Certificate	Can $10.00
Cost for a certified Marriage Certificate	Can $10.00
Cost for a wallet-size Marriage Certificate	Can $10.00
Cost for a certified Death Certificate	Can $10.00

The Division of Vital Statistics has some birth records from 1898 and complete records from 1925. Birth and marriage certificates are issued in a wallet size and framing size. The framing size is a more complete document. A photocopy of the original birth or marriage certificate is also available but it is a restricted document. If your request is urgent please enclose an additional fee of Can $2.00.

The Yukon Archives (P.O. Box 2703, Whitehorse Y1A 2C6; Tel. 403-667-5321; FAX 403-667-4253) also has materials of interest.

The National Archives of Canada (395 Wellington Street, Ottawa, K1A 0N3; Tel. 613-995-5138) and the National Library of Canada (same address; Tel. 613-995-9481; FAX 613-996-4424) have extensive holdings.

The Family History Library of The Church of Jesus Christ of Latter-day Saints in Salt Lake City, Utah has microfilmed original and published vital records and church registers of the Yukon. For further details on their holdings please consult your nearest Family History Center.

APPLICATION FOR
CERTIFICATE OR SEARCH

Health and Social Services
DIVISION OF VITAL STATISTICS
BOX 2703
WHITEHORSE, YUKON Y1A 2C6
PH. (403) 667-5207

PLEASE INDICATE
TYPE & NUMBER
OF CERTIFICATES
REQUIRED ↓

IF BIRTH CERTIFICATE(S) REQUIRED COMPLETE THIS SECTION (PLEASE PRINT)

B I R T H

SURNAME (IF MARRIED SURNAME AT BIRTH)	(GIVEN NAMES)	SEX	QUANTITY/SIZE

WALLET

YEAR	MONTH BY NAME	DAY	PLACE OF BIRTH (CITY, TOWN OR VILLAGE)	PROVINCE/TERRITORY

FRAMING

SURNAME OF FATHER	(GIVEN NAMES)	BIRTHPLACE OF FATHER

RESTRICTED PHOTOCOPY

SURNAME OF MOTHER AT BIRTH	(GIVEN NAMES)	BIRTHPLACE OF MOTHER

DATE OF REGISTRATION	PLACE OF REGISTRATION	REGISTRATION NUMBER
SEARCHED	RESEARCHED	VERIFIED	CERT. NO.	AMENDMENT NO.

IF MARRIAGE CERTIFICATE(S) REQUIRED COMPLETE THIS SECTION (PLEASE PRINT)

M A R R I A G E

QUANTITY/SIZE
WALLET

SURNAME OF GROOM	(GIVEN NAMES)	BIRTHPLACE OF GROOM

FRAMING

SURNAME OF BRIDE AT BIRTH	(GIVEN NAMES)	BIRTHPLACE OF BRIDE

RESTRICTED PHOTOCOPY

YEAR	MONTH BY NAME	DAY	PLACE OF MARRIAGE (CITY, TOWN OR VILLAGE)	PROVINCE/TERRITORY

DATE OF REGISTRATION	PLACE OF REGISTRATION	REGISTRATION NUMBER
SEARCHED	RESEARCHED	VERIFIED	CERT. NO.	AMENDMENT NO.

IF DEATH CERTIFICATE(S) REQUIRED COMPLETE THIS SECTION (PLEASE PRINT)

D E A T H

SURNAME OF DECEASED	(GIVEN NAMES)	AGE	SEX	QUANTITY/SIZE

YEAR	MONTH BY NAME	DAY	PLACE OF DEATH (CITY, TOWN OR VILLAGE)	PROVINCE/TERRITORY	FRAMING

PERMANENT RESIDENCE OF DECEASED PRIOR TO DEATH	MARITAL STATUS

DATE OF REGISTRATION	PLACE OF REGISTRATION	REGISTRATION NUMBER
SEARCHED	RESEARCHED	VERIFIED	CERT. NO.	AMENDMENT NO.

PLEASE INDICATE THE REASON FOR APPLICATION:

STATE RELATIONSHIP TO PERSON NAMED:

SIGNATURE OF APPLICANT:

FOR OFFICE USE ONLY

REMARKS

X

DATE YR.	MO.	DAY	FEE ENCLOSED WITH THIS APPLICATION $

MAILING ADDRESS

NAME

STREET ADDRESS

CITY	PROVINCE	POSTAL CODE

REFUND

DATE MAILED

YG (3385) NC2 REV 04/91

CAPE VERDE

Direccao Geral dos Registos e Notariado
Ministerio de Justica
C.P. 204
Praia, Cape Verde

Records date from 1803.

CAYMAN ISLANDS

Registrar General
Tower Building
George Town
Grand Cayman, Cayman Islands, BWI

(809) 949-7900

Cost for a Birth or Death Certificate	US $3.75
Cost for a Marriage Certificate	US $8.75

CENTRAL AFRICAN REPUBLIC

Center for the Civil Status
(Town), Central African Republic

Registration began in 1940 for French citizens and foreigners. By 1966 registration expanded to the entire population.

CHAD

Civil Registrar
Direction de la Statistique
B.P. 453
N'Djamena, Chad

Cost for a Birth, Marriage, or Death Certificate	75F CFA

Registration began in 1961. Divorce records are kept by the court that issued the decree. Registration is not complete.

CHILE

Director General del Servicio de Registro Civil e Identificacion
Ministerio de Justicia
Hurfanos 1570
Santiago, Chile

(011) (562) 698-2546

Cost for a Birth, Marriage, or Death Certificate   Ch$ 260.

Registration began January 1, 1885. There is no divorce in Chile.

CHINA

Send your requests to:

Population Registration
Ministry of Public Security
(City), China

Cost for a certified Birth Certificate	Price Varies
Cost for a certified Marriage Certificate	Price Varies
Cost for a certified Death Certificate	Price Varies

China uses a household registration system to record and identify each person in China. The registration is handled by the local police office. Current vital registration is considered to be 90 percent complete. When writing include two International Postal Reply Coupons, available at your local post office, with your request.

The Family History Library of The Church of Jesus Christ of Latter-day Saints in Salt Lake City, Utah has microfilmed original and published records of China. For further details on their holdings please consult your nearest Family History Center.

（用于涉外公证）

出 生 公 证 申 请 表

证号（　）沪　字第　　号

<table>
<tr><td colspan="7">

填 表 须 知

填表人必须如实填写本表所列各栏。如发现有不真实内容，除拒绝办理公证外，将根据情节和后果，建议有关部门作必要处理。
</td></tr>
<tr><td colspan="7">申请公证用途,画√表示 定居　　探亲　　留学　　工作　　公证书使用于　　　　国家或地区</td></tr>
<tr><td rowspan="4">申请人</td><td>姓　名</td><td>曾用名、别名</td><td>外文名</td><td>性别</td><td>出生日期</td><td colspan="2">工作单位和地址（或原）</td></tr>
<tr><td></td><td></td><td></td><td></td><td></td><td colspan="2"></td></tr>
<tr><td colspan="2">住　　　　　址</td><td>联系电话</td><td colspan="2">邮政编码</td><td colspan="2">居民身份证编号</td></tr>
<tr><td colspan="2"></td><td></td><td colspan="2"></td><td colspan="2"></td></tr>
<tr><td colspan="2">申请人已住境外者，出境年月日</td><td></td><td colspan="2">出境前户籍所在地</td><td colspan="2"></td></tr>
<tr><td colspan="2">住境外者回沪临时住址</td><td></td><td colspan="2">过去办过何种公证</td><td colspan="2"></td></tr>
<tr><td colspan="7">申请人出生地点（详填门牌号码或医院）</td></tr>
<tr><td rowspan="3"></td><td>姓　名</td><td>出生日期</td><td>健在否</td><td colspan="4">现 住 址 或 生 前 住 址</td></tr>
<tr><td>生父</td><td></td><td></td><td colspan="4"></td></tr>
<tr><td>生母</td><td></td><td></td><td colspan="4"></td></tr>
<tr><td colspan="4">生父母现住境外的，在沪最后户籍所在地及离沪日期</td><td colspan="3">生父母出境前若住外省市的地址</td></tr>
<tr><td>生父</td><td colspan="3"></td><td colspan="3"></td></tr>
<tr><td>生母</td><td colspan="3"></td><td colspan="3"></td></tr>
<tr><td rowspan="2">代申请人</td><td>姓　名</td><td>性别</td><td>出生日期</td><td>与申请人关系</td><td>联 系 地 址</td><td>邮政编码</td><td>电话</td></tr>
<tr><td></td><td></td><td></td><td></td><td></td><td></td><td></td></tr>
<tr><td colspan="7">申请人提供由公证处收下证件登记，原件画（○）、复印件及其他材料画（√）表示</td></tr>
<tr><td>身份证</td><td>户口本</td><td>护照</td><td>出入境通行证</td><td>境外身份证</td><td>委托书（信）</td><td>单位证明</td><td>照　片</td></tr>
<tr><td></td><td></td><td></td><td></td><td></td><td></td><td></td><td>寸
张</td></tr>
<tr><td colspan="7">填表人：　　　　　　　　　19　　年　　月　　日</td></tr>
</table>

接待人　　　　　　　　　　　　　上海市司法局公证管理处制(91)表十八

（用于涉外公证）

结婚（　）离婚（　）未婚（　）未再婚（　）公证申请表

填 表 须 知

填表人必须如实填写本表所列各栏，如发现有不真实内容，除拒绝办理公证外，将根据情节和后果，建议有关部门必要处理。

| 申请公证用途，画√表示 | 定居 | 探亲 | 留学 | 工作 | 公证书使用于 | | 国家或地区 |

申请人	姓名	曾用别名	外文名	性别	出生日期	工作单位和地址（或原单位）		
	住　　　　址			联系电话	邮政编码	居民身份证编号		

| 申请人已住境外者，出境年月 | | 出境前户籍所在地址 | |

| 现婚姻状况，画√表示 | 未婚 | 结婚 | 离婚 | 丧偶 | 未再婚 | 过去办过何公证 |

结婚情况	结婚日期	年　月　日	结婚地点		登记或批准机关	
	配偶姓名	外文名	出生日期		住址	

离婚情况	离婚日期	年　月　日	离婚地点		登记或批准机关	
	原配偶姓名	出生日期		住址		

丧偶情况	配偶姓名	出生日期	死亡日期、地点	
	生前住址		原结婚日期、地点	

代申请人	姓名	性别	出生日期	与申请人关系	联系地址	邮政编码	电话

申请人提供由公证处收下证件登记，原件画（○）复印件及其他证明材料画（√）表示

身份证	户口本	护照	出入境通行证	境外身份证	委托书	未婚证明	结婚证明	离婚证或判决书调解书	死亡证明	未再婚证明	其他
（　份）	（　份）										

填表人：　　　　　　　　　　19　年　月　日

接待人：　　　　　　　　　　上海市司法局公证管理处制（91）表二十

公 证 申 请 表

证号（　　）沪　　字第　　　号

<table>
<tr><td rowspan="8">申请人</td><td>姓名</td><td></td><td>性别</td><td>出生日期</td><td></td><td>文化程度</td><td>工作单位及地址</td><td></td></tr>
<tr><td>住址</td><td></td><td>电话</td><td></td><td>邮编</td><td></td><td>身份证号码</td><td></td></tr>
<tr><td>姓名</td><td></td><td>性别</td><td>出生日期</td><td></td><td>文化程度</td><td>工作单位及地址</td><td></td></tr>
<tr><td>住址</td><td></td><td>电话</td><td></td><td>邮编</td><td></td><td>身份证号码</td><td></td></tr>
<tr><td>姓名</td><td></td><td>性别</td><td>出生日期</td><td></td><td>文化程度</td><td>工作单位及地址</td><td></td></tr>
<tr><td>住址</td><td></td><td>电话</td><td></td><td>邮编</td><td></td><td>身份证号码</td><td></td></tr>
</table>

<table>
<tr><td rowspan="2">代申请人</td><td>姓名</td><td></td><td>性别</td><td>出生日期</td><td></td><td>文化程度</td><td>工作单位及地址</td><td></td></tr>
<tr><td>住址</td><td></td><td>电话</td><td></td><td>邮编</td><td></td><td>身份证号码</td><td></td></tr>
</table>

申请公证的目的、用途		代申请人与申请人关系	

申请公证的内容	

需要说明的情况	

申请人提供由公证处收下证件登记：

填表人：　　　　　　　　　　　　　19　　年　　月　　日

接待人：　　　　　　　　　　　上海市司法局公证管理处制（91）表一

CHINA—HONG KONG

Send your requests to:

General Register Office
3/F, Low Block
Queensway Government Offices
66 Queensway
Hong Kong

(011) (852) 829-3579, FAX (011) (852) 824-1133

Cost for a certified Birth Certificate	HK $40.00
Cost for a certified Marriage Certificate	HK $55.00
Cost for a certified Divorce Record	HK $50.00
Cost for a certified Death Certificate	HK $40.00

While church registers date from the colonial period, vital registration in Hong Kong began in 1872. Current registration is considered to be complete. Divorces are registered by the Registrar of the Supreme Court. There is a HK $12.40 fee to send each certificate by registered airmail and an additional charge of HK $20.00 to search for a record.

The Family History Library of The Church of Jesus Christ of Latter-day Saints in Salt Lake City, Utah has microfilmed original and published records of Hong Kong and China. For further details on their holdings please consult your nearest Family History Center.

Immigration Department
Births and Deaths Registry

人民入境事務處
生死註冊處

APPLICATION FOR BIRTH CERTIFICATE(S)
出 生 證 明 書 申 請 表

Note: Please read 'Explanatory Notes' overleaf before completing this form.
注意：填寫此表格前，請詳閱背頁所載的附註。

1. Name of applicant
   申請人姓名 _____

2. Identity card/passport no. of applicant
   申請人身份證 / 護照號碼 _____

3. Address of applicant
   申請人住址 _____

   _____ Daytime Tel. no.
   日間聯絡電話號碼 _____

4. Relationship of applicant with the birth certificate holder
   申請人與出生者關係 _____

5. Particulars of application
   申請事項

Date of Birth 出生日期			Name of birth certificate holder 出生者姓名	Name of parents 父母親姓名	Copies applied for 申請張數
(Day) (日)	(Month) (月)	(Year) (年)			

Signature of applicant
申請人簽名 _____

Date
日期 _____

For Official Use Only
此節由辦理機關填寫

Application no.:   Birth Entry no.:

Documents produced in support of application:

Name and signature of accepting officer: _____

Date: _____

Serial no. of birth certificate allotted:

Date of allotment:

Fee paid:

Receipt no.:

Name and signature of issuing officer: _____

Date: _____

Remarks:

B.D.R. 87 (3/91)

BIRTHS AND DEATHS REGISTRY
HONG KONG
香港生死註冊處

APPLICATION FOR SEARCH OF RECORD OF BIRTH
查閱出生登記冊籍申請書

APPLICATION FOR
SEARCH OF
RECORD OF BIRTH

FEE: HK$20.00

for Registrar of Births & Deaths

Date

Name (English) .... (Chinese)
姓名 (英文) (中文)

Sex .... H K identity card no (if any) .... Verified *(Yes/No)
性別 香港身份證號碼 (如有的話)

Date of birth .... / .... / .... (in Gregorian/Lunar Calendar)
出生日期 (Day 日) (Month 月) (Year 年) 陽曆/陰曆

Address of birth or hospital ....
出生地址或醫院

Name of father .... Name of mother ....
父親姓名 母親姓名

Name of midwife, if any ....
如係由助產婦接生者，請將其姓名及地址

Name of applicant .... Daytime tel no ....
申請人姓名 日間聯絡電話號碼

Address of applicant ....
申請人地址

FOR OFFICIAL USE ONLY 以下由辦理機關填寫

1.   District and years searched: ....

2.   Search result: ☐ No record found on information provided   ☐ Record lost.

      ☐ Similar hospital/midwife record found   ☐ Birth entry no.
         but birth not yet registered. Please
         advise applicant to approach GRO for   * Name of
         application of CPR.   child/parent

3.   Remarks ....

Searched by: ....   Result issued by: ....
                (Name & signature)   (Name & signature)

      Date: ....   Date: ....

* Delete where inapplicable

BDR 40 (Rev 12/91)

BIRTHS AND DEATHS REGISTRY
HONG KONG
香港生死註冊處

Application for Search of Record of Birth
查閱出生登記冊籍申請書

Name ....
姓名

Fee: HK$20.00 received
費用：港幣貳拾圓正收訖

for Registrar of Births & Deaths
生死註冊官

Date 日期 ....

Application form received on
申請書收到日期 ....

for Registrar of Births & Deaths
生死註冊官

RESULT 查閱結果

Name ....
姓名
Sex ....
性別
Date of birth ....
出生日期

* No record found on information provided
   據存查無紀錄

* Record lost
   紀錄遺失

* Similar hospital/midwife record found but birth
   not yet registered
   有相似的醫院 / 助產所紀錄但出生未經登記

* Birth entry no
   出生登記號碼 ....

for Registrar of Births & Deaths
生死註冊官

* Delete where inapplicable

BDR 40 (Rev 12/91)

Control No. ....

APPLICATION FOR SEARCH OF MARRIAGE RECORDS AND/OR
ISSUE OF CERTIFIED COPY OF MARRIAGE CERTIFICATE
翻查結婚記錄 / 領取婚姻證書認證副本申請表

	Male Party 男 方	Female Party 女 方
Surname & Name (in English) 英 文 姓 名		
Surname & Name (in Chinese) 中 文 姓 名		
H.K. Identity Card/Travel Document No. 香港身份證 / 旅行證件號碼		
Date & Place of Marriage 結 婚 日 期 及 註 冊 地 點		

Name of Applicant 申 請 人 姓 名	
H.K. Identity Card/Travel Document No. 香港身份證 / 旅行證件號碼	
Address 住 址	
No. of Marriage Certificate Required 申 請 張 數	Tel. No. 電話號碼
Signature of Applicant 申 請 人 簽 署	Date 日 期

Official Fee:

1. $20.00 for search for a specified entry of a marriage.

2. $40.00 for a certified copy of a marriage certificate, and in addition, $15.00 where the application is by post outside Hong Kong, together with a sum equivalent to the airmail postage at the normal rate.

收費：

一、翻查一項結婚記錄的費用為港幣二十元正。

二、領取一份婚姻證書認證副本的費用為港幣四十元正。倘從海外以郵寄方式提出申請，則須另繳港幣十五元，及
　　一筆相等於標準空郵郵費的款項。

FOR OFFICIAL USE ONLY　此 欄 由 辦 理 機 關 填 寫

(1) Result of Search

    a.   M/C No. .... Date of Marriage ....

    b.   No Record .... Date ....

(2) Duplicate copy of M/C prepared by ....

(3)

Fee	Receipt No.	Date	Amount
Search of Record			
Certified copy of M/C			

MR 10 (3/91)

Immigration Department

Births and Deaths Registry

人民入境事務處

生死註冊處

APPLICATION FOR DEATH CERTIFICATE(S)
死 亡 證 明 書 申 請 表

Note: Please read 'Explanatory Notes' overleaf before completing this form.

注意：填寫此表格前，請詳閱背頁所載的「附註」。

1. Name of applicant
   申請人姓名 _____

2. Identity card/passport no. of applicant
   申請人身份證 / 護照號碼 _____

3. Address of applicant
   申請人住址 _____

   _____ Daytime Tel. no.
   日間聯絡電話號碼 _____

4. Particulars of application
   有關申請的詳情

Date of Death 死亡日期			Name of deceased person 死者姓名	Relationship with applicant 與申請人關係	Copies applied for 申請簽發張數
(Day) (日)	(Month) (月)	(Year) (年)			

Signature of applicant
申請人簽名 _____

Date
日期 _____

For Official Use Only
此節由辦理機關填寫

Application no.:

Death entry no.:

Documents produced in support of application:

Name and signature of accepting officer: _____

Date: _____

Serial no. of death certificate allotted:

Date of allotment:

Fee paid:

Receipt no.:

Name and signature of issuing officer: _____

Date: _____

Remarks:

BDR 62 (1/92)

BIRTHS AND DEATHS REGISTRY
HONG KONG
香港生死註冊處

Application for Search of Record of Death
查閱死亡登記冊籍申請書

Fee: HK$20.00

Name of deceased (English) .... (Chinese)
死者 姓 名 （英文） 姓名 （中文）

Sex .... Age at death .... Hong Kong Identity card no. (if any) ....
性別 死時年齡 香港身份證號碼（如有的話）

Date of death ....
死亡日期 (Day 日) (Month 月) (Year 年) (In *Gregorian/Lunar Calendar)
西曆/陰曆

Place of death ....
死亡地點

Name of applicant .... Daytime tel. no. ....
申請人姓名 日間聯絡電話號碼

Address of applicant ....
申請人地址

FOR OFFICIAL USE ONLY 以下由辦理機關填寫

1. District and years searched: ....

2. Search result: ☐ Death entry no. .... Name of deceased ....
   ☐ No record found on information provided. ☐ Record lost.

3. Remarks: ....

Searched by: .... Result issued by: ....
(Name & Signature) (Name & Signature)

Date: .... Date: ....

* Delete where inapplicable

BDR 41 (Rev. 7/92)

BIRTHS AND DEATHS REGISTRY
HONG KONG
香港生死註冊處

Application for Search of Record of Death
查閱死亡登記冊籍申請書

Application for Search of Record of Death

Fee: HK$20.00 received
費用：港幣貳拾圓正收妥

Name ....
姓名

for Registrar of Births & Deaths （代行）
生死註冊官

Date ....
日期

Application form received on ....
申請表格收到日期：

for Registrar of Births & Deaths （代行）
生死註冊官

RESULT 查閱結果

Name ....
姓名

Sex ....
性別

Date of death ....
死亡日期

* Death entry no. ....
死亡登記號碼

* No record found on information provided.
據查並無紀錄

* Record lost.
紀錄遺失

for Registrar of Births & Deaths （代行）
生死註冊官

* Delete where inapplicable

BDR 41 (Rev. 7/92)

CHINA—MACAU

Direccao de Servicos de Justica
Secretario-Adjunto para a Administracao
Rua da Praia Grande, No. 26
Edificio B.C.M., 8,9,10 Andares
Macau

Cost for a Birth Certificate   MOP 25.00
Cost for a Marriage or Death Certificate   MOP 35.00

While church registers date from the colonial period, the vital registration office in Macau has birth records from 1890 and marriage and death records from 1900. The codes have been changed over the years with a new code going into effect in May 1987. The office is adding photocopies of church registers from January 1, 1900 to the official records.

CHINA—MONGOLIA

Population Registration
Ministry of Public Security
(City), Mongolia

Mongolia uses a household registration system to record and identify each person in the country. The registration is handled by the local police office. Current vital registration is considered to be 85 percent complete.

CHINA—TAIWAN

Send your requests to:

Civil Registration Service
Department of Civil Affairs
Taipei City Government Offices
39 Chang An West Road
Taipei, Taiwan
Republic of China

(011) (886) (2) 383-2741

Cost for a certified Birth Certificate	NT $10.00
Cost for a certified Marriage Certificate	NT $10.00
Cost for a certified Death Certificate	NT $10.00
Cost for a certified Household Registration	NT $10.00

China uses a household registration system to record and identify each person in China. The registration is handled by the local police office. Current vital registration is considered to be complete.

Materials of interest are also found at The National Central Library, located at 20 Chungshan South Road, Taipei, Taiwan, Republic of China; Tel. (011) (886) (02) 361-9132.

The Family History Library of The Church of Jesus Christ of Latter-day Saints in Salt Lake City, Utah has microfilmed original and published records of China. For further details on their holdings please consult your nearest Family History Center.

出生登記申請書

本期申請書之順序編號

| 戶號 | 統一號碼 | | | | |

出生者

姓名 ‧ 出生別 (）男 1 (）女 2

出生別：遵服子 1 ‧ 非婚生已認領 3 ‧ 非婚生未認領 4 ‧ 養子 5 ‧ 其他 3

接生者身分：醫生 1 ‧ 助產士 2 ‧ 其他 3

出生日期：民國 年 月 日 出生時體重 公克

出生地點：省市 縣市 鄉鎮區市 村里 鄰

胎位：單 1 □ 雙 2 □ 多 3 □ ‧ 出生身分：同胞 □ 自己 □ 其他 □

附繳證件：□出生證明書 □戶籍登記簿 □戶口校正簿 □戶口卡片 □其他

父

姓名 ‧ 統一號碼

行業

住址：省市 縣市 鄉鎮區市 村里 鄰 路街 段 巷 弄 號 樓之 號

出生日期：民國 年 月 ‧ 同生父本籍 □ 本籍 □ ‧ 教育程度

母

姓名 ‧ 統一號碼

行業

住址

出生日期：民國 年 月 ‧ 教育程度

生父母結婚（同居）日期：民國 年 月 日

申請人與出生者之關係 ‧ 戶長姓名及與本人關係

記事

申請日期：民國 年 月 日

申請人住址：台北市 區 里 鄰 路街 段 巷 弄 號 樓之 號（簽章）

申請人：

承辦人 ‧ 主任 ‧ 審核

填寫說明：
1. 出生別、出生日期、胎次、胎次序等均填數字填寫。
2. 出生身分、胎別、胎位、同胞胎數、出生生父、出生地點、接生者身分、本籍、出生者身分、教育程度、行業、職業等欄請依實情形填寫，至其後面的小欄則由戶政事務所專人填註其代號。
3. 教育程度、行業、職業等欄請按審核情形填寫，至其後面的小欄則由戶政事務所專人填註其代號。

凡各欄通用同法伯數字填於適當地號及同法伯數字填寫；戶號及統一號碼兩欄通用各欄請在適當項目"□"內以"✓"選擇之，或加填適當文字。

80. 4. 4,000本

結婚登記申請書

本件申請書之順序編號

| 夫妻別 | 原戶號 | 現 |

結婚當事人

夫
- 姓名
- 教育程度
- 生父姓名
- 生母姓名
- 統一號碼
- 出生日期：民國　年　月　日　出生別（　）男
- 婚前婚後婚狀況：□未婚1　□夫偶2　□離婚3　□重婚4
- 原配偶姓名
- 婚前住址：□同申請人住址／□不同而更→　省市　縣市　鄉鎮區市　村里　路街　段　巷　弄　號
- 婚後住址：□同申請人住址／□不同而更→　省市　縣市　鄉鎮區市　村里　路街　段　巷　弄　號

妻
- 姓名
- 教育程度
- 生父姓名
- 生母姓名
- 統一號碼
- 出生日期：民國　年　月　日　出生別（　）女
- 婚前婚後婚狀況：□未婚1　□夫偶2　□離婚3　□重婚4
- 原配偶姓名
- 婚前住址：□同申請人住址／□不同而更→　省市　縣市　鄉鎮區市　村里　路街　段　巷　弄　號
- 婚後住址：□同申請人住址／□不同而更→　省市　縣市　鄉鎮區市　村里　路街　段　巷　弄　號

記事

- 結婚日期：民國　年　月　日
- 結婚儀式舉行地點
- 夫之原戶長姓名及與其關係
- 妻之原戶長姓名及與其關係
- 與戶長之關係
- 1.約定事項：□冠夫（妻）姓　□不冠夫（妻）姓

證人姓名　1.　2.
住址　1.　2.

附繳證件：□戶籍登記簿　□戶口查察簿　□戶口卡片　□結婚證書　□軍人結婚報告表　□其他

婚姻類別：□普通婚姻1　□招贅婚姻2

其他5　□法院4　□教堂3　□飯店2　□賓館1

申請人

- 申請日期：民國　年　月　日
- 申請人（　　　　　）（簽章）
- 申請人住址：省市　縣市　鄉鎮區市（　）村里　路街　段　巷　弄　號

承辦人　審核　主任

戶籍登記簿　日登記
戶口查察簿　民國　年　月　日整理記
戶口卡片　　　年　月　日註記

村里收件　樓之　號

填寫說明：1.出生日期、結婚日期及申請日期等日期欄各欄應使用阿拉伯數字清晰地填寫；戶籍及統一號碼兩欄應使用英文字母及阿拉伯數字填寫。
2.婚前婚後婚狀況、婚前及婚後住址、結婚儀式舉行地點、婚姻類別、約定事項及附繳證件各欄請在適當項目「□」內以「ˇ」選擇之，或加填適當文字。
3.教育程度、職業、行業等欄請按實際情形填寫，至其他各欄則由戶政事務所承辦人據實詳人據註代號。

81. 9. 1.500本

離婚登記申請書

本册申請書之順序編號

戶 號				

稱別

夫

姓 名	統一號碼			出生日期 民國 年 月 日	出生別 ( ) 男

生父姓名	生母姓名		原配偶姓名及存歿欄

教育程度	統一號碼		出生別

妻

姓 名			出生日期 民國 年 月 日	原配偶姓名及存歿欄

離婚前住址 □申請人同而是 □不是	省 市	縣 市	鄉鎮 區市	村里	鄰	街 路	段	巷	弄	號	樓之

離婚後住址 □同離婚前住址是 □不是	省 市	縣 市	鄉鎮 區市	村里	鄰	街 路	段	巷	弄	號	樓之

事

生父姓名	離婚前住址 □申請人同而是 □不是	離婚後住址 □同離婚前住址是 □不是	職業

生母姓名			行業

教育程度		行業

當

住址	省 市	縣 市	鄉鎮 區市	村里	鄰	街 路	段	巷	弄	號	樓之

事

人

結婚日期 民國 年 月 日	本次結婚生育子女數 男 女	戶長姓名

離婚日期 民國 年 月 日	離婚種類 □1.由夫監護之子女姓名： □2.由妻監護之子女姓名：	附繳證件 □3.離婚協議書 □法院判決書及判決確定證明書 □離婚冠夫（妻）姓 □4.其他

記

事

申請日期	民國 年 月 日

申請人住址	( ) 省 市 ( ) 縣 市 ( ) 鄉鎮 區市 村里 鄰 街 路 段 巷 弄 號 樓之

主任	審核	承辦人	戶籍登記簿 戶口查察簿 戶口卡片	鄉鎮 區市 民國 年 月 日	村里收件 日登記 日登理記 日註册

填寫說明：1.出生日期、出生別、結婚日期、生育子女數、離婚日期及申請日期各欄應使用阿拉伯數字清晰地填寫；戶號及統一號碼兩欄應使用英大寫字母及阿拉伯數字填寫。
2.離婚前（後）本籍、離婚種類、附繳證件及記事各欄，應就應填查項目以"✓"內以"✓"選擇之，或加填查詢文字。
3.教育程度、行業、職業、離婚前（後）住址等欄請按實際情形填寫，至夫妻接面兩小欄則由戶政事務所事人檯註代號。

81. 9. 400本

死亡 死亡宣告登記申請書

戶號					本類申請書之順序編號

死亡	姓名	統一號碼			
死亡宣告	出生日期	民國前 年 月 日	出生別 ( )男 1 ( )女 2	婚姻狀況 未婚 1 有配偶 2 有偶 2 離婚 3 離婚 4	配偶姓名
			死亡或推定死亡日期	死亡或推定死亡地點	
	教育程度		死亡或推定死亡日期 民國 年 月 日	死亡或推定死亡地點	

死亡	本籍	□同申請人住址	□不同 → 台北市 省 市 縣 市 鄉鎮 市 區 村 里 鄰 戶長姓名		
宣告	戶籍所在地址	□同申請人住址	□不同 → 台北市 省 市 縣 市 鄉鎮 市 區 村 里 鄰	死亡原因 (直接經過) 附繳證件	□死亡登記 □死亡宣告裁判書 □軍方死亡通報文件 □戶籍登記簿 □整理改記 □村里狀体 □其他

申請日期	民國 年 月 日	申請人與死亡者關係 死亡者之	申請人	

申請人住址	( )省 ( )縣 市 ( )鄉鎮 區 市 ( )村 里 路 街 段 巷 弄 號 樓之	(各章)

主任	審核	承辦人	戶籍登記簿 民國 年 月 日 註記	戶口卡片 民國 年 月 日 註記

填寫說明：
1. 出生日期、出生別、婚姻狀況、死亡日期及死亡地點、本籍及戶籍所在地、死亡原因等欄請按實際情形填寫，至其後面兩小欄則由戶政事務所人員註記。
2. 出生別、婚姻狀況、戶籍所在地、死亡原因等欄，應按各欄所列號碼填寫。
3. 教育程度、行業、職業及死亡原因各欄所列項目，請就適當項目於"□"內以"✓"選擇之，或加填適當文字。
4. 死亡宣告登記應在記事欄內填寫法院裁判之時間及文號。

78. 8. 1,200本

戶 016

戶籍謄記簿閱覽本申請書

申請日期：民國　年　月　日

說明	主任	費　規	證	附	申請種類	被申請者	申請人

説明：

一、被申請者姓名住址、申請種類及申請份數各欄，請在適當項目「□」內劃「✓」號，或加填適當文字。

二、附繳證明文件欄，請領本人之謄本者免填。委託申請欄，親自申請者免填。

三、合計張數、發文字號、規費及收據號碼等欄由戶政事務所人員填寫。

四、如辦理籍別、出生、認領、收養、結婚、離婚、死亡、遷入、變更、更正或撤銷登記後，即時申請戶籍謄本時，應在申請書備註欄註明其登記類別及日期。

主任

費　規
新台幣　百　拾　元

核審
碼號據收

字發號文
發文　年　月　日　辦理　登記

複印或抄錄
理受

證件　附繳

申請種類
□現行戶籍謄本
□民國　年除戶謄本
□日據時期調查簿謄本
□閱覽戶籍登記簿

備註

委託申請
委託人：
地址：
身分證統一號碼：
蓋章：

份數
□全部謄本　份
□部分謄本　份

合計
張數
（由本所填寫）　張

被申請者
姓名住址
戶長：
□同申請人住址
□不同而是↓
縣市　鄉鎮市區　里村　鄰　街路　段　巷　弄　號　樓之

申請（受託）人
姓名住址
姓名　　　　　簽章
縣市　鄉鎮市區　里村　鄰　街路　段　巷　弄　號　樓之
等　名

81.10.8,000本

COLOMBIA

Superintendencia de Notariado y Registro Civil
Ministerio de Justicia
Calle 26 #13-49, Interior 201
Bogota, Colombia

(011) (57) (1) 284-8976

Cost for a Birth, Marriage, or Death Certificate $100.00.

Records began June 3, 1852 and were kept by parish priests. Government registries were set up in 1934. Death records have been kept since 1969.

COMOROS

Registrar General
Moroni, Comoros

Comoros became independent from France in 1975.

CONGO

Direction Nationale de l'Etat Civil
Ministere de l'Interieur
B.P. 880
Brazzaville, Congo

Vital registration began in 1922.

COSTA RICA

Dirección de Registro Civil y Notariado
Tribunal Supremo de Eleciones
AP 10218-1000
San José, Costa Rica

Cost for a Birth, Marriage, or Death Certificate Colon 15.50

Registration began in 1881 and is considered to be complete.

CROATIA

Civil Registration Office
(Town), Croatia

Vital records are on file from 1946.

CUBA

Directora de Registros y Notarias
Registro Civil
Ministerio do Justicia
Calle O No. 216
Havana, Cuba 10400

International Operator (053) 32-4536

Cost for a Birth, Marriage, or Death Certificate   P2.00.

Registration began June 17, 1870 with key changes in 1885 and January 1, 1986.

CYPRUS

Registrar
District Office
(Town), Cyprus

Birth and death records began in 1895, marriage records in 1923.

CZECH REPUBLIC

Ministry of the Interior
Archivni Sprava
Tridadr. Milady Horakove
133, 166 21 Prague, Czech Republic

Cost for a Birth, Marriage, or Death Certificate $15

The Archives charges an hourly fee for a search. Registration began in 1919, and church records are available from 1785. Records are also available at the Narodni Knihovna v Praz (National Library), located at Klementinum 190, 110 01 Prague, Czech Republic; Tel. (011) (42) (2) 266-541; FAX (011) (42) (2) 261-775.

DENMARK

Send your requests to:

Lutheran Pastor
(Town), Denmark

The Central Office can also advise you:

Central Office of Civil Registration
Ministry of the Interior
Datavej 20
P.O. Box 269
3460 Birkerød, Denmark

(011) (45) 82-7200, FAX (011) (45) 82-5110

For further assistance contact:

Ministry of Ecclesiastical Affairs
Frederiksholms Kanal 21
DK 1220 Copenhagen, Denmark

(011) (45) 3392-3390, FAX (011) (45) 3392-3913

Cost for a certified Birth Certificate	Free
Cost for a certified Marriage Certificate	Free
Cost for a certified Death Certificate	Free

Civil registration is administered by the Lutheran Church. Church registers are on file from the 1600s. The Central Office does not make their records public but can advise you on where to write.

The Family History Library of The Church of Jesus Christ of Latter-day Saints in Salt Lake City, Utah has microfilmed original and published records of Denmark. For further details on their holdings please consult your nearest Family History Center.

DEN DANSKE FOLKEKIRKE

Personnr. _____

FØDSELS- og DÅBSATTEST
for

Efternavn: _____

For- og mellemnavne: _____

Registreringssted for fødslen (sogn og kommune):	
Fødselsår og -dag:	
Kirken, hvori dåben eller fremstillingen efter hjemmedåb har fundet sted:	
Dåbsår og -dag samt – ved fremstilling efter hjemmedåb – år og dag for fremstillingen:	
Forældrenes eller adoptiv- forældrenes fulde navne:	
Anmærkning angående optagelse i eller udtrædelse af folkekirken:	

Overensstemmelsen med ministerialbogen bevidnes

_____
Sted og dato

Embedsstempel

Ki 22 (1-1-1988)

DEN DANSKE FOLKEKIRKE

VIELSESATTEST

Vielsesår og dag | Vielsessted

KVINDEN

Efternavn

Eget efternavn

For- og mellemnavne

Registreringssted for fødslen (sogn og kommune)

Personnummer el. fødselsår og -dag

Anvender eget efternavn som mellemnavn foran giftenavn

Nej ☐   Ja ☐

MANDEN

Efternavn

Eget efternavn

For- og mellemnavne

Registreringssted for fødslen (sogn og kommune)

Personnummer el. fødselsår og -dag

Anvender eget efternavn som mellemnavn foran giftenavn

Nej ☐   Ja ☐

Overensstemmelsen med ministerialbogen bevidnes

_____   _____
Sted og dato

Embedsstempel

Ki 26 (1-1-1988)

DEN DANSKE FOLKEKIRKE

DØDS- og BEGRAVELSESATTEST

Efternavn:	
Eget efternavn:	
For- og mellemnavne:	
Registreringssted for fødslen (sogn og kommune):	
Personnummer eller fødselsår og -dag:	

Registreringssted for døds-faldet (sogn og kommune):	
Dødsår og -dag:	
År og dag for jordpåkastelsen:	
Begravelsesstedet:	

Efterlevende eller tidligere afdøde ægtefælles fulde navn:	
Ægtefællens personnummer eller fødselsår og -dag:	

Overensstemmelsen med ministerialbogen bevidnes

_____
Sted og dato

Embedsstempel

Ki 28 (1-1-1988)

DJIBOUTI

Direction de la Population
Ministere de l'Interieur des
    Postes et Telecommuncations
B.P. 2383
Djibouti, Djibouti

Formerly known as French Somalia and later as the French Territory of the Affars and the Issas, Djibouti became independent in 1977. The registration is not considered to be complete.

DOMINICA

Registrar General's Office
Supreme Court
Bay Front
P.O. Box 304
Rouseau, Commonwealth of Dominica
West Indies

(809) 448-2401

Cost for a Birth or Death Certificate	US $2.00
Cost for a Marriage Certificate	US $3.00

Dominica became independent in 1978. The Registrar General's Office has records from April 2, 1861 but the office was burned in June 1979, with the loss of many records. Current registration is considered to be complete.

DOMINICAN REPUBLIC

Seccion de Actas del Estado Civil
Junta Central Electoral
Avenida Luperon
Santo Domingo, Dominican Republic

For records before 1930 write to:

Archivo General de la Nación
Cesar Nicolas Penson 91
Plaza de la Cultura
Santo Domingo, Dominican Republic

Cost for a Birth, Marriage or Death Certificate	RD $.50

Registration began January 1, 1828 and is not considered to be complete.

ECUADOR

Director General de Registro Civil,
    Identificación y Cedulacin
Ministerio de Gobierno
Av. Amazonas 743 y Veintimilla
Ed. Espinosa
Quito, Ecuador

Older records are available at the Archivo Municipal (National Museum Building, Quito, Ecuador). Modern vital registration began January 1, 1901. The National Library also has records. Contact them at Universidad Central del Ecuador, P.O. Box 166, Quito.

EGYPT

Department of Civil Registration
Ministry of Interior
Abassia, Cairo, Egypt

While Egypt had the world's first vital records registration program, dating from Ramses II in 1250 B.C., current registration began in 1839. Only births and deaths are registered. Marriages are kept by the religious denomination and divorces are kept by the court issuing the decree. The National Library and Archives also has records. Contact them at Corniche El-Nil Street, Boulac, Cairo.

EL SALVADOR

Registro Civil
Alcaldía Municipal
(City), El Salvador

The Central Office can also assist you:

Dirección General de Estadistica y Censos
Ministerio de Economia
43a. Avenida Norte y la. Calle Ponient
AP 2670
San Salvador, El Salvador

(011) (503) 23-1520

Records begin in 1860 and are recorded in each town. Divorces are recorded on the original marriage certificate.

EQUATORIAL GUINEA

District Judge
Ministerio de Justica, Culto y Registro
Malabo, Equatorial Guinea

Equatorial Guinea, the only Spanish-speaking nation in Africa, became independent in 1968.

ERITREA

Registrar
Ministry of the Interior
Asmara, Eritrea

Vital registration is not considered to be comprehensive.

ESTONIA

Russian-American Genealogical Archival Service (RAGAS)
P.O. Box 236
Glen Echo, Maryland 20812

(202) 501-5206

Cost for a Birth, Marriage, or Death Certificate $20.00

By an agreement between the United States National Archives Volunteer Association and the Archives of Russia Society RAGAS receives and processes requests for vital records in some of the former Soviet republics. Although at this time RAGAS is able to deal mainly with Russia, Belarus, and Ukraine they might be able to help you with your inquiries regarding Estonia. There is a $20 charge per document with a $2.00 shipping fee per document. The service also is available at an hourly rate. (See Russia for application forms.)

Records are also available at the National Library (Eesti Rahvusraamatukogu), located at Tonismagi 2, Tallinn, Estonia EE0106; Tel. (011) (7) (142) 442-094.

ETHIOPIA

	Registrar
Urban areas:	Ministry of Housing and Urban Development
	Addis Ababa, Ethiopia

	Registrar
Rural areas:	Ministry of the Interior
	Addis Ababa, Ethiopia

Vital registration is not considered to be comprehensive.

FIJI

Registrar General
Crown Law Office
Box 2213
Suva, Fiji

(011) (679) 211-598

Cost for a Birth, Marriage, or Death Certificate   Fiji $1.00

Registration began in 1874. Records are also available at the National Archives, P.O. Box 2125, Suva, Fiji; Tel. (011) (679) 304-144; FAX (011) (679) 302-379.

FINLAND

Send your requests to:

Pastor	or	Registrar
Lutheran Church		District Registrar
(Town), Finland		(Town), Finland

Records from the local parishes and the registrars are forwarded to:

Population Register Center
Ministry of the Interior
PL 7
SF-00521 Helsinki, Finland

(011) (358) (0) 189-3909

Cost for a certified Birth Certificate	Price Varies
Cost for a certified Marriage Certificate	Price Varies
Cost for a certified Death Certificate	Price Varies

Over 90 percent of Finland's vital records are registered by the Lutheran Church. Non-Lutherans have been allowed to register with their respective churches or the government since 1917. These records are forwarded to the Population Register Center and *are not open to public inspection*. A file is kept on every resident of Finland, immigrant or citizen, as well as those who have emigrated from Finland. Current registration is considered to be complete. Church registers date back to 1686.

When writing include two International Postal Reply Coupons, available at your local post office.

The Family History Library of The Church of Jesus Christ of Latter-day Saints in Salt Lake City, Utah has microfilmed many of the original and published vital records and church registers of Finland. For further details on their holdings please consult your nearest Family History Center.

FRANCE

Le Marie
(Town), France

Vital records are on file from the late 1700s. Current registration is considered to be complete.

GABON

Registrar of Births, Marriages and Deaths
Ministeres de l'Interieur et de la Justice
Libreville, Gabon

Registration began in 1940 for French citizens and in 1972 for the entire population. Currently the registration is not considered to be complete.

GAMBIA

Medical and Health Department
Ministry of Health
Banjul, Gambia

Gambia became independent in 1970. Vital registration is 50 percent complete for births and 10 percent complete for deaths. The National Library also has records; write P.O. Box 552, Banjul, Gambia.

GEORGIA

Russian-American Genealogical Archival Service (RAGAS)
P.O. Box 236
Glen Echo, Maryland 20812

(202) 501-5206

Cost for a Birth, Marriage, or Death Certificate $20.00

By an agreement between the United States National Archives Volunteer Association and the Archives of Russia Society RAGAS receives and processes requests for vital records in some of the former Soviet republics. Although at this time RAGAS is able to deal mainly with Russia, Belarus, and Ukraine they might be able to help you with your inquiries regarding Georgia. There is a $2.00 shipping fee per document. The service also is available at an hourly rate. (See Russia for application forms.)

Records are also available at The National Library (Gruzinskaia Gosudarstvennaia Respublikanskaia Biblioteka), located at ul. Ketskhoveli 5, 38007 Tbilisi, Georgia; Tel (011) (7) (883) 22.

GERMANY

Send your requests to:

> Standesamt
> (Town), Germany

Cost for a certified Birth Certificate	Varies
Cost for a certified Marriage Certificate	Varies
Cost for a certified Death Certificate	Varies

Write to the Civil Registration District Office or the parish church in the town where the event occurred. Vital records are on file as early as 1809 but usually from 1875. Current registration is considered to be complete.

When writing include two International Postal Reply Coupons, available at your local post office.

The Family History Library of The Church of Jesus Christ of Latter-day Saints in Salt Lake City, Utah has microfilmed many of the original and published vital records and church registers of Germany. For further details on their holdings please consult your nearest Family History Center.

GHANA

Send your requests for births and deaths to:

> Registrar of Births and Deaths
> Central Registry Office
> Ministry of Local Government
> P.O. Box M270
> Accra, Ghana

Send your requests for marriages to:

> Registrar of Marriages
> Registrar General's Department
> P.O. Box 118
> Accra, Ghana

Cost for a certified Birth Certificate	US $5.00
Cost for a certified Marriage Certificate	US $5.00
Cost for a certified Death Certificate	US $5.00

A system for registration began in 1888 in Accra and Christianborg and was expanded to other principal towns in 1912; however, registration for the entire nation did not begin until 1965. Births are on file from 1912 and deaths from 1888.

When writing include two International Postal Reply Coupons, available at your local post office.

The Family History Library of The Church of Jesus Christ of Latter-day Saints in Salt Lake City, Utah has microfilmed original and published vital records and church registers of Ghana. For further details on their holdings please consult your nearest Family History Center.

BIRTHS AND DEATHS REGISTRY
APPLICATION FOR CERTIFIED COPY OF ENTRY IN BIRTH
REGISTER

Full Name: ....

Relationship to the child:...

Postal Address:..

B. PARTICULARS OF THE BIRTH

Entry Number...

Full Name and Sex:...

Date and Place of Birth:...

Date and Place of Registration:..

Mother's Full Name:..

Mother's Maiden Name:,,,

Father's Full Name:..

Purpose of search..

Date:.....................................

                                        ....
                                        SIGNATURE OF APPLICANT

                    C   FOR OFFICE USE

Type of Search:..

Number of copies required:...

Date of collection:..

Amount paid and C.R.No: ....

Date:.....................................

                                        ....
                                        SIGNATURE OF OFFICER

Report of Search:..

Extract(s) prepared, checked and sealed for signature

on: ....

....

BIRTHS AND DEATHS REGISTRY
APPLICATION FOR CERTIFIED COPY OF ENTRY IN DEATH REGISTER

A. APPLICANT

1. Full Name:...

2. Postal Address and Telephone No: ....

B. PARTICULARS OF DEATH

3. Full Name of Deceased..

4. Sex................5: Date of Death................................

6. Place of Death: ....
   ....
   (State Town/Village, Local Authority Area and Region)

7. Date of Registration: ....

8. Place of Registration...
   ....
   (State Town/Village, Local Authority Area and Region)

9. Date of Burial:...

10. Place of Burial:...
                    (Give Name of Cemetery and Town/Village)

C. DOCUMENTARY EVIDENCE AND DECLARATION

11. Applicant's Relationship to the Deceased: ....

12. Purpose of request for Extract, Search............................
    ....

13. Number of copies of Extract Requested..............................

14. Documentary Evidence, Authority, Declarations etc. attached(to be
    listed...
    ....

15. Date............-..

                                    SIGNATURE OR MARK OF APPLICANT

D. FOR OFFICE USE

16. Type of Search:..

17. Date of collection: ....

18. Amount paid and C.R.No...

19. Date:.....................

                                    SIGNATURE OF SEARCH OFFICER

20. Report of Search...

21. Extract(s) prepared, checked and sealed for signature on:..........

22. Extract(s) signed...

GIBRALTAR

Send your requests for births and deaths to:

Registrar General
Registry of Births, Deaths and Marriages
277 Main Street
Gibraltar

(011) (350) 7-2289

Send your requests for divorce records to:

Registrar
Supreme Court of Gibraltar
277 Main Street
Gibraltar

Cost for a Birth, Marriage, Divorce, or Death Certificate	£5.00

The Registrar has birth records from October 3, 1848, stillbirth records from November 24, 1951, marriage records from April 10, 1862, and death records from September 1, 1859. Registration was not compulsory for births until January 20, 1887, for marriages until July 17, 1902, and for deaths until January 1, 1869.

Current vital registration is considered to be more than 90 percent complete. The Supreme Court has divorce records on file from November 6, 1890.

Payment must be made by certified check payable to "Gibraltar Government Account."

GREECE

Registrar
Civil Registry Office
(Town), Greece

Vital registration started in 1924. Current registration is considered to be complete. The Division on Citizenship of the Ministry of the Interior (14 Euripidou Street, Athens 105 59, Greece) directs the work of the local registrars.

GRENADA

Send your requests for births and deaths to:

Registrar General's Office
Ministry of Health
Church Street
St. George's, Grenada
West Indies

(809) 440-2030

Cost for a certified Birth Certificate	$20.00
Cost for a certified Marriage Certificate	$20.00
Cost for a certified Death Certificate	$20.00

The Registrar General has records from January 1, 1866. Current vital registration is considered to be complete. The local churches also have their own records.

When writing include two International Postal Reply Coupons, available at your local post office.

The Family History Library of The Church of Jesus Christ of Latter-day Saints in Salt Lake City, Utah has microfilmed original and published records of Grenada. For further details on their holdings please consult your nearest Family History Center.

GRENADA

Application for a Search and Certificate Extract from Register of Births, Deaths and Marriages

———————

The Registrar General

PLEASE cause a search to be made for the Birth/Death/Marriage of

.... which took place on or about

.... in the parish of ....

and furnish me with a certified copy of the entry under your hand and seal.

In the case of an application for a Birth Certificate the following particulars are required:

Father's Name ....

Mother's Name ....

Where Born ....

Date of Birth ....

Mother's Name (before Marriage) ....

....

Date ....

Address ....

....

B 56.

GUATEMALA

Director
Registro Civil
(Town), Guatemala

Vital registration began January 1, 1877 and is recorded in the Office of Civil Registration in each town. Current vital registration is considered to be complete.

GUINEA

Direction generale de l'identification et du Registre Civile
Ministere de la Justice
Conakry, Guinea

Registration began in 1979 and is not complete.

GUINEA-BISSAU

Direction generale de l'identification et du Registre Civile
Ministere de la Justice
Bissau, Guinea-Bissau

Vital registration began in 1976 and is not complete.

GUYANA

Registrar
General Register Office
Ministry of Home Affairs
G.P.O. Building
Robb Street
Georgetown, Guyana

Cost for a Birth, Marriage, or Death Certificate $.50

Registration in Guyana began in 1880 and is not complete. The National Library also has records. Contact them at P.O. Box 10240, Georgetown.

HAITI

Service National de l'Inspection
et de Controle de l'Etat Civil
Ministere de la Justice
Port au Prince, Haiti

Registration began in 1880 and is not complete.

HONDURAS

Archivo Nacional de Honduras
6a Avenida 408
Tegucigalpa, Honduras

Registration began January 1, 1881. The National Library also has records. Contact them at 6a Avenida Salvador Mendieta, Tegucigalpa.

HUNGARY

Civil Registration Office
(Town), Hungary

Vital records are on file from 1895. The National Archives also has records; contact Magyar Orszagos Leveltar, Becsi kapu ter 4, Budapest 1 H-1250; Tel. (011) (36) (1) 156-5811.

ICELAND

Send your requests to:

Hagstofa Islands Pjooskra
The National Registry
Skuggasund 3
150 Reykjavik, Iceland

(011) (354) (1) 609-800, FAX (011) (354) (1) 623-312

Cost for a certified Birth Certificate	US $6.50
Cost for a certified Marriage Certificate	US $6.50
Cost for a certified Death Certificate	US $6.50

The National Registry has records on all residents of Iceland from 1953. They maintain these records as part of a national identity system. Prior to this time records were kept by the local, usually Lutheran, church. These church registers go back to 1785. The current vital registration is considered to be complete.

The Family History Library of The Church of Jesus Christ of Latter-day Saints in Salt Lake City, Utah has microfilmed original and published records of Iceland. For further details on their holdings please consult your nearest Family History Center.

Ísland

Iceland / Islande / IJsland

Hagstofa Íslands - Þjóðskrá
The National Registry
Skuggasundi 3
150 Reykjavík

Sími /tel. +354-1-609800
Telefax: +354-1-623312

Fæðingarvottorð

Fødselsattest / Extract of the register of births / Auszug aus dem Geburtsregister / Extrait des registres de l´état civil concernant une naissance / Extracto del registro de nacimientos / Estratto del registro delle nascite / Uittreksel uit de geboortearchieven

Nafn navn / name / Name / nom / nombre / nome / naam	
Fæðingardagur fødselsdato / date of birth / Geburtsdatum / date de naissance / fecha de nacimiento / data di nascita / geboortedatum	
Kyn køn / sex / Geschlecht / sexe / sexo / sesse / geslacht	
Fæðingarstaður fødested / place of birth / Geburtsort / lieu de naissance / lugar de nacimiento / luogo di nascito / geboorteplaats	
Nafn föður faders navn / name of the father / Name des Vaters / nom du père / nombre del padre / nome del padre / naam van de vader	
Nafn móður moders navn / name of the mother / Name der Mutter / nom de la mère / nombre de la madre / nome della madre / naam van de moeder	

Dagsetning, undirskrift og stimpill embættis

udgivelsesdato, underskrift og myndigheds stempel
date of issue, signature and seal of keeper
Ausstellungsdatum, Unterschrift und Dienstsiegel des Registerführers
Date de délivrance, signature et sceau du dépositaire
fecha de expedición, firma y sello del depositario
data in cui è stato rilasciato l´atto, con firma e bollo dell´ufficio
afgiftedatum, handtekening en ambtelijk stempel

Reykjavík, _____

_____

D2451 Gutenberg

Hjónavígsluvottorð óskast

Fullt nafn karls _____

Fæðingardagur hans _____ Fæðingarstaður _____

Fullt nafn konu _____

Fæðingardagur hennar _____ Fæðingarstaður _____

Hjónavígsludagur _____ Hjónavígslustaður _____

Ísland

Iceland / Islande / IJsland

Hagstofa Íslands - Þjóðskrá
The National Registry
Skuggasund 3   Sími / tel. +354-1-609800
150 Reykjavík   Telefax: +354-1-623312

Hjúskaparvottorð

Vielsesattest / Extract of the register of marriages / Auszug aus dem Eheregister / Extrait des registres de l´état civil concernant un mariage / Extracto del registro de matrimonios / Estratto del registro dei matrimoni / Uittreksel uit huwelijksarchieven

Nafn brúðguma brudgommens navn / name of the bridegroom / Name des Bräutigam / nom du marié/ nombre del novio / nome dello sposo / naam van de echtgenoot	
Fæðingardagur fødselsdato / date of birth / Geburtsdatum / date de naissance / fecha de nacimiento / data di nascita / geboortedatum	
Fæðingarstaður fødested / place of birth / Geburtsort / lieu de naissance / lugar de nacimiento / luogo di nascito / geboorteplaats	
Nafn brúðar brudens navn / name of the bride / Name der Braut / nom de la mariée / nombre de la novia / nome della sposa / naam van de echtgenote	
Fæðingardagur fødselsdato / date of birth / Geburtsdatum / date de naissance / fecha de nacimiento / data di nascita / geboortedatum	
Fæðingarstaður fødested / place of birth / Geburtsort / lieu de naissance / lugar de nacimiento / luogo di nascito / geboorteplaats	
Hjónavígsludagur og -staður sted og dato for vielsen / date and place of the marriage / Datum und Ort der Eheschließung / date et lieu du mariage / fecha y lugar del matrimonio / data e luogo della celebration del matrimonio / datum en plaats van het huwelijk	

Dagsetning, undirskrift og stimpill embættis   Reykjavík, _____

udgivelsesdato, underskrift og myndigheds stempel
date of issue, signature and seal of keeper
Ausstellungsdatum, Unterschrift und Dienstsiegel des Registerführers
Date de délivrance, signature et sceau du dépositaire
fecha de expedición, firma y sello del depositario
data in cui è stato rilasciato l´atto, con firma e bollo dell´ufficio
afgiftedatum, handtekening en ambtelijk stempel

D2450 Steindórsprent Gutenberg hf

Beiðni um staðfestingu á dánardegi

Nafn hins látna _____

Fæðingardagur og -ár _____ Hjúskaparstétt _____

Lögheimili _____

Dánardagur _____

Ísland

Iceland / Islande / IJsland

Hagstofa Íslands - Þjóðskrá
The National Registry
Skuggasundi 3
150 Reykjavík   Sími / tel. (9)1 - 609800

D á n a r v o t t o r ð

Dødsattest / Extract of the register of deaths / Auszug aus dem Todesregister / Extrait des registres de l´état civil concernant un décès / Extracto del registro de defunciones / Estratto del registro delle morti / Uittreksel uit het overlijdensarchief

Nafn navn / name / Name / nom / nombre / nome / naam	
Fæðingardagur og -staður fødselsdato og fødested / date and place of birth / Geburtsdatum und Geburtsort / date et lieu de naissance / fecha y lugar de nacimiento / data e luogo di nascita / geboortedatum en geboorteplaats	
Kyn køn / sex / Geschlecht / sexe / sexo / sesse / geslacht	
Hjúskaparstaða civilstand / marital status / Familienstand / situation de famille / estado civil / stato di civile / burgerlijke staat	
Heimilisfang sidste bopæl / last residence / letzter Wohnsitz / dernier domicile / ultimo domicilio / ultimo domicilio / laatste woonplaats	
Dánardagur dødsdato / date of death / Todesdatum / date de décès / fecha de fallecimiento / data della morte / datum van overlijden	
Dánarstaður dødested / place of death / Todesort / lieu de décès / lugar de fallecimiento / luogo della morte / plaats van overlijden	

Dagsetning, undirskrift og stimpill embættis
udgivelsesdato, underskrift og mydigheds stempel
date of issue, signature and seal of keeper
Ausstellungsdatum, Unterschrift und Dienstsiegel des Registerführers
Date de délivrance, signature et sceau du dépositaire
fecha de expedición, firma y sello del depositario
data in cui è stato rilasciato l´atto, con firma e bollo dell´ufficio
afgiftedatum, handtekening en ambtelijk stempel

Reykjavík, _____

_____

INDIA

Chief Registrar of Births, Deaths and Marriages
(Capital City; State, Union or Territory), India

Cost for a Birth or Death Certificate   Rs. 1 to 20 (varies)
Cost for a certified Marriage Certificate   No Charge

Records began in the mid-1800s for Europeans. The Christian Marriage Act took effect in 1872, the Parsee in 1936, and the Hindu in 1955. The Bengal Births and Deaths Registration Act took effect in 1873 and the Births, Deaths, and Marriages Registration Act in 1886.

INDONESIA

Burgerlijke Stand
(Town), Indonesia

Records began in 1815. All Indonesians in Jakarta were registered in 1929. Births and deaths are with the Minister of Internal Affairs and in each town on individual forms called triplikats. Marriages and divorces are filed with the denomination and the vital registration office, and in the Indonesian Department of Religious Affairs.

IRAN

Civil Registration Organization
Ministry of the Interior
Eman Khomaini Street
Central Building No. 184
Teheran, Iran 11374

ID cards have been required for Iranian men since 1918, and now every Iranian is issued an ID card. Marriage and divorce records are kept by the Notarial Office and Court of Justice.

IRAQ

Director of Vital and Health Statistics
Ministry of Health
Alwiyah, Baghdad, Iraq

Records began in 1947. Marriages are recorded by the religious denomination and divorces are kept by the court that issued the decree.

IRELAND

Send your requests to:

Registrar General
Joyce House
8-11 Lombard Street East
Dublin 2, Ireland

(011) (353) (1) 711-000, FAX (011) (353) (1) 711-243

Cost for a certified Birth Certificate	Ire £3.00
Cost for a short form Birth Certificate	Ire £3.50
Cost for a certified Marriage Certificate	Ire £5.50
Cost for a certified Death Certificate	Ire £5.50
Cost for a duplicate copy, when ordered at the same time	Ire £4.00

The Registrar General has records from January 1, 1864. Vital registration is considered to be complete. (For Northern Ireland see United Kingdom—Northern Ireland.)

The Family History Library of The Church of Jesus Christ of Latter-day Saints in Salt Lake City, Utah has microfilmed many of the original and published vital records and church registers of Ireland's cities and counties. For further details on their holdings please consult your nearest Family History Center.

<table>
<tr><td>

General Register Office

Joyce House,
8 – 11 Lombard Street East, Dublin 2
</td><td>

</td><td>

Oifig an Ard-Chláraitheora

(Office of the Registrar General)
Teach Sheoighe,
8 – 11 Sráid Lombaird Thoir, Baile Átha Cliath 2
</td></tr>
</table>

TEL. (01) 711000 EXTN.
TELEX: 33451
FAX. (01) 711243

Our Ref.:

Your Ref.:

FAX NO. (01) 711243

With reference to your application for a birth certificate the information requested below should be provided as accurately as possible and the form returned to this Office with the necessary fee. All Cheques, Postal or Money Orders should be made payable to "THE REGISTRAR-GENERAL".

Please complete in BLOCK CAPITALS.

FEES

Full Birth Certificate (including search fee)........................... IR£5.50

Short Birth Certificate (including search fee) .... IR£3.50

If more than one certificate relating to the birth of the same person is required an additional fee of IR£4.00 should be forwarded for each extra full certificate or IR£2.00 for each extra short certificate.

SURNAME of PERSON whose Birth Certificate is required _____

FIRST NAME(S)in full _____

Date of Birth _____

Place of Birth
(If in a town, name of street to be given) _____

Father's Name _____

Father's Occupation _____

Mother's First Name(s) and Maiden Surname _____

Has the Person whose Birth record is required been legally adopted: YES/NO _____

Name of Applicant ....

Address ....

....

Date ....19.....

Oifig an Ard-Chláraitheora

Joyce House,
8-11 Lombard Street East, Dublin 2

Oifig an Ard-Chláraitheora

Teach Sheoighe,
8-11 Sráid Lombaird Thoir, Baile Átha Cliath 2

TEL. (01) 711000 EXTN.
TELEX 28451

Our Ref.:

Your Ref.:

FAX NO. (01) 711243

With reference to your application for a marriage certificate the information requested below should be provided as accurately as possible and the form returned to this Office with the necessary fee. All Cheques, Postal or Money Orders should be made payable to "THE REGISTRAR-GENERAL".

Please complete in BLOCK CAPITALS.

<u>FEES</u>

Marriage Certificate (including search fee)...............................IR£5.50

If more than one certificate relating to the marriage of the same person is required an additional fee of £4.00 should be forwarded to each exta certificate.

NAME and ADDRESS of the Parties Married (to be written in full in each case).

(a) _____

_____

_____

(b) _____

_____

_____

<u>Date of Marriage</u> _____

<u>Where Married</u> _____

Name of Applicant ....

Address ....

....

Date ....19.....

TEL. (01) 711000 EXTN.
TELEX: 33451
260

Our Ref.:

Your Ref.:

FAX NO. (01) 711243

With reference to your application for a death certificate the information requested below should be provided as accurately as possible and the form returned to this Office with the necessary fee. All Cheques, Postal or Money Orders should be made payable to the "THE REGISTRAR-GENERAL".

Please complete in BLOCK CAPITALS.

_____

FEES

Death Certificate (including search fee) ....IR£5.50

If more than one certificate relating to the death of the same person is required an additional fee of £4.00 should be forwarded for each extra certificate.

SURNAME of DECEASED _____

FIRST NAME(S) in full _____

Date of Death _____

Place of Death
(If in a town, name of street to be given _____

Age of Deceased _____

Occupation of Deceased _____

State whether Single, Married, Widow, Widower _____

Name of Applicant ....

Address ....

....

Date ....19.....

ISRAEL

Registrar
Immigration Services and Population Registration
Ministry of the Interior
P.O. Box 2420
Jerusalem, Israel

For marriage records write to the Rabbinate in the town where the event took place.

ITALY

Stato Civile
(Town), Italy

Vital records are on file for most areas from the early 1800s, but are more generally available from 1870 to the present. Older records are often on deposit at the State Archives.

IVORY COAST

Registrar
Ministries of Interior and Justice
Abidjan 01, Ivory Coast

Registration began in 1933 for French citizens, expanded in 1950 to include residents within 15 miles of registration centers, and in 1964 was extended to the entire nation. Current registration is not complete.

JAMAICA

Registrar General
Registrar General's Office
Spanish Town, Jamaica

(809) 984-3041

Cost for a Birth, Marriage, or Death Certificate   Jam 45¢ plus postage

Vital registration began January 1, 1878.

JAPAN

Send your requests to:

> Director General
> Second Division
> Civil Affairs Bureau
> Ministry of Justice
> 1-1-1 Kasumigaseki, Chiyoda-ku
> Tokyo 100, Japan

(011) (81) (3) 3580-4111

Cost for a certified Birth Certificate	¥ 400
Cost for a certified Marriage Certificate	¥ 400
Cost for a certified Divorce Certificate	¥ 400
Cost for a certified Death Certificate	¥ 400
Cost for a certified Abstract	¥ 200
Cost for a certified Abstract from Old Form	¥ 300
Cost for a certificate from Old Form	¥ 500
Cost for a certificate on Rice Paper	¥ 10,000

Japan instituted its system of KOSEKI or family registers on February 1, 1872. Current registration is considered to be complete. Japan also requires each resident to have a national identification card. Both of these systems are administered by the Ministry of Justice.

The Family History Library of The Church of Jesus Christ of Latter-day Saints in Salt Lake City, Utah has microfilmed original and published records of Japan. For further details on their holdings please consult your nearest Family History Center.

本　籍

名　氏

生出

母

父

生出

母

父

生出

母

父

出生届

平成　年　月　日届出

　　　　　　長　殿

	受理	平成　年　月　日		発送	平成　年　月　日
		第　　　　号			第　　　　号　　　長印
	送付	平成　年　月　日			
		第　　　　号			
	書類調査	戸籍記載	記載調査	調査票	附票	住民票	通知

(1)	子の氏名	（よみかた）					
		氏		名		□嫡出子	平成　年　月　日
						□嫡出でない子	□男 □女
(2)	生まれたとき	平成　年　月　日　午前・午後　時　分					
(3)	生まれたところ				番地 番 号		
(4)	住所（住民登録をするところ）			番地 番 号			
		世帯主の氏名	世帯主との続き柄				
(5)	父母の氏名・生年月日（子が生まれたときの年齢）	父	母				
		平成　年　月　日（満　歳）	年　月　日（満　歳）				
(6)	本籍（外国人のときは国籍だけを書いてください）		番地 番				
		筆頭者の氏名					
(7)	同居を始めたとき	年　月（結婚式をあげたとき、または、同居を始めたときのうち早いほうを書いてください）					
(8)	子が生まれたときの世帯のおもな仕事と父母の職業	□1. 農業だけまたは農業とその他の仕事を持っている世帯 □2. 自由業・商工業・サービス業等を個人で経営している世帯 □3. 企業・個人商店等（官公庁は除く）の常用勤労者世帯で勤め先の従業者数が1人から99人までの世帯（日々または1年未満の契約の雇用者は5） □4. 3にあてはまらない常用勤労者世帯及び会社団体の役員の世帯（日々または1年未満の契約の雇用者は5） □5. 1から4にあてはまらないその他の仕事をしている者のいる世帯 □6. 仕事をしている者のいない世帯					
(9)	父母の職業	（国勢調査の年…　　年…の4月1日から翌年3月31日までに子が生まれたときだけ書いてください）					
		父の職業		母の職業			
	その他						

届出人	□1. 父 □2. 法定代理人（　　） □3. 同居者 □4. 医師 □5. 助産婦 □6. その他の立会者
	住所　　　　　　　　　　　　　番地 番 号
	本籍　　　　　　　　　　　番地 番　筆頭者の氏名
	署名　　　　　　　　　　　㊞　　　　　年　月　日生

事件簿番号

出生証明書

(10)	子の男女の別、氏名及び体重	1 男 2 女	氏名		体重	グラム
(11)	双子以上の場合	1 双子 2 三つ子以上 3 四つ子以上 （　　子）	出産順位	1 第一子 2 第二子 3 第三子 4 第四子以上（第　子）		
(12)	出生の年月日時／出生の場所	平成　年　月　日　午前・午後　時　分				
		1 病院 2 診療所 3 助産所 4 自宅 5 その他（　）		番地 番 号		
(13)	及びその種別／妊娠週数及び母の氏名	1.2.3の名称	妊娠満　週	母の氏名		
(14)	この母の出産した子の数／出生子（この出生子及び出生後死亡した子を含む）	出生子（この出生子及び出生後死亡した子を含む）　　人 妊娠満22週（妊娠第6月）以後の死産児　　胎				
(15)	上記のとおり記の日時場所で出生したことを証明する。	住所		番地 番 号		
		平成　年　月　日	1 医師 2 助産婦 3 その他	氏名 押印	㊞	

連絡先　　　　　　　番　方

婚姻届

平成　　年　　月　　日届出

　　　　　　　長　殿

受理	平成　年　月　日	発送	平成　年　月　日
	第　　　　号		第　　　　号
送付	平成　年　月　日		長　印
	第　　　　号		
書類調査	戸籍記載	記載調査	調査票	附票	住民票	通知

		夫になる人	妻になる人
(1)	氏　名	氏　　　名	氏　　　名
	生年月日	年　月　日	年　月　日
(2)	住　所 (住民登録をしているところ)	番地番　号	番地番　号
		世帯主の氏名	世帯主の氏名
(3)	本　籍	番地番	番地番
	(外国人のときは国籍だけを書いてください)	筆頭者の氏名	筆頭者の氏名
	父母の氏名父母との続き柄 (他の養父母は その他の欄に書いてください)	父	母	続き柄 男	父	母	続き柄 女
(4)	婚姻後の夫婦の氏・新しい本籍	□夫の氏　□妻の氏	新本籍	番地番
(5)	同居を始めたとき	（結婚式をあげたとき、または同居を始めたときのうち早いほうを書いてください） 年　月
(6)	初婚・再婚の別	□初婚　□再婚（□死別 □離別） 年　月　日	□初婚　□再婚（□死別 □離別） 年　月　日
(7)	同居を始める前の夫妻のそれぞれの世帯のおもな仕事と	1. 農業だけまたは農業とその他の仕事を持っている世帯 2. 自由業・商工業・サービス業等を個人で経営している世帯 3. 企業・個人商店等（官公庁は除く）の常用勤労者世帯で勤め先の従業者数が1人から99人までの世帯 4. 3にあてはまらない常用勤労者世帯及び会社団体の役員の世帯 5. 1から4にあてはまらないその他の仕事をしている者のいる世帯 6. 仕事をしている者のいない世帯
(8)	夫妻の職業	夫の職業	妻の職業
	（国勢調査の年…　　年…の4月1日から翌年3月31日までに届出をするときだけ書いてください）		
	その他		
	届出人署名押印	夫	印	妻	印
	事件簿番号		

記入の注意

鉛筆や消えやすいインキで書かないでください。

この届は、あらかじめ用意し、結婚式をあげる日または同居を始める日に出すようにすることもできますし、この用紙のほかに郵送で出すこともできます。この場合、宿直等で取扱います。

とくに急ぐ人または本人になる人の本籍地に出すときは2通、その他のところに出すときは3通出してください。（あらかじめ用意するとき。）

この届が本籍地でない役場に出すときは、戸籍の謄本が必要ですから、あらかじめその用意をしてください。（謄本でもけっこうです。）

証		人
署名押印		印		印
生年月日	年　月　日	年　月　日
住　所	番地番　号	番地番　号
本　籍	番地番	番地番

「筆頭者の氏名」には、戸籍のはじめに記載されている人の氏名を書いてください。

父母がいま婚姻しているときは、母の氏は書かないで、名だけを書いてください。

養父母については、その他の欄に同じように書いてください。

ここには、あてはまるものの□のように□のしるしをつけてください。

外国人と婚姻する人か、まだ戸籍の筆頭者となっていない場合は、新しい戸籍がつくられますので、希望する本籍を書いてください。

再婚のときは、直前の婚姻について書いてください。内縁のものはふくまれません。

◎ 署名は必ず本人が自署してください
◎ 印は各自別々の印を押して下さい
◎ 届出人の印を御持参下さい

連絡先	
電話（　　）	番
自宅・勤務先・呼出	方

離婚届

記入の注意

鉛筆や消えやすいインキで書かないで下さい。

筆頭者の氏名欄には、戸籍のはじめに記載されている人の氏名を書いて下さい。

本籍地でない役場に出すときは、2通または3通出して下さい。

そのほかに必要なもの

調停離婚のとき —— 調停調書の謄本

審判離婚のとき —— 審判の謄本と確定証明書

同決離婚のとき —— 判決の謄本と確定証明書

証　人

署名　印

生年月日　年　月　日

住所

本籍　番地番

（平成　年　月　日届出）

長　殿

	夫	妻
(1) 氏　名	氏　名	氏　名
生年月日		
住所		
本籍		
(2) 父母の氏名　父母との続き柄	父　母　続き柄　男	父　母　続き柄　女
(3) 離婚の種別	協議離婚　調停　審判　和解　請求の認諾　判決	
(4) 婚姻前の氏にもどる者の本籍	夫　妻　もとの戸籍にもどる　新しい戸籍をつくる	
(5) もとの戸籍の筆頭者の氏名		
(6) 同居の期間		
(7) 別居する前の住所		
(8) 別居する前の世帯のおもな仕事と		
(9) 夫妻の職業	夫の職業	妻の職業

届出人　夫　妻
署名押印

死亡診断書（死体検案書）

氏　名		1 男　2 女	生年月日	明治 大正 昭和 平成　　年　　月　　日

(13) 発病年月日　平成　　年　　月　　日　午前・午後　　時　　分

(14) 死亡年月日時分　平成　　年　　月　　日　午前・午後　　時　　分

(15) 死亡したところ及びその種別（注意(1)参照）
1 病院　2 診療所　3 老人保健施設　4 助産所　5 自宅　6 その他
死亡したところ 番地 番 号

死亡の種類
1 病及び自然死
2 不慮の外因死　外因死 3 その他の災害死 4 自殺 5 他殺 6 その他及び不詳
7 その他及び不詳（1〜4の名称）

(16) 死亡の原因
イ 直接死因
ロ （イ）の原因
ハ （ロ）の原因
II その他の身体状況（注意(2)参照）
手術の年月日　平成　　年　　月　　日
解剖の主要所見

(17) 外因死の追加事項
傷害発生の年月日時　平成　　年　　月　　日　午前・午後　　時　　分
傷害発生のところ　場所名の具体的記載欄
手段及び状況

(18) 生後168時間未満で死亡した場合の母体の状況（注意(4)参照）
妊娠・分娩時における母体の状況
1 従業中　2 従業中でない時

(19) 上記の通り診断（検案）する
病院、診療所若しくは老人保健施設の名称及び所在地又は医師の住所
（氏名）　　　　　医師　印
平成　　年　　月　　日　番地 番 号

死亡診断書記入の注意
(1) 死亡の場所の種別では、老人ホームにおいて死亡した場合において、住民票に記載された住所地が当該ホームであるときは5を、その他のときは6を〇で囲んでください。
(2) I欄では、I欄記載の原因と直接の関係はないが、病的経過に悪影響を与えたと思われる身体の状況を書いてください。なお妊娠満何週の死亡では「妊娠満何月」、分娩中の死亡では「妊娠満何週」の分娩中、産後42日以内の死亡では「妊娠満何週」産後何日目、と書いてください。
(3) 傷害発生の場所はたとえば「自宅の風呂場」、「鉱山の坑内」のように具体的に書いてください。
(4) 妊娠・分娩時に母又は同一の病院・診療所で出生した場合にのみ書いてください。

死　亡　届

平成　　年　　月　　日届出

受理	平成　　年　　月　　日 第　　号
送付	平成　　年　　月　　日 第　　号
書類調査	戸籍記載	記載調査	調査票	附票	住民票	通知

長　殿　　　長印

(1) 氏名　　□男　□女

(2) 生年月日　平成　　年　　月　　日（生まれてから30日以内に死亡したときは午前・午後　　時　　分）

(3) 死亡したとき　平成　　年　　月　　日　午前・午後　　時　　分

(4) 死亡したところ　番地 番 号

(5) 住所（住民登録をしているところ）　番地 番 号
世帯主の氏名

(6) 本籍（外国人のときは国籍だけを書いてください）　番地 番
筆頭者の氏名

(7) 死亡した人の夫または妻　□いる（満　　歳）　□いない　□未婚　□死別　□離別

(8) 死亡した人の届出（生まれてから8日以内に死亡したときだけ書いてください）
都道府県　役所　役場に届出

(9) 世帯のおもな仕事と
□1. 農業だけまたは農業とその他の仕事を持っている世帯
□2. 農業とその他の仕事を持っている世帯
□3. 店舗などの事業所を持っている自由業・商工業・サービス業などを個人で経営している世帯
□4. 管理・事務・技術者・教員・販売・外交・医療保健技術者・旧専門学校卒業以上の技術者などの勤労者世帯（日々または1年未満の契約の雇用者は6）
□5. 4にあてはまらない勤労者世帯（日々または1年未満の契約の雇用者は6）
□6. その他の世帯

(11) 職業・産業（国勢調査の年…年4月1日から翌年3月31日までに死亡したときだけ書いてください）　職業　産業

(12) その他

届　住所　番地 番
本籍　番地 番
筆頭者の氏名

出　署名　印　平成　　年　　月　　日生

人　事件簿番号

記入の注意
鉛筆や消えやすいインキで書かないでください。
死亡したことを知った日からかぞえて7日以内に出してください。
死亡者の本籍地でない役場に出すときは、2通提出してください。
「筆頭者の氏名」には、戸籍のはじめに記載されている人の氏名を書いてください。
内縁のものはふくまれません。
□には、あてはまるものに〇のようにしるしをつけてください。
死亡者について書いてください。

JORDAN

Registrar
Department of Civil Status
Ministry of the Interior
P.O. Box 2740
Amman, Jordan

Vital registration began in 1926 and is considered to be complete for births and about 60 percent for deaths.

KAZAKHSTAN

Russian-American Genealogical Archival Service (RAGAS)
P.O. Box 236
Glen Echo, Maryland 20812

(202) 501-5206

Cost for a Birth, Marriage, or Death Certificate $20.00

By an agreement between the United States National Archives Volunteer Association and the Archives of Russia Society RAGAS receives and processes requests for vital records in some of the former Soviet republics. Although at this time RAGAS is able to deal mainly with Russia, Belarus, and Ukraine they might be able to help you with your inquiries regarding Kazakhstan. There is a $2.00 shipping fee per document. The service also is available at an hourly rate. (See Russia for application forms.)

The National Library also has records; contact Kazakhskaia Biblioteka, ul. Abaia 14, 480013 Alma-Ata, Kazakhstan; Tel. (011) (7) (327) 696-586.

KENYA

Send your requests to:

Registrar General
P.O. Box 30031
Nairobi, Kenya

(011) (254) (2) 7461

Cost for a certified Birth Certificate	KSh. 10.00
Cost for a short form Birth Certificate	KSh. 5.00
Cost for a certified Marriage Certificate	KSh. 10.00
Cost for a certified Death Certificate	KSh. 10.00

Although church registers were kept from colonial times, modern vital registration for Europeans did not begin until 1904. Registration was expanded to include Asians in 1906 and the entire population by 1971. Currently, registration is not considered to be complete. When writing please include two International Postal Reply Coupons, available at your local post office. The Registrar will accept an international bank draft payable in U.S. dollars.

Kenya is divided into districts; the original birth and death certificates are kept at the District Registry. Duplicates are sent to the Central Registry.

The Family History Library of The Church of Jesus Christ of Latter-day Saints in Salt Lake City, Utah has microfilmed records of Kenya and Africa. For further details on their holdings please consult your nearest Family History Center.

REPUBLIC OF KENYA

No. ....

APPLICATION FOR A BIRTH/MARRIAGE/ DEATH CERTIFICATE

Insert name and address of applicant.

I, ...

of ....

Delete as necessary.

hereby apply for Certificate(s) of Birth / Marriage / Death particulars whereof are given below.

I attach the sum of Sh. .... being the prescribed fee payable at the rate of

Sh. 10 for each certificate required.

Full Name	Where Born, Married or Died	Date of Birth, Marriage or Death	Entry No. (To be completed at District Registry)
....	....	....	....
....	....	....	....
....	....	....	....
....	....	....	....

(For use in Registrar's Department only)

	Date	*Initials*
Application received with fee as above	....	
Certificate issued	....	

TO THE REGISTRAR-GENERAL

P.O. BOX 30031,

NAIROBI.

KIRIBATI

Registrar General of Births, Deaths and Marriages
Civil Registration Office
P.O. Box 55
Bairiki, Tarawa, Kiribati

Cost for a certified Death Certificate   Aus $2.00

Civil registration began in the late 19th century. Records are also available at The National Archives and Library; write to the following address for information: P.O. Box 6, Bairiki, Tarawa, Kiribati; Tel. (011) (686) 21-337; FAX (011) (686) 28- 222.

KOREA—NORTH

Police Department
(Town), North Korea

Korea has maintained national population registers from the time of the United Silla Kingdom (668-935 A.D.). In 1896 a law on population registration was issued that required the registers to be updated annually. Currently, individuals register and update their family listings with the local police department.

KOREA—SOUTH

Director General
Bureau of Registry
Ministry of Court Administration
37, Sosomoon-dong, Chung-ku
Seoul, 110-310, Korea

or to: Registrar
Ministry of Home Affairs
(Town of current residence), Korea

Cost for a Birth, Marriage, or Death Certificate   8,000 Won

Korea has maintained national population registers from the time of the United Silla Kingdom (668-935 A.D.). In 1896 a law on population registration was issued that required the registers to be updated annually.

Currently individuals may register and update their family listings at either the Ministry of Home Affairs' office in the town where they now live or at the Ministry of Court Administration's offices in the family's recognized "hometown" or "ancestral home." This dual registration system means that both registers need to be searched for copies of vital records.

KUWAIT

Department of Central Civil Registration
Ministry of Public Health
P.O. Box 5286
13053 Safat, Kuwait

Birth, marriage, divorce, and death records are available from 1964. A new system of national identity cards was established in 1988.

KYRGYZSTAN

Russian-American Genealogical Archival Service (RAGAS)
P.O. Box 236
Glen Echo, Maryland 20812

(202) 501-5206

Cost for a Birth, Marriage, or Death Certificate $20.00

By an agreement between the United States National Archives Volunteer Association and the Archives of Russia Society RAGAS receives and processes requests for vital records in some of the former Soviet republics. Although at this time RAGAS is able to deal mainly with Russia, Belarus, and Ukraine they might be able to help you with your inquiries regarding Kyrgyzstan. There is a $2.00 shipping fee per document. The service also is available at an hourly rate. (See Russia for application forms.)

The National Library also has records; contact them at Gosudarstvennaia Respublikanskaia Biblioteka, ul. Ogonbaeva 242, 720873 Bishkek, Kyrgyzstan.

LAOS

Laos does not have an organized system of vital registration.

LATVIA

Russian-American Genealogical Archival Service (RAGAS)
P.O. Box 236
Glen Echo, Maryland 20812

(202) 501-5206

Cost for a Birth, Marriage, or Death Certificate $20.00

By an agreement between the United States National Archives Volunteer Association and the Archives of Russia Society RAGAS receives and processes requests for vital records in some of the former Soviet republics. Although at this time RAGAS is able to deal mainly with Russia, Belarus, and Ukraine they might be able to help you with your inquiries regarding Latvia. There is a $2.00 shipping fee per document. The service also is available at an hourly rate. (See Russia for application forms.)

The National Library also has records; contact them at Kr. Barona iela 14, Riga, Latvia 226011; Tel. (011) (7) 280-851.

LEBANON

Lebanon, with the changes in government, does not have an organized system of vital registration.

LESOTHO

Registrar General
The Law Office
Office of the Prime Minister
P.O. Box 33
Maseru 100, Lesotho

Vital registration began in 1880.

LIBERIA

Bureau of Health and Vital Statistics
Ministry of Health and Social Welfare
P.O. Bag 3762
Monrovia, Liberia

Liberia gained its independence in 1847. While the system of vital registration has been worked on for years, including a United Nations project to improve the process, the registration is not complete. Limited records are available for the past 20 years.

LIBYA

Registrar
Civil Registration Section
Secretariat of Utilities
Tripoli, Libya

During the period of Italian control, vital registration was begun in urban areas. Modern vital registration began in 1968. Currently births and deaths are computerized but are not complete. Marriage and divorce records are kept by the religious law courts.

Each household in Libya is required to keep a family registration booklet, which gives the vital information on each person in the family. These booklets have serial numbers and are copied and registered at the local Civil Records Office. All changes must be recorded with the government.

LIECHTENSTEIN

Amtsvorstand/Zivilstandsamt
des Furstentums Liechtenstein
St. Florinsgasse 3
FL-9490 Vaduz, Liechtenstein

The National Archives also has copies of vital records; contact them at Liechtensteinisches Landesarchiv, 9490 Vaduz, Liechtenstein; Tel. (011) (41) (75) 66111. Vital records are available from 1878.

LITHUANIA

Russian-American Genealogical Archival Service (RAGAS)
P.O. Box 236
Glen Echo, Maryland 20812

(202) 501-5206

The Lithuanian National Archives has early vital records:

Centrinis Valstybinis Istorijos Archyvas
Gerosios Vilties Gatve 10
232015 Vilnius, Lithuania

Cost for a Birth, Marriage, or Death Certificate $20.00

By an agreement between the United States National Archives Volunteer Association and the Archives of Russia Society RAGAS receives and processes requests for vital records in some of the former Soviet republics. Although at this time RAGAS is able to deal mainly with Russia, Belarus, and Ukraine they might be able to help you with your inquiries regarding Lithuania. There is a $2.00 shipping fee per document. The service also is available at an hourly rate. (See Russia for application forms.)

The National Library also has records; contact them at Lietuvos nacionaline Martyno Mazvydo Bibliotek, Gedimino pr. 51, 2635 Vilnius, Lithuania; Tel. (011) (7) 629-023; FAX (011) (7) 627-129.

LUXEMBOURG

Registrars of the Civil Status
(Town), Luxembourg

Send your requests for events before 1979 to:

Luxembourg State Archives
BP 6
L-2010 Luxembourg, Luxembourg

(011) (352) 478-480

Vital records are generally on file from 1795.

MACEDONIA

Civil Registration Office
(Town), Macedonia

Vital records are on file from 1946. Records before that were kept by the local churches.

MADAGASCAR

Direction du Controle et de la Tutelle des Collectivites
Ministere de l'Interieur
Antananarivo, Madagascar

Vital registration began in July 1878. Currently registration coverage is estimated to be about 80 percent for births and 50 percent for deaths.

MALAWI

Registrar General
Ministry of Justice
P.O. Box 100
Blantyre, Malawi

Cost for a Birth, Marriage, or Death Certificate   Free

The Registrar General has birth and death records from 1886, marriage records from 1903, and divorce records from 1905. These early records are mostly from Europeans living in Malawi.

MALAYSIA

National Registration Department
Ministry of Home Affairs
Wisma Pendaftaran
Jalan Persiaran Barat
46551 Petaling Jaya
Selangor, Malaysia
(011) (60) (3) 756-0044

Cost for a Birth, Marriage, Divorce, or Death Certificate   MR 2.00

Records begin in the 1800s. The National Registration Department, established in 1948 and computerized in 1990, requires everyone 12 and older to carry a national ID. Marriage and divorce records are handled differently depending on religion and part of the country where the event occurred.

MALDIVES

For Birth and Death Records write to:

Health Information Unit
Ministry of Health
Male, Maldives

For Marriage and Divorce Records write to:

Registrar
Ministry of Justice
Male, Maldives

Registration began in the 1500s but the modern system did not begin until the 1950s.

MALI

Direction Nationale de l'Administration Territoriale
Ministere d'Etat Charge de l'Administration
Territoriale et de la Securite Interieur
Bamako, Mali

Vital registration began in 1938 but is not considered to be complete.

MALTA

Send your requests to:

Director
Public Registry
Ministry of Justice and Parliamentary Affairs
197, Merchants Street
Valletta, Malta

(011) (356) 225-291

Cost for a certified Birth Certificate	M .40
Cost for a certified Marriage Certificate	M .40
Cost for a certified Death Certificate	M .40

The Public Registry has records from 1863. No separate divorce records are kept. Divorce information is annotated onto the marriage record. Current vital registration is considered to be complete.

The Family History Library of The Church of Jesus Christ of Latter-day Saints in Salt Lake City, Utah has microfilmed original and published records of Malta. For further details on their holdings please consult your nearest Family History Center.

MALTA GOVERNMENT

Name & Surname of Applicant ....

Address ....

....

Director of Public Registry
197, Merchants Street,
Valletta, MALTA.

APPLICATION FOR A BIRTH CERTIFICATE

Name & Surname (person's required Certificate) ....

Place of Birth ....

Exact Date of Birth ....

Father's Name ....

Mother's name & Maiden surname ....

MALTA GOVERNMENT

Name & Surname of Applicant ....

Address ....

....

Director of Public Registry
197, Merchants Street,
Valletta - MALTA

APPLICATION FOR A MARRIAGE CERTIFICATE

Name & Surname of Husband ....

Name & Maiden Surname of wife ....

Date of Marriage ....

Place of Marriage ....

MALTA GOVERNMENT

Name & Surname of Applicant ....

Address ....

....

Director of Public Registry
197, Merchants Street
Valletta - MALTA

APPLICATION FOR A DEATH CERTIFICATE

Name & Surname of Deceased Person ....

Place of Death .... Date of Death ....

Name & Surname of Father ....

Name & Maiden Surname of Mother ....

If married (Name & Surname of Spouse) ....

MARSHALL ISLANDS

Chief Clerk of Supreme Courts
Republic of the Marshall Islands
Majuro, Marshall Islands

Cost for a Birth, Marriage, or Death Certificate $.25

Records begin November 12, 1952, with some earlier records at the Hawaii State Bureau of Vital Statistics (see Hawaii). Personal checks are not accepted.

Information is also available from the Alele Museum of the Marshall Islands, P.O. Box 629, Majuro, Marshall Islands 98960; Tel. (011) (692) 625-3550; FAX (011) (692) 625-3226.

MAURITANIA

Ministere de l'Interieur, des Postes et Telecommunications
B.P. 240
Nouakchott, Mauritania

Vital registration began in 1933 for French citizens as well as all residents within 15 miles of the registration centers.

MAURITIUS

Registrar General
Civil Status Office
Prime Minister's Office
Emmanuel Anquetil Building, 7th Level
Port Louis, Mauritius

The Registrar General has birth and death records from 1539, marriage records from 1579, and divorce records from 1793. The law of April 1667 formally established registration there. Mauritius is one of the few countries in Sub-Saharan Africa where the modern registration of births and deaths is considered to be complete.

MEXICO

Send your requests to:

Oficina del Registro Civil
(Town, State), Mexico

Further assistance can also be obtained from:

Director General
Dirección General del Registro Nacional de Poblacion e Identificacion Personal
Albaniles No. 18
Col. Ampliación Penitenciaria
C.P. 15350
Mexico D.F., Mexico

(011) (52) (5) 789-5331 or 789-4543; FAX (011) (52) (5) 789-5250

Cost for a certified Birth Certificate	Varies
Cost for a certified Marriage Certificate	Varies
Cost for a certified Death Certificate	Varies

Records begin in 1859. Mexico currently requires each resident to have a national identity card. This office also registers all births, marriages, divorces, and deaths. The registration is considered to be 90 percent complete for births and 72 percent for deaths.

The National Archives of Mexico has many of the early records; contact them at Archivo General de la Nacion, Eduardo Molina y Albaniles 15350, Mexico D.F., Mexico. For further information see their published series, *Archives Estatales y Municipales de Mexico.*

The Family History Library of The Church of Jesus Christ of Latter-day Saints in Salt Lake City, Utah has microfilmed original and published records of Mexico. For further details on their holdings please consult your nearest Family History Center.

TARIFAS ACTUALES POR COPIAS CERTIFICADAS, 1992.

ENTIDAD FEDERATIVA	TARIFA POR COPIA CERTIFICADA DE:				PROMEDIO DE LAS TARIFAS
	NACIMIENTO	MATRIMONIO	DEFUNCION	DIVORCIO	
E.U.M.					
AGUASCALIENTES	$2,000	$2,000	$2,000	$2,000	$2,000
BAJA CALIFORNIA	$17,000	$17,000	$17,000	$17,000	$17,000
BAJA CALIFORNIA SUR	$8,663	$8,663	$8,663	$8,663	$8,663
CAMPECHE	$6,000	$6,000	$6,000	$6,000	$6,000
COAHUILA	$10,000	$10,000	$10,000	$10,000	$10,000
COLIMA	$6,240	$6,240	$6,240	$6,240	$6,240
CHIAPAS	$7,000	$7,000	$7,000	$7,000	$7,000
CHIHUAHUA	$1,700	$8,700	$8,700	$8,700	$6,950
DISTRITO FEDERAL	$1,600	$1,600	$1,600	$1,600	$1,600
DURANGO	$2,000	$2,000	$2,000	$2,000	$2,000
GUANAJUATO	$15,000	$15,000	$15,000	$15,000	$15,000
GUERRERO	$9,500	$9,500	$9,500	$9,500	$9,500
HIDALGO	$6,500	$6,500	$6,500	$6,500	$6,500
JALISCO	$8,500	$8,500	$8,500	$8,500	$8,500
MEXICO	$3,500	$3,500	$3,500	$3,500	$3,500
MICHOACAN	$3,000	$3,000	$3,000	$3,000	$3,000
MORELOS	$10,000	$10,000	$10,000	$10,000	$10,000
NAYARIT	$7,800	$7,800	$7,800	$7,800	$7,800
NUEVO LEON	$5,000	$5,000	$5,000	$5,000	$5,000
OAXACA	$1,200	$1,200	$1,200	$1,200	$1,200
PUEBLA	$6,000	$6,000	$6,000	$6,000	$6,000
QUERETARO	$6,150	$6,150	$6,150	$6,150	$6,150
QUINTANA ROO	$13,800	$19,600	$13,000	$56,800	$25,800
SAN LUIS POTOSI	$3,000	$3,000	$3,000	$3,000	$3,000
SINALOA	$3,057	$3,057	$3,057	$3,057	$3,057
SONORA	$5,000	$5,000	$5,000	$5,000	$5,000
TABASCO	$5,000	$5,000	$5,000	$5,000	$5,000
TAMAULIPAS	$5,600	$5,600	$5,600	$5,600	$5,600
TLAXCALA	$13,896	$16,672	$16,672	$16,672	$15,978
VERACRUZ	$10,900	$10,900	$10,900	$10,900	$10,900
YUCATAN	$1,100	$1,100	$1,100	$1,100	$1,100
ZACATECAS	$6,000	$6,000	$6,000	$6,000	$6,000
PROMEDIO DE LAS TARIFAS	$6,616	$7,103	$6,896	$8,265	$7,220

FUENTE: UNIDADES COORDINADORAS ESTATALES DEL REGISTRO CIVIL.

TARIFAS EN PESOS ANTIGÜOS

ESTADOS UNIDOS MEXICANOS

FOLIO

REGISTRO CIVIL

ACTA DE NACIMIENTO

ENTIDAD FEDERATIVA

CURP
PREIMPRESA

| OFICIALIA | LIBRO No | ACTA No | L O C A L I D A D | FECHA DE REGISTRO |
| | | | | DIA | MES | AÑO |

MUNICIPIO O DELEGACION | ENTIDAD FEDERATIVA

DATOS DEL REGISTRADO

SEXO: MASCULINO ①   FEMENINO ②

NOMBRE (S)   PRIMER APELLIDO   SEGUNDO APELLIDO

FECHA DE NACIMIENTO _____ DIA MES AÑO   HORA DE NACIMIENTO HORAS MINUTOS

LUGAR DE NACIMIENTO LOCALIDAD   MUNICIPIO O DEL.   ENTIDAD   PAIS

FUE REGISTRADO   VIVO (1)   MUERTO (2)   NUMERO DE CERTIFICADO DE NACIMIENTO _____

COMPARECIO.   EL PADRE (1)   LA MADRE (2)   AMBOS (3)   REGISTRADO (4)   PERSONA DISTINTA (5)

PADRES

CLAVE

NOMBRE DEL PADRE _____ EDAD AÑOS

DOMICILIO HABITUAL _____ NOMBRE DE LA CALLE Y No. EXT. E INT.

LOCALIDAD   MUNICIPIO O DEL.   ENTIDAD   PAIS

FECHA DE NACIMIENTO _____ DIA MES AÑO NACIONALIDAD   CERTIFICADA SI (1) NO (2)

CLAVE

NOMBRE DE LA MADRE _____ EDAD AÑOS

DOMICILIO HABITUAL _____ NOMBRE DE LA CALLE Y No. EXT. E INT.

LOCALIDAD   MUNICIPIO O DEL.   ENTIDAD   PAIS

FECHA DE NACIMIENTO: _____ DIA MES AÑO NACIONALIDAD   CERTIFICADA SI (1) NO (2)

ABUELOS

PATERNO   NOMBRE   NACIONALIDAD

PATERNA   NOMBRE   NACIONALIDAD

DOMICILIO (S)

MATERNO   NOMBRE   NACIONALIDAD

MATERNA   NOMBRE   NACIONALIDAD

DOMICILIO (S)

TESTIGOS

DOMICILIO   NOMBRE   NACIONALIDAD   EDAD AÑOS

DOMICILIO   NOMBRE   NACIONALIDAD   EDAD AÑOS

PERSONA DISTINTA DE LOS PADRES QUE PRESENTA AL REGISTRADO

CLAVE   NACIONALIDAD

NOMBRE (S) _____ EDAD AÑOS   PARENTESCO

DOMICILIO

FIRMAS DE LOS PADRES O DE LA PERSONA DISTINTA QUE PRESENTA AL REGISTRADO

FIRMA DE LOS TESTIGOS

LA PRESENTE ACTA TIENE ANEXAS LAS ANOTACIONES SIGUIENTES:

HUELLA DIGITAL
PULGAR DERECHO

SE DIO LECTURA A LA PRESENTE ACTA Y CONFORMES CON SU CONTENIDO LA RATIFICAN Y FIRMAN QUIENES EN ELLA INTERVINIERON Y SABEN HACERLO Y QUIENES NO, IMPRIMEN SU HUELLA DIGITAL DOY FE.

EL OFICIAL _____ DEL REGISTRO CIVIL

NOMBRE _____ FIRMA _____

SELLO DE LA
OFICIALIA DEL
REGISTRO CIVIL

DATOS COMPLEMENTARIOS DE LOS PADRES

1.- TIPO DE NACIMIENTO   (1) SIMPLE   (2) DOBLE   (3) TRIPLE O MAS   2.- NUMERO DE PARTO   (1) (2) (3) (4) (5) (6) (7) (8) (9) (10 O MAS)

NUMERO DE HIJOS E HIJAS NACIDOS VIVOS
   3.- DE LA MADRE INCLUYENDO _____   4.- HIJOS E HIJAS _____
     AL QUE SE ESTA REGISTRANDO   QUE AUN VIVEN

5.- LUGAR DE ATENCION DEL PARTO: (1) HOSPITAL O CLINICA OFICIAL   (2) HOSPITAL O CLINICA PRIVADA   (3) CASA PARTICULAR   (4) OTRO LUGAR ESPECIFIQUE _____

6.- PERSONA QUE ATENDIO EL PARTO: (1) MEDICO   (2) ENFERMERA   (3) PARTERA   (4) OTRA ESPECIFIQUE _____

7.- TIPO DE LA UNION DE LA MADRE: (1) SOLTERA   (2) CASADA   (3) UNION LIBRE   (4) SEPARADA   (5) DIVORCIADA   (6) VIUDA

DEL PADRE	DE LA MADRE
8-ESCOLARIDAD	9-ESCOLARIDAD:
(1) SIN ESCOLARIDAD (5) SECUNDARIA O EQUIVALENTE	(1) SIN ESCOLARIDAD (5) SECUNDARIA O EQUIVALENTE
(2) DE 1 A 3 AÑOS DE PRIMARIA (6) PREPARATORIA O EQUIVALENTE	(2) DE 1 A 3 AÑOS DE PRIMARIA (6) PREPARATORIA O EQUIVALENTE
(3) DE 4 A 5 AÑOS DE PRIMARIA (7) PROFESIONAL	(3) DE 4 A 5 AÑOS DE PRIMARIA (7) PROFESIONAL
(4) PRIMARIA COMPLETA (8) OTRA	(4) PRIMARIA COMPLETA (8) OTRA
10-SITUACION LABORAL:	11-SITUACION LABORAL:
(1) TIENE TRABAJO O ESTA BUSCANDOLO (4) JUBILADO O PENSIONADO	(1) TIENE TRABAJO O ESTA BUSCANDOLO (4) JUBILADO O PENSIONADO
(2) ESTUDIANTE (5) INCAPACITADO PERMANENTE-MENTE PARA TRABAJAR	(2) ESTUDIANTE (5) INCAPACITADO PERMANENTE-MENTE PARA TRABAJAR
(3) DEDICADO A QUEHACE-RES DEL HOGAR (6) OTRA	(3) DEDICADO A QUEHACE-RES DEL HOGAR (6) OTRA
12-POSICION EN SU TRABAJO	13-POSICION EN SU TRABAJO
(1) OBRERO (4) TRABAJADOR POR SU CUENTA	(1) OBRERO (4) TRABAJADOR POR SU CUENTA
(2) EMPLEADO	(2) EMPLEADO
(3) JORNALERO O PEON (5) PATRON O EMPRESARIO	(3) JORNALERO O PEON (5) PATRON O EMPRESARIO
(6) TRABAJADOR FAMILIAR NO REMUNERADO	(6) TRABAJADOR FAMILIAR NO REMUNERADO

ESTADOS UNIDOS MEXICANOS.

REGISTRO CIVIL

ENTIDAD FEDERATIVA

FOLIO

ACTA DE MATRIMONIO

CLAVE UNICA DEL REGISTRO DE POBLACION

EL

ELLA

OFICIALIA	LIBRO No	ACTA No	L O C A L I D A D	FECHA DE REGISTRO
				DIA MES AÑO

MUNICIPIO O DELEGACION

ENTIDAD FEDERATIVA

DATOS DE LOS CONTRAYENTES

NOMBRE DEL CONTRAYENTE

NOMBRE (S) — PRIMER APELLIDO — SEGUNDO APELLIDO

LUGAR DE NACIMIENTO

LOCALIDAD — MUNICIPIO O DEL. — ENTIDAD — PAIS

EDAD [ ] AÑOS FECHA DE NACIMIENTO [ ] DIA MES AÑO — NACIONALIDAD

DOMICILIO HABITUAL — OCUPACION

LOCALIDAD — MUNICIPIO O DEL. — ENTIDAD — PAIS

NOMBRE DE LA CONTRAYENTE

NOMBRE (S) — PRIMER APELLIDO — SEGUNDO APELLIDO

LUGAR DE NACIMIENTO

LOCALIDAD — MUNICIPIO O DEL. — ENTIDAD — PAIS

EDAD [ ] AÑOS FECHA DE NACIMIENTO [ ] DIA MES AÑO — NACIONALIDAD

DOMICILIO HABITUAL — OCUPACION

LOCALIDAD — MUNICIPIO O DEL. — ENTIDAD — PAIS

PADRES DEL CONTRAYENTE

NOMBRE DEL PADRE — OCUPACION — NACIONALIDAD

NOMBRE DE LA MADRE — OCUPACION — NACIONALIDAD

DOMICILIO (S)

PADRES DE LA CONTRAYENTE

NOMBRE DEL PADRE — OCUPACION — NACIONALIDAD

NOMBRE DE LA MADRE — OCUPACION — NACIONALIDAD

DOMICILIO (S)

TESTIGOS DE LOS CONTRAYENTES

NOMBRE — NACIONALIDAD — EDAD [ ] AÑOS

DOMICILIO — PARENTESCO

ESTADO CIVIL — OCUPACION

NOMBRE — NACIONALIDAD — EDAD [ ] AÑOS

DOMICILIO — PARENTESCO

ESTADO CIVIL — OCUPACION

NOMBRE — NACIONALIDAD — EDAD [ ] AÑOS

DOMICILIO — PARENTESCO

ESTADO CIVIL — OCUPACION

NOMBRE — NACIONALIDAD — EDAD [ ] AÑOS

DOMICILIO — PARENTESCO

ESTADO CIVIL — OCUPACION

NOMBRE (S) DE LA (S) PERSONA (S) QUE DA (N) SU CONSENTIMIENTO POR MINORIA DE EDAD DEL (OS) CONTRAYENTE (S)

AUTORIZACION DE LA SECRETARIA DE GOBERNACION EN EL CASO DE CONTRAYENTE (S) EXTRANJERO (S)

ESTE CONTRATO DE MATRIMONIO ESTA SUJETO AL REGIMEN DE SOCIEDAD CONYUGAL (1) SOC. LEGAL O COMUNIDAD DE BIENES (2) SOC. VOLUNTARIA O CONVENCIONAL (3) SEPARACION DE BIENES (4) MIXTO (5)

LA PRESENTE ACTA TIENE ANEXAS LAS ANOTACIONES SIGUIENTES:

	EL	ELLA	
F I R M A S	CONTRAYENTES		HUELLA DIGITAL DEL CONTRAYENTE
	PADRES		HUELLA DIGITAL DE LA CONTRAYENTE
	TESTIGOS		

HABIENDO INTERROGADO A LOS CONTRAYENTES EN LOS TERMINOS QUE LA LEY ORDENA Y NO EXISTIENDO IMPEDIMENTO LEGAL O HABIENDO SIDO DISPENSADO EL EXISTENTE PARA LA CELEBRACION DEL MATRIMONIO, LOS DECLARO EN NOMBRE DE LA LEY Y ANTE LA SOCIEDAD UNIDOS EN MATRIMONIO Y SU CONTRATO MATRIMONIAL PERFECTO Y LEGITIMO PARA TODOS LOS EFECTOS LEGALES, PREVIA LECTURA QUE DI AL MISMO, LO RATIFICAN Y FIRMAN EN UNION DEL SUSCRITO QUIENES EN EL INTERVINIERON Y SABEN HACERLO, Y QUIENES NO, IMPRIMEN SU HUELLA DIGITAL. DOY FE.

EL C. OFICIAL_____ DEL REGISTRO CIVIL

SELLO DE LA OFICIALIA DEL REGISTRO CIVIL

NOMBRE — FIRMA

DATOS COMPLEMENTARIOS DE LOS CONTRAYENTES

EL	ELLA
1.- ESCOLARIDAD	**2.- ESCOLARIDAD**
(1) SIN ESCOLARIDAD (5) SECUNDARIA O EQUIVALENTE	(1) SIN ESCOLARIDAD (5) SECUNDARIA O EQUIVALENTE
(2) DE 1 A 3 AÑOS DE PRIMARIA (6) PREPARATORIA O EQUIVALENTE	(2) DE 1 A 3 AÑOS DE PRIMARIA (6) PREPARATORIA O EQUIVALENTE
(3) DE 4 A 5 AÑOS DE PRIMARIA (7) PROFESIONAL	(3) DE 4 A 5 AÑOS DE PRIMARIA (7) PROFESIONAL
(4) PRIMARIA COMPLETA (8) OTRA	(4) PRIMARIA COMPLETA (8) OTRA
3.- SITUACION LABORAL	**4.- SITUACION LABORAL**
(1) TIENE TRABAJO O ESTA BUSCANDOLO (4) JUBILADO O PENSIONADO	(1) TIENE TRABAJO O ESTA BUSCANDOLO (4) JUBILADO O PENSIONADO
(2) ESTUDIANTE (5) INCAPACITADO PERMANENTEMENTE PARA TRABAJAR	(2) ESTUDIANTE (5) INCAPACITADO PERMANENTEMENTE PARA TRABAJAR
(3) DEDICADO A LOS QUEHACERES (6) OTRO DEL HOGAR	(3) DEDICADO A LOS QUEHACERES (6) OTRO DEL HOGAR
5.- POSICION EN SU TRABAJO	**6.- POSICION EN SU TRABAJO**
(1) OBRERO (4) TRABAJADOR POR SU CUENTA	(1) OBRERO (4) TRABAJADOR POR SU CUENTA
(2) EMPLEADO (5) PATRON O EMPRESARIO	(2) EMPLEADO (5) PATRON O EMPRESARIO
(3) JORNALERO O PEON (6) TRABAJADOR FAMILIAR NO REMUNERADO	(3) JORNALERO O PEON (6) TRABAJADOR FAMILIAR NO REMUNERADO
7.- CONTRAJO MATRIMONIO CIVIL ANTERIORMENTE SI (1) NO (2)	**8.- CONTRAJO MATRIMONIO CIVIL ANTERIORMENTE** SI (1) NO (2)
9. CUANTAS VECES (1) (2) (3) (4) (5 O MAS)	**10.- CUANTAS VECES** (1) (2) (3) (4) (5 O MAS)
11.- FECHA DE LA MAS RECIENTE DISOLUCION DIA MES AÑO	**12.- FECHA DE LA MAS RECIENTE DISOLUCION** DIA MES AÑO

ESTADOS UNIDOS MEXICANOS

REGISTRO CIVIL

ENTIDAD FEDERATIVA

CLAVE UNICA DEL REGISTRO DE POBLACION

EL

ELLA

OFICIALIA	LIBRO No	ACTA No	L O C A L I D A D	FECHA DE REGISTRO
				DIA MES AÑO

MUNICIPIO O DELEGACION   ENTIDAD FEDERATIVA

DATOS DEL DIVORCIADO

NOMBRE _____

NOMBRE (S)   PRIMER APELLIDO   SEGUNDO APELLIDO

EDAD ☐ AÑOS   FECHA DE NACIMIENTO ☐☐☐☐☐☐   NACIONALIDAD _____
                    DIA MES AÑO

DOMICILIO HABITUAL _____   OCUPACION _____

LOCALIDAD ☐☐☐   MUNICIPIO O DEL ☐☐☐   ENTIDAD ☐☐   PAIS ☐☐☐

DATOS DE LA DIVORCIADA

NOMBRE _____

NOMBRE (S)   PRIMER APELLIDO   SEGUNDO APELLIDO

EDAD ☐ AÑOS   FECHA DE NACIMIENTO ☐☐☐☐☐   NACIONALIDAD _____
                    DIA MES AÑO

DOMICILIO HABITUAL _____   OCUPACION _____

LOCALIDAD ☐☐☐   MUNICIPIO O DEL. ☐☐☐   ENTIDAD ☐☐   PAIS ☐☐☐

DATOS DEL ACTA DE MATRIMONIO DE LOS DIVORCIADOS

OFICIALIA	LIBRO No	ACTA No	LOCALIDAD	FECHA DE REGISTRO
				DIA MES AÑO

MUNICIPIO O DELEGACION   ENTIDAD FEDERATIVA   PAIS

REGIMEN PATRIMONIAL

SOCIEDAD CONYUGAL (1)   SOC LEGAL O COMUNIDAD DE BIENES (2)   SOC. VOLUNTARIA O CONVENCIONAL (3)   SEPARACION DE BIENES (4)   MIXTO (5)

RESOLUCION ADMINISTRATIVA

FECHA DE RESOLUCION   DIA MES AÑO

FIRMAS DEL DIVORCIO VOLUNTARIO POR VIA ADMINISTRATIVA

_____   _____

EL DIVORCIADO   LA DIVORCIADA

LA PRESENTE ACTA TIENE ANEXAS LAS ANOTACIONES SIGUIENTES

SE DIO LECTURA A LA PRESENTE ACTA Y CONFORMES CON SU CONTENIDO LA RATIFICAN Y FIRMAN QUIENES EN ELLA INTERVINIERON Y SABEN HACERLO Y QUIENES NO IMPRIMEN SU HUELLA DIGITAL DOY FE

EL C. OFICIAL _____ DEL REGISTRO CIVIL

SELLO DE LA

OFICIALIA DEL

REGISTRO CIVIL

N O M B R E   F I R M A

DATOS COMPLEMENTARIOS DE LOS DIVORCIADOS

1 DURACION DEL MATRIMONIO

AÑOS ☐☐   MESES ☐☐

EL	ELLA
2 - ESCOLARIDAD	3 - ESCOLARIDAD
(1) SIN ESCOLARIDAD (5) SECUNDARIA ó EQUIVALENTE	(1) SIN ESCOLARIDAD (5) SECUNDARIA ó EQUIVALENTE
(2) DE 1 A 3 AÑOS DE PRIMARIA (6) PREPARATORIA ó EQUIVALENTE	(2) DE 1 A 3 AÑOS DE PRIMARIA (6) PREPARATORIA ó EQUIVALENTE
(3) DE 4 A 5 AÑOS DE PRIMARIA (7) PROFESIONAL	(3) DE 4 A 5 AÑOS DE PRIMARIA (7) PROFESIONAL
(4) PRIMARIA COMPLETA (8) OTRA	(4) PRIMARIA COMPLETA (8) OTRA
4 - SITUACION LABORAL	5 - SITUACION LABORAL
(1) TIENE TRABAJO ó ESTA BUSCANDOLO (4) JUBILADO ó PENSIONADO	(1) TIENE TRABAJO ó ESTA BUSCANDOLO (4) JUBILADO ó PENSIONADO
(2) ESTUDIANTE (5) INCAPACITADO PERMANENTEMENTE PARA TRABAJAR	(2) ESTUDIANTE (5) INCAPACITADO PERMANENTEMENTE PARA TRABAJAR
(3) DEDICADO A LOS QUEHACERES DEL HOGAR (6) OTRA	(3) DEDICADA A LOS QUEHACERES DEL HOGAR (6) OTRA
6 - POSICION EN SU TRABAJO	7 - POSICION EN SU TRABAJO
(1) OBRERO (4) TRABAJADOR POR SU CUENTA	(1) OBRERO (4) TRABAJADOR POR SU CUENTA
(2) EMPLEADO (5) PATRON ó EMPRESARIO	(2) EMPLEADO (5) PATRON ó EMPRESARIO
(3) JORNALERO ó PEON (6) TRABAJADOR FAMILIAR NO REMUNERADO	(3) JORNALERO ó PEON (6) TRABAJADOR FAMILIAR NO REMUNERADO

ESTADOS UNIDOS MEXICANOS

REGISTRO CIVIL

ENTIDAD FEDERATIVA

FOLIO

ACTA DE DIVORCIO JUDICIAL

CLAVE ÚNICA DEL REGISTRO DE POBLACIÓN

EL:

ELLA:

OFICIALIA	LIBRO No.	ACTA No.	L O C A L I D A D	FECHA DE REGISTRO
				DIA	MES	AÑO

MUNICIPIO O DELEGACION   ENTIDAD FEDERATIVA

DATOS DEL DIVORCIADO

NOMBRE _____

NOMBRE (S)   PRIMER APELLIDO   SEGUNDO APELLIDO

EDAD [ ] AÑOS   FECHA DE NACIMIENTO [ ][ ][ ]   NACIONALIDAD _____
DIA MES AÑO

DOMICILIO HABITUAL _____   OCUPACION _____

LOCALIDAD [ ]   MUNICIPIO O DEL. [ ]   ENTIDAD [ ]   PAIS [ ]

DATOS DE LA DIVORCIADA

NOMBRE _____

NOMBRE (S)   PRIMER APELLIDO   SEGUNDO APELLIDO

EDAD [ ] AÑOS   FECHA DE NACIMIENTO [ ][ ][ ]   NACIONALIDAD _____
DIA MES AÑO

DOMICILIO HABITUAL _____   OCUPACION _____

LOCALIDAD [ ]   MUNICIPIO O DEL. [ ]   ENTIDAD [ ]   PAIS [ ]

DATOS DEL ACTA DE MATRIMONIO DE LOS DIVORCIADOS

OFICIALIA	LIBRO No	ACTA No.	LOCALIDAD	FECHA DE REGISTRO
				DIA	MES	AÑO

MUNICIPIO O DELEGACION   ENTIDAD FEDERATIVA   PAIS

REGIMEN PATRIMONIAL

SOCIEDAD CONYUGAL (1)   SOC. LEGAL O COMUNIDAD DE BIENES (2)   SOC. VOLUNTARIA O CONVENCIONAL (3)   SEPARACION DE BIENES (4)   MIXTO (5)

PARTE RESOLUTIVA DE LA SENTENCIA JUDICIAL

TIPO DE DIVORCIO JUDICIAL   VOLUNTARIO (1)   NECESARIO (2)   QUIEN LO PROMOVIO   EL (1)   ELLA (2)   AMBOS (3)

FECHA DE INICIO: [ ][ ][ ]   FECHA DE LA RESOLUCION [ ][ ][ ]
DIA MES AÑO   DIA MES AÑO

AUTORIDAD QUE LA DICTO: _____

CAUSA(LES) DEL DIVORCIO :
1 RA. _____ [ ]
2 RA. _____ [ ]
3 RA. _____ [ ]

LA PRESENTE ACTA TIENE ANEXAS LAS ANOTACIONES SIGUIENTES :

LO QUE SE ASIENTA EN LA PRESENTE ACTA PARA QUE SURTA SUS EFECTOS LEGALES, DOY FE.

EL C. OFICIAL _____ DEL REGISTRO CIVIL

SELLO DE LA OFICIALIA DEL REGISTRO CIVIL

_____   _____
N O M B R E   F I R M A

DATOS COMPLEMENTARIOS DE LOS DIVORCIADOS

1. DURACION DEL MATRIMONIO: AÑOS [ ] MESES [ ]

2. NUMERO DE HIJOS DEL MATRIMONIO: (1) (2) (3) (4) (5) (6) (7) (8) (9) (10 O MAS)

3. ¿EN QUIEN RECAYO LA CUSTODIA Y NUMERO DE HIJOS CORRESPONDIENTES? PADRE ( ) MADRE ( ) OTRO ( ) ESPECIFIQUE: _____

EL	ELLA
4 ESCOLARIDAD	5 ESCOLARIDAD
(1) SIN ESCOLARIDAD (5) SECUNDARIA O EQUIVALENTE	(1) SIN ESCOLARIDAD (5) SECUNDARIA O EQUIVALENTE
(2) DE 1 A 3 AÑOS DE PRIMARIA (6) PREPARATORIA O EQUIVALENTE	(2) DE 1 A 3 AÑOS DE PRIMARIA (6) PREPARATORIA O EQUIVALENTE
(3) DE 4 A 5 AÑOS DE PRIMARIA (7) PROFESIONAL	(3) DE 4 A 5 AÑOS DE PRIMARIA (7) PROFESIONAL
(4) PRIMARIA COMPLETA (8) OTRA	(4) PRIMARIA COMPLETA (8) OTRA
6 SITUACION LABORAL	7 SITUACION LABORAL
(1) TIENE TRABAJO O ESTA SUBEMPLEO (4) JUBILADO O PENSIONADO	(1) TIENE TRABAJO O ESTA SUBEMPLEO (4) JUBILADO O PENSIONADO
(2) ESTUDIANTE (5) INCAPACITADO PERMANENTEMENTE PARA TRABAJAR	(2) ESTUDIANTE (5) INCAPACITADO PERMANENTEMENTE PARA TRABAJAR
(3) DEDICADO A LOS QUEHACERES DEL HOGAR (6) OTRA	(3) DEDICADO A LOS QUEHACERES DEL HOGAR (6) OTRA
8 POSICION EN SU TRABAJO	9 POSICION EN SU TRABAJO
(1) OBRERO (4) TRABAJADOR POR SU CUENTA	(1) OBRERO (4) TRABAJADOR POR SU CUENTA
(2) EMPLEADO (5) PATRON O EMPRESARIO	(2) EMPLEADO (5) PATRON O EMPRESARIO
(3) JORNALERO O PEON (6) TRABAJADOR FAMILIAR NO REMUNERADO	(3) JORNALERO O PEON (6) TRABAJADOR FAMILIAR NO REMUNERADO

ESTADOS UNIDOS MEXICANOS

REGISTRO CIVIL

FOLIO

ACTA DE DEFUNCION

ENTIDAD FEDERATIVA

CLAVE UNICA DEL REGISTRO DE POBLACION

| OFICIALIA BRO. No | ACTA No | L O C A L I D A D | FECHA DE REGISTRO |
| | | | DIA | MES | AÑO |

MUNICIPIO O DELEGACION | ENTIDAD FEDERATIVA

DATOS DEL FINADO

SEXO: MASCULINO (1) FEMENINO (2)

NOMBRE(S) — PRIMER APELLIDO — SEGUNDO APELLIDO

ESTADO CIVIL — NACIONALIDAD — EDAD AÑOS MESES DIAS HORAS — FECHA NAC DIA MES AÑO

DOMICILIO HABITUAL

NOMBRE DE LA CALLE Y No. EXTERIOR E INTERIOR

LOCALIDAD — MUNICIPIO O DEL — ENTIDAD — PAIS

LUGAR DE NACIMIENTO

LOCALIDAD — MUNICIPIO O DEL — ENTIDAD — PAIS

NOMBRE DEL CONYUGE — NACIONALIDAD

NOMBRE DEL PADRE

NOMBRE DE LA MADRE

FALLECIMIENTO

FECHA DE LA DEFUNCION — DIA MES AÑO — HORA — MINUTO

LUGAR DE FALLECIMIENTO — LOCALIDAD — MUNICIPIO O DEL — ENTIDAD — PAIS

DESTINO DEL CADAVER: INHUMACION (1) CREMACION (2) NOMBRE DEL PANTEON O CREMATORIO

UBICACION — ORDEN No.

DONDE FALLECIO (1) HOSPITAL O CLINICA OFICIAL (2) HOSPITAL O CLINICA PRIVADA (3) CASA PARTICULAR (4) VIA PUBLICA (5) LUGAR DE TRABAJO (6) OTRO ESPECIFIQUE

CAUSA(S) DE LA MUERTE: A

B

C

TIPO DE DEFUNCION: NATURAL O POR ENFERMEDAD (1) ACCIDENTAL O VIOLENTA (2) NUMERO DE CERTIFICADO DE DEFUNCION

NOMBRE DEL MEDICO QUE CERTIFICA LA DEFUNCION — NUMERO DE CEDULA PROFESIONAL

DOMICILIO

DECLARANTE

NOMBRE — EDAD AÑOS

NACIONALIDAD — PARENTESCO

DOMICILIO — OCUPACION

TESTIGOS

NOMBRE — NACIONALIDAD — EDAD AÑOS

DOMICILIO — OCUPACION — PARENTESCO

NOMBRE — NACIONALIDAD — EDAD AÑOS

DOMICILIO — OCUPACION — PARENTESCO

LA PRESENTE ACTA TIENE ANEXAS LAS SIGUIENTES ANOTACIONES:

FIRMAS

TESTIGO — DECLARANTE — TESTIGO

SE DIO LECTURA A LA PRESENTE ACTA Y CONFORMES CON SU CONTENIDO LA RATIFICAN Y FIRMAN QUIENES EN ELLA INTERVINIERON Y SABEN HACERLO Y QUIENES NO, IMPRIMEN SU HUELLA DIGITAL DOY FE.

SELLO DE LA OFICIALIA DEL REGISTRO CIVIL

EL OFICIAL _____ DEL REGISTRO CIVIL

NOMBRE _____ FIRMA _____

DATOS COMPLEMENTARIOS

1 – TUVO EL FALLECIDO ASISTENCIA MEDICA EN SU ULTIMA ENFERMEDAD? SI (1) NO (2) NO SABE (3)

DATOS DEL FALLECIDO CUANDO ESTE TENGA 12 AÑOS Y MAS, EN CASO CONTRARIO CORRESPONDERAN AL JEFE DEL HOGAR

2.- SITUACION LABORAL

(1) TENIA TRABAJO O ESTABA BUSCANDOLO   (3) DEDICADO A LOS QUEHACERES DEL HOGAR   (5) INCAPACITADO PERMANENTEMENTE PARA TRABAJAR

(2) ESTUDIANTE   (4) JUBILADO O PENSIONADO   (6) OTRO

CUANDO EL FALLECIDO HAYA SIDO MENOR DE 12 AÑOS DE EDAD, LOS SIGUIENTES DATOS CORRESPONDEN AL JEFE DEL HOGAR

3 –

SEXO DEL JEFE DEL HOGAR   MASCULINO (1)   FEMENINO (2)

4 – ESCOLARIDAD:

(1) SIN ESCOLARIDAD   (3) DE 4 A 5 AÑOS DE PRIMARIA   (5) SECUNDARIA O EQUIVALENTE   (7) PROFESIONAL

(2) DE 1 A 3 AÑOS DE PRIMARIA   (4) PRIMARIA COMPLETA   (6) PREPARATORIA O EQUIVALENTE   (8) OTRA

5 – POSICION EN SU TRABAJO:

(1) OBRERO   (3) JORNALERO O PEON   (5) PATRON O EMPRESARIO

(2) EMPLEADO   (4) TRABAJADOR POR SU CUENTA   (6) TRABAJADOR FAM. NO REMUNERADO

MICRONESIA — Federated States of Micronesia

Send your requests to:

Clerk of Courts
State of Losrae
Lelu, Losrae, ECI 96944

Clerk of Courts
State of Truk, FSM
Moen, Truk, ECI 96942

Clerk of Courts
State of Pohnpei, FSM
P.O. Box 1449
Kolonia, Pohnpei, ECI 96941

Clerk of Courts
State of Yap, FSM
Colonia, Yap WCI 96943

Cost for a certified Birth Certificate	$ .25
Cost for a certified Marriage Certificate	$ .25
Cost for a certified Death Certificate	$ .25

Records begin November 12, 1952, with some earlier records at the Hawaii State Bureau of Vital Statistics (see Hawaii). Personal checks are not accepted, and there is a typing charge of $.10 per every 100 words.

The Family History Library of The Church of Jesus Christ of Latter-day Saints in Salt Lake City, Utah has microfilmed original and published records of Micronesia and the Pacific. For further details on their holdings please consult your nearest Family History Center.

MOLDOVA

Russian-American Genealogical Archival Service (RAGAS)
P.O. Box 236
Glen Echo, Maryland 20812

(202) 501-5206

Cost for a Birth, Marriage, or Death Certificate $20.00

By an agreement between the United States National Archives Volunteer Association and the Archives of Russia Society RAGAS will receive and process requests for vital records in the former Soviet republics. Although at this time RAGAS is able to deal mainly with Russia, Belarus, and Ukraine they might be able to help you with your inquiries regarding Moldova. There is a $2.00 shipping fee per document. (See Russia for application forms.)

The National Library of Moldova also has records; contact them at Bibliotea Nationala al Republicii Moldova, ul 31 August 78a, 2776112 Chisinau, Moldova; Tel. (011) (7) (042) 22-1475.

MONACO

Mairie de Monaco
Bureau of the Civil Status
Monte Carlo, Monaco

Cost for a Birth, Marriage, or Death Certificate 10.00 F

Monaco began vital registration in 1793. Current vital registration is considered to be complete.

MONTENEGRO

Civil Registration Office
(Town), Montenegro

Records begin in 1946. The National Library (Narodna Biblioteka, P.O. Box 57, 81250 Cetinje, Montenegro) also has records.

MONTSERRAT

Registrar General's Office
Judicial Department
P.O. Box 22
Plymouth, Montserrat, W.I.

(809) 491-2129

Cost for a Birth, Marriage, or Death Certificate EC $5.00, plus US $1.15 for postage
A general search costs EC $20.00.

Records begin February 12, 1862. Your request should state in which of the three districts the event occurred. Registration is complete.

MOROCCO

Chef
Division d'Etat Civil
Ministere de l'Interieur
Rabat, Morocco

Records begin in 1915 for the French and foreign population. In 1931 registration was extended to all Moroccans. With independence in 1956, registration became formalized for the entire country. Morocco began a major effort in 1987 to computerize all of its records. Marriages and divorces are kept by the denomination or court of record.

MOZAMBIQUE

Direccao Nacional dos Registros e Notoriados
Av. Vladimir Lenine n. 565, 2 Andar
C.P. 2157
Maputo, Mozambique

Vital registration is not considered to be complete.

MYANMAR

Registrar
Health Department
Ministry of Health
Yangon, Myanmar

Formerly known as Burma, Myanmar has a centralized vital registration program which is considered to be complete.

NAMIBIA

Vital Registration Department
Government House
Windhoek, Namibia

Namibia became independent in 1990.

NAURU

Registrar General
Republic of Nauru
Nauru Island

Nauru's current vital registration is considered to be complete. Nauru uses the Australian dollar as currency.

NEPAL

Registrar
Civil Registration and Vital Statistics Office
Ministry of Home Affairs
Singha Durba, Katmandu, Nepal

Although there are earlier records from the colonial period, modern vital registration has been nearly comprehensive only in the past ten years. Marriages began to be kept centrally in 1983 and divorces in 1985.

THE NETHERLANDS

Send your requests to:

Burgerlijke Stand
(Town), The Netherlands

Cost for a certified Birth Certificate	Fr 14.55
Cost for a certified Marriage Certificate	Fr 14.55
Cost for a certified Death Certificate	Fr 14.55

Current records are kept by the town Burgerlijke Stand. Older records are usually deposited in the Provincial or Municipal Archives. Vital records are on file from 1811. Current vital registration is considered to be complete.

The Royal Library, Netherlands National Library, also has records. Contact them at Koninklijke Bibliotheek, Postbus 90407, 2509 LK, The Hague; Tel. (011) (31) (70) 314-0911; FAX (011) (31) (70) 314-0450.

The Family History Library of The Church of Jesus Christ of Latter-day Saints in Salt Lake City, Utah has microfilmed original and published records of The Netherlands. For further details on their holdings please consult your nearest Family History Center.

Aan de ambtenaar van de burgerlijke stand te

_____

Zeist, _____

Hierbij verzoek ik u mij toe te zenden een uittreksel uit het register van

geboorten
huwelijken
echtscheidingen   x) ten name van
overlijden

_____

geboren
gehuwd   op _____
gescheiden
overleden

Dit uittreksel is nodig voor _____

en kan worden toegezonden aan

_____

adres: _____

_____

Voor kosten van leges en toezending gelieve u hierbij 1 girobetaalkaart c.q. bankcheque van ƒ 14,55 aan te treffen*.
U gelieve mij te berichten op welke wijze de betaling kan geschieden.

                                        De aanvrager,

* s.v.p. doorhalen wat niet   _____
  van toepassing is

NEW ZEALAND

Send your requests to:

Registrar General's Office
Department of Justice
Levin House
191 High Street
P.O. Box 31-115
Lower Hutt, Wellington, New Zealand

(011) (64) (4) 569-4489, FAX (011) (64) (4) 566-5311

Cost for a certified Birth Certificate	NZ $13.35
Cost for a certified Marriage Certificate	NZ $13.35
Cost for a certified Death Certificate	NZ $13.35

The Registrar General has birth and death records from January 1, 1848 and marriage records from 1854. Current vital registration is considered to be complete. The fee plus postage costs may be paid in your local currency to the New Zealand Consulate, which will then forward your application to the Registrar General. Application forms sent directly to the Registrar General must be accompanied by an international bank draft payable in New Zealand dollars.

The National Archives of New Zealand also has records; contact them at P.O. Box 6148, Te Aro, Wellington; Tel. (011) (64) 485-6109; FAX (011) (64) 482-8789.

The Family History Library of The Church of Jesus Christ of Latter-day Saints in Salt Lake City, Utah has microfilmed original and published records of New Zealand. For further details on their holdings please consult your nearest Family History Center.

R.G.93

DEPARTMENT OF JUSTICE
Application for Birth, Death or Marriage Certificate

Tick one box
POST
COLLECT

Please supply a certificate for which particulars are given below.   ALL FEES MUST BE PREPAID.

Enclosed is a money order/cheque/cash for $ ....

Applicant: ....   Address: ....
          (Please print or write clearly)

Date: ....

PLEASE READ CAREFULLY

NOTE 1: Applications for birth and death certificates can be made at the office where the registration was made or at the Registrar-General's Office 191 High Street.
P.O. Box 31115, LOWER HUTT. Phone 5694-489.

NOTE 2: Applications for marriage certificates can be made as follows:
(i)   Church marriages can only be obtained from the Registrar General's Office, Lower Hutt.
(ii)   Registry Office marriages can be obtained from the office where marriage performed or from Registrar-General's Office.
(iii) Other celebrant marriages can be obtained from the office which issued the licence or from Registrar-General's Office.

NOTE 3: Dates — Show the exact date if possible. If the entry is not found in the year stated an extended search can be made on request. If you require an extended search the years to
be covered should be stated (e.g. 1926-1935) and search fees paid in addition to the certificate fee.

BIRTH	Surname or Family Name	First Names	Date & Year of Birth	Place of Birth	Father's Full Name	Mother's Full Name
PLEASE SHOW NAME AT BIRTH						(continue overleaf)

DEATH	Surname or Family Name	First Names	Date & Year of Death	Place of Death	To Whom Married	Names of Parents
						(continue overleaf)

MARRIAGE		Surname or Family Name	First Names		Date of Marriage	Place of Marriage
	BRIDEGROOM					
	BRIDE	Surname or Family Name	First Names			(continue overleaf)

2000X50/8-92/2684WP

BIRTH

PLEASE SHOW
NAME AT BIRTH

Surname or Family Name	First Names	Date & Year of Birth	Place of Birth	Father's Full Name	Mother's Full Name

DEATH

Surname or Family Name	First Names	Date & Year of Death	Place of Death	To Whom Married	Names of Parents

MARRIAGE

BRIDEGROOM		BRIDE			
Surname or Family Name	First Names	Surname or Family Name	First Names	Date of Marriage	Place of Marriage

NICARAGUA

Dirección General del Registro
Ministerio de Justicia
Managua, Nicaragua

Although church registers date from the 1500s, vital registration in Nicaragua did not begin until 1867.

NIGER

Directeur de l'Etat Civil et de la Population
Ministere de l'Interieur
B.P. 622
Niamey, Niger

Registration began in 1933 for French citizens and expanded in 1950 to include everyone within 15 miles of the registration centers.

NIGERIA

Vital Registration Department
National Population Commission
P.M.B. 12628
Lagos, Nigeria

Records begin in 1867 for Lagos Island, and expand in 1901 to include Ebute, Metta, and the island of Iddo. By 1903 records include all of Southern Nigeria. The Laws of 1918 and 1979 have helped but the registration is still not complete.

NIUE

Births and Deaths:
Registrar General's Office
Department of Administration
P.O. Box 67
Alofi, Niue

Marriages and Divorces:
Registrar of Marriages
Department of Justice
Alofi, Niue

Cost for a Birth, Marriage, or Death Certificate	NZ $14.00
Cost for a short form Birth Certificate	NZ $ 6.00

Requests may be sent to a New Zealand Consulate. Requests sent directly to Niue must be paid in New Zealand currency. Records are on file from 1845.

The National Archives of Niue also has records; contact them at P.O. Box 77, Alofi, Niue; Tel. (011) (683) 4019; FAX (011) (683) 4010.

NORTHERN MARIANA ISLANDS

Vital Statistics
Superior Court
P.O. Box 307
Saipan, CNMI 96950

(011) (670) 234-6401, FAX (011) (670) 234-8010

Cost for a Birth, Marriage, or Death Certificate $3.00

Birth and death records are available from 1945, marriage records from 1954. Some records are at the Hawaii State Bureau of Vital Statistics. Money orders or cashiers checks should be payable to CNMI Treasury.

NORWAY

Pastor
Lutheran Church
(Town), Norway

Records begin in the 1600s. Early registers are available at the Norwegian Emigration Center, Bergjelandsgate 30, N-4012 Stavanger, Norway; Tel. (011) (474) 501-274; FAX (011) (474) 501-290. Divorce licenses are kept by the County Commissioner or local court that granted the divorce. The Lutheran pastor in each town holds all vital records for the town.

Norway uses a national personal identification numbering system administered by the Central Population Register Central Bureau of Statistics (P.O. Box 8131 Dep, 0033 Oslo 1, Norway). This computerized office maintains vital records on all persons in Norway as of November 1, 1960 or later. These records are *not* available to the public.

OMAN

Ministry of Health
Muscat, Oman

The Omani Heritage Library (Ministry of National Heritage, P.O. Box 668, Muscat, Oman) can also be of assistance.

PAKISTAN

Directorate General of Registration
Civil Registration Organization
7 Civil Center, Near GPO
Islamabad, Pakistan

Registration began in 1863. Birth, marriage, divorce, and death records are kept by the Directorate.

PALAU

Chief Clerk of Supreme Courts
Republic of Palau
P.O. Box 248
Koror, Palau 96940

(011) (680) 488-2461, FAX (011) (680) 488-1597

Cost for Birth, Marriage, Divorce, or Death Certificate   US $1.00

The Court has records from November 12, 1952. Some records are at the Hawaii State Bureau of Vital Statistics (see Hawaii). Personal checks are not accepted.

PANAMA

Send your requests to:

Dirección General del Registro Civil
Betania, La Gloria, Calle I No. 195
A.P. 5281
Panama 5, Republic of Panama

Cost for a certified Birth Certificate	US $15.00
Cost for a certified Marriage Certificate	US $15.00
Cost for a certified Death Certificate	US $15.00

Although church registers date from the 1500s, modern vital registration in Panama did not begin until 1917. The current registration is considered to be complete for births and 75 percent complete for deaths. Money orders should be made payable to Tesoro Nacional. When writing to the Registro Civil please include two International Postal Reply Coupons, available at your local post office.

The Family History Library of The Church of Jesus Christ of Latter-day Saints in Salt Lake City, Utah has microfilmed original and published records of Panama. For further details on their holdings please consult your nearest Family History Center.

TRIBUNAL ELECTORAL

REGISTRO CIVIL

SOLICITUD DE CERTIFICADO   No. _____

Nombre _____

Fecha de: Nacimiento)
          Defunción) _____
          Matrimonio)   Día   Mes   Año

Lugar _____

PROVINCIA _____ TOMO _____ FOLIO _____ ASIENTO

Fecha _____ 19 ____ Recibido por: _____

Fecha de reclamo _____

Llene los dos primeros renglones - subraye el certificado deseado.

PAPUA NEW GUINEA

Registrar General of Births, Deaths and Marriages
Department of Justice
P.O. Box 1281
Port Moresby, Papua New Guinea

Divorces to: Registrar of the Court
National Court of Justice
Port Moresby, Papua New Guinea

Vital registration began in British New Guinea in 1892, but with a limited registration organization, registration of vital records is very incomplete.

Information is also available from The National Archives and Public Records Service of Papua New Guinea, P.O. Box 1089, Boroki, National Capital District, Papua New Guinea; Tel. (011) (675) 254-4332; FAX (011) (675) 254-4648.

PARAGUAY

Director
Oficina de Registro del Estado Civil de las Personas
Ministerio de Justicia y Trabajo
Herrera 875
Asunción, Paraguay

Although church registers date from the 1500s, vital registration in Paraguay did not begin until September 26, 1880.

PERU

Registro Civil
(Town), Peru

Dirección General de Registro Civil
Instituto Nacional de Estadistica e Informatica
Presidencia del Consejo de Ministros
Av. 28 de Julio 1056
Lima 1, Peru

(011) (51) (14) 334-223, FAX (011) (51) (14) 333-159

Cost for a Birth, Marriage, or Death Certificate   S 6.00

Civil registration began in 1852, and modern vital registration in Peru began in 1936. Adoptions, legitimizations, and recognition of illegitimate children are recorded in the birth registers. Divorces are recorded in the marriage registers.

PHILIPPINES

Send your requests to:

> Civil Registrar General
> National Statistics Office
> Archives Management Section
> P.O. Box 779
> Sta. Mesa, Manila, Philippines

(011) (63) (61-3645 to 54)

or to the:

> Local Civil Registrar
> Municipal Building
> (Town) Philippines

Cost for a certified Birth Certificate	$5.00
Cost for a certified Marriage Certificate	$5.00
Cost for a certified Death Certificate	$5.00

Vital registration began in 1898—although church registers begin much earlier—and is now centrally administered by the Civil Registrar. Birth, marriage, divorce, and death records from 1945 are on file at the central office. Earlier records are on file with the local civil registrars.

The National Library and Archives has microfilmed original and published vital records and church registers of the Philippines; contact them at T. M. Kalaw Street, Manila; Tel. (011) (63) (2) 491-114.

The Family History Library of The Church of Jesus Christ of Latter-day Saints in Salt Lake City, Utah has microfilmed original and published records of The Philippines. For further details on their holdings please consult your nearest Family History Center.

☐ RUSH

☐ ORDINARY

For Birth Certificate Only

For NSO use only

Application No.	:	_____
Date of filing	:	_____
Number of copies	:	_____
Date of release	:	_____
O. R. Number	:	_____
Amount paid	:	_____

Verification Status

DOCUMENT/CERTIFICATION NOT CLAIMED WITHIN THIRTY (30) WORKING DAYS FROM DATE OF RELEASE WILL BE DISPOSED OF

To be filled up by applicant
(Print all entries)

Name : _____

           First   *Middle*   *Last*

Date of Birth : _____

Place of Birth : _____

           (Town)   *(Province)*

Name of Father : _____

Name of Mother : _____

Registered late?

☐   Yes,   When : _____

☐   No

Requested by : _____

Address : _____ Tel. No.: _____

Purpose : _____
(If for travel, specify country/countries.)

_____

Received by : _____

NOTE:

1. AUTHORIZATION and ID of the document owner ARE REQUIRED if the person is NOT any of the following:

    a. the owner of the document
    b. his parents
    c. his spouse
    d. his direct descendents
    e. his guardian/institution in charge, if minor

2. This office may or may not have the document being requested.

☐ RUSH

☐ ORDINARY   For Marriage Certificate Only

For NSO use only

		Verification Status
Application No.	_____	
Date of filing	_____	
Number of copies	_____	
Date of release	_____	
O. R. Number	_____	
Amount paid	_____	

To be filled up by applicant
(Print all entries)

Name of Husband : _____
                     First   Middle   Last

Name of Wife : _____
                  First   Middle   Last

Date of Marriage : _____

Place of Marriage : _____
                      (Town)   (Province)

Requested by : _____

Address : _____

Purpose : _____
(If for travel, specify country/countries.)

_____

Received by : _____

NOTE:

This office may or may not have the document being requested.

DOCUMENT/CERTIFICATION NOT CLAIMED WITHIN THIRTY (30) WORKING DAYS FROM DATE OF RELEASE WILL BE DISPOSED OF.

Republic of the Philippines
NATIONAL STATISTICS OFFICE
Manila

☐ **RUSH**
☐ **ORDINARY**

For Death Certificate Only

For NSO use only

Application No.   : _____

Date of filing   : _____

Number of copies   : _____

Date of release   : _____

O. R. Number   : _____

Amount paid   : _____

Verification Status

To be filled up by applicant
  (*Print all entries*)

Name of Deceased : _____
                        First   *Middle*   *Last*

Date of Death   : _____

Place of Death   : _____
                              (*Town*)   (*Province*)

Requested by   : _____

Address : _____ Tel. No.: _____

Purpose : _____
(*If for travel, specify country/countries.*)

_____

Received by   : _____

NOTE:

This office may or may not have the document being requested.

---

*DOCUMENT/CERTIFICATION NOT CLAIMED WITHIN THIRTY (30) WORKING
DAYS FROM DATE OF RELEASE WILL BE DISPOSED OF.*

POLAND

Send your requests to:

Urzad Stanu Cywilnego
[Civil Registration Office]
(Town), Poland

Help is also available from the National Archives:

Naczelnik Wydziahu Wspolpracy z Zagranica
Archiwow Pantswowych
ul. Dluga 6
Skrytka Pocztowa 1005
00-950 Warsaw, Poland

Cost for a certified Birth Certificate	Price Varies
Cost for a certified Marriage Certificate	Price Varies
Cost for a certified Death Certificate	Price Varies

There is no central office for vital records in Poland. To obtain copies of birth, marriage, and death certificates write to the Civil Registration District Office (Urzad Stanu Cywilnego) in the town where the event occurred. Vital records are on file from 1809. Current vital registration is considered to be complete. Many older vital records are on deposit at the National Archives.

The Family History Library of The Church of Jesus Christ of Latter-day Saints in Salt Lake City, Utah has microfilmed original and published records of Poland. For further details on their holdings please consult your nearest Family History Center.

PORTUGAL

Los Registros Civiles
(Town), Portugal

Cost for a Birth, Marriage, or Death Certificate   Pr $200

Vital records are on file from 1911. Some local registrars have records from 1832; most older records have been transferred to the District Archives.

The Direccao-Geral dos Registos e do Notariado (Ministry of Justice, Av. Almirante Reis 101, 197 Lisboa Codex, Portugal) directs the work of the local registrars.

QATAR

For certificates from 1959 write to: Registrar of Births
                                              Ministry of Public Health
                                              P.O. Box 9374
                                              Doha, Qatar

For other requests write to: Age Estimation Committee
                                              Ministry of Public Health
                                              Qatar

Cost for a Birth or Death Certificate   Free

Birth records are available from 1959. Marriages are recorded by the denomination performing the wedding. It is the standard practice to petition the Age Estimation Committee to determine a person's age.

ROMANIA

Civil Registration Office
(Town), Romania

Vital records are on file from 1865 and in many areas begin much earlier.

RUSSIA

Send your requests to:

Russian-American Genealogical Archival Service (RAGAS)
P.O. Box 236
Glen Echo, Maryland 20812

(202) 501-5206

Cost for a certified Birth Certificate	$20.00
Cost for a certified Marriage Certificate	$20.00
Cost for a certified Death Certificate	$20.00

By an agreement between the United States National Archives Volunteer Association and the Archives of Russia Society RAGAS will receive and process requests for vital records in Russia. There is a $2.00 shipping fee per document. The service also is available at an hourly rate.

The Family History Library of The Church of Jesus Christ of Latter-day Saints in Salt Lake City, Utah has microfilmed original and published records of Russia. For further details on their holdings please consult your nearest Family History Center.

RAGAS
Box 236
Glen Echo, MD 20812

AUTHORIZATION FORM

I authorize a minimum fifty (50) hours of research at the rate of $6.00 per hour for the purpose of securing pertinent genealogical information as stated on the Fuller Genealogical Search Form sent to RAGAS.

In the event of a positive search, the $50.00 amount attached to the search form will be deducted from the total sum accrued.

Signed_____

Date_____

RAGAS
Box 236
Glen Echo, MD 20812

SPECIFIC INFORMATION FORM

PLEASE PRINT OR TYPE (пожалуйста, пишите печатными буквами)

It is realized that you may not have answers to some questions. Fill in to the best of your knowledge.
(Возможно, Вы не сможете ответить на все вопросы. Постарайтесь ответить как можно более подробно)

Search for information about a specific event or a specific document.

Record to be searched:	☐ **Birth** Рождение	☐ **Baptism** Крещение	☐ **Marriage** Брак	☐ **Death** Смерть
	☐ Military Service Records О Военной Службе	☐ Civil Service Records О Гражданской Службе	☐ Property Records Об Имущественной Собственности	

Approximate date (within 5 years) & place of event (guberniya/region, district, town, village, parish; in large cities - ward, quarter, parish, street, house)
Дата (приблизительно – в пределах 5 лет) и место события (губерния/область, уезд /район, волость, стан, округаж город, село, деревня, церковный приход, синагога; в крупных городах - район, участок=. церковный приход, улица, дом)

First name Имя	Patronymic Отчество	Last name Фамилия	Sex Пол

All other names used at any time (including maiden name if married) Другие имена (включая девичью фамилию)

Variant spelling Возможные разночтения фамилии, имени, отчества

Citizenship Гражданство	Ethnic group Национальность	Religion Вероисповедание	Class: Сословие
			☐ Nobility Дворянство ☐ Clergy Духовенство ☐ Middle Class Мещанство ☐ Merchant class Купечество ☐ Peasantry Крестьянство ☐ Working class Рабочий класс ☐ Foreign national working in Russia Иностранцы на русской службе

P A R E N T S (РОДИТЕЛИ)

Father ОТЕЦ	Full name Фамилия, имя, отчество	Date of birth Дата рождения	Place of birth Место рождения	Other information Дополнительная информация
Mother МАТЬ	Full name Фамилия, имя, отчество	Date of birth Дата рождения	Place of birth Место рождения	Other information Дополнительная информация

B R O T H E R S   A N D   S I S T E R S (БРАТЬЯ И СЕСТРЫ)

Name including maiden name Фамилия, имя, отчество (включая девичью фамилию)	Sex Пол	Date of Birth Дата рождения	Place of Birth Место рождения	Other information Дополнительная информация

SPOUSE(S) OF PERSON TO BE SEARCHED (МУЖЬЯ, ЖЕНЫ)

Name including maiden name Фамилия, имя, отчество (включая девичью фамилию)	Date of birth Дата рождения	Place of birth Место рождения	Other information Дополнительная информация

C H I L D R E N (ДЕТИ)

Name Имя	Date of birth Дата рождения	Place of birth Место рождения	Other information Дополнительная информация

P L A C E S   O F   R E S I D E N C E (МЕСТО ЖИТЕЛЬСТВА)

	Place of residence Место жительства	~~Time~~ Время проживания
1.		
2.		

AME AND ADDRESS OF THE REQUESTER

АМИЛИЯ И АДРЕС ЗАЯВИТЕЛЯ

AGAS
ox 236
len Echo, MD 20812

FULLER GENEALOGICAL SEARCH FORM
PLEASE PRINT OR TYPE (пожалуйста, пишите печатными буквами)

It is realized that you may not have answers to some questions. Fill in to the best of your knowledge. (Возможно, Вы не сможете ответить на все вопросы. Постарайтесь ответить как можно более подробно)

FOCUS OF SEARCH: ☐ To link several generations (Установить связи между несколькими поколениями)

ЦЕЛЬ ПОИСКА ☐ To link family members within a generation (Установить связи между членами семьи одного поколения)

☐ To confirm several events in the life of a single individual (Подтвердить определенные события из жизни одного человека)

First name Имя	Patronymic Отчество	Last name Фамилия	Sex Пол	Date of birth Дата рождения
All other names used at any time (including maiden name if married) Другие имена			Place of birth Место рождения	
Variant spelling Возможные разночтения фамилии, имени, отчества				

Citizenship Гражданство	Ethnic group Национальность	Religion Вероисповедание	Class: Сословие ☐ Nobility Дворянство ☐ Clergy Духовенство ☐ Middle Class Мещанство ☐ Merchant class Купечество ☐ Peasantry Крестьянство ☐ Working class Рабочий класс ☐ Foreign national working in Russia Иностранцы на русской службе Transfer from one class to another Переход из одного класса в другой

PARENTS (РОДИТЕЛИ)

Father ОТЕЦ	Full name Фамилия, имя, отчество	Date of birth Дата рождения	Place of birth Место рождения	Other information Дополнительная информация
Mother МАТЬ	Full name Фамилия, имя, отчество	Date of birth Дата рождения	Place of birth Место рождения	Other information Дополнительная информация

BROTHERS AND SISTERS (БРАТЬЯ И СЕСТРЫ)

Name including maiden name Фамилия, имя, отчество (включая девичью фамилию)	Sex Пол	Date of Birth Дата рождения	Place of Birth Место рождения	Other information Дополнительная информация

SPOUSE(S) OF PERSON TO BE SEARCHED (МУЖЬЯ, ЖЕНЫ)

Name including maiden name Фамилия, имя, отчество (включая девичью фамилию)	Date of birth Дата рождения	Place of birth Место рождения	Other information Дополнительная информация

C H I L D R E N (ДЕТИ)

Name Имя	Date of birth Дата рождения	Place of birth Место рождения	Other information Дополнительная информация

P L A C E S O F R E S I D E N C E (МЕСТО ЖИТЕЛЬСТВА)

	Place of residence Место жительства	Date Время проживания
1.		
2.		

O T H E R I N F O R M A T I O N (ДОПОЛНИТЕЛЬНАЯ ИНФОРМАЦИЯ)

Education (Name and address of institution)
Образование (Название и адрес учебного заведения)

Place of service or work
Место службы или работы

Titles, Ranks, Awards
Звания, чины, награды

Real estate ownership
Земельные владения

Adoption, guardianship
Усыновление, опекунство

Legal actions
Нахождение под судом

Place and date of emigration
Место и дата эмиграции

Membership in organizations (cultural, fraternal)
Членство в организациях (культурных, общественных)

Military service (rank, organization, dates)
Военная служба (звание, название части, время службы)

Other information that might help in identification
Дополнительная информация, которая могла бы облегчить поиски

AME AND ADDRESS OF THE REQUESTER
АМИЛИЯ И АДРЕС ЗАЯВИТЕЛЯ

RAGAS
Box 236
Glen Echo, MD 20812

RWANDA

Direction Generale des Affaires Politiques et Administratives
Ministère de l'Interieur et du Dcvoloppemont Communal
BP 446
Kigali, Rwanda

Cost for a Birth or Marriage Certificate 50 Frws.
Cost for a Divorce or Death Certificate 600 Frws.

Vital registration began May 4, 1895.

ST. CHRISTOPHER/NEVIS

Registrar General's Office
Health Department
P.O. Box 236
Basseterre, St. Christopher/Nevis

(809) 465-2521

Cost for a Birth, Marriage, or Death Certificate US $2.00

The Registrar General has records from St. Christopher from January 1, 1859 and Nevis from August 1, 1869.

ST. LUCIA

Registrar General
Registry Department
Castries, St. Lucia

(809) 452-1257

Cost for a Birth, Marriage, or Death Certificate US $2.55

The Registrar General has records from January 1, 1869. Current registration is considered to be complete.

ST. VINCENT and the GRENADINES

Registrar General's Office
Registry Department
Courthouse
Kingstown, St. Vincent and the Grenadines

(809) 457-1424

Cost for a Birth, Marriage, or Death Certificate US $1.75

Records are available from July 1, 1874.

SAMOA

Registrar General
Justice Department
P.O. Box 49
Apia, Samoa

(011) (685) 22-671

Cost for Birth, Marriage/Divorce, or Death Certificate   S $7.50

Registration began in the mid 1800s. The Registrar of the Supreme Court is required to send copies of all divorces to the Registrar General.

SAN MARINO

Parish Priest
(Parish), San Marino

Vital records are available from the Roman Catholic parish churches in San Marino.

SAO TOME and PRINCIPE

Departamento do Registo Civil
Ministerio de Justicia e Funcao Publica
C.P. 4
Sao Tome, Sao Tome and Principe

Sao Tome and Principe were under Portuguese control until independence in 1975. Vital registration is complete.

SAUDI ARABIA

Registrar
Department of Preventive Medicine
Ministry of Health
Airport Road
Riyadh 11176, Saudi Arabia

Registration is considered complete.

SENEGAL

Division de l'Etat Civil
Direction de la Statistique
Ministere des Finances et des Affaires Economiques
B.P. 116
Dakar, Senegal

Vital registration of births and deaths began in 1916 for most French citizens; modern vital registration in Senegal began in 1961. Currently, the registration is not considered to be complete.

SERBIA

Civil Registration Office
(Town), Serbia

Vital records are on file from 1946.

SEYCHELLES

Send your requests to:

Civil Status Office
Ministry of Administration and Manpower
Management and Information Systems Division
P.O. Box 206
Victoria, Seychelles

(011) (248) 2-4041, FAX (011) (248) 2-5339

Cost for a certified Birth Certificate	R 25
Cost for a certified Marriage Certificate	R 25
Cost for a certified Death Certificate	R 25

The Civil Status Office has records from 1902 to the present. For records from 1794 to 1902 contact the National Archives, P.O. Box 720, La Bastille, Mahe, Seychelles.

Seychelles is one of the few countries in Sub-Saharan Africa where the registration of births and deaths is considered to be complete.

The Family History Library of The Church of Jesus Christ of Latter-day Saints in Salt Lake City, Utah has microfilmed original and published records of Seychelles and Africa. For further details on their holdings please consult your nearest Family History Center.

APPLICATION FOR BIRTH CERTIFICATE

FULL NAME:..

SURNAME:..

DATE OF BIRTH:..

PLACE OF BIRTH:...

NAME OF FATHER:...

NAME OF MOTHER:...

MOTHER'S MAIDEN SURNAME:....................................

APPLICATION FOR MARRIAGE CERTIFICATE

HUSBAND'S NAME:...

HUSBAND'S SURNAME:..

WIFE'S NAMES:...

WIFE'S SURNAME:...

DATE OF MARRIAGE :..

PLACE OF MARRIAGE:..

APPLICATION FOR DEATH CERTIFICATE

NAME OF DECEASED:...

MAIDEN SURNAME: ....

PLACE OF DEATH: ....

DATE OF DEATH: ....

SIERRA LEONE

Send your requests to:

Office of Chief Registrar
Births and Deaths Office
Ministry of Health
3 Wilberforce Street
Freetown, Sierra Leone

Cost for a certified Birth Certificate	Varies
Cost for a certified Marriage Certificate	Varies
Cost for a certified Death Certificate	Varies

Registration began as early as 1801 in Freetown and Granville. Currently, the registration is considered to be incomplete.

The Family History Library of The Church of Jesus Christ of Latter-day Saints in Salt Lake City, Utah has microfilmed original and published records of Sierra Leone and Africa. For further details on their holdings please consult your nearest Family History Center.

SINGAPORE

Send your requests to:

Registrar of Births and Deaths
National Registration Department
Ministry of Home Affairs
1 Colombo Court #02-01
Singapore 0617

(011) (65) 330-7668, FAX (011) (65) 338-8935

Send your requests for Marriage Records to:

Registrar of Marriages
National Registration Department
Canning Rise
Singapore 0617

(011) (65) 338-9987, FAX (011) (65) 339-3328

Send your requests for Divorce Records to:

Registry
Supreme Court
St. Andrew's Road
Singapore 0617

Cost for a certified Birth Certificate	S $ 8.00
Cost for a Marriage or Divorce Certificate	S $10.00
Cost for a certified Death Certificate	S $ 8.00

Singapore has birth and death records from 1872, marriage records from 1875, and divorce records from 1937. Muslim marriage records are not filed with the Registrar but are kept by their religious leaders.

The Singapore Archives also has records; contact them at 17-18 Lewin Terrace, Fort Canning, Singapore 0167; Tel. (011) (65) 338-3954 or 337-7314.

The Family History Library of The Church of Jesus Christ of Latter-day Saints in Salt Lake City, Utah has microfilmed original and published records of Singapore. For further details on their holdings please consult your nearest Family History Center.

APPLICATION FORM FOR A SEARCH AND/OR CERTIFIED EXTRACT FROM REGISTER OF BIRTHS

Part A	Birth Registration No.	Number of Copies Applied For

SUBJECT'S PARTICULARS

Name	

Sex	Date of Birth	Identification Document and No.

Part B	To be completed only if the applicant is unable to furnish the birth registration number or subject is holding a foreign identification document.

BIRTH PARTICULARS

Date of Registration	
Place & Address of Birth	
Birth Registered At	

FATHER'S PARTICULARS

Identification Document & No.	
Name	
Alias (if any)	

MOTHER'S PARTICULARS

Identification Document & No.	
Name	
Alias (if any)	

Part C	Identification Document and No.

APPLICANT'S PARTICULARS

Name in full	Relationship to Child
Address	Telephone No.

Reasons for Application

....
DATE   SIGNATURE/THUMB IMPRESSIONS OF APPLICANT

Part D	SEARCH	EXTRACT

FOR OFFICIAL USE ONLY

SEARCH		EXTRACT	
Fee Paid $		Fee Paid $	
Receipt No. And Date		Receipt No. And Date	
Search Conducted By		Application No.	
Result of Search TRACED/UNTRACED	Application No.	Extract No. And Date	
Notified Applicant On		Extract Issued On	

Entered By : ....   Date : ....   BD 40

APPLICATION FORM FOR A SEARCH AND/OR CERTIFIED EXTRACT FROM REGISTER OF DEATHS

Part A	Death Registration No.	Number of Copies Applied For

	DECEASED'S PARTICULARS	
	Name	
	Alias (if any)	
	Sex	Date of Death	Identification Document and No.

Part B	To be completed only if the applicant is unable to furnish the death registration No.

	SUPPLEMENTARY INFORMATION		
	Date of Birth/Age	Race/Dialect Group	Nationality
	Address of Death		
	Death Registered At		

Part C	Identificatin Document & No.

	APPLICANT'S PARTICULARS	
	Name in full	Relationship to Deceased
	Address	Telephone No.
	Reasons for Application	

_____   _____
DATE   SIGNATURE/THUMB IMPRESSIONS OF APPLICANT

Part D	SEARCH	EXTRACT

	FOR OFFICIAL USE ONLY		
	Fee Paid $		Fee Paid $
	Receipt No. And Date		Receipt No. And Date
	Search Conducted By		Application No.
	Result of Search TRACED/UNTRACED	Application No.	Extract No. And Date
	Notified Applicant On		Extract Issue On

BD 41

Entered By : ....   Date : ....

SLOVAKIA

Ministry of the Interior
Department of Archives
Krizkova 7
811 04 Bratislava, Slovakia

Slovakia, formerly part of Czechoslovakia, became independent in January 1993. The Archives charges an hourly fee of US $15.00 for a search. Church records are available in the Czech Republic and Slovakia from 1785. Modern civil registration began in 1919.

SLOVENIA

Civil Registration Office
(Town), Slovenia

Vital records are on file from 1946. Records before that were kept by the local churches.

SOLOMON ISLANDS

For Birth and Death Records write to:

Ministry of Health and Medical Services
P.O. Box G11
Honiara, Solomon Islands

For Marriage and Divorce Records write to:

Ministry of Police and Justice
Magistrates Division
Honiara, Solomon Islands

Cost for a Birth, Marriage, or Death Certificate   A $.50

Current vital registration is considered to be 75 percent complete. Information is also available from the Solomon Islands National Archives, Ministry of Home Affairs, P.O. Box 781, Honiara, Solomon Islands; Tel. (011) (677) 21-399; FAX (011) (677) 21-397.

SOMALIA

There is currently no organized vital registration program in Somalia.

SOUTH AFRICA

Send your requests to:

Registration Office
Department of Home Affairs
Private Bag X114
Pretoria, 0001, Republic of South Africa

(011) (27) (123) 148-911

Cost for a certified Birth Certificate	No Charge
Cost for a certified Marriage Certificate	No Charge
Cost for a certified Death Certificate	No Charge

The Registration Office has records from 1924. The Director-General of Internal Affairs can, at his discretion, approve or refuse to issue a certificate. A computer printout of the certificate will be issued unless you request an "unabridged" certificate.

The Family History Library of The Church of Jesus Christ of Latter-day Saints in Salt Lake City, Utah has microfilmed original and published records of South Africa. For further details on their holdings please consult your nearest Family History Center.

DEPARTMENT OF HOME AFFAIRS

APPLICATION FOR BIRTH CERTIFICATE
(VIr Afrikaans sien koorcy)
(Complete in block letters please)

N.B.—For use in the Republic of South Africa an abridged birth certificate, or where possible, a computer printed certificate of birth particulars is normally issued. Such a certificate usually complies with the requirements for which a birth certificate is required.

An unabridged certificate is available on request and is issued mainly for overseas purposes. If such a certificate is required, indicate with a X in the block hereunder and state fully the purpose for which the certificate is required.

☐ Purpose for which required ....

....

....

I. PARTICULARS OF PERSON CONCERNED

1. Identity Number ☐☐☐☐☐☐ ☐☐☐☐ ☐☐ ☐

2. Surname ....

3. Maiden name if a married woman ....

4. Forenames in full ....

5. Date of birth ....

6. District of birth ....

II. PARTICULARS OF FATHER AND MOTHER

1. Full name of father ....

2. Surname of father ....

3. Full name of mother ....

4. Maiden name..

III. PARTICULARS OF APPLICANT

1. Name of applicant ....

2. Address of applicant ....

3. Postal code .... 4. Tel. No.: W .... H.........................

5. .... 6. ....
   Signature   *Date*

APPLICATION FOR MARRIAGE CERTIFICATE

(Complete in block letters please)

Indicate in the appropriate square whether an abridged or a full certificate is required.

N.B.—An abridged certificate generally answers the purpose for which a marriage certificate is required in the Republic of South Africa. A full certificate is issued mainly for *overseas* purposes.

If a full certificate is required, state fully the purpose for which it is required:

....

....

....

☐ **Abridged certificate**   ☐ **Full certificate**

Full names and surname of husband ....

....

Identity number of husband

Date of birth of husband ....

Full names and maiden name of wife ....

....

Identity number of wife

Date of birth of wife ....

Date of marriage ....

Name of church or magistrate's office ....

Place where marriage took place ....

Name of marriage officer (if married in church) ....

Name of applicant ....

Address of applicant ....

....

....

Postal code ....   Tel. No.: Work...

                                                                      Home..

....
            Signature

Date ....

APPLICATION FOR DEATH CERTIFICATE

(Complete in block letters please)

Identity number: ☐☐☐☐☐ ☐☐☐☐ ☐☐ ☐

Surname ....

Maiden name if a married woman ....

Forenames in full ....

Population group ....

Date of birth ....

Date of death ....

District where death occurred ....

N.B.—Two types of certificates are issued, viz. an abridged certificate and a full certificate.

An abridged certificate usually answers the purpose for which it is required in the Republic of South Africa.

A full certificate is issued mainly for overseas purposes.

Make a cross (X) in the appropriate block if a full certificate is required and state the purpose for which it is required.

☐ A full certificate is required for ....

....

....

Name of applicant ....

Address of applicant ....

....

....

Postal code ....   Tel. No.: Work ....

Home ....

....
Signature

Date ....

SPAIN

Registro Civil
(Town), Spain

Records are on file from 1870 and in some areas much earlier. The Direccion General de los Registros y de Notariado (Ministerio de Justicia, San Bernardo 62, 28071 Madrid, Spain) directs the work of the local registrars.

SRI LANKA

Registrar General of Marriages, Births and Deaths
Ministry of Home Affairs
340, R.A. De Mel Mawatha
Colombo 3, Sri Lanka

Cost for a Birth, Marriage, or Death Certificate   R 2.00

Registration began in the Dutch period and by 1867 included the entire population. Marriages are kept separately by religion. Muslims keep separate divorce records. Kandyan divorces are kept by District Registrars and all others are kept by the District Courts. Each person obtains a national identity card at age 18. Records are prepared at the local level and are held by the District Registrars and the Registrar General.

SUDAN

Registrar
Ministry of Health
Khartoum, Sudan

Vital registration only began recently and is not uniform throughout the country. The Sudan became independent in 1956.

SURINAME

Registrar General
Central Bureau of Civil Registration
Ministry of Interior Affairs
Coppenamelaan 177
Paramaribo, Suriname

The Registrar is computerizing the vital records concentrating on the Marowijne, Brokopondo, and Sipaliwini districts.

SWAZILAND

Registrar General
Ministry of Justice
P.O. Box 460
Moabane, Swaziland

Registration began in 1900 for the foreign population and expanded to the entire nation in 1927.

SWEDEN

Pastor
Lutheran Church
(Town), Sweden

Cost for a Birth, Marriage, or Death Certificate   Kr 1.00

While there is no central office for vital records, a national personal identification number has been assigned to every person living in Sweden since January 1, 1947. These numbers are administered by the National Tax Board, Department for Civil Registration and Elections, Ministry of Finance, S-171 94 Solna, Sweden. The national government and each county maintain a register of their respective jurisdictions.

The local pastor serves as the registrar of this system and of the national census. To obtain copies of birth, marriage, and death certificates write to the pastor of the local Lutheran congregation in the town where the event occurred. Church registers are on file from the 1600s.

SWITZERLAND

Zivilstandsamt
(Town), Switzerland

Records date from January 1, 1876. The Office Federal de l'Etat Civil (Department of Justice, Bundesgasse 32, CH-3003 Berne, Switzerland) directs the work of the local registrars.

SYRIA

Director
General Directorate of Civil Registration
Ministry of Interior Affairs
Fardos Street
Damascus, Syria

Registration began in 1923.

TAJIKISTAN

Russian-American Genealogical Archival Service (RAGAS)
P.O. Box 236
Glen Echo, Maryland 20812
(202) 501-5206

Cost for a Birth, Marriage, or Death Certificate $20.00

By an agreement between the United States National Archives Volunteer Association and the Archives of Russia Society RAGAS will receive and process requests for vital records in the former Soviet republics. Although at this time RAGAS deals mainly with Russia, Belarus, and Ukraine they might be able to help you with your inquiries regarding Tajikistan. There is a $2.00 shipping fee per document. There is also an hourly rate. (See Russia for application forms.)

TANZANIA

Registrar General
Ministry of Justice
Office of the Administrator General
P.O. Box 9183
Dar Es Salam, Tanzania

(011) (255) (51) 28-811

Cost for a Birth, Divorce or Death Certificate	T.Shs. 600/=
Cost for a Marriage Certificate	T.Shs. 700/=

There is a T.Shs. 100/= charge for postage per certificate

Registration began in 1917 for Europeans; it expanded to Asians in 1923 and to the major towns in 1966. The Registrar General has birth and death records from 1917, marriage and divorce records from 1921.

THAILAND

Director
Administrative and Civil Registration Division
Department of Local Administration
Ministry of Interior
Nakhon Sawan Road
Bangkok 10300, Thailand

Cost for a Birth, Marriage, Divorce, or Death Certificate	Free

Registration began in 1909. In 1956 family registration was also required, and in 1982 a computerized national identification card system was implemented to centralize data on all individuals.

TOGO

Division des Affaires Politiques et Administratives
Ministere de l'Interieur
Lome, Togo

Vital registration in Togo began in 1923 in the larger urban areas; it was not expanded to the entire nation until 1962. Current registration is not considered to be complete.

The Family History Library of The Church of Jesus Christ of Latter-day Saints in Salt Lake City, Utah has microfilmed records of Togo and Africa. For further details on their holdings please consult your nearest Family History Center.

TONGA

Registrar General
Registrar of the Supreme Court
Justice Department
P.O. Box 11
Nuku'alofa, Tonga

(011) (676) 23 599, FAX (011) (676) 23 098

Cost for a Birth, Marriage, or Death Certificate	T $2.00
Cost for a Divorce Certificate	T $3.00

The Registrar General has birth and death records from 1867, marriage records from 1892, and divorce records from 1905. Current vital registration is considered to be 95 percent complete for births and 90 percent complete for deaths.

The Family History Library of The Church of Jesus Christ of Latter-day Saints in Salt Lake City, Utah has microfilmed records of Tonga. For further details on their holdings please consult your nearest Family History Center.

TRINIDAD and TOBAGO

Send your requests to:

Registrar General's Office
Ministry of Legal Affairs
Red House
St. Vincent Street
Port of Spain, Trinidad and Tobago

(809) 623-5793

Cost for a certified Birth Certificate	TT $25.00
Cost for a certified Marriage Certificate	TT $25.00
Cost for a certified Death Certificate	TT $25.00

The Registrar General has records for Trinidad from January 1, 1848 and for Tobago from January 30, 1868. Trinidad and Tobago were united in 1889. Current registration is considered to be complete. The local churches also have their own records.

The Family History Library of The Church of Jesus Christ of Latter-day Saints in Salt Lake City, Utah has microfilmed records of Trinidad and the Caribbean. For further details on their holdings please consult your nearest Family History Center.

REQUEST FOR A DEATH CERTIFICATE

Particulars:—

Death of ....

Date of Death ....

Place of Death ....

....
Applicant

For Official use

Year........................ Volume ....

Folio .... Entry No. ....

....
Search Clerk

Fee of $ ..12.50.. .... in stamps received and affixed
on Certificate No.

....
Cashier

G.P., Tr./To.—F1495—20,000— /89

REQUEST FOR A MARRIAGE CERTIFICATE

Particulars:

    (a) Civil   *(b)* Hindu

    (c) Muslim   *(d)* In Extremis

Names   (i) ....

of

Parties   (ii) ....

Date of Marriage ....

....
Applicant

For Official Use

Year........................ Volume ....

Folio .... Entry No. ....

....
Search Clerk

Fee of $ ..12.50.. .... in stamps received and affixed
on Certificate No.

....
Cashier

G.P., Tr./To.—F3300—30,000 /89

REQUEST FOR A BIRTH CERTIFICATE

(Particulars of person for whom Certificate is required)

Particulars:

Birth of ....

Date of Birth ....

Father's Name ....

Mother's Maiden Name ....

Place of Birth ....

....
Applicant

For Official use

Year........................ Volume ....

Folio .... Entry No. ....

....
Search Clerk

Fee of $ ..12.50.. ....in stamps received and affixed on
Certificate No.

....
Cashier

G.P., Tr./To.—I 1528—100,000— /92

TUNISIA

Registrar
Centres d'Etat Civil
(Town), Tunisia

Registration began in 1958.

TURKEY

General Directorate of Population and Citizenship Affairs
Ministry of Internal Affairs
T.C. Icisleri Bakanligi
Nufus ve Vatandaslik Isleri Gn. Md.
Bakanliklar
Ankara, Turkey

Turkey was founded in 1923. Over 98 percent of the people are Sunni Muslim. Efforts have been made to expand vital registration but currently it is not considered to be comprehensive.

TURKMENISTAN

Russian-American Genealogical Archival Service (RAGAS)
P.O. Box 236
Glen Echo, Maryland 20812

(202) 501-5206

Cost for a Birth, Marriage, or Death Certificate $20.00

By an agreement between the United States National Archives Volunteer Association and the Archives of Russia Society RAGAS will receive and process requests for vital records in the former Soviet republics. Although at this time RAGAS is able to deal mainly with Russia, Belarus, and Ukraine they might be able to help you with your inquiries regarding Turkmenistan. There is a $2.00 shipping fee per document. There is also an hourly rate. (See Russia for application forms.)

TURKS and CAICOS ISLANDS

Send your requests to:

Registrar General's Office
Post Office Building
Front Street
Grand Turk, Turks and Caicos
British West Indies

(809) 946-2791, FAX (809) 946-2821

Cost for a certified Birth Certificate	US $1.68
Cost for a certified Marriage Certificate	US $1.00
Cost for a certified Death Certificate	US $1.68

The Registrar General has records from January 2, 1863. Current registration is considered to be more than 90 percent complete. The local churches also have their own records.

The Family History Library of The Church of Jesus Christ of Latter-day Saints in Salt Lake City, Utah has microfilmed records of Turks and Caicos and the Caribbean. For further details on their holdings please consult your nearest Family History Center.

APPLICATION FOR BIRTH CERTIFICATE

TO: Registrar of Births

            Registrar General's Office

            Grand Turk

       I desire to have a search made for and .... certified copy/ies supplied of the Registrar of Birth of

....
(Enter all names)

Born at ....

in the Parish of ....

in or about the year ....

Father's full name ....

Mother's full name ....

                       Name of applicant

                       Mr/Mrs/Miss

                       Date   ....

Entry No ....

Stamp Duty Required	80¢
Office fees	88¢
	$1.68

APPLICATION FOR MARRIAGE CERTIFICATE

TO: Registrar of Marriages

         Registrar General's Office

         Grand Turk

     I desire to have a search made for and .... certified copy/ies supplied of the Registrar of Marriages of

....
                 (enter all names)

Place of marriage ....

in the Parish of ....

in or about the year ....

                       Name of Applicant

                       Mr/Mrs/Miss

                       Date ....

Entry No............

Office fees $1.00
                    $1.00

APPLICATION FOR DEATH CERTIFICATE

TO: Registrar of Death
          Registrar General's Office
          Grand Turk

          I desire to have a search made for and .... certified copy/ies
supplied of the Registrar of Death of

....
                   (Enter all names)

Died at...
in the Parish of ....
in or about the year............................

                   Name of Applicant

                   Mr/Mrs/Miss

                   Date   ....

Entry No ....

Stamp Duty Required   80¢
Office fees   88¢
                        $1.68

TUVALU

Registrar General
Medical Division
Office of the Prime Minister
Fanafuti, Tuvalu

You can also find information at the National Archives and Library of Tuvalu, P.O. Box 67, Fuanafuti, Tuvalu; Tel. (011) (688) 711; FAX (011) (688) 819.

UGANDA

Registrar General of Births and Deaths
Ministry of Home Affairs
Kampala, Uganda

Registration began in 1905 for Europeans, in 1915 for Asians, and in 1973 for the rest of the population.

UKRAINE

Russian-American Genealogical Archival Service (RAGAS)
P.O. Box 236
Glen Echo, Maryland 20812

(202) 501-5206

Cost for a Birth, Marriage, or Death Certificate $20.00

By an agreement between the United States National Archives Volunteer Association and the Archives of Russia Society RAGAS will receive and process requests for vital records in Ukraine. There is a $2.00 shipping fee per document. There is also an hourly rate. (See Russia for application forms.)

UNITED ARAB EMIRATES

Registration Central Preventive
  Medicine Directorate
Ministry of Health
Abu Dhabi, United Arab Emirates

Efforts have been made to implement vital registration but currently it is not considered to be comprehensive.

UNITED KINGDOM—ENGLAND and WALES

Present your requests in person to:

General Register Office
St. Catherines House
10 Kingsway
London WC2B 6JP, England

(011) (44) 071-242-0262

Send your requests by mail to:

Postal Applications Section
Office of Population Censuses and Surveys
Smedley Hydro
Southport
Merseyside PR8 2HH, England

(011) (44) 051-471-4371

When requested in person:

Cost for a certified Birth, Marriage, or Death Certificate	£ 5.50
Cost for a short form Birth Certificate	£ 3.50

When requested by mail:

Cost for a certified Birth, Marriage, or Death Certificate	£15.00
Cost for a duplicate copy, when ordered at the same time	£ 5.50
Cost for a short form Birth Certificate	£13.00
If the index citation is given	£10.00
Cost for a duplicate copy, when ordered at the same time	£ 3.50

The General Register Office has records from July 1, 1837. If your request is urgent there is an additional £14.50 fee.

The Family History Library of The Church of Jesus Christ of Latter-day Saints in Salt Lake City, Utah has microfilmed many of the original and published vital records and church registers of the United Kingdom. For further details on their holdings please consult your nearest Family History Center.

COPIES
....
....

 OPCS
OFFICE OF POPULATION
CENSUSES & SURVEYS

PAS

APPLICATION FOR BIRTH CERTIFICATE

Office of Population Censuses and Surveys, General Register Office, Smedley Hydro, Southport, Merseyside PR8 2HH

Applicant

Mr/Mrs/Miss	
Full postal address	

Number of certificates required
.... Full Certificate   ....Short certificate

Please tick approplate box
☐ Birth Register
☐ Adoption Register

Particulars of the person whose certificate is required.
Remember, we need full details to ensure a positive search.
PLEASE COMPLETE IN BLOCK CAPITALS

Surname at Birth
Forenames
Date of birth
Place of birth
Fathers surname
Fathers forenames
Mothers maiden surname
Mothers forenames

X Reference information from OPCS Index

Qtr/Year	Vol.No.	Page No.	District

APPLICANT TO COMPLETE

Amount Submitted ....

Signature ....

Address label (please use BLOCK LETTERS)

Enter in this space the name and full postal address to which the certificate should be sent

COPIES Please allow .... days for despatch of certificates

PAS

APPLICATION FOR MARRIAGE CERTIFICATE

Office of Population Censuses and Surveys, General Register Office, Smedley Hydro, Southport, Merseyside PR8 2HH

Number of certificates required
First certificate
.... certificate at £15.00
.... certificate at £12.00 (See Notes)*

Additional copies of the same certificate can
be issued at the same time at a fee of
.... £5.50 each copy

Particulars of the persons whose certificate is required.
Remember, we need full details to ensure a positive search.
PLEASE COMPLETE IN BLOCK CAPITALS.

amount received
£ _____

Applicant

PAS

Mr/Mrs/Miss	
Full postal address	

Man's	Surname	
	Forenames	
Woman's	Surname	
	Forenames	
Date of marriage		
Place of marriage		
Name of man's father		
Name of woman's father		

X

Reference information from OPCS Index			
Qtr/Year	Vol.No.	Page No.	District

FOR OFFICE USE ONLY

Sub-District					
LB MB	CB	MD	City of	County of	
Entry	Year	M	J	S	D
	Year	M	J	S	D
	Year	M	J	S	D
D/S	Year	M	J	S	D
Yes	Year	M	J	S	D
No	Restricted to				

NOTES

THIS OFFICE HOLDS RECORDS OF MARRIAGES REGISTERED IN ENGLAND AND WALES SINCE 1ST JULY 1837.

If you attend St Catherines House, 10 Kingsway, London WC2B 6JP and make the search personally, the certificate may be collected on the fourth working day after the application was accepted or be posted direct to your home address. The fees are £5.50 for a full certificate or £3.50 for a short certificate.

You can also obtain certificates on application in person or by post to the Officiating Minister of the Church where the marriage took place or to the Superintendent Registrar of the same district.

* **Variable Fee** - The lower postal fee of £12.00 applies to applicants who can complete at **X** the exact reference information from OPCS Index.

METHODS OF PAYMENT

Cheques, postal orders, etc should be made payable to "**The Registrar General**". Payment from abroad may be made by cheque, international money order, or draft in favour of "**The Registrar General.**" Orders, cheques and drafts should always be expressed in STERLING and bear the name and address of a London clearing bank. PLEASE DO NOT SEND CASH.

Searching by OPCS Staff

If the search is likely to be too time consuming because of lack of identifying details, or if the search to be made is a general one (eg. to trace a family tree), we cannot undertake the task. The applicant should conduct the search personally or arrange for someone else to search on their behalf, at the Public Search Rooms, St. Catherines House, London.

If we cannot find the entry, a fee of £9.50 will be retained.

Amount Received	
Fees Certificates	
Total charge	
Refund	
Despatched	

Address label (please use BLOCK LETTERS)

Enter in this space the name and full postal address to which the certificate should be sent

SB23/3 6/91

PAS 8M

APPLICATION FOR DEATH CERTIFICATE

Office of Population Censuses and Surveys, General Register Office, Smedley Hydro, Southport, Merseyside PR8 2HH

Number of certificates required
First certificate
.... certificate at £15.00
.... certificate at £12.00 (See Notes)*

Additional copies of the same certificate can
be issued at the same time at a fee of
.... £5.50 each copy

amount received
£ _____

Applicant

PAS

Mr/Mrs/Miss

Full postal address

**Particulars of the person whose certificate is required.
Remember, we need full details to ensure a positive search.
PLEASE COMPLETE IN BLOCK CAPITALS**

Surname	
Forename(s)	
Date of death	
Place of death	
Age at death	
Occupation of Deceased	
Marital status of Deceased (if female)	

X Reference information from OPCS Index

Qtr/Year	Vol.No.	Page No.	District

Notes

THIS OFFICE HOLDS RECORDS OF DEATHS REGISTERED IN ENGLAND AND WALES SINCE 1ST JULY 1837.

If you attend St Catherines House, 10 Kingsway, London WC2B 6JP and make the search personally, the certificate may be collected on the fourth working day after the application was accepted or be posted direct to your home address. The fees are £5.50. for a full certificate or £3.50 for a short certificate.

You can also obtain certificates on application in person or by post to the Superintendent Registrar for the district where the death occurred.

*Variable Fee - The lower postal fee of £12.00 applies to applicants who can complete at **X** the exact reference information from OPCS Index.

METHODS OF PAYMENT
Cheques, postal orders, etc should be made payable to **"The Registrar General"**. Payment from abroad may be made by cheque, international money order, or draft in favour of **"The Registrar General."** Orders, cheques and drafts should always be expressed in STERLING and bear the name and address of a London clearing bank. PLEASE DO NOT SEND CASH.

Searching by OPCS Staff
If the search is likely to be too time consuming because of lack of identifying details, or if the search to be made is a general one (eg. to trace a family tree), we cannot undertake the task. The applicant should conduct the search personally or arrange for someone else to search on their behalf, at the Public Search Rooms, St. Catherines House, London.

If we cannot find the entry, a fee of £9.50 will be retained.

FOR OFFICE USE ONLY

Sub-District					
LB MB	CB	MD	City of	County of	
Entry	Year	M	J	S	D
	Year	M	J	S	D
	Year	M	J	S	D
D/S	Year	M	J	S	D
Yes	Year	M	J	S	D
No	Restricted to				

Amount Received	
Fees	Certificates
Total charge	
Refund	
Despatched	

Address label (please use BLOCK LETTERS)

Enter in this space the name and full postal address to which the certificate should be sent

PAS 8D

SB23/5 6/91

UNITED KINGDOM—NORTHERN IRELAND

Send your requests to:

General Register Office
Department of Health and Social Services
Oxford House
49-55 Chichester Street
Belfast BT1 4HL, Northern Ireland

(011) (44) 232-235-211

Cost for a certified Birth Certificate	£5.50
Cost for a short form Birth Certificate	£3.50
Cost for a certified Marriage Certificate	£5.50
Cost for a certified Death Certificate	£5.50
Cost for a duplicate copy, when ordered at the same time	£3.50

The General Register Office has birth and death records from January 1, 1864 and marriage records from April 1, 1845 (with Roman Catholic marriage records from January 1, 1864).

The Family History Library of The Church of Jesus Christ of Latter-day Saints in Salt Lake City, Utah has microfilmed many of the original and published vital records and church registers of Northern Ireland. For further details on their holdings please consult your nearest Family History Center.

Application for birth certificate / search

Office use	
Serial no.	Date / /
Related nos.	
Reference no.	

- Please complete in CAPITAL letters Parts 1 and 2
- For the certificate of an adopted child, please complete Parts 1 **and** 3

Part 1 Applicant

Full name   Mr / Mrs / Miss

Address

Postcode   Tel no.

I enclose   £   payable to **'Registrar General'**

Signed   Date   /   /

Part 2 Certificate / Details of the person whose certificate is required

	Surname at birth	Forename(s)	Date of birth	Place of birth Hospital or address
Details of person			/ /	
Father				

	Surname	Forename(s)	Maiden surname	Mother's residence (at time of child's birth)
Mother				

Part 3 Certificate / Search from Adopted Children Register (from 1 July 1930 only)

	Surname	Forename(s)	Date of birth
Adopted person			/ /
Name(s) of adopters			

	Name of court which made the order	Date of the order
Adoption Order		/ /

Number and type of certificate(s) required

[Number]   **Full**   [Number]   **Short**

and for statutory reasons: *(Please tick)*   Child Benefit ☐   Education and Libraries Order ☐

Social Security Act ☐

Please return to   **The Registrar General, Oxford House, 49 / 55 Chichester Street, BELFAST BT1 4HL**
Telephone **(0232) 235211**   *Opening Hours 9.30 - 3.30*

Office use   **Birth**

Notes

....

....

....

....

....

....

....

....

....

....

....

....

....

....

Entry to be offered   *Action taken*

....

....

....

....

....

....

Fees

Number

Full	£	
Short	£	
Stat	£	
Other	£	

APP Form

TOTAL DUE | £ |

Completed /
checked by .... Date / /

Receipt

Certificate
checked by .... Date / /

TOTAL REC'D

Cheq / Cash / PO	£	
Extra fees. Cheq / Cash / PO	£	
GRAND TOTAL	£	
TOTAL DUE	£	
Refunds / Retained fees / Postage	£	

Cashier /
AA   .... Date / /

Cashier /
Postal Clerk .... Date / /

REFUND

Schedule no. ....

Received by ....

Certificate
stamped by .... Date / /

Cashier /
AA   .... Date / /

Finance
Officer   .... Date / /

HMSO 8091921 C800 11/91 GP155 59102

APPLICATION FOR A
SEARCH/MARRIAGE CERTIFICATE

To: The Registrar General
Oxford House, 49-55 Chichester Street
Belfast BT1 4HL (Tel. No. 235211)

PLEASE COMPLETE PARTS A & B

A

PLEASE USE BLOCK CAPITALS

Name of Applicant
Mr.
Mrs. ....
Miss   (STATE NAME IN FULL)

Full postal address ....

.... Tele. No. ....

I enclose cheque/postal order for ....

Date .... Signature ....

MAN	WOMAN	
Surname	Maiden Surname	Any other surname before this marriage
Christian or Forenames	Christian or Forenames	

PLACE OF MARRIAGE	DATE OF MARRIAGE		
Full Address	Day	Month	Year

B

I require .... certificate(s)
        (Number)

GRO 42

FIRST SEARCH

Result ....

....

Date ....Searched by ....

CHECK SEARCH

Result ....

....

Date ....Searched by ....

Notes

....

....

....

....

....

Entry to be offered	Action taken
....	....
....	....
....	....
....	....
....	....
....	....

Fees payable

Number

£   p

..........Full @ ....

Checked by ....

Date ....

Stamped by ....

Date ....

Total _____

	£	p
In	:	
	:	

	£	p
Out	:	
	:	
	:	

By ....

Recd. ....

Cashier ....

Date ....

By ....

Receipt

Dd. 8093831 20M 6/90 LPC Ltd. Gp. 198/1

APPLICATION FOR A
SEARCH/DEATH CERTIFICATE

To: The Registrar General,
Oxford House, 49 - 55 Chichester Street,
Belfast BT1 4HL. (Tel. No. 235211)

FIRST COMPLETE PART A THEN FILL IN WHICHEVER OTHER PART REFERS TO THE TYPE OF CERTIFICATE YOU REQUIRE

A   PLEASE USE BLOCK CAPITALS

Name of Applicant   Mr.
Mrs. ....
Miss. ....   (STATE NAME IN FULL)

Full postal address .... Tele. No. ....

I enclose cheque/postal order for ....

Date ....   Signature ....

PARTICULARS OF THE PERSON WHOSE CERTIFICATE IS REQUIRED

Christian or Forenames

Surname

Date of Death

Place of Death	Usual Residence

Date of Birth, or age at Death

If person was married or widowed at time of death - Name of Spouse

If Death occurred in last three years,
was Death reported to Coroner?

B   Full Certificate

I require .... full certificate(s).
(Number)

C   Certificate for purposes of Friendly Societies Acts

I require .... certificate(s) for the following Registered Friendly Society:

....

D   CERTIFICATE FOR CERTAIN OTHER STATUTORY PURPOSES

I require a certificate for each undermentioned purpose against which I have placed a cross.

STATUTORY PURPOSE OF CERTIFICATE	INSERT X IF REQD.	STATUTORY PURPOSE OF CERTIFICATE	INSERT X IF REQD.
Child Benefit Order		National Savings Bank	
Social Security Act		Premium Savings Bonds	
Government Annuities		Trustee Savings Bank	
Savings Contracts		Ulster Savings Certificates	
		War & National Savings Certificates	

G.R.O. 41

FIRST SEARCH

Result ....

....

: _____

Date ....Searched by...............................

CHECK SEARCH

Result ....

....

Date ....Searched by...............................

Notes

....

....

....

....

....

Entry to be Offered	Action Taken
....	....
....	....
....	....
....	....
....	....
....	....

Fees Payable

Number   £   p

...............Full @ ....

                                                          ....

...............Stat Purposes @ ....

                              Total _____

	£	p.
In	:	
	:	

	£	p.
Out	:	
	.	
	:	

Checked by ....

Date ....

Stamped by ....

Date ....

By ....

Recd. ....

Cashier ....

Date ....

By ....

Receipt

Dd 8093832 C200 6/90 GP153 CPC

UNITED KINGDOM—SCOTLAND

Send your requests to:

General Register Office for Scotland
New Register House
Edinburgh EH1 3YT, Scotland

(011) (44) 31-334-0380, FAX (011) (44) 31-314-4400

Cost for a certified Birth, Marriage, Divorce or Death Certificate

Ordered in person	£ 8.00
Ordered by mail	£10.50
Cost for a duplicate copy, when ordered at the same time	£ 5.50

The General Register Office has records from governmental registers from January 1, 1855. In addition, they hold many old parish registers dating back to 1553. These are indexed. The Office has divorce records from May 1, 1984. Divorces before that date are noted on the Registrar's copy of the marriage certificate. Include the estimated airmail postage with your fee. International Postal Reply Coupons are not accepted as payment.

The Family History Library of The Church of Jesus Christ of Latter-day Saints in Salt Lake City, Utah has microfilmed many of the original and published vital records and church registers of Scotland. For further details on their holdings please consult your nearest Family History Center.

General Register Office for Scotland

Postal Search Unit

New Register House Edinburgh EH1 3YT

Telephone direct line   031-314 4440, 4441, 4451
Switchboard   031-334 0380
Facsimile   031-314 4400

To:

Date

Dear Applicant

Your letter is returned as no money was enclosed to cover the cost.

Please complete the application overleaf and return it to this office with the cost. Details of charges are given on the enclosed leaflet.

Please indicate in the appropriate box(es) below the number of extracts or certificates required.

1. ☐ Abbreviated certificate of birth. This shows the person's name surname, sex, date and place of birth. Not applicable to records before 1855.   Cost   £

2. ☐ Extract of Birth. This is a full copy of the entry in the birth register and is used for all purposes. (For adoption or original birth certificates see notes below)   Cost   £

3. ☐ Extract of Death   Cost   £

4. ☐ Extract of Marriage   Cost   £

5. ☐ Extract of Divorce (see note below)   Cost   £

Note that if more than one copy of the same entry is ordered at the same time, there is a reduced charge.

If you order an extract(s) by post, you may pay by Sterling cheque. ALL CHEQUES SHOULD BE CROSSED AND MADE PAYABLE TO "THE REGISTRAR GENERAL". **PLEASE DO NOT SEND CASH**. You can also if you wish, quote your Visa or Mastercard number (plus the cardholder's name, the expiry date and your signature, as they appear on the card) since this enables us to charge you exactly the right amount. (We do not know wether a document fee will be payable until we have actually traced the entry). If you order by fax, you must pay by Visa or Mastercard.

Cardholder's Name: ....   Cardholder's Signature ....

Card Number: ☐☐☐☐☐ ☐☐☐☐☐ ☐☐☐☐☐ ☐☐☐☐☐

Expiry Date: _ _ / _ _

If you overpay us by more than £2.50, we will refund the overpayment by a cheque in pounds Sterling, but it is not economic for us to make refunds of smaller amounts.

Overseas applicants should include airmail postage. International Reply Coupons are not acceptable as payment.

An adoption birth certificate is the legal birth certificate which can be used for all purposes. If a copy of the original birth entry is required please complete the original details only overleaf.,

Yours sincerely

Note: DIVORCE:

When a decree of divorce was granted by the Court of Session, it was formerly the practice to enter a note on the marriage entry to show that the marriage had ended in divorce. This practice was discontinued on 1 May 1984. Where a divorce was notified to the Registrar General on or after that date, there will be no note regarding divorce on the corresponding marriage entry or on any extract of the entry.

Prior to 1.5.1984 an extract of divorce granted in Scotland is obtainable from the Court where the decree was granted or from 1.5.1984 the General Register Office, New Register House, Edinburgh EH1 3YT.

BIRTH	ADOPTION	MARRIAGE	DIVORCE	DEATH

BIRTH / ADOPTION

- • Surname at Birth/Adoption (delete as relevant)
- Forenames
- • MALE/FEMALE
- Place (town or parish) in which Birth occurred (adopted persons please state date of adoption, if known)
- • PARENTS/ADOPTIVE PARENTS
- Father's forenames
- Father's surname
- Mother's maiden surname
- Mother's forenames

Date of Birth		
DAY	MONTH	YEAR

Date of application ....

Signature ....

FOR OFFICE USE		
RD No	YEAR	Entry No
RCE		

MARRIAGE

- Groom's surname
- Forenames
- Bride's surname
- Forenames
- Place (town or parish) in which Marriage occurred
- Widow or Divorcee please state former married name
- • PARENTS/ADOPTIVE PARENTS
- Father's surname
- Father's forenames
- Mother's maiden surname
- Mother's forenames

Date of Marriage		
DAY	MONTH	YEAR

Date of Divorce (if applicable)		
DAY	MONTH	YEAR

Date of application ....

Signature ....

FOR OFFICE USE		
RD No	YEAR	Entry No
RCE		

DEATH

- Surname
- Forenames
- Age at Death
- Place (town or parish) in which Death occurred
- • PARENTS/ADOPTIVE PARENTS
- Father's surname
- Father's forenames
- Mother's maiden surname
- Mother's forenames

Date of Death		
DAY	MONTH	YEAR

Date of application ....

Signature ....

FOR OFFICE USE		
RD No	YEAR	Entry No
RCE		

URUGUAY

Dirección General del Registro del Estado Civil
Ministerio de Educación y Cultura
Av. Uruguay 933
11.100 Montevideo, Uruguay

Registration began July 1, 1879.

UZBEKISTAN

Russian-American Genealogical Archival Service (RAGAS)
P.O. Box 236
Glen Echo, Maryland 20812

(202) 501-5206

Cost for a Birth, Marriage, or Death Certificate $20.00

By an agreement between the United States National Archives Volunteer Association and the Archives of Russia Society RAGAS will process requests for vital records in the former Soviet republics. Although at this time RAGAS is able to deal mainly with Russia, Belarus, and Ukraine they might be able to help you with your inquiries regarding Uzbekistan. There is a $2.00 shipping fee per document. There is also an hourly rate. (See Russia for application forms.)

VANUATU

Registrar General
Civil Registration Office
Ministry of Home Affairs
Private Bag 050
Port Vila, Vanuatu

Vital registration was not formally introduced to Vanuatu until 1975, and so the Registrar General's Office has initiated a program to retroactively register each birth and marriage.

The National Archives of Vanuatu also has information; write to P.O. Box 184, Port Vila, Vanuatu; Tel. (011) (678) 22-498; FAX (011) (678) 23-142.

VENEZUELA

Dirección de Registro y Notaria
Ministerio de Justicia
Torre Norte, Centro Simon Bolivar, Piso 20
Caracas, Venezuela

Registration began in 1873.

VIETNAM

Registrar
Police Station
(Town), Vietnam

Cost for a Birth, Marriage, or Death Certificate   10,000 D

Vietnam has a personal identity card, family registration, and a vital registration system. The family register is the basic document and is registered at the police station.

YEMEN

Registrar General
Ministry of Justice and AWQAF
P.O. Box 5030
Maalla, Aden, Yemen

Vital registration is not considered to be comprehensive.

ZAIRE

Etat Zairois
Ministere de l'Administration du Territoire
Kinshasa, Zaire

Registration began in 1958.

ZAMBIA

Registrar General
Department of National Registration, Passport and Citizenship
Kundalila House
P.O. Box 32311
Lusaka, Zambia

Registration is not considered to be complete.

ZIMBABWE

Registrar General of Zimbabwe
Central Registry
Ministry of Home Affairs
Bag 7734
Causeway, Harare, Zimbabwe

Registration is not considered to be complete.